lonely planet

İstanbul

"All you've got to do is decide to go
and the hardest part is over.

So go!"

THIS EDITION WRITTEN AND RESEARCHED BY
Virginia Maxwell, James Bainbridge

Contents

(left) **Subterranean Basilica Cistern** p76
....
(above) **Streets of the Galata District** p127
....
(right) **Gate detail, Topkapı Palace** p61
....

Welcome to İstanbul

This magical meeting place of East and West has more top-drawer attractions than it has minarets (and that's a lot).

Art & Architecture

The conquering armies of ancient times tended to ransack the city rather than endow it with artistic treasures, but all that changed with the Byzantines, who adorned their churches and palaces with mosaics and frescoes. Miraculously, many of these remain. Their successors, the Ottomans, were quick to launch an ambitious building program and the magnificently decorated imperial mosques that resulted are architectural triumphs that together form one of the world's great skylines. In recent years, local banks and business dynasties have reprised the Ottomans' grand ambitions and endowed İstanbul with an impressive array of galleries, museums and festivals for all to enjoy.

Living History

İstanbul's strategic location has attracted many marauding armies over the centuries. The Greeks, Romans and Venetians took turns ruling before the Ottomans stormed into town and decided to stay – physical reminders of their various tenures are found across the city. The fact that the city straddles two continents wasn't its only drawcard – it was the final stage on the legendary Silk Road linking Asia with Europe, and many merchants who came here liked it so much that they, too, decided to stay. In so doing, they gave the city a cultural diversity that it retains to this day.

Culinary Heritage

'But what about the food?' we hear you say. We're happy to report that the city's cuisine is as diverse as its heritage, and delicious to boot. Locals take their eating and drinking seriously – the restaurants here are the best in the country. You can eat aromatic Asian dishes or Italian classics if you so choose, but most visitors prefer to sample the succulent kebaps, flavoursome mezes and freshly caught fish that are the city's signature dishes, washing them down with the national drink, rakı (grape spirit infused with aniseed), or a glass or two of locally produced wine.

Local Life

Some ancient cities are the sum of their monuments, but İstanbul factors a lot more into the equation. Chief among its manifold attractions are the locals, who have an infectious love of life and generosity of spirit. This vibrant, inclusive and expanding community is full of people who work and party hard, treasure family and friendships, and have no problem melding tradition and modernity in their everyday lives. Joining them in their favourite haunts – *çay bahçesis* (tea gardens), *kahvehans* (coffeehouses), *meyhanes* (Turkish taverns) and *kebapçıs* (kebap restaurants) – will be a highlight of your visit.

Why I Love İstanbul

By Virginia Maxwell, Writer

Why do I love this city? Let me count the ways. I love the locals, who have an endless supply of hospitality and good humour at their disposal. I love the fact that when I walk down a city street, layers of history unfold before me. I love listening to the sound of the *müezzins* duelling from their minarets and I love seeing the sun set over the world's most beautiful skyline. I love the restaurants, the bars and the tea gardens. But most of all, I love the fact that, in İstanbul, an extraordinary cultural experience lies around every corner.

For more about our writers, see p256

For more about our writers, see p256

Top: Prayer Hall, Blue Mosque (p72)

İstanbul's
Top 10

Aya Sofya (p54)

1 History resonates when you visit this majestic Byzantine basilica. Built by order of the Emperor Justinian in the 6th century AD, its soaring dome, huge nave and glittering gold mosaics contribute to its reputation as one of the world's most beautiful buildings, and its long and fascinating history as church, mosque and museum make it the city's most revealing time capsule. Looted by marauding Crusaders in the 13th century, stormed by Ottoman invaders during the Conquest in 1453 and visited by millions of tourists since becoming a museum, it is Turkey's greatest treasure.

◉ *Sultanahmet & Around*

Topkapı Palace (p61)

2 The secrets of the seraglio will be revealed during your visit to this opulent Ottoman palace complex occupying the promontory of İstanbul's Old City. A series of mad, sad and downright bad sultans lived here with their concubines and courtiers between 1465 and 1830, and extravagant relics of their centuries of folly, intrigue, excess, patronage, diplomacy and war are everywhere you look. Highlights include the huge Harem (private quarters), impressive Imperial Council Chamber, object-laden Imperial Treasury and picturesque Marble Terrace.

◉ *Sultanahmet & Around*

Bosphorus Ferry Trip *(p163)*

3 Climbing aboard one of the city's famous flotilla of ferries is the quintessential İstanbul experience. The trip between Asia and Europe on a commuter ferry is hard to beat, but the Bosphorus tourist ferries that travel the great strait from Eminönü towards the mouth of the Black Sea are even better, offering passengers views of palaces, parks and ornate timber mansions on both the Asian and European shores. It doesn't matter whether you opt for a long or short cruise, as either is sure to be memorable.

🏃 *Day Trips*

Shopping in the Bazaars *(p93)*

4 The chaotic and colourful Grand Bazaar is the best-known shopping destination on the Historic Peninsula, but it certainly isn't the only one. After exploring its labyrinthine lanes and hidden caravanserais, follow the steady stream of local shoppers heading downhill into the busy shopping precinct of Tahtakale, which has at its hub the seductively scented Spice Bazaar, pictured left. From there, head back up towards the Blue Mosque and its attached *arasta* (row of shops by a mosque), where you may well find a lasting memento of your trip.

🛍 *Bazaar District*

Süleymaniye Mosque *(p96)*

5 Dominating the Old City's skyline, Süleyman the Magnificent's most notable architectural legacy certainly lives up to its patron's name. The fourth imperial mosque built in İstanbul, the Süleymaniye was designed by Mimar Sinan, the most famous of all Ottoman architects, and was built between 1550 and 1557. Its extensive and largely intact *külliye* (mosque complex) buildings illustrate aspects of daily Ottoman life and are still used by the local community, making this a sight that truly lives up to the tag of 'living history'.

👁 *Bazaar District*

Kariye Museum (p114)

6 Tucked away in the shadow of Theodosius II's monumental land walls, Kariye Museum is a tiny Byzantine building located in the little-visited Western Districts of the city. It's adorned with mosaics and frescoes that were created in the 14th century and illustrate the lives of Christ and the Virgin Mary. These are among the world's best examples of Byzantine art, rivalled only by mosaics adorning churches in Ravenna, Italy. Put simply, it's impossible to overpraise the exquisite interior here – visiting it is sure to be a highlight of your trip.

👁 *Western Districts*

Wining & Dining in Beyoğlu (p51)

7 Breathtaking views of the Bosphorus and Old City from the rooftop terraces of a constellation of glamorous bars are just one of the enticements on offer in bohemian Beyoğlu. Locals come here to carouse in traditional *meyhanes* (taverns), eat kebaps in *ocakbaşıs* (fireside kebap restaurants), sample modern Turkish cuisine in sophisticated bistros and relax in casual European-style cafes and clubs. It's the eating and entertainment epicentre of the city – don't miss it.

🍴 *Beyoğlu*

EMILE CHAIX/GETTY IMAGES ©

Basilica Cistern *(p76)*

8 When the Byzantine emperors decided to build something, they certainly didn't cut corners! This extraordinary subterranean cistern, located opposite Aya Sofya, features a wildly atmospheric forest of columns (336 to be exact), vaulted brick ceilings, mysterious carved Medusa-head column bases (pictured) and ghostly patrols of carp. A testament to the ambitious town planning and engineering expertise of the Byzantines, the cistern has played a starring role in innumerable motion pictures (remember *From Russia with Love*?) and is now one of the city's best-loved tourist attractions.

◉ *Sultanahmet & Around*

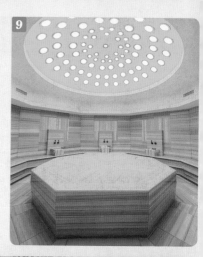

Visiting a Hamam *(p46)*

9 In life, there aren't too many opportunities to wander seminaked through a 16th-century Ottoman monument. Unless you visit İstanbul, that is. The city's world-famous hamams offer a unique opportunity to immerse yourself in history, architecture, warm water and soap suds all at the same time. A hamam treatment offers a relaxing finale to a day spent pounding the city's pavements and gives a fascinating insight into the life and customs of Ottoman society. You can surrender to the steam at baths on both side of the Galata Bridge.

🏃 *Hamams & Spas*

Blue Mosque *(p72)*

10 The city's signature building was the grand project of Sultan Ahmet I, who urged its architect and builders on in the construction process before his untimely death in 1617, aged only 27. The mosque's wonderfully curvaceous exterior features a cascade of domes and six tapering minarets. Inside, the huge space is encrusted with thousands of the blue İznik tiles that give the building its unofficial but commonly used name. Beloved by tourists and locals alike, it and Aya Sofya bookend Sultanahmet Park in a truly extraordinary fashion.

👁 *Sultanahmet & Around*

What's New

Balat Renewal

The run-down streets and buildings of this historic neighbourhood on the Golden Horn are finally being revitalised, with atmosphere-laden Vodina Caddesi being the current centre of attention. (p112)

Palace Kitchens, Topkapı Palace

Lavish imperial feasts were once prepared in the huge kitchens at Topkapı, and now they've reopened after a painstaking renovation. (p61)

Museum of Turkish Jews

Celebrating its move to a new building attached to the Neve Shalom synagogue, this excellent museum in Galata uses multimedia displays to document the long history of the Jewish people in Turkey. (p127)

Hünkâr Kasrı

Sultans once rested in this elevated pavilion attached to the New Mosque, and now its gorgeous tile-encrusted interior is open to the rest of us for two weeks every month. (p99)

Palace Collections Museum

Housed in the recently restored Matbah-ı Amire (former kitchens) of Dolmabahçe Palace, this museum showcases costumes, furniture, porcelain, textiles and many other objects from the palace collection. (p150)

Nuruosmaniye Mosque

The restoration of this baroque mosque took years, but has been well worth the wait; don't miss the unique rear courtyard. (p100)

Grand Bazaar Scavenger Hunt

Book the kids into this enjoyable activity in the historic Grand Bazaar, one of a number of unusual offerings by Alternative City Tours. (p111)

Babylon Bomonti

The city's best-loved live-music venue has moved to new digs in a converted beer factory in the arty enclave of Bomonti, north of Taksim Meydani (Taksim Square; p154).

Levent and Boğaziçi Üniversitesi Metro Link

The new M6 branch line running between Levent and Boğaziçi Üniversitesi has made accessing suburbs on the European shore of the Bosphorus much easier.

Tophane Design Precinct

The Depo cultural centre (p129) and Hiç design store (p144) led the way, and now the streets north of the Tophane tram stop have become a magnet for designer boutiques.

Yeldeğirmeni

Street art, cultural venues, boutiques and cafes are sprouting in this once-dishevelled quarter near Haydarpaşa, reinforcing Kadıköy's claim to the title of İstanbul's hippest neighbourhood. (p155)

Golden Horn Tour

Following the success of its hop-on, hop-off Bosphorus ferry tour, the Dentur Avraysa company has introduced a similar service on the Golden Horn. (p171)

For more recommendations and reviews, see **lonelyplanet. com/Istanbul**

Need to Know

For more information, see Survival Guide (p207)

Currency
Türk Lirası (Turkish lira; ₺)

Language
Turkish

Visas
Not required for some (predominantly European) nationalities; most other nationalities can obtain a 90-day visa electronically at www.evisa.gov.tr.

Money
ATMs are widespread. Credit cards accepted at most shops, hotels and upmarket restaurants.

Mobile Phones
Most European and Australasian phones work here; some North American phones don't. Check with your provider. Prepaid SIM cards must be registered when purchased.

Time
Eastern European Time (UTC/GMT) plus three hours.

Tourist Information
Tourist offices operate in Sultanahmet, Sirkeci, Taksim, Atatürk International Airport and Sabiha Gökçen International Airport. See p217 for their addresses and opening hours.

Daily Costs

Budget: Less than €60
➡ Dorm bed: €10 to €25
➡ Kebap or pide dinner: €6
➡ Beer at a neighbourhood bar: €5
➡ Tram, bus or ferry ride: €1.19

Midrange: €60 to €200
➡ Double room: from €90
➡ *Lokanta* (eatery serving ready-made food) lunch: €8
➡ *Meyhane* (tavern) dinner with wine: €25
➡ Taxi from Sultanahmet to Beyoğlu: €5

Top End: More than €200
➡ Double room: from €200
➡ Restaurant dinner with wine: €35
➡ Cocktail in a rooftop bar: €12
➡ Hamam experience: from €50

Advance Planning

Three months before If you're travelling in spring, autumn or over Christmas, make your hotel booking as far in advance as possible.

Two months before İstanbul's big-ticket festivals and concerts sell out fast. Book your tickets online at Biletix (p40).

Two weeks before Ask your hotel to make dinner reservations.

Useful Websites

Canım İstanbul (http://canimistanbul.com/blog/en) Lifestyle-focused blog that's heavy on listings and events.

İstanbul Eats (http://istanbul eats.com) Fab foodie blog.

Lonely Planet (www.lonely planet.com /istanbul) Destination ifnromation, hotel bookings, traveller forum and more.

Not Only İstanbul (www.notonlyistanbul.com) Curated guide to the city's art, food and culture, with plenty of video content.

Yabangee (www.yabangee.com) Expats' guide to the city, with loads of events listings.

YellAli (www.yellali.com) Useful site for expats and long-stay visitors.

WHEN TO GO

Spring and autumn are ideal, as the weather is good and festivals are in full swing. Summer can be unpleasantly hot and winter bone-chillingly cold.

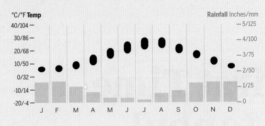

Arriving in İstanbul

Atatürk International Airport (p208) Metro and tram to Sultanahmet (₺8, 6am to midnight); Havataş bus to Taksim Meydanı (₺11, 4am to 1am); taxi ₺45 to Sultanahmet, ₺55 to Beyoğlu.

Sabiha Gökçen International Airport (p209) Havataş bus to Taksim Meydanı (₺14, 3.30am to 1am), from where a funicular (₺4) and tram (₺4) travel to Sultanahmet; Havataş bus to Kadıköy (₺9, 4am to 1am); taxi ₺155 to Sultanahmet and ₺140 to Beyoğlu.

For much more on **arrival** see p208

Safe Travel

➡ Recently, political tensions within the country and the region have led to a violent, ultimately unsuccessful military coup d'état. There have also been terrorist incidents including bomb attacks in areas and facilities frequented by tourists. Visitors should monitor their country's travel advisories and stay alert at all times.

➡ Always employ common sense when exploring city neighbourhoods. Be particularly careful near the historic city walls, as these harbour vagrants and people with substance-abuse problems – don't walk here alone or after dark.

➡ As a pedestrian, always give way to vehicles; the sovereignty of the pedestrian is recognised in law but not out on the street. Footpaths (sidewalks) and road surfaces are often in a poorly maintained state and some shops have basements that are accessed from the footpath via steep steps without barriers – watch where you are walking!

Sleeping

Accommodation choices in İstanbul are diverse and plentiful. During peak tourism periods such as spring, autumn and Christmas it's important to book ahead.

➡ **Boutique hotels** The city's fastest-growing hotel trend; often in historic buildings and usually with high levels of service and amenities.

➡ **Suite hotels** Spacious rooms with kitchenettes, daily maid service and stylish fittings; great for families.

➡ **Hotels** Everything from small family-run *pansiyons* (pensions) to slick business hotels; mid-range options predominate.

➡ **Luxury hotels** World-class options mostly located in Beyoğlu and along the Bosphorus.

➡ **Hostels** Small and friendly options in Sultanahmet, Beyoğlu and Kadıköy; most offer both dorms and private rooms.

For much more on **sleeping** see p177

First Time İstanbul

For more information, see Survival Guide (p207)

Checklist

➡ Check if you need a visa; these should be organised electronically before your arrival.

➡ Make sure your passport is valid for at least six months.

➡ Check your airline's baggage restrictions; when packing, make sure you reserve some of your allowance for holiday purchases.

➡ Arrange travel insurance.

What to Pack

➡ Sturdy walking shoes or sandals – İstanbul's footpaths are often cobbled and uneven.

➡ Females will need a scarf or shawl to cover head and shoulders when visiting mosques; also a bikini to wear in hamams (optional).

➡ Males should bring at least one pair of long pants to wear in mosques.

➡ Electrical adaptors (see p214).

Top Tips for Your Trip

➡ Plan your itinerary – although İstanbul's public transport system is excellent, criss-crossing the city will eat into your time. Instead, choose just one or two neighbourhoods to explore in a single day.

➡ When you have prepared your itinerary, estimate how much museum entries will cost and then compare this figure to the cost of a Museum Pass İstanbul – you may save money (and time) by purchasing one of these.

➡ Most major museums are closed on Monday; the exceptions are Topkapı Palace (Tuesday), the Kariye Museum (Wednesday) and the Museum of Turkish Jews (Saturday). The İstanbul Archaeological Museums, Museum of Turkish & Islamic Arts and Basilica Cistern are open every day. Dolmabahçe and Beylerbeyi Palaces are closed on both Monday and Thursday. The Grand Bazaar is closed on Sunday.

➡ Even if you're only here for a few days, it's a good idea to purchase an İstanbulkart to use on public transport.

What to Wear

İstanbul's weather can be variable, so pack an umbrella and sweater (jumper) or jacket.

Mosque visits involve certain dress conventions. In other situations, you can dress as you would in Europe, North America or Australasia.

Walking Tours

If you have a guidebook and don't have specialist interests, there's no compelling reason to organise a tour guide. That said, there are a number of companies in the city offering excellent walking tours that give an in-depth introduction to neighbourhoods. These include the history-focused İstanbul Walks (p89), food-focused İstanbul Eats (p89), photography-focused Alternative City Tours (p111) and art-focused Artwalk Istanbul (p146).

See the Sports & Activities sections in our Explore chapters for reviews of other recommended companies.

Bargaining

The non-negotiable price tag reigns supreme in most of the city's retail outlets these days, and bargaining is becoming a dying art. Most exceptions to this rule can be found in the Grand Bazaar, especially in its carpet shops, where shopkeepers continue to take pride in practising the ancient art of bargaining (p44).

Tipping

➡ **Hamams** Around 10% for the masseuse/masseur in a hamam, but only if you are happy with their service.

➡ **Meyhanes** At least ₺10 per person for musicians in *meyhanes*.

➡ **Restaurants & bars** Usually 10% in restaurants, *meyhanes* (taverns) and upmarket bars; not usually necessary in *lokantas* (eateries serving ready-made food) or fast-food joints.

➡ **Taxis** Round taxi fares up to the nearest lira.

Etiquette

➡ Be punctual for all appointments.

➡ If you invite someone to dine, it is assumed that you will pay the bill.

➡ Avoid eating and drinking on the street during daylight hours in Ramazan (Ramadan).

➡ Don't blow your nose in public.

➡ Never point the soles of your feet towards a person.

➡ Don't use the OK sign as here it is sign language for calling someone homosexual.

BORIS STROUJKO/SHUTTERSTOCK ©

Tram on İstiklal Caddesi (p125)

City Geography

İstanbul is the world's only city to straddle two continents, separated by the Sea of Marmara. You'll spend most of your time on the European side exploring Sultanahmet's sights and Beyoğlu's restaurants and bars, but a trip to the city's Asian side is highly recommended for the scenic ferry ride between the two shores and for the fascinating glimpse into local life that a visit to suburbs such as Kadıköy and Üsküdar imparts.

Language

The vast majority of people working in İstanbul's tourist sector speak English. However, it goes almost without saying that locals appreciate visitors making the effort to master a few Turkish phrases.

See p218 for our language section.

Getting Around

For more information, see Transport (p208)

Ferry

The most atmospheric way to travel between the Old City and Beyoğlu to the Asian, Golden Horn or Bosphorus suburbs; services operate from 7am to 10pm (approximately).

Tram

The easiest way to travel between Sultanahmet and Beyoğlu; services operate every five minutes between 6am and midnight.

Metro

The best way to travel from Atatürk International Airport to the Old City and from Taksim Meydanı (Taksim Sq) to suburbs in the north of the city. A new line links the Old City and Asian shore via a tunnel under the Sea of Marmara. Services operate from 6am to midnight.

Bus

Used when travelling along both sides of the Bosphorus and from Eminönü to the Western Districts. Services operate between 6am and 11pm (approximately).

Key Phrases

Dentur Avrasya Private ferry company

Dolmuş Shared minibus

Funıküler Funicular

İskele Ferry dock

İstanbul Şehir Hatları The city's main ferry service; government-run

İstanbulkart Rechargeable travel card (see p210 for more)

Jeton Transport token

Mavi Marmara Private ferry line to/from the Princes' Islands, operated by Dentur Avraysa

Otobüs Bus

Otogar Bus station

Teleferic Cable car

Tramvay Tramway

Tünel Literally, 'tunnel'; name for funicular between Karaköy and Tünel Meydanı (Tünel Sq)

Turyol Private ferry company

Key Routes

F1 Funicular between Kabataş and Taksim Meydanı (Taksim Sq).

M1A Metro line linking Atatürk International Airport with Yenikapı near Sultanahmet.

M2 Metro line linking Yenikapı with Hacıosman. Stops at Vezneciler (near the Grand Bazaar), on the new bridge across the Golden Horn (Haliç) and at Şişhane and Taksim Meydanı (Taksim Sq) in Beyoğlu.

Marmaray Newly opened metro line that travels from Kazlıçeşme and Yenikapı to Sirkeci near Eminönü and then under the Sea of Marmara to Üsküdar and Ayrılık Çeşme on the Asian shore.

T1 Tram line between Bağcılar/Cevizlibağ and Kabataş via Zeytinburnu (for airport and otogar metro connections), Sultanahmet, the Grand Bazaar, Eminönü and Karaköy.

Tünel Funicular between Karaköy and Tünel Meydanı.

TOP TIPS

➡ Purchase an İstanbulkart (p210) to save nearly 50% on the standard ticket price every time you take a ferry, tram, metro, funicular or bus ride, and even more on connecting journeys.

➡ If travelling from the Grand Bazaar or Süleymaniye Mosque to Beyoğlu, consider taking the metro from Vezneciler rather than the slower tram service.

➡ To pick up a handy public transport map of the city or to request transport information, go to the extremely helpful İstanbul Büyükşehir Belediyesi (İstanbul Municipality) Information Office between the Harem and Kadıköy *iskeles* at Eminönü.

When to Travel

➡ İstanbul is a busy city and even though public transport services are frequent, they are often crowded. Try to avoid rush hours (8am to 10am and 4pm to 6pm) if possible.

➡ If you need to get to Taksim Meydanı (Taksim Sq) from the Asian or Bosphorus suburbs after services have finished for the night, you should be able to take a dolmuş.

➡ All Bosphorus and Princes' Islands ferry services are jam-packed on weekends; consider exploring on a weekday if possible.

Etiquette

➡ Have your İstanbulkart or *jeton* ready before you go through the ticket turnstile – locals are well practised at moving through ticket barriers without breaking pace.

➡ If you want to stay stationary on an escalator, stand on the right-hand side; you'll need to walk if you are on the left.

➡ Turks are usually very polite and will give their seats to older passengers, disabled people, pregnant women or parents carrying babies or toddlers if there are no spare seats available. You should do the same.

➡ Queuing to board public transport is honoured in principle rather than in reality. Be proactive but not pushy.

How to Hail a Taxi

➡ Taxis are plentiful and are usually hailed in the street. Round fares up to the nearest lira.

➡ See the Transport chapter (p208) for more information on taxis.

Tickets & Passes

➡ *Jetons* can be purchased from ticket machines or offices at tram stops, *iskelesi* and funicular and metro stations, but it's much cheaper and easier to use an İstanbulkart (p210).

➡ You must have an İstanbulkart to use a bus.

➡ Pay the driver when you take a dolmuş (shared minibus); fares vary according to destination and length of trip.

➡ Ticket prices are usually the same on public and private ferry services; İstanbulkarts can be used on some private ferries, but not all.

➡ İstanbulkarts cannot be used to pay for Bosphorus ferry tours.

For much more on **getting around** see p210 ➡

Top Itineraries

Day One

Sultanahmet & Around (p52)

Head to Aya Sofya Meydanı (Aya Sofya Sq) and work out which of the museums and mosques in the immediate area will be on your visiting list. Don't miss **Aya Sofya**, the **Blue Mosque** and the **Basilica Cistern**. After your visits, wander through the **Hippodrome**, where chariot races were held in ancient times.

> **Lunch** Join local workers at one of the humble *lokantas* (eateries serving ready-made food) in the area – Sefa Restaurant (p82) is a popular choice.

Sultanahmet & Around (p52)

Diverge from the crowded tourist trail and follow our walking tour down into the Küçük Ayasofya neighbourhood. Afterwards, source some souvenirs in the historic **Arasta Bazaar**.

> **Dinner** Have fish at Balıkçı Sabahattin (p84) or kebaps at Hamdi Restaurant (p105).

Sultanahmet & Around (p52)

After dinner, claim a table at **Derviş Aile Çay Bahçesi** or **Cafe Meşale**, where you can enjoy tea, nargile (water pipe) and a free (but very touristy) whirling-dervish performance. Alternatively, head to the **A'YA Rooftop Lounge** at the ritzy Fours Seasons Hotel. In winter a treatment at one of the Old City's **Ottoman-era hamams** is a relaxing and warm alternative.

Day Two

Sultanahmet & Around (p52)

It's time to investigate the lifestyles of the sultans at **Topkapı Palace**. You'll need a half-day to explore the palace Harem, marvel at the precious objects in the Treasury, admire the recently renovated palace kitchens and wander through the pavilion-filled grounds.

> **Lunch** Investigate the excellent cheap eateries on Sirkeci's Hocapaşa Sokak; old-fashioned Hocapaşa Pidecisi (p83) is one of our favourites.

Beyoğlu (p123)

Explore the streets, cafes and boutiques of **Galata**, **Tophane**, **Karaköy** and **Çukurcuma** and consider a visit to the eclectic **Pera Museum** or nostalgic **Museum of Innocence**.

> **Dinner** Beyoğlu is the city's eating and drinking hotspot. Enjoy a pre-dinner drink at a hipster bar in Asmalımescit before enjoying fine *meyhane*-style food at Eleos (p135) or modern Turkish cuisine at Neolokal (p133).

Beyoğlu (p123)

The night is still young! Hit the bars and clubs in **Asmalımescit**, on **İstiklal Caddesi** or in **Harbiye** and **Cihangir**. Those who are still hungry should instead head to **Karaköy** for a ate-night baklava fix at **Karaköy Güllüoğlu**.

Day Three

Bazaar District (p91)

Get ready to explore the city's famous Bazaar District. After visiting the most magnificent of all Ottoman mosques, the **Süleymaniye**, make your way to the world-famous **Grand Bazaar** to explore its labyrinthine lanes and hidden caravanserais, picking up a few souvenirs along the way.

Lunch Grab a cheap eat in or around the Grand Bazaar; head to Dürümcü Raif Usta (p107) or Dönerci Şahin Usta (p107) for kebap, and Bena Dondurmaları (p107) for something sweet.

Bazaar District (p91)

After lunch follow the steady stream of local shoppers making their way down the hill to the **Spice Bazaar**. While there, seek out the exquisite **Rüstem Paşa Mosque**, camouflaged in the midst of a busy produce market. As the sun starts to set, walk across **Galata Bridge** towards the eating and entertainment district of Beyoğlu.

Dinner Beyoğlu has restaurants, *meyhanes* and street food aplenty – explore these on a night-time food tour with İstanbul Eats (p89), İstanbul on Food (p146) or Urban Adventures (p103).

Beyoğlu (p123)

Listen to some live jazz at **Nardis** or **Salon**. Alternatively, take a taxi to **Babylon Bomonti**, the city's best-known live-music venue.

Day Four

The Bosphorus (p162)

Board the **Long Bosphorus Tour** (Uzun Boğaz Turu) for a one-way trip up the Bosphorus and then make your way back to town by bus, visiting museums and monuments along the way. Alternatively, take the Dentur Avraysa **hop-on, hop-off tour** from Beşiktaş and visit the **Sakıp Sabancı Museum** in Emirgan and the Ottoman-era **Küçüksu Kasrı** and **Beylerbeyi Palace**.

Lunch If the weather is fine, enjoy a light lunch in the Hıdiv Kasrı Garden Cafe (p169). In cooler weather try one of the cafes in the shadow of majestic Rumeli Hisarı – we particularly like the casual Sade Kahve (p169).

Beyoğlu (p123)

If you take a 90-minute cruise on a Bosphorus excursion boat rather than the full-day or hop-on, hop-off trip, you can devote the afternoon to investigating Beyoğlu's exciting contemporary-art scene. Don't miss the **İstanbul Modern, ARTER** and **Pera Museum**.

Dinner It's time to sample the national dish, kebaps – head to Antiochia (p134) or Zübeyir Ocakbaşı (p135) to enjoy a meaty feast.

Beyoğlu (p123)

Bid farewell to the city over a post-dinner drink at one of Beyoğlu's rooftop bars or make your way to **Akarsu Yokuşu** in Cihangir to wind down in one of its many bohemian cafes.

If You Like...

Markets

Grand Bazaar One of the world's oldest – and most atmospheric – shopping complexes. (p93)

Spice Bazaar Has been supplying locals with spices and sugary treats for nearly 400 years. (p98)

Kadıköy Produce Market İstanbul's most enticing fresh-food market is found near the Kadıköy İskelesi (Kadıköy Ferry Dock; p157)

Çarşamba Pazarı A bustling local street market held every Wednes-day in the streets surrounding the Fatih Mosque. (p118)

Women's Bazaar Located beneath the Aqueduct of Valens and specialising in produce from Turkey's southeast. (p100)

Museums

İstanbul Archaeology Museums Eclectic collection of artefacts from the imperial collections, including outstanding classical sculptures. (p74)

Museum of Turkish & Islamic Arts An internationally renowned collection of antique carpets, plus exquisite examples of calligraphy. (p77)

Pera Museum A splendid collection of paintings featuring Turkish Orientalist themes plus top-notch international shows. (p126)

Sakıp Sabancı Museum Wonderful calligraphy and blockbuster international exhibitions in a scenic Bosphorus location. (p168)

Museum of Innocence Orhan Pamuk's quirky collection of objects evoking 20th-century İstanbul. (p131)

IZZVET/SHUTTERSTOCK ©

Mosaics, Museum of Great Palace Mosaics (p78)

Ottoman Mosques

Süleymaniye Mosque Crowning the Old City's third hill, this magnificent Ottoman mosque complex is an architectural triumph. (p96)

Blue Mosque Possesses more minarets and visual pizzazz than any mosque should rightly lay claim to. (p72)

Atik Valide Mosque This majestic building is the most impressive of Üsküdar's many Ottoman mosques. (p160)

Rüstem Paşa Mosque Notable for its utterly exquisite İznik tilework, which adorns both interior and exterior walls. (p99)

Nuruosmaniye Mosque Designed in Ottoman baroque style, with a huge dome and unique polygonal rear courtyard. (p100)

Şemsi Ahmed Paşa Mosque Pretty mosque complex with a wonderful location on the waterfront in Üsküdar. (p160)

Views

Topkapı Terraces Sequestered in the Topkapı palace complex, the sultans must have loved the views from its panoramic terraces. (p61)

Galata Bridge Snapshots of local life and unbeatable views reward those walking between Sultanahmet and Beyoğlu. (p101)

Yavuz Sultan Selim Mosque The terrace of this mosque perched atop the Old City's fifth hill overlooks the Golden Horn. (p118)

Rooftop Bars Glamorous bars and clubs on rooftops across Beyoğlu offer sensational views from their outdoor terraces. (p140)

Byzantine History

Kariye Museum A concentration of Byzantine mosaics unrivalled here or perhaps anywhere in the world. (p114)

Aya Sofya This ancient basilica has witnessed history unfold and its interior tells many stories. (p54)

İstanbul Archaeology Museums The city's largest collection of Byzantine artefacts is on display at this excellent museum. (p74)

Great Palace Mosaic Museum A remarkably intact and visually arresting remnant of the Great Palace of Byzantium. (p78)

Little Aya Sofya This former church is one of the most beautiful Byzantine structures in the city. (p81)

Palaces & Pavilions

Topkapı Palace Home to the sultans for centuries, this cluster of ornately decorated pavilions houses treasures galore. (p61)

Dolmabahçe Palace This essay in decorative excess was built alongside the Bosphorus in the 19th century. (p149)

Beylerbeyi Palace Nestled under the Bosphorus Bridge, this 30-room imperial holiday shack is set in pretty gardens. (p164)

Küçüksu Kasrı This Ottoman hunting lodge on the shore of the Bosphorus is as pretty as a picture. (p165)

Hünkâr Kasrı Built into an archway attached to the New Mosque, with an extraordinary array of İznik tiles. (p99)

For more top İstanbul spots, see the following:
➡ Eating (p29)
➡ Drinking & Nightlife (p36)
➡ Entertainment (p39)
➡ Shopping (p42)
➡ Hamams & Spas (p46)

PLAN YOUR TRIP IF YOU LIKE...

Contemporary Art

ARTER Four floors of cutting-edge visual art on İstiklal Caddesi. (p129)

The Empire Project One of the many impressive commercial galleries in the city. (p131)

İstanbul Modern The city's pre-eminent art museum, with a huge permanent collection of Turkish artworks and world-class temporary exhibitions. (p127)

Mixer An exciting showcase of emerging artists from across Turkey. (p130)

Galeri Nev One of the city's oldest and most impressive commercial galleries. (p130)

Ferry Trips

Crossing the Continents Sail to Asia on a ferry from Eminönü, Karaköy or Kabataş. (p163)

The Bosphorus One of the city's signature experiences, offering magnificent museums, mansions and meals along its length. (p163)

The Golden Horn Hop on and off the commuter ferry that services the city's western districts. (p171)

Princes' Islands Escape the city and head towards these vehicle-free islands in the Sea of Marmara. (p174)

Month by Month

March

It's cold at the start of the month, but as the weather improves the festival season kicks off. Good hotel deals are on offer early in the month; high-season prices from Easter onwards.

☆ Akbank Short Film Festival

Beloved by the black-clad Beyoğlu bohemian set, this arty film-culture event is held at the Akbank Culture & Arts Centre (www.akbanksanat.com).

April

Locals are well and truly into the springtime swing of things by April.

Highlights include the blooming of tulips across the city and the arrival of fresh *kılıç* (swordfish) on restaurant menus.

☆ International İstanbul Film Festival

If you're keen to view the best in Turkish film, this is the event (http://film.iksv.org/en) to attend. Held early in the month in cinemas around town, it programs retrospectives and recent releases from Turkey and abroad.

◉ İstanbul Tulip Festival

The tulip *(lâle)* is one of İstanbul's traditional symbols, and the local government celebrates this fact by planting more than 10 million of them annually. They bloom in mid-April, enveloping almost every street and park in vivid spring colours.

May

Enginar (artichoke) comes into season and takes pride of place on meze trays across the city. Days start to heat up, although evenings can still be chilly.

🏃 Chill-Out Festival

Featuring a concept stage, cultural and artistic activities, yoga programs and plenty of music, this two-day event (www.chilloutfest.com) at Life Park on the Bosphorus has a growing profile.

☆ Parkfest

A relatively new addition to the events circuit, this one-day music festival is held in KüçükÇiftlik Park in Maçka. Check its Twitter feed for details.

June

It's summertime and, yes, the living is easy. There's an abundance of sweet cherries and sour green plums in the produce markets and the open-air nightclubs on the Bosphorus start to hit their strides.

☆ İstanbul Music Festival

The city's premier arts festival (http://muzik.iksv.org/en) includes performances of opera, dance, orchestral concerts and chamber recitals. Acts are often internationally renowned and much of the

ISLAMIC HOLIDAYS & EVENTS

Islamic religious holidays and events are celebrated according to the Muslim lunar Hejira calendar, so their dates change every year. The most important event of the year is the holy month of **Ramazan** (called Ramadan in other countries), when Muslims fast from dawn until dusk and then sit with friends, family and community members to enjoy *iftar* (the meal that breaks the fast). It runs between May and June from 2017 to 2019. These *iftar* meals are sometimes held in streets or in large tents within the grounds of mosques. A three-day festival called **Ramazan Bayramı** (also known as Şeker, or Sugar, Bayramı because it involves lots of candy consumption) celebrates the completion of Ramazan.

The four- or five-day **Kurban Bayramı** is the most significant religious holiday of the year. It celebrates the biblical and Kur'anic account of Abraham's near-sacrifice of his son on Mt Moriah. In 2017 it will be in September; in 2018, August.

odd-numbered years from mid-September to mid-November. An international curator or panel of curators nominates a theme and puts together a cutting-edge program that is then exhibited in a variety of venues around town.

October

The year's final festivals take everyone's minds off the impending arrival of winter. Ruby-red pomegranates come into season at the end of the month and are juiced at stands across the city.

☆ Akbank Jazz Festival

This older sister to the International İstanbul Jazz Festival is a boutique event (www.akbanksanat.com), with a program featuring traditional and avant-garde jazz. Venues are scattered around town.

🕺 İstanbul Design Biennial

A reasonably recent addition to the İstanbul Foundation for Culture & Arts' (İKSV) stellar calendar of festivals, this event (http://istanbuldesignbiennial.iksv.org) sees the city's design community celebrating its profession and critically discussing its future. It's held in even-numbered years.

action takes place in atmosphere-laden Aya İrini.

July

It can be as hot as Hades at this time of year, so many locals decamp to beaches on the Mediterranean coast. Those left in town keep the heat under control with a liberal dose of cool jazz.

☆ İstanbul Jazz Festival

This festival (http://caz.iksv.org/en) programs an exhilarating hybrid of conventional jazz, electronica, drum 'n' bass, world music and rock. Venues include Salon in Şişhane and parks around the city.

☆ Efes Pilsen One Love

This one-day music festival (www.oneloveistanbul.com) is organised by the major promoter of rock and pop concerts in Turkey, Pozitif. International headline acts play everything from punk to pop, electronica to disco.

September

Autumn's cool breezes usher in an influx of tourists, and hotels revert to their high-season rates. Arty types are in seventh heaven when the internationally acclaimed art biennial is launched.

🕺 İstanbul Biennial

The city's major visual-arts shindig (http://bienal.iksv.org/en) takes place in

With Kids

İstanbul is a great destination for a family-friendly break. Children will be happy by the fantastic baklava, lokum *(Turkish Delight)* and dondurma *(ice cream) on offer, as well as the castles, underground cisterns and parks waiting to be explored.*

For Toddlers

Playgrounds & Parks

There are good playgrounds in Gülhane Park (p81) and in the waterside park near the Fındıklı tram stop in Beyoğlu. Open areas such as the Hippodrome (p77) and Yıldız Park (p151) also offer loads of space in which toddlers can expend energy.

For Bigger Kids

Rahmi M Koç Museum

Junior members of the family will go crazy (in a good way) when they encounter all of the trains, planes, boats and automobiles on exhibit at this museum (p172) in Hasköy.

Grand Bazaar Scavenger Hunt

Forget shopping – exploring the Grand Bazaar on a scavenger hunt offered by Alternative City Tours (p111) is much more fun.

Rumeli Hisarı

This huge castle (p165) on the Bosphorus is a hit with most children. Just be sure that your junior knights and princesses

are careful when they clamour up the battlements.

Princes' Islands

Your kids will love taking *fayton* (horse-drawn carriage; p174) rides around the islands, or hiring bicycles to get around under their own steam.

Basilica Cistern

It's creepy, and children can explore the walkways suspended over the water (p76). Way cool.

For Teenagers

Cooking Courses

Some teenagers see the kitchen as offering more than a refrigerator just waiting to be raided. Book yourself and your aspiring chef into a cooking class such as the one offered by Cooking Alaturka (p90) in Sultanahmet.

Ice Cream

They may try to appear sophisticated, but teenagers almost inevitably lose their attitude and get excited when they sample the *dondurma* sold at the many Mado ice cream shops (www. mado.com.tr) found throughout the city. There's a strategically located branch next to the Sultanahmet tram stop, and another at 121 İstiklal Caddesi in Beyoğlu.

Need to Know

➡ **Museums** Children under 12 receive free or discounted entry to most museums and monuments.

➡ **Transport** Children under seven travel free on public transport.

➡ **Strollers** Most footpaths are cobbled or uneven, so strollers aren't very useful.

➡ **Nappies** Disposable nappies (diapers) and formula are easy to purchase.

➡ **Restaurants** Children are almost inevitably made welcome in restaurants, although high chairs and kids' menus are the exception rather than the rule.

Like a Local

İstanbul's 14 million residents enjoy a lifestyle crammed with culture, backdropped by history and underpinned by family and faith. Head off the tourist trails to experience the city as they do.

Keyif

İstanbullus have perfected the art of *keyif* (quiet relaxation), and practise it at every possible opportunity. *Çay bahçesi* (tea gardens) and nargile (water pipe) cafes are *keyif* central, offering patrons pockets of tranquillity off crowded streets. Games of *tavla* (backgammon), glasses of tea, nargiles and quiet conversations are the only distractions on offer.

The İskele

Traffic in İstanbul is nightmarish, so it's sensible to take to the waters wherever possible. The city's famous flotilla of ferries transports thousands of commuters daily. Many of these passengers spend time before or after their journey enjoying a glass of tea or a snack at the *iskele* (ferry dock), making these often ramshackle places wonderful pockets of local life.

The Mosque

İstanbul's magnificent Ottoman mosques may be important tourist destinations, but their primary function is religious. Observe these rules when visiting:

➡ Remove your shoes before walking on the mosque's carpet; you can leave shoes on shelves near the mosque door or carry them with you in a plastic bag.

➡ Women should always cover their heads and shoulders with a shawl or scarf; both women and men should dress modestly.

➡ Avoid visiting mosques within 30 minutes of when the *ezan* (call to prayer) sounds from the mosque minaret; and also around Friday lunch, when weekly sermons and group prayers are held.

➡ Speak quietly and don't use flashes on your camera if people are praying (and never photograph people praying).

Street Snacking

Locals love to eat, and do so at regular intervals throughout the day. In busy areas around town (*iskeles*, bazaars, shopping strips), street carts and stands sell a huge variety of quick and cheap eats. The most popular of these are fish sandwiches and döner kebap or *kokoreç* (seasoned grilled intestines) stuffed in bread, but other favourites include roasted chestnuts, grilled corn on the cob, *midye dolma* (stuffed mussels) and *tavuk pilav* (rice with chickpeas and chicken).

Produce Markets

Locals love to shop and, although there seems to be a swish modern mall unveiled every few weeks, the hundreds of traditional street markets across the city retain loyal followings. To see local life at its most vibrant head to the streets around the Spice Bazaar, to the Kadınlar Pazarı in Fatih, the famous produce market in Kadıköy every day except Sunday, or to the streets surrounding the Fatih Mosque on Wednesday.

Sunday Brunch

A chance for friends and extended families to get together over an inexpensive meal, this ever-growing phenomenon has plenty of local devotees. Popular options include Namlı Gurme (p133), Aheste (p136), Dandin (p133) and Cuma (p140) in Beyoğlu; Akdenız Hatay Sofrası (p103) in Aksaray; Forno (p122) in Fener; Sütiş (p170), Lokma (p170) and Sade Khave (p169) on the Bosphorus; and Teras Restaurant (p176) on Büyükada.

For Free

The hippies and backpackers who flocked to İstanbul in the 1960s and 1970s would certainly blow their meagre budgets if they headed this way today. Fortunately, the ever-increasing price of hotel rooms, transport and meals is counterbalanced by an array of top-drawer sights that can be visited at no cost.

Mosques

Topping the seven hills of the Old City and adorning many of its streets, İstanbul's Ottoman mosques (p54) are the jewels in the city's crown. Entry to these architectural wonders is open to everyone regardless of their religion. The *türbes* (tombs) attached to these mosques are often sumptuously decorated with İznik tiles and can also be visited; head to the Aya Sofya Tombs (p78) to see some great examples.

Museums & Galleries

The recent trend for İstanbul's banks and business dynasties to endow private art galleries and cultural centres is the best thing to hit the city since the tulip bulb arrived. Most are on or near İstiklal Caddesi (p125) in Beyoğlu and charge no entry fees. The Pera Museum (p126) offers free admission every Friday between 6pm and 10pm; on Wednesday admission is also free for students. On the Bosphorus, the Sakıp Sabancı Museum (p168) offers free entry on Wednesday. In Eminönü, the tile-adorned Hünkâr Kasrı (p99) charges no entry fees.

Parks & Gardens

Picnicking and promenading are two favourite local pastimes, so it's fortunate that there are so many wonderful parks and gardens open to the public. Particularly beautiful or historic examples include Gülhane Park (p81) and the Hippodrome (p77) in Sultanahmet, Yıldız Park (p151) in Beşiktaş, and Hıdiv Kasrı (p168) and Emirgan Korusu (woods; p168) on the Bosphorus.

Churches

There are a surprising number of still-functioning Christian churches in İstanbul, many of which are of great historical significance and none of which charge an official entry fee. The best known of these is the Patriarchal Church of St George (p117) in Fener, the symbolic headquarters of the Greek Orthodox church.

Byzantine Monuments

Many of the city's Byzantine churches were converted into mosques after the Conquest and still function as such. Other Byzantine monuments that can be visited at no charge include the beautifully restored cistern in the basement of the Nakkaş (p82) carpet store in Sultanahmet and the historic city walls built during the reign of Emperor Theodosius II. The best place to see the latter is at Edirnekapı in the Western Districts.

Street stall selling fish sandwiches (*balık ekmek*; p106)

 # Eating

In İstanbul, meals are events to be celebrated. There's an eating option for every budget, predilection and occasion – all made memorable by the use of fresh seasonal ingredients and a local expertise in grilling meat and fish that has been honed over centuries. When you eat out here, you're sure to finish your meal replete and satisfied.

NEED TO KNOW

Price Ranges

The following symbols indicate the average cost of a main course in the reviewed restaurant or eatery.

€ less than ₺20

€€ ₺20–35

€€€ more than ₺35

Opening Hours

Standard opening hours for restaurants and cafes:

Breakfast 7.30am to 10.30am

Lunch noon to 2.30pm

Dinner 6.30pm to 10pm

Reservations

Friday and Saturday nights are busy at all popular restaurants. Be sure to book at least a week in advance.

Alcohol

Many simple eateries in İstanbul don't serve alcohol. In our reviews, we have indicated if a place is alcohol free.

Tipping

In restaurants, bistros and *meyhanes*, a 10% tip is standard if you have been satisfied with the service. There's usually no expectation that customers will tip at cafes, *lokantas*, *kebapçıs*, *köftecıs* and *pidecis*.

What's on the Menu?

The local cuisine has been refined over centuries and is treated more reverently than any museum collection in the country. That's not to say it's fussy, because what differentiates Turkish food from other national noshes is its rustic and honest base. Here mezes (small tapas-like dishes) are simple, kebaps uncomplicated, salads unstructured and seafood unsauced. Flavours explode in your mouth because ingredients are grown locally and used when they are in season.

MARVELLOUS MEZES

Mezes aren't just a type of dish, they're a whole eating experience. In *meyhanes* (Turkish taverns), waiters heave around

Turkish Delight (*lokum*; p44) – comes in a variety of flavours

enormous trays full of cold meze dishes that customers can choose from; hot meze dishes are usually chosen from the menu.

Mezes are usually vegetable based, though seafood dishes also feature.

MEAT – THE TURKISH WAY

Overall, the Turks are huge meat eaters. Beef, lamb, mutton, liver and chicken are prepared in a number of ways and eaten at home, in *kebapçıs* (kebap restaurants) and in *köftecisi* (meatball restaurants).

The most famous meat dish is the kebap – *şiş* and döner – but *köfte, saç kavurma* (stir-fried cubed-meat dishes) and *güveç* (meat and vegetable stews) are just as common.

The most popular sausage in Turkey is the spicy beef *sucuk*. Garlicky *pastırma* (pressed beef preserved in spices) is regularly used as an accompaniment to egg dishes; it's occasionally served with warm hummus as a meze.

A few İstanbul restaurants serve the central Anatolian dish of *mantı* (Turkish ravioli stuffed with beef mince and topped with yogurt, garlic tomato and butter).

FRESH FROM THE SEA

Fish is wonderful here, but can be pricey. In a *balık restoran* (fish restaurant), you should always choose your own fish from the display. The eyes should be clear and the flesh under the gill slits near the eyes should be bright red. After choosing, ask the approximate price. The fish will be weighed, and the price computed at the day's per-kilogram rate. Try to avoid eating *lüfer* (bluefish) when the fish are small

Above: Pide (Turkish-style pizza) is perfect for snacking on

Right: Fresh vegetables are available from markets all over the city

LOKANTAS

These casual eateries serve *hazır yemek* (ready-made food) kept warm in bains-marie, and usually offer a range of vegetable dishes alongside meat options. The etiquette when eating at one of these places is to check out what's in the bain-marie and tell the waiter or cook behind the counter what you would like to eat. You can order one portion *(bir porsiyon)*, a *yarım* (half) porsiyon or a plate with a few different choices. You'll be charged by the portion.

(less than 24cm in length), as overfishing is endangering the future of this much-loved local species. The best time of the year for local fish is winter.

VEGETABLES & SALADS

Turks love vegetables, eating them fresh in summer and pickling them for winter (pickled vegetables are called *turşu*). There are two particularly Turkish ways of preparing vegetables: the first is known as *zeytinyağlı* (sautéed in olive oil) and the second as *dolma* (stuffed with rice or meat).

Simplicity is the key to a Turkish *salata* (salad), with crunchy fresh ingredients being eaten with gusto as a meze or as an accompaniment to a meat or fish main course. The most popular summer salad is *çoban salatası* (shepherd's salad), a colourful mix of chopped tomatoes, cucumber, onion and pepper.

Sweets

Turks don't usually finish their meal with a dessert, preferring to serve fruit as a finale. Most of them love a midafternoon sugar hit though, and will often pop into a *muhallebici* (milk pudding shop), *pastane* (patisserie) or *baklavacı* (baklava shop) for a piece of syrup-drenched baklava, a plate of chocolate-crowned profiteroles or a *fırın sütlaç* (rice pudding) tasting of milk, sugar and just a hint of exotic spices. Other Turkish sweet specialities worth sampling are *dondurma,* the local ice cream; *kadayıf,* dough soaked in syrup and topped with a layer of *kaymak* (clotted cream); *künefe,*

layers of *kadayıf* cemented together with sweet cheese, doused in syrup and served hot with a sprinkling of pistachio; and *katmer* (flaky pastry stuffed with pistachios and *kaymak*).

FAST FOOD

The nation's favourite fast food is undoubtedly döner kebap – lamb slow-cooked on an upright revolving skewer and then shaved off to be stuffed into bread. Soggy cold French fries and green chillies are sometimes included; at other times salad and a sprinkling of slightly sour sumac are the accompaniments.

Coming a close second in the popularity stakes is pide, the Turkish version of pizza. It has a canoe-shaped base topped with *peynir* (cheese), *yumurta* (egg) or *kıymalı* (minced meat). A *karaşık* pide has a mixture of toppings. You can sit down to eat these in a *pideci* (Turkish pizza parlour) or ask for your pide *paket* (wrapped to go). *Lahmacun* (Arabic-style pizza) has a thinner crust than pide and is usually topped with chopped lamb, onion and tomato.

Börek (filled pastries) are usually eaten in the morning and are distinguished by their filling, cooking method and shape. They come in square, cigar or snail shapes and are filled with *peynir, ıspanaklı* (spinach), *patates* (potatoes) or *kıymalı*. Bun-shaped *poğaca* are glazed with sugar or stuffed with cheese and olives. *Su böreği,* a melt-in-the-mouth, lasagne-like layered pastry laced with white cheese and parsley, is the most popular of all *börek* styles.

Gözleme (thin savoury crepes cooked with cheese, spinach or potato) are also great quick snacks.

STREET FOOD

Street vendors pound pavements across İstanbul, pushing carts laden with artfully arranged snacks to satisfy the appetites of commuters. You'll see these vendors next to ferry and bus stations, on busy streets and squares,and even on the city's bridges.

Some of their snacks are innocuous – freshly baked *simits* (bread rings studded with sesame seeds), golden roasted *mısır* (corn on the cob), refreshing chilled and peeled *salatalık* (cucumber) – but others are more confrontational for non-Turkish palates. These include *midye*

Baklava – this traditional sweet needs no introduction

dolma (stuffed mussels) and *kokoreç* (seasoned lamb or mutton intestines wrapped around a skewer and grilled over charcoal).

VEGETARIANS & VEGANS

Though it's normal for Turks to eat a vegetarian (*vejeteryen*) meal, the concept of vegetarianism is quite foreign. Say you're a vegan and most Turks will either look mystified or assume that you're 'fessing up to some strain of socially aberrant behaviour. There is a sprinkling of vegetarian restaurants in Beyoğlu, a couple of which serve some vegan meals, but the travelling vegetarian certainly can't rely on specialist restaurants.

The meze spread is usually vegetable based, and meat-free salads, soups, pastas, omelettes and *böreks,* as well as hearty vegetable dishes, are all readily available. Ask '*Etsiz yemekler var mı?*' (Is there something to eat that has no meat?) to see what's on offer.

SELF-CATERING

İstanbul has many small supermarkets (DIA, Gima, Makro) sprinkled on the streets around Beyoğlu, with giant cousins (such as Migros) in the suburbs. These sell most of the items you will need if you plan to self-cater. Then there is the ubiquitous *bakkal* (corner shop), which stocks bread, milk, basic groceries and usually fruit and vegetables.

The best places to purchase fresh produce are undoubtedly the street markets. In Eminönü the streets around the Spice Bazaar (p98; Mısır Çarşısı) sell fish, meat, vegetables, fruit, spices, sweets and much more. In Beyoğlu the Balık Pazarı (p128; Fish Market) off İstiklal Caddesi is a great, if expensive, little market. As well as its fish stalls, it has greengrocers selling a wide range of fruit and vegetables, shops selling sweets and pickles, and delicatessens (*şarküteri*) selling cheeses, *pastırma,* pickled fish, olives, jams and preserves. Larger produce markets are found near the *iskele* in Kadıköy from Monday to Saturday; in Fatih on Wednesday; in Beşiktaş and Feriköy on Saturday; and in Kasımpaşa (in Piyalepaşa Bulvarı) on Sunday. The best of these are the Kadıköy Produce Market (p157), the

Eating by Neighbourhood

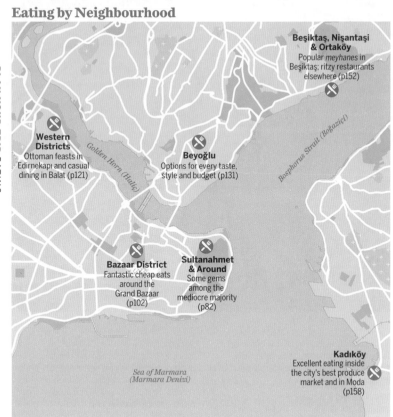

Beşiktaş, Nişantaşı & Ortaköy
Popular *meyhanes* in Beşiktaş; ritzy restaurants elsewhere (p152)

Western Districts
Ottoman feasts in Edirnekapı and casual dining in Balat (p121)

Beyoğlu
Options for every taste, style and budget (p131)

Bazaar District
Fantastic cheap eats around the Grand Bazaar (p102)

Sultanahmet & Around
Some gems among the mediocre majority (p82)

Kadıköy
Excellent eating inside the city's best produce market and in Moda (p158)

Golden Horn (Haliç)

Bosphorus Strait (Boğaziçi)

Sea of Marmara (Marmara Denizi)

Feriköy organic farmers market on Saturday and the Inebolu Produce Market in Kasimpaşa on Sunday.

COOKING COURSES & TOURS

Ask İstanbullus what makes their city special and the answer usually comes straight from their stomachs. The local cuisine has a fan club as numerous as it is vociferous, and its members enjoy nothing better than introducing visitors to the foods, eateries and provedores of the city. In short, this is a dream destination for everyone who loves to eat, cook and shop for food, particularly as plenty of cooking courses and food-focused walking tours are on offer, including the following:

➡ **Cooking Alaturka** (p90) Runs popular classes suitable for all skill levels.

➡ **İstanbul Eats** (p89) Fantastic food tours and a one-day cooking class in the fascinating Kurtuluş neighbourhood.

➡ **İstanbul on Food** (p146) A newly launched company offering food tours.

➡ **Turkish Flavours** (p160) Walking tours and excellent cooking classes held in a private residence on the Asian side of town. If requested, the course can focus on a Sephardic menu.

➡ **Urban Adventures** (p103) A variety of food tours.

Lonely Planet's Top Choices

Antiochia (p134) Southeastern dishes that look as good as they taste.

Çiya Sofrası (p158) Casual eatery showcasing Turkish regional cuisine.

Develi Baklava (p102) The baklava is great, but wait until you try the Gaziantep-style *katmer*...

Eleos (p135) Greek-style tavern specialising in seafood.

Hayvore (p134) Delectable dishes from the Black Sea region.

Zübeyir Ocakbaşı (p135) The city's most famous *ocakbaşı* (grill house) for good reason.

Best by Budget

€

Fatih Damak Pide (p103) It's a trek to get here, but the piping hot pides are worth it.

Hayvore (p134) Beyoğlu's best lunch venue.

€€

Antiochia (p134) Tangy mezes and succulent meat dishes.

Karaköy Lokantası (p133) One of İstanbul's most popular *meyhanes*.

€€€

Eleos (p135) Wonderful food and a view to match.

Neolokal (p133) Refined modern Turkish cuisine in swish surrounds.

Best Regional Eateries

Antiochia (p134) Specialises in dishes from the southeastern city of Antakya (Hatay).

Çiya Sofrası (p158) Seasonally inspired dishes from the southeast.

Hayvore (p134) Delicious dishes from the Black Sea.

Siirt Şeref Büryan Kebap (p105) Tender slow-cooked lamb from the southeastern city of Siirt.

Best Kebaps

Antiochia (p134) The best *şiş et* (grilled lamb) in town.

Zübeyir Ocakbaşı (p135) Locals flock here for the succulent meats cooked over coals.

Hamdi Restaurant (p105) Excellent meat, panoramic views and a bustling atmosphere.

Best Lokantas

Çiya Sofrası (p158) Bainsmarie full of unusual dishes from Turkey's southeastern region.

Erol Lokantası (p82) Simple food in the heart of Sultanahmet.

Hayvore (p134) *Hazır yemek* and pides popular with shoppers and workers in Beyoğlu.

Hünkar (p152) Upmarket choice with top-notch food and service.

Sefa Restaurant (p82) A reliable eatery close to the Grand Bazaar.

Best Meyhanes

Agora Meyhanesi (p121) Recently reinvented city institution known for its seafood.

Asmalı Cavit (p136) Good mezes and a convivial atmosphere.

Eleos (p135) Ultrafresh and flavourful Greek-style delicacies.

Karaköy Lokantası (p133) Stylish surrounds, a loyal clientele and excellent food.

Best Mezes

Meze by Lemon Tree (p135) Unusual and delicious meze spread.

Sahrap (p135) There are plenty of surprises on the modern meze menu at this stylish eatery.

Eleos (p135) Seafood-dominated meze spread that looks great and tastes even better.

Best Baklava

Develi Baklava (p102) Tiny space with a huge (and well-deserved) reputation.

Karaköy Güllüoğlu (p131) The perfect baklava stop at any time of day.

Pare Baklava Bar (p152) The genuine article flown in from Gaziantep daily.

Best Cafe Food

Cuma (p140) Seasonally driven menu and casually chic surrounds.

İnci Pastanesi (p134) Home of the city's best chocolate profiteroles.

Kantın (p152) Early and much-loved adaptor of the slow food philosophy.

Drinking & Nightlife

At the end of the working day, İstanbullus love nothing more than heading to a fashionable bar, convivial cafe or atmospheric çay bahçesi (tea garden) to catch up with friends and agree on which of the city's many clubs or live-music venues they will kick on to later in the evening.

Nonalcoholic Drinks

Drinking *çay* (tea) is the national pastime. Sugar cubes are the only accompaniment and they're needed to counter the effects of long brewing. No self-respecting Turk would dream of drinking *elma çay*, the sweet 'apple tea' made from chemicals that is offered to many tourists.

Surprisingly, *Türk kahve* (Turkish coffee) isn't widely consumed. A thick and powerful brew, it's drunk in a couple of short sips. If you order a cup, you will be asked how sweet you like it – *çok şekerli* means 'very sweet'; *orta şekerli*, 'middling'; *az şekerli*, 'slightly sweet' and *şekersiz* or *sade,* 'not at all'.

Freshly squeezed *portakal suyu* (orange juice) and *nar suyu* (pomegranate juice) are extremely popular drinks. In *kebapçıs* (kebap restaurants) patrons often drink *ayran* (a refreshing yogurt drink made by whipping yogurt with water and salt) or *şalgam suyu* (sour turnip juice).

If you're here during winter, you should try delicious and unusual *sahlep,* a hot drink made from crushed orchid-root extract.

Alcoholic Drinks

Turkey's most beloved tipple is rakı, a grape spirit infused with aniseed. Similar to Greek ouzo, it's served in long thin glasses and is drunk neat or with water, which turns the clear liquid chalky white. If you want to add ice *(buz),* do so after adding water, as dropping ice straight into rakı kills its flavour.

Bira (beer) is also popular. The most common local drop, Efes, is a perky pilsner that comes in bottles, cans and on tap.

Turkey grows and bottles its own *şarap* (wine), which has greatly improved over the past decade but is quite expensive due to high government taxes. If you want red wine, ask for *kırmızı şarap*; for white ask for *beyaz şarap*. There are four main grape-growing regions: Thrace, the Aegean, eastern Turkey and central Anatolia. As a general guide, you should consider whites from Thrace and the Aegean, and reds from the Aegean, eastern Turkey and central Anatolia. The best vintages of recent times are 2008, 2010 and 2015.

Labels to look out for include Sarafin (chardonnay, Fumé Blanc, sauvignon blanc, cabernet sauvignon, shiraz and merlot); Karma (cabernet sauvignon, shiraz and merlot); Kav Tuğra (*narince, kalecik karası* and *öküzgözü*); and DLC (most grape varieties). All are produced by **Doluca** (www.doluca.com). Its major competitor, **Kavaklidere** (www.kavaklidere.com), is known for the wines it puts out under the Pendore, Ancyra and Prestige labels (the Pendore *boğazkere* is particularly good), as well as its eminently quaffable Çankaya white blend.

Together, Doluca and Kavaklidere dominate the market, but producers such as **Vinkara** (www.vinkara.com) and **Kayra** (www.kayrasaraplari.com) are starting to build strong reputations. Seek out Vinkara's Narince Reserve and also its Yaşasın sparkling wine. From Kayra, the Buzbağ Reserve *öküzgözü-boğazkere* blend and the vintages it puts out under its Terra and Leona labels (try the Terra *öküzgözü*) are notable.

In recent years Thrace has become a wine-making hotspot. The vintages that are being released from estates such as **Arcadia** (www.arcadiavineyards.com), **Barbare** (www.barbarewines.com), **Suvla** (www.suvla.com.tr) and **Gali** (www.gali.com.tr) are well worth sampling.

The standout Aegean wineries are **Urla** (www.urlasarapcilik.com.tr), **Corvus** (www.corvus.com.tr) and **Sevilen** (http://sevilengroup.com). If you get the chance, sample Urla's Vourla red blend, Sevilen's late-harvest *misket* (muscat) and Corvus' Corpus red blend and passito.

Nargiles

While in town, consider visiting a *çay bahçesi* (tea garden). These atmosphere-rich venues are frequented by locals who don't drink alcohol, but enjoy smoking nargiles (water pipes).

When ordering a nargile, you'll need to specify what type of tobacco you would like. Most people opt for *elma* (when the tobacco has been soaked in apple juice, giving it a sweet flavour and scent), but it's possible to order it unadulterated (*tömbeki*). A nargile will cost between ₺20 and ₺30 and can be shared; you'll be given individual plastic mouthpieces.

Drinking & Nightlife by Neighbourhood

➡ **Sultanahmet & Around** (p84) A limited choice of cafes and *çay bahçesis* (tea gardens), but a few bars worth considering.

➡ **Bazaar District** (p106) An atmospheric array of *çay bahçesis* and nargile cafes, but no nightlife of which to speak.

➡ **Beyoğlu** (p140) The city's entertainment hub, with hundreds of bars, cafes and clubs from which to choose.

➡ **Beşiktaş, Nişantaşi & Ortaköy** (p153) A string of upmarket cafes, bars and clubs alongside the Bosphorus.

➡ **Kadıköy** (p159) A vibrant cafe and bar scene.

NEED TO KNOW

Opening Hours

➡ Opening hours of cafes, *çay bahçesi* (tea gardens), bars and clubs vary wildly; we have included specific hours in our reviews.

➡ Clubs are busiest on Friday and Saturday nights, and the action doesn't really kick off until 1am. Cover charges are levied at many clubs on these nights.

➡ Many Beyoğlu clubs close from June or July until the end of September. Most of the Bosphorus clubs close for part of winter.

Dress Code

When İstanbullus go out clubbing, they dress to kill. If you don't do the same, you'll be unlikely to get past the door staff at the Bosphorus clubs or into the rooftop bars and clubs in Beyoğlu. Fortunately, what you're wearing won't affect entry at the live-music venues, *meyhanes* (taverns) or grungier clubs.

Nightlife Rip-Offs

Foreigners, especially single foreign males, are sometimes targets for a classic İstanbul rip-off whereby they are approached by a friendly local, or group of locals, who asks them if they would like to visit a bar or nightclub. Unfortunately these guys are luring their victims into places run by organised crime groups, where drinks and the company of hostesses cost an absolute fortune and where refusing to pay the bill can lead to nasty, often physical confrontations. Be very wary of any such invitations.

Where to Party

The superclubs in the Golden Mile between Ortaköy and Kuruçeşme on the Bosphorus attract the wealthy and celebrity obsessed. Bohemian types tend to gravitate to the venues in Beyoğlu's Karaköy, Cihangir, Asmalımescit and Nevizade enclaves. Students hang out on or near Balo Sokak in Beyoğlu, or head over to Kadıköy, where they can be found drinking, dancing and listening to live gigs on Kadife Sokak, aka Barlar Sokak (Bar St).

Lonely Planet's Top Choices

Erenler Nargile ve Çay Bahçesi (p106) Alcohol free but atmosphere rich.

Fazıl Bey (p159) An esssential stop for lovers of Turkish coffee.

Federal Coffee Company (p137) İstanbul's best espresso.

Indigo (p141) Four-floor electronic-music temple.

Mikla (p140) Spectacular views and a stylish clientele.

Best Coffee

Coffee Department (p122) Bean-besotted business in Balat.

Fazıl Bey (p159) Perfecting the art of coffee making since 1927.

Federal Coffee Company (p137) Espresso made with house-roasted beans.

Kronotrop (p137) Ultrafashionable Cihangir coffee bar.

Manda Batmaz (p141) Popular pit stop off İstiklal Caddesi.

Best Çay Bahçesis

Cafe Grand Boulevard (p141) The only old-style tea garden left on İstiklal Caddesi.

Derviş Aile Çay Bahçesi (p85) Enjoy a million-dollar Blue Mosque view with your çay.

Erenler Nargile ve Çay Bahçesi (p106) Popular hangout near the Grand Bazaar.

Mistanbul Hancı Cafe (p160) Next to the water in Üsküdar.

Pierre Loti Café (p122) Favourite weekend destination for couples and families.

Best Clubs

CUE İstiklal (p142) Cocktails and dancing high above Beyoğlu.

Indigo (p141) The city's electronic-music temple.

Klein (p153) Where energetic locals come to dance the night away.

Kloster (p142) Three floors, three different stages and a rooftop terrace.

Best Gay & Lesbian Venues

Haspa (p142) Popular Taksim bar.

Love Dance Point (p153) The most Europhile of the local gay venues.

Tek Yön (p142) The city's largest gay dance floor.

Best Neighbourhood Bars

Unter (p140) In the centre of the fashionable Karaköy neighbourhood.

Cihangir 21 (p142) Popular haunt of Cihangir locals.

Geyik (p137) Coffee during the day, cocktails into the wee hours.

Karga Bar (p159) The best-loved bar in Kadıköy.

Smyrna (p142) Long-standing favourite of arty types.

Best Rooftop Bars & Cafes

A'YA Rooftop Lounge (p85) Luxurious retreat overlooking Aya Sofya and the Blue Mosque.

Leb-i Derya (p141) The prototype for the famous portfolio of rooftop bars in Beyoğlu.

Mikla (p140) Scenery and style overload (in a good way).

Mimar Sinan Teras Cafe (p106) A student hangout near İstanbul University.

360 (p141) Panoramic view, mixed clientele and weekend club vibe.

Topless Teras (p142) Start with a cocktail and stay for a dance.

Entertainment

It's rare to have a week go by without a range of special events, festivals and performances being staged in İstanbul. Locals adore listening to live music (jazz is a particular favourite), attend multiplex cinemas on a regular basis and support a small but thriving number of local theatre, opera and dance companies.

Seeing the Dervishes Whirl

If you thought the Hare Krishnas or the Harlem congregations were the only religious groups to celebrate their faith through music and movement, think again. Those sultans of spiritual spin known as the 'whirling dervishes' have been twirling their way to a higher plane ever since the 13th century and show no sign of slowing down.

There are a number of opportunities to see dervishes whirling in İstanbul. The best known of these is the weekly ceremony in the *semahane* (whirling dervish hall) in the Galata Mevlevi Museum (p143) in Tünel. This one-hour ceremony is held on Sunday at 5pm and costs ₺70 per person. Come early to buy your ticket.

Another much longer and more authentic ceremony is held at the **EMAV Silivrikapı Mevlana Cultural Center** (EMAV Silivrikapı Mevlana Kültür Merkezi; ☑0212-588 5780; www.emav.org; Yeni Tavanlı Çeşme Sokak 6, Silivrikapı; 🚇Çapa-Şehremini) on Thursday evening between 7.30pm and 11pm. This includes a Q&A session (in Turkish), prayers and a *sema* (ceremony). You'll need to sit on the ground for a long period. Admission is by donation. Those wishing to have an English-language introduction to the *sema*, be accompanied by a guide and be taken there and back by minibus from Sultanahmet should book through Les Arts Turcs (p88).

For a more touristy experience, the Hodjapasha Culture Centre (p88), housed in a beautifully converted 15th-century hamam near Eminönü, presents whirling dervish performances at least three evenings per week throughout the year.

Remember that the ceremony is a religious one – by whirling, the adherents believe they are attaining a higher union with God. So don't talk, leave your seat or take flash photographs while the dervishes are spinning or chanting.

Cultural Centres

Beyoğlu is home to a swathe of high-profile cultural centres where film events and live music, theatre and dance performances are staged. These include Akbank Art (p131), Borusan Art (p143), Depo (p129), Salon (p143), SALT Galata (p129) and Garajistanbul (p143).

Mall Venues

Most of the city's cinemas are operated by **Cinemaximum** (www.cinemaximum.com.tr) and are located in modern shopping malls. They include multiscreen venues at the **Zorlu Center** (☑0212-924 0124; www.zorlucenter.com; Beşiktaş; 🅼Gayrettepe) in Beşiktaş, Kanyon (p154) in Levent and City's Nişantaşı (p154) in Nişantaşı. Zorlu also has a state-of-the-art performing arts centre where musicals are staged and big-name international acts perform.

Dervishes whirl at a *sema* (whirling-dervish ceremony)

NEED TO KNOW

What's On

The **Canım Istanbul** (http://canim istanbul.com/blog/en), **The Guide** (www.theguideistanbul.com) and **Yabangee** (http://yabangee.com) websites feature events information.

Booking Tickets

Biletix (☑0216-556 9800; www.biletix. com) is the number-one web-based resource to use when sourcing tickets for concerts, festivals and performance events across the city.

Entertainment by Neighbourhood

➡ **Sultanahmet & Around** (p88) Whirling dervish and Turkish dance performances at the Hodjapasha Cultural Centre, but nothing else of note.

➡ **Beyoğlu** (p142) The city's entertainment hub, with performance venues, cinemas and live-music clubs galore. Also home to the Galata Mevlevi Museum, where a weekly *sema* (Whirling dervish ceremony) is held.

➡ **Beşiktaş, Nişantaşi & Ortaköy** (p154) Home to the city's major orchestral music hall, the **İstanbul Lütfi Kırdar ICEC** (Map p250; ☑0212-373 1100; www.icec.org; Gümüş Caddesi 4, Harbiye; Ⓜ Taksim); while the much-loved Babylon Bomonti music venue is only a short distance away.

➡ **Kadıköy** (p159) The city's bijou Süreyya Opera House is located here, as are a couple of smaller venues in the Yeldeğirmeni district.

Lonely Planet's Top Choices

Babylon Bomonti (p154) Eclectic music program and bohemian surrounds.

Borusan Art (p143) Small but prestigious music hall.

Garajistanbul (p143) About as edgy as the city's performance scene gets.

Nardis Jazz Club (p143) The city's pre-eminent jazz venue.

Salon (p143) Intimate space operated by İstanbul Foundation for Culture & Arts (İKSV).

Zorlu Center (p39) Two theatres where musicals are staged and big-name acts perform.

Best Cinemas

Başka Sinema (p143) Art-house cinema on İstiklal Caddesi in Beyoğlu.

Cinemaximum Zorlu Center (p39) Fourteen state-of-the-art screens.

Best Jazz Venues

Borusan Art (p143) Limited but top-drawer performance program.

Nardis Jazz Club (p143) Beloved of true aficionados.

Salon (p143) Strong on jazz, but also hosts alternative, experimental and world music.

Best Classical Music Venues

Akbank Art (p131) Where the Akbank Chamber Orchestra performs.

İstanbul Lütfi Kırdar ICEC (p40) Main venue for the Borusan İstanbul Philharmonic Orchestra.

Süreyya Opera House (p159) Home to the İstanbul State Opera and Ballet.

Best Popular & Alternative Music Venues

Babylon Bomonti (p154) Alternative and arty.

Borusan Art (p143) Classical, jazz, world and new music.

Garajistanbul (p143) Pop, alt rock, jazz and experimental music.

Salon (p143) World, jazz and experimental music.

Zorlu Center (p39) Blockbuster musicals and big-name international acts.

PLAN YOUR TRIP ENTERTAINMENT

The Grand Bazaar (p93) grew from a small warehouse in the 15th century

Shopping

İstanbullus have perfected the practice of shopping over centuries, and most visitors to the city are quick to follow their lead. Historic bazaars, colourful street markets and an ever-expanding portfolio of modern shopping malls cater to every desire and make sourcing a souvenir or two both easy and satisfying.

What to Buy

ANTIQUES

The grand Ottoman-era houses of İstanbul are still surrendering treasures. Head to the antique shops of Çukurcuma or the Grand Bazaar to find something to take home, but note that it is officially illegal to take anything over 100 years old out of the country. In reality, though, officials are only worried about objects from the classical, Byzantine or early Ottoman eras.

BATH WARES

Attractive towels, *peştemals* (bath wraps) and bathrobes made on hand looms in southern Turkey are sold in designer bath-wares shops around the city. Other popular purchases include olive-oil soaps and hamam sets with soap, shampoo, an exfoliation glove and a hamam bowl.

CARPETS & KILIMS

Asking locals for a recommendation when it comes to rug shops can be something of a knotty subject. This industry is rife with commissions, fakes and dodgy merchandise, so you need to be very careful when making a purchase. Don't fall for the shtick of touts on the street – these guys never, ever work for the truly reputable dealers.

Scam artists abound in the carpet trade. Be extremely wary in all of your negotiations and dealings.

CERAMICS
Turkish ceramics are beautiful and the standard fare fits within most budgets. Many of the tiles you see in the tourist shops have been painted using a silk-screen printing method and this is why they're cheap. Hand-painted bowls, plates and other pieces are more expensive; the best have original designs and are painted without the use of a carbon-paper pattern. Head to the Arasta Bazaar (p88) or Grand Bazaar (p93) to find good examples.

FASHION
The local fashion industry is thriving and there are plenty of chains, department stores and boutiques to investigate. Head to Nişantaşı, Tophane and Karaköy to find the most interesting boutiques.

GLASSWARE
İstanbul produces some unique glasswork, a legacy of the Ottoman Empire's affection for this delicate and intricate art. Paşabahçe shops around the city sell attractive glassware that is mass produced at its factory on the upper Bosphorus.

INLAID WOOD
Local artisans make jewellery boxes, furniture and chess and backgammon boards that are inlaid with different-coloured woods, silver or mother-of-pearl. Make sure the piece really does feature inlay. These days alarmingly accurate decals exist. Also check the silver: is it really silver, or does it look like aluminium or pewter? And what about that mother-of-pearl? It is in fact 'daughter-of-polystyrene'?

JEWELLERY
İstanbul is a wonderful place to buy jewellery, especially pieces made by the city's growing number of artisans creating contemporary pieces inspired by local culture. You'll find great examples around and inside the Grand Bazaar, and in Beyoğlu and Nişantaşı.

PLAN YOUR TRIP SHOPPING

NEED TO KNOW

Opening Hours

The most common shopping hours are from 10am to 7pm Monday to Saturday, but this is by no means always the case. We have indicated specific hours in most reviews.

Taxes & Refunds

Turkey has a value-added tax (VAT), known as the *katma değer vergisi* (KDV). This means that a tax of between 1% and 60% is included in the price of most goods and services. Rates vary wildly – eg alcohol is taxed at 18% (producers also pay a tax of 50%), whereas food and books are taxed at 8%.

If you buy an item costing more than ₺118 from a shop that participates in the national 'Global Refund: Tax Free Shopping' scheme, you are entitled to a refund of the KDV at your point of departure. At the airport, remember to have customs inspect your purchase(s) and stamp your tax-free form before you go through immigration; you can then collect your refund near the food court in the departure lounge.

SHAWLS
Those keen on buying a shawl should be aware of the difference between a pashmina and a shahtoosh. Pashminas use cashmere from Himalayan goats that is blended with silk, whereas shahtooshs are woven from the hair of the endangered Tibetan antelope. Antelope wool is usually obtained after the animal's death, so we believe that shahtoosh purchase should be avoided. Neither bear any resemblance to the cheap, faux pashminas that are sold by stores in the Grand Bazaar, which are made from synthetic fibre.

TEXTILES
Turkey's southeast region is known for its textiles, and there are examples aplenty on show in the Grand Bazaar (p93). You can also find top-quality cotton, linen and silk there.

Collectors of antique textiles will be in seventh heaven when inspecting the decorative tribal textiles that have made their way here from Central Asia. These are often sold in carpet shops.

TURKISH DELIGHT

Lokum (Turkish Delight) makes a great present for those left at home, but is even better to scoff on the spot. It's sold in speciality shops around the city and comes in flavours such as *cevizli* (walnut), *fıstıklı* (pistachio), *bademli* (almond) and *roze* (rose water). Ask for a *çeşitli* (assortment) if you want to sample the various types. The largest concentration of quality outlets is around (but not in) the Spice Bazaar at Eminönü.

The Dying Art of Bargaining

The elaborate etiquette of the Ottoman Empire lingers in many day-to-day rituals still observed in its greatest creation, İstanbul. Until recently the art of bargaining was one of these. Times have changed, though, and these days the non-negotiable price tag reigns supreme in most of the city's retail outlets. Here, as in many former stops along the legendary Silk Road, the days of camel caravans have long gone, supplanted by multinational retailers, sleek supply-chain management and an increasingly homogeneous shopping experience.

Perhaps the only exception to this rule can be found in the city's carpet shops, particularly those located in the Grand Bazaar (p93). Many of these still take pride in practising the ancient art of bargaining.

If you are visiting İstanbul and are keen to buy a carpet or rug in the bazaar, keep the following tips in mind:

➡ The 'official' prices have almost always been artificially inflated to allow for a bargaining margin, with 20% to 30% the rule of thumb.

➡ Shopping here involves many aspects of Ottoman etiquette. You will drink tea, exchange polite greetings and size up the trustworthiness of the shopkeeper. He, in turn, will drink tea, exchange polite greetings and size up your gullibility.

➡ Never feel pressured to buy something. Tea and conversation are gratis. If you accept them, you don't need to buy anything in exchange.

➡ It's important to do your research. Always shop around to compare quality and pricing.

➡ Before starting to bargain, decide how much you like the carpet or rug and how much you are prepared to pay for it. It's important that you stick to this. The shopkeepers here are professional bargainers and have loads of practise in talking customers into purchases against their better judgement.

➡ Your first offer should be around 60% of the initial asking price. The shopkeeper will laugh, look offended or profess to be puzzled, which is all part of the ritual.

➡ He will then make a counter offer of 80% to 90%. You should look disappointed, explain that you have done your research and say that you are not prepared to pay that amount. Then you should offer around 70%.

➡ By this stage you and the shopkeeper should have sized each other up. He will cite the price at which he is prepared to sell and, if it corresponds with what you were initially happy to pay, you can agree to the deal. If not, you should smile, shake hands and walk away.

The same rules also apply in some textile, jewellery and antique shops in the bazaar, but they don't apply to all. The fashionable stores in Halıcılar Çarşışı Sokak started the trend towards set pricing here a number of years ago and many other shops have followed their lead.

Shopping by Neighbourhood

➡ **Sultanahmet & Around** (p88) Top-notch ceramics, rug and bath-ware stores are found in and around the Arasta Bazaar.

➡ **Bazaar District** (p108) Options galore in the Grand Bazaar, the Spice Bazaar and streets between the two.

➡ **Beyoğlu** (p143) Galata, Cihangir, Karaköy and Çukurcuma are bursting with fashion boutiques, designer homewares stores and antique shops.

➡ **Beşiktaş, Nişantaşı & Ortaköy** (p154) International and local designer fashion can be sourced from the upmarket boutiques in Nişantaşı.

Lonely Planet's Top Choices

Hiç (p144) Designer homewares made by local and international artisans.

Jennifer's Hamam (p88) Top-quality hamam items, including towels, *peştemals* (bath wraps) and *keses* (exfoliating cloth mittens).

Nahıl (p145) Felting, lacework, embroidery and all-natural soaps made by economically disadvantaged women in Turkey's rural areas.

Özlem Tuna (p88) Artisan-designed and artisan-made jewellery and homewares.

Abdulla Natural Products (p108) Top-quality soap, towels and wraps.

Best for Bath Wares

Abdulla Natural Products (p108) Olive-oil soaps, cotton towels and a large range of *peştemals* (bath wraps).

Derviş (p109) Soaps, towels and wraps to beautify your bathroom.

Eyüp Sabri Tuncer (p144) Well-priced colognes, soaps and lotions.

Jennifer's Hamam (p88) Towels, robes and wraps produced on old-style shuttled looms.

Best for Fashion

Antijen Design (p145) Sculptural pieces made to measure.

Arzu Kaprol (p145) Sleek and sophisticated women's ensembles.

Gönul Paksoy (p154) Exquisite Ottoman-influenced creations.

Misela (p145) Ultrafashionable handbags.

Vakko İndirim (p111) Bargains galore for men and women.

Best for Homewares

Hamm (p144) Stylish showcase of contemporary Turkish furniture and lighting.

Hiç (p144) Artisan-made rugs, cushions, furniture and ceramics.

NYKS (p144) Elegantly packaged olive-oil candles.

Özlem Tuna (p88) Super-stylish bowls, coffee cups and platters.

Best for Jewellery

Özlem Tuna (p88) Contemporary designs with Turkish accents.

Necef Antik & Gold (p108) Byzantine- and Ottoman-inspired pieces in the Grand Bazaar.

Selda Okutan (p144) Avant-garde designer based in Karaköy.

Ümit Berksoy (p109) Artisan jeweller based in the Grand Bazaar.

Best for Turkish Delight

Ali Muhıddin Hacı Bekir (p109) Family-run business established in the city more than two centuries ago.

Altan Şekerleme (p109) Selling cheap and delicious Turkish delight since 1865.

Hafız Mustafa (p109) An İstanbul institution, with branches across the Old City.

Lokum Istanbul (p154) Gorgeous packaging makes for sophisticated gifts.

Şekerci Aytekin Erol Caferzade (p160) Old-fashioned shop known for its unusual flavours.

Best for Textiles

Mehmet Çetinkaya Gallery (p89) Antique pieces in the Arasta Bazaar.

Mekhann (p109) Handwoven silk from Uzbekistan, plus a range of finely woven shawls.

Muhlis Günbatti (p110) Specialises in *suzani* fabrics from Uzbekistan.

Yazmacı Necdet Danış (p109) Richly hued bolts of fabric and a range of scarves.

Cocoon (p89) Striking textiles and handicrafts from Central Asia.

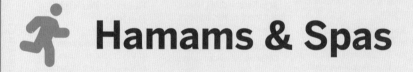 Hamams & Spas

Succumbing to a soapy scrub in a steamy hamam is one of İstanbul's quintessential experiences. Not everyone feels comfortable with baring all (or most) of their body in public, though. If you include yourself in this group, a number of the city's spas offer private hamam treatments.

Hamams

The concept of the steam bath was passed from the Romans to the Byzantines and then on to the Turks, who named it the hamam. They've even exported the concept throughout the world, hence the term 'Turkish bath'. Until recent decades, many homes in İstanbul didn't have bathroom facilities and, due to Islam's emphasis on personal cleanliness, the community relied on the hundreds of hamams throughout the city, often as part of the *külliye* (mosque complex) of a mosque. Now that most people have bathrooms in İstanbul, hamams are nowhere near as popular, but some carry on due to their roles as local meeting places. Others have become successful tourist attractions.

The city's hamams vary enormously. Some are dank dives where you may come out dirtier than you went in (remember, Turks call cockroaches 'hamam insects'); others are plain and clean, servicing a predominantly local clientele. A small number have built a reputation as gay meeting places (we're talking truly steamy here), and an increasing number are geared exclusively towards tourists. A number of hotels in the city have hamams, too. These include Sirkeci Mansion (p181), Arcadia Blue Hotel (p182), **Hayriye Hanım Konağı** (HHK Hotel; Map p242; ☑0212-513 0026; www.hhkhotel. com; Hayriye Hanım Sokak 19, Süleymaniye; s/d €148/158; ☀✳☎☑; ⓜHaliç), Pera Palace

Hotel (p184), Four Seasons Istanbul at the Bosphorus (p184), **Sumahan on the Water** (☑0216-422 8000; www.sumahan.com; Kuleli Caddesi 43, Çengelköy; r €200-330, ste €300-620; ☀✳@☎; ☑15, 15F & 15P from Üsküdar) and Vault Karaköy (p183).

We haven't reviewed any gay hamams, as the current socio-political climate makes their legal status ambiguous.

BATH PROCEDURE

Upon entry you are shown to a *camekan* (entrance hall or space), where you will be allocated a dressing cubicle *(halvet)* or locker and given a *peştemal* (bath wrap) and *plastik çarıklar* (plastic sandals) or *takunya* (wooden clogs). Store your clothes and don the *peştemal* and footware. An attendant will then lead you through the *soğukluk* (intermediate section) to the *hararet* (steam room), where you sit and sweat for a while, relaxing and loosening up, perhaps on the *göbektaşı* (central, raised platform atop the heating source).

Soon you will be half asleep and as soft as putty from the steamy heat. The cheapest bath is the one you do yourself, having brought your own soap, shampoo and towel. But the real Turkish bath experience is to have an attendant wash, scrub and massage you.

If you have opted for the latter, an attendant douses you with warm water and lathers you with a sudsy sponge. Next you are scrubbed with a *kese* (coarse cloth mitten), loosening dirt you never suspected you had. After a massage (these yo-yo between being enjoyable, limp-wristed or mortally dangerous) comes a shampoo and another dousing with warm water, followed by one with cool water.

When the scrubbing is over, relax in the *hararet* or head to the *camekan*, where you can get dressed or have a rest; at some hamams you can order something to eat or drink. The average hamam experience takes around one hour.

Spas

Most of İstanbul's five-star hotels have spas where a hamam exists alongside facilities such as saunas, steam rooms, plunge pools and rain-shower rooms. Hamam treatments in these spas are private and often incorporate added extras such as facials, foot massages, hair treatments and body wraps. Some also offer remedial massages.

Lonely Planet's Top Choices

Four Seasons İstanbul at the Bosphorus (p184) The best of the luxury spas.

Kılıç Ali Paşa Hamamı (p146) Magnificently restored 16th-century hamam in Beyoğlu.

Ambassador Spa (p90) An expert masseur makes this modest place worth considering.

Ayasofya Hürrem Sultan Hamamı (p90) Dating to 1556 it offers the most luxurious traditional bath experience in the Old City.

Best Hamam Interiors

Kılıç Ali Paşa Hamamı (p146) Magnificently restored 16th-century hamam in Beyoğlu.

Ayasofya Hürrem Sultan Hamamı (p90) Built by order of Süleyman the Magnificent, and meticulously restored.

Cağaloğlu Hamamı (p90) The most beautiful of the city's Ottoman hamams.

Çemberlitaş Hamamı (p111) An architecturally splendid Ottoman hamam.

NEED TO KNOW

Opening Hours

Most of the tourist hamams and hotel spas are open from 8am to 11pm or midnight. Local hamams with only one bath have one set of hours for females and another for males; generally they close earlier than the tourist hamams.

Practicalities

Soap, shampoo and towels are provided at all of the hamams we've reviewed. If you're only having a bath, you'll need to pay for the soap and shampoo separately; it's always included in the cost of full treatments. You'll get drenched, so make sure you take a comb, toiletries, make-up and (if you choose to wear underwear during the massage) a dry pair of replacement underpants. There are usually hairdryers available for customer use.

Modesty

Traditional Turkish baths have separate sections for men and women, or have only one set of facilities and admit men and women at different times.

Bath etiquette requires that men remain covered with a *peştemal* at all times. Most women wear a bikini or a pair of knickers (Turks tend to do the latter). Some tourist hamams don't mind women baring all. During the bathing, everyone washes their private parts themselves, without removing the *peştemal* or underclothes.

In tourist areas there are a couple of hamams with only one bath area that allow foreign men and women to bathe together. In these cases, women should wear a bikini.

Tipping

This is discretionary. Don't feel obliged to tip if your treatment was cursory or substandard.

Explore İstanbul

Frescoes, Kariye Museum (p114)

İSTANBUL'S TOP SIGHTS

Neighbourhoods at a Glance

Many visitors to İstanbul never make it out of Sultanahmet. And while this is a shame, it's hardly surprising. After all, not many cities have such a concentration of historic sights, shopping precincts, hotels and eateries within easy walking distance. Ideally suited to exploration by foot, the neighbourhood is a showcase of the city's glorious past, crammed as it is with mosques, palaces, churches and houses dating from Roman, Byzantine and Ottoman periods.

This beguiling district is home to the Grand Bazaar and Spice Bazaar. Amid the thousands of shops that surround these

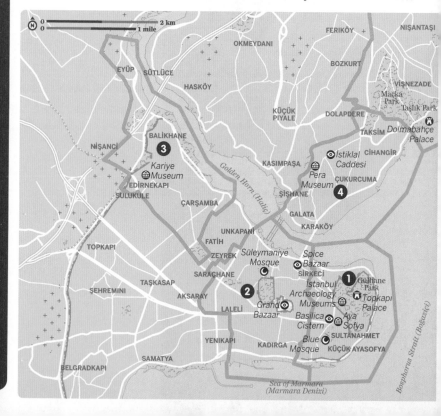

centuries-old marketplaces are magnificent Ottoman mosques, historic hamams and atmospheric *çay bahçesis* (tea gardens) where locals smoke nargiles (water pipes) and play games of *tavla* (backgammon). The streets between the bazaars are a popular stamping ground for İstanbullus, and seem to crackle with a good-humoured and infectious energy.

❸ Western Districts p112

A showcase of İstanbul's ethnically diverse and endlessly fascinating history, this neighbourhood to the west of the Historic Peninsula contains synagogues built by the Jews in Balat and churches constructed by the Greeks in Fener. In recent times migrants from eastern Turkey have settled here, attracted by the vibrant Wednesday street market in Fatih and the presence of two important Islamic pilgrimage sites: the tombs of Mehmet the Conqueror and Ebu Eyüp el-Ensari.

Kadıköy Produce Market (700m)

❹ Beyoğlu p123

The high-octane hub of eating, drinking and entertainment in the city, Beyoğlu is where visitors and locals come in search of good restaurants and bars, live-music venues, hip hotels and edgy boutiques. Built around the major boulevard of İstiklal Caddesi, it incorporates a mix of bohemian residential districts such as Çukurcuma and Cihangir, bustling entertainment enclaves such as Asmalımescit and historically rich pockets such as Tophane, Galata and Karaköy that have morphed into style centres.

❺ Beşiktaş, Nişantaşı & Ortaköy p147

Nineteenth-century French writer Pierre Loti described the stretch of the Bosphorus shore between Beşiktaş and Ortaköy as featuring 'a line of palaces white as snow, placed at the edge of the sea on marble docks'. Fortunately, his description remains as accurate as it is evocative. North of this palace precinct is the 'Golden Mile', a string of upmarket nightclubs running between Ortaköy and Kuruçeşme. These once-humble fishing villages are now pockets of prime waterfront real estate. Inland, join the İstanbul glitterati as they shop, dine and party in chichi Nişantaşı.

❻ Kadıköy p155

In recent years, locals have been decamping from the European side of town to Asia in ever-increasing numbers, setting up home in the suburbs that are strung south from the Bosphorus Bridge. Of these, bustling Kadıköy and its annex Moda are of the most interest to visitors, being home to İstanbul's best produce market, great eateries, convivial cafes, grunge bars and a progressive vibe.

Sultanahmet & Around

Neighbourhood Top Five

1 Aya Sofya (p54) Standing beneath the magnificent dome, imagining what it would have been like to attend a candlelit service in the greatest of all Byzantine churches.

2 Topkapı Palace (p109) Uncovering the secrets of the Harem in this opulent complex, which evokes the exotic, savage, *Game of Thrones*–like customs of the Ottoman court.

3 Blue Mosque (p118) Gazing up at the six minarets and many domes of the Ottoman masterpiece.

4 Basilica Cistern (p76) Exploring the atmospheric Byzantine cistern's watery depths.

5 Ayasofya Hürrem Sultan Hamamı (p90) Surrendering to the steam and admiring the historic surrounds in a restored Ottoman hamam such as this 16th-century beauty, commissioned by Süleyman the Magnificent and designed by the great Mimar Sinan.

For more detail of this area see Map p238 and p240 ➡

Explore Sultanahmet & Around

With so many significant monuments and museums in close proximity, devising an itinerary helps to make the most of your time. You'll need at least three days (four or five would be better) to do the neighbourhood justice.

Plan to visit one of the major museums (Aya Sofya, Topkapı Palace, the İstanbul Archaeology Museums, the Museum of Turkish & Islamic Arts) each day and then add the less time-intensive sights into your itineraries. For instance, it makes sense to visit the İstanbul Archaeology Museums and Gülhane Park together on one day and Aya Sofya, the Blue Mosque and the Basilica Cistern on another.

Don't worry if your plan of attack doesn't recall the military precision of the Ottomans' capture of Constantinople in 1453: retracing your steps is a pleasure when you pass the likes of Aya Sofya.

The ever-present battalions of tour groups tend to visit the museums first thing in the morning or after lunch – you will find that queues are shorter and exhibits less crowded if you visit during lunchtime or later in the afternoon.

This isn't a part of town where many locals live. Restaurants, cafes and shops are geared towards tourists and prices reflect this.

Local Life

➡ **Produce markets** There are weekly street markets in Cankurtaran on Wednesdays and in nearby Kadırga on Thursdays.

➡ **Backgammon** Head to Derviş Aile Çay Bahçesi (p85) or Cafe Meşale (p85) to join locals in smoking nargiles (water pipes), drinking tea and playing backgammon.

➡ **Promenade** On weekends, make like the local families who promenade through the Hippodrome (p77) and picnic in Gülhane Park (p81).

➡ **Küçük Ayasofya** Walking the quiet back streets of this residential neighbourhood gives a glimpse of everyday life beyond the tourist haunts.

Getting There & Away

➡ **Tram** The easiest way to reach Sultanahmet from Beyoğlu. The route crosses the Galata Bridge from Kabataş (where a funicular climbs to Taksim) and Karaköy (where a funicular climbs to Tünel) to the stops at Eminönü (terminal for ferries over the Bosphorus and up the Golden Horn), Sirkeci, Gülhane, Sultanahmet, Çemberlitaş and Beyazıt-Kapalı Çarşı (Grand Bazaar). Sultanahmet is the best stop for most of the sights in this area.

Lonely Planet's Top Tip

If you are spending a few days in the city and plan to visit the major museums in Sultanahmet, the **Museum Pass İstanbul** (www.muze.gov.tr/en/museum-card) will save you money and enable you to jump ticket queues.

Best Museums

➡ Aya Sofya (p54)

➡ Topkapı Palace (p61)

➡ Museum of Turkish & Islamic Arts (p77)

➡ İstanbul Archaeology Museums (p74)

➡ Carpet Museum (p79)

For reviews, see p77.➡

Best Places to Eat

➡ Deraliye (p84)

➡ Balıkçı Sabahattin (p84)

➡ Hocapaşa Sokak (p82)

➡ Cooking Alaturka (p84)

➡ Sefa Restaurant (p82)

For reviews, see p82.➡

Best Places to Shop

➡ Galeri Kayseri (p89)

➡ Özlem Tuna (p88)

➡ Jennifer's Hamam (p88)

➡ İznik Classics (p89)

➡ Mehmet Çetinkaya Gallery (p89)

➡ Khaftan (p89)

For reviews, see p88.➡

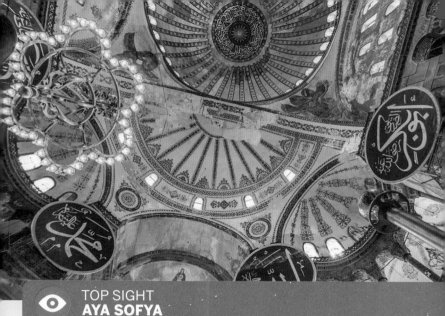

TOP SIGHT
AYA SOFYA

There are many important monuments in İstanbul, but this venerable structure – commissioned by the great Byzantine emperor Justinian, consecrated as a church in 537, converted to a mosque by Mehmet the Conqueror in 1453 and declared a museum by Atatürk in 1935 – surpasses the rest due to its innovative architectural form, rich history, religious importance and extraordinary beauty.

Entering the Building

Known as Hagia Sophia in Greek, Sancta Sophia in Latin and the Church of the Divine Wisdom in English, Aya Sofya has a history that's as long as it is fascinating. It was constructed on the site of Byzantium's acropolis, which was also the site of two earlier churches of the same name, one destroyed by fire and another during the Nika riots of AD 532.

On entering his commission for the first time, Justinian exclaimed, 'Glory to God that I have been judged worthy of such a work. Oh Solomon! I have outdone you!' Entering the building today, his hubris is understandable. The less impressive exterior offers little preparation for the sublimely beautiful interior, with its magnificent domed roof soaring heavenward.

Enter the building and walk straight ahead through the outer and inner narthexes to reach the **Imperial Door**, which is crowned with a striking mosaic of **Christ as Pantocrator** (Ruler of All). Christ holds a book that carries the inscription 'Peace be With You. I am the Light of the

DON'T MISS

→ *Christ as Pantocrator*
→ *Virgin and Christ Child*
→ *Deesis*
→ *Virgin Mary, Emperor John Comnenus II and Empress Eirene*
→ *Constantine the Great, Virgin Mary and the Emperor Justinian*

PRACTICALITIES

→ Hagia Sophia
→ Map p240, F1
→ ☎0212-522 0989, 0212-522 1750
→ http://ayasofya muzesi.gov.tr/en
→ Aya Sofya Meydanı 1
→ adult/child under 12yr ₺40/free
→ ⏰9am-7pm Tue-Sun mid-Apr–mid-Oct, to 5pm mid-Oct–mid-Apr, last entry 1hr before closing
→ 🚊Sultanahmet

World.' At his feet an emperor (probably Leo VI) prostrates himself. The Virgin Mary is on Christ's left and to his right is the Archangel Gabriel.

Through the Imperial Door is the building's main space, famous for its dome, huge nave and gold mosaics. Unfortunately, a huge scaffolding tower erected for restoration works has marred the interior for more than a decade.

Nave

Made 'transparent' by its profusion of windows and columned arcades, Aya Sofya's nave is as visually arresting as it is enormous.

The **chandeliers** hanging low above the floor are Ottoman additions. In Byzantine times, rows of glass oil lamps lined the balustrades of the gallery and the walkway at the base of the dome.

The focal point at this level is the **apse**, with its magnificent 9th-century mosaic of the **Virgin and Christ Child**. The *mimber* (pulpit) and the *mihrab* (prayer niche indicating the direction of Mecca) were added during the Ottoman period. The mosaics above the apse once depicted the archangels Gabriel and Michael; today only fragments remain.

The Byzantine emperors were crowned while seated on a throne placed within the **omphalion**, the section of inlaid marble in the main floor. The ornate **library** behind the omphalion was built by Sultan Mahmut I in 1739.

The large 19th-century **medallions** inscribed with gilt Arabic letters are the work of master calligrapher Mustafa İzzet Efendi, and give the names of God (Allah), Mohammed and the early caliphs Ali and Abu Bakr. Though impressive works of art in their own right, they seem out of place here, detracting from the austere magnificence of the building's interior.

The curious elevated kiosk screened from public view is the **imperial loge** (*hünkar mahfili*). Sultan Abdül Mecit I had this built in 1848 so he could enter, pray and leave unseen, thus preserving the imperial mystique.

Looking up towards the northeast (to your left if you are facing the apse), you should be able to see three mosaics at the base of the northern tympanum (semicircle) beneath the dome, although they were obscured by scaffolding when we visited. These are 9th-century portraits of **St Ignatius the Younger**, **St John Chrysostom** and **St Ignatius Theodorus of Antioch**. To their right, on one of the pendentives (concave triangular segments below the dome), is a 14th-century mosaic of the face of a **seraph** (six-winged angel charged with the caretaking of God's throne).

MOSAICS

In Justinian's day, the great dome, the semi-domes, the north and south tympana and the vaults of the narthexes, aisles and galleries were all covered in gold mosaics. Remnants exist, but one can only imagine what the interior looked like when overlaid with glittering and gleaming tesserae (small glass tiles incorporating gold leaf). There were no figurative mosaics at this time – these date from after the iconoclastic period, which ended in the early 9th century. When the church was converted into a mosque, the mosaics were considered inappropriate; fortunately, most were covered with plaster and not destroyed. Some were uncovered and restored during building works in the mid-19th century, and, though once again covered (by paint), were left in good condition for a final unveiling after the mosque was deconsecrated.

Vikings are said to have left the 'Eric woz here'-type graffiti that is carved into the balustrade in the upstairs south gallery. You'll find it near the *Deesis* mosaic.

AYA SOFYA – Ground Floor & Upstairs Galleries

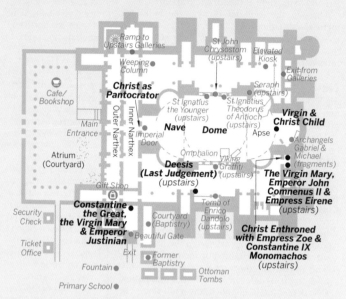

In the side aisle at the bottom of the ramp to the upstairs galleries is a column with a worn copper facing pierced by a hole. According to legend, the pillar, known as the **Weeping Column**, was blessed by St Gregory the Miracle Worker and putting one's finger into the hole is said to lead to ailments being healed if the finger emerges moist. Nearby, informative **films** are shown about Aya Sofya's structure and history.

Dome

Aya Sofya's dome is 30m in diameter and 56m in height. It's supported by 40 massive ribs constructed of special hollow bricks, and these ribs rest on four huge pillars concealed in the interior walls. On its completion, the Byzantine historian Procopius described it as being 'hung from heaven on a golden chain', and it's easy to see why. The great Ottoman architect Mimar Sinan, who spent his entire professional life trying to design a mosque to match the magnificence and beauty of Aya Sofya, used the same trick of concealing pillars and 'floating' the dome when designing the Süleymaniye Mosque almost 1000 years later.

Upstairs Galleries

To access the galleries, walk up the switchback ramp at the northern end of the inner narthex. In the south gallery (straight ahead and then left through the 6th-century marble door) are the remnants of a magnificent **Deesis** (Last Judgement). This 13th-century mosaic depicts Christ with the Virgin Mary on his right and John the Baptist on his left.

Close by is the **Tomb of Enrico Dandolo**, a blind Venetian doge who led the Sack of Constantinople during the Fourth Crusade (1202–04) and died soon

Mosaics

THE BUTTRESSES

The original building form designed by Aya Sofya's architects, Anthemios of Tralles and Isidoros of Miletus, has been compromised by the addition of 24 buttresses, added to reinforce the building and its enormous dome. Some date from Byzantine times, others from the Ottoman period; seven buttresses are on the eastern side of the building, four on the southern, four on the northern and five on the western. The remaining four support the structure as weight towers.

afterwards. The marker was laid in the 19th century by an Italian restoration team, the original having been destroyed by the Ottomans.

Further on, at the eastern (apse) end of the gallery, is an 11th-century mosaic depicting **Christ Enthroned with Empress Zoe and Constantine IX Monomachos**. When this portrait was started, Zoe (r 1028–50) was 50 years old and newly married (for the first time) to the aged Romanus III Argyrus. Upon Romanus' death in 1034, she had his face excised from the mosaic and replaced it with that of her virile new husband and consort, Michael IV. Michael died eight years later and Zoe, aged 64, wed the eminent senator Constantine IX Monomachos (r 1042–55), whose portrait was added here and remains only because he outlived the empress.

To the right of Zoe and Constantine is a 12th-century mosaic depicting the **Virgin Mary, Emperor John Comnenus II and Empress Eirene**. The emperor, who was known as 'John the Good', is on the Virgin's left and the empress, who was known for her charitable works, is to her right; both are giving money to Aya Sofya. Their son **Alexius** is depicted next to Eirene; he died soon after this portrait was made. Eirene's stone sarcophagus is downstairs in the outer narthex.

Outbuildings

Exit the inner narthex through the **Beautiful Gate**, a magnificent bronze gate dating from the

The last Byzantine Emperor, Constantine XI, prayed in Aya Sofya just before midnight on 28 May 1453. Hours later he was killed while defending the city walls from the attack being staged by the army of Mehmet II. The city fell to the Ottomans on the 29th, and Mehmet's first act of victory was to make his way to Aya Sofya and declare that it should immediately be converted to a mosque.

Aya Sofya

TIMELINE

537 Emperor Justinian, depicted in one of the church's famous **mosaics** ❶, presides over the consecration of Byzantium's new basilica, Hagia Sophia (Church of the Holy Wisdom).

557 The huge **dome** ❷, damaged during an earthquake, collapses and is rebuilt.

843 The second Byzantine Iconoclastic period ends and figurative **mosaics** ❸ begin to be added to the interior. These include a depiction of the Empress Zoe and her third husband, Emperor Constantine IX Monomachos.

1204 Soldiers of the Fourth Crusade led by the Doge of Venice, Enrico Dandolo, conquer and ransack Constantinople. Dandolo's **tomb** ❹ is eventually erected in the church whose desecration he presided over.

1453 The city falls to the Ottomans; Mehmet II orders that Hagia Sophia be converted to a mosque and renamed Aya Sofya.

1577 Sultan Selim II is buried in a specially designed tomb, which sits alongside the **tombs** ❺ of four other Ottoman Sultans in Aya Sofya's grounds.

1847–49 Sultan Abdül Mecit I orders that the building be restored and redecorated; the huge **Ottoman Medallions** ❻ in the nave are added.

1935 The mosque is converted into a museum by order of Mustafa Kemal Atatürk, president of the new Turkish Republic.

2009 The face of one of the four **seraphs** ❼ is uncovered during major restoration works in the nave.

2012 Restoration of the exterior walls and western upper gallery commences.

TOP TIPS

Bring binoculars if you want to properly view the mosaic portraits in the apse and under the dome.

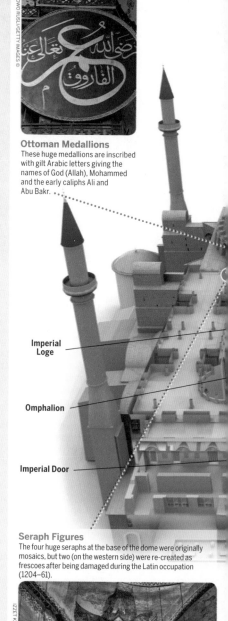

Ottoman Medallions
These huge medallions are inscribed with gilt Arabic letters giving the names of God (Allah), Mohammed and the early caliphs Ali and Abu Bakr.

Imperial Loge

Omphalion

Imperial Door

Seraph Figures
The four huge seraphs at the base of the dome were originally mosaics, but two (on the western side) were re-created as frescoes after being damaged during the Latin occupation (1204–61).

Dome

Soaring 56m from ground level, the dome was originally covered in gold mosaics but was decorated with calligraphy during the 1847–49 restoration works overseen by Swiss-born architects Gaspard and Giuseppe Fossati.

Christ Enthroned with Empress Zoe and Constantine IX Monomachos

This mosaic portrait in the upper gallery depicts Zoe, one of only three Byzantine women to rule as empress in their own right.

Ottoman Tombs

The tombs of five Ottoman sultans and their families are located in Aya Sofya's southern corner and can be accessed via Babıhümayun Caddesi. One of these occupies the church's original Baptistry.

Aya Sofya Tombs

Former Baptistry

Muvakkithane (place where prayer hours were determined)

Ablutions Fountain

Exit

Primary School

Main Entrance

Grave of Enrico Dandolo

The Venetian doge died in 1205, only one year after he and his Crusaders had stormed the city. A 19th-century marker in the upper gallery indicates the probable location of his grave.

Constantine the Great, the Virgin Mary and Emperor Justinian

This 11th-century mosaic shows Constantine (right) offering the Virgin Mary the city of Constantinople. Justinian (left) is offering her Hagia Sophia.

2nd century BC. This originally adorned a pagan temple in Tarsus and was brought to İstanbul by Emperor Theophilos in 838.

As you reach the gate, be sure to look back to admire the 10th-century mosaic of **Constantine the Great, the Virgin Mary and the Emperor Justinian** on the lunette of the inner doorway. Constantine (right) is offering the Virgin, who holds the Christ Child, the city of İstanbul; Justinian (left) is offering her Aya Sofya.

The doorway to your left just after the Beautiful Gate leads into a small courtyard that was once part of a 6th-century **baptistry**. In the 17th century the baptistry was converted into a tomb for Sultans Mustafa I and İbrahim I. The huge stone basin displayed in the courtyard is the original **font**.

To the right after you exit the main building is a recently restored rococo-style *şadırvan* (ablutions fountain) dating from 1740. Next to it is a small *sibyan maktab* (primary school) also dating from 1740. The small structure next to the gate is the *muvakkithane* (place where prayer hours were determined), built in 1853.

The first of Aya Sofya's minarets was added by order of Mehmet the Conqueror. Sinan designed the other three between 1574 and 1576.

After exiting the museum grounds, walk east (left) and turn left again on Babıhümayun Caddesi to visit the Aya Sofya Tombs (p78).

TOP SIGHT
TOPKAPI PALACE

Topkapı Palace (Topkapı Sarayı) is the subject of more colourful stories than most of the world's museums put together. Libidinous sultans, ambitious courtiers, beautiful concubines and scheming eunuchs lived and worked here between the 15th and 19th centuries when it was the court of the Ottoman Empire. Visiting its opulent pavilions, jewel-filled Treasury and sprawling Harem gives a fascinating glimpse into their lives.

First Court

Before you enter the **Imperial Gate of Topkapı**, take a look at the ornate structure in the cobbled square just outside. This is the rococo-style **Fountain of Sultan Ahmet III**, built in 1728 by the sultan who so favoured tulips. As you pass through the Imperial Gate, you enter the First Court, known as the Court of the Janissaries or the Parade Court. On your left is the Byzantine church of Hagia Eirene, more commonly known as Aya İrini (p79).

Mehmet the Conqueror had built the first stage of the palace shortly after the Conquest in 1453, and lived in the compound behind the Imperial Gate until his death in 1481. The Ottoman sultans continued to live in Topkapı's rarefied environment until the 19th century, when they moved to ostentatious European-style palaces such as Dolmabahçe, Çırağan and Yıldız that were built on the shores of the Bosphorus.

Second Court

The **Middle Gate** (Ortakapı or Bab-üs Selâm) led to the palace's Second Court, used for the business of running the

DON'T MISS

➡ Imperial Council Chamber

➡ Outer Treasury

➡ Harem

➡ Audience Chamber

➡ Imperial Treasury

➡ Marble Terrace

➡ Palace Kitchens

PRACTICALITIES

➡ Map p238, C3

➡ ☎0212-512 0480

➡ www.topkapisarayi. gov.tr/en

➡ Babıhümayun Caddesi

➡ palace adult/child under 12yr ₺40/free, Harem adult/child under 6yr ₺25/free

➡ ⊙9am-6.45pm Wed-Mon mid-Apr–Oct, to 4.45pm Nov–mid-Apr, last entry 1hr before closing

➡ Ⓜ Sultanahmet

WOMEN OF THE HAREM

Islam forbade enslaving Muslims, so the concubines in Topkapı's Harem were foreigners or infidels. Girls were bought as slaves or were received as gifts from nobles and potentates. Many of the girls were from Eastern Europe and all were noted for their beauty. The most famous was Haseki Hürrem (Joyous One), more commonly known as Roxelana, who was the consort of Süleyman the Magnificent. The daughter of a Ruthenian (Ukrainian) Orthodox priest, she was captured by Crimean Tatars, who brought her to Constantinople to be sold in the slave market.

The chief black eunuch, the sultan's personal representative in administration of the Harem and other important affairs of state, was the third most powerful official in the empire, after the grand vizier and the supreme Islamic judge.

empire. Only the sultan and his mother, the *valide sultan,* were allowed through the Middle Gate on horseback. Everyone else, including the grand vizier, had to dismount. Scale models just inside the gate give a good sense of the palace's layout and sheer size.

Like the First Court, the Second Court has an attractive park-like setting. Unlike typical European palaces, which feature one large building with outlying gardens, Topkapı is a series of pavilions, kitchens, barracks, audience chambers, kiosks and sleeping quarters built around a central enclosure.

The great **Palace Kitchens** on the right (east) as you enter have finally reopened following years of restoration. The ornate contents of the palace cupboards are on display, ranging from poreclain perfume bottles to a gold-plated copper jug owned by Tiryâl, one of Mahmut II's many consorts. Also here is a small portion of Topkapı's vast collection of Chinese celadon porcelain, valued by the sultans for its beauty but also because it was reputed to change colour if touched by poisoned food.

On the left (west) side of the Second Court is the ornate **Imperial Council Chamber** (Dîvân-ı Hümâyûn). The council met here to discuss matters of state, and the sultan sometimes eavesdropped through the gold grille high in the wall. The room to the right showcases clocks from the palace collection.

North of the Imperial Council Chamber is the **Outer Treasury**, where an impressive collection of Ottoman and European arms and armour is displayed, including a 14th-century Hungarian sword fit for a giant.

Harem

The entrance to the Harem is beneath the Tower of Justice on the western side of the Second Court. If you decide to visit – and we highly recommend that you do – you'll need to buy a dedicated ticket. The visitor route through the Harem changes when rooms are closed for restoration or stabilisation, so some of the areas mentioned here may not be open during your visit.

As popular belief would have it, the Harem was a place where the sultan could engage in debauchery at will. In more prosaic reality, these were the imperial family quarters, and every detail of Harem life was governed by tradition, obligation and ceremony. The word 'harem' literally means 'forbidden' or 'private'.

The sultans supported as many as 300 concubines in the Harem, although numbers were usually lower than this. Upon entering the Harem, the girls

TOPKAPI PALACE (TOPKAPI SARAYI)

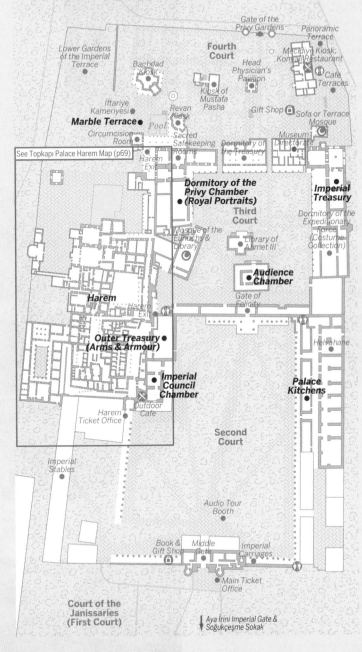

Topkapı Palace

DAILY LIFE IN THE IMPERIAL COURT

A visit to this opulent palace compound, with its courtyards, harem and pavilions, offers a fascinating glimpse into the lives of the Ottoman sultans. During its heyday, royal wives and children, concubines, eunuchs and servants were among the 4000 people living within Topkapı's walls.

The sultans and their families rarely left the palace grounds, relying on courtiers and diplomats to bring them news of the outside world. Most visitors would go straight to the magnificent **Imperial Council Chamber** ❶, where the sultan's grand vizier and Dîvân (Council) regularly met to discuss affairs of state and receive foreign dignitaries. Many of these visitors brought lavish gifts and tributes to embellish the **Imperial Treasury** ❷.

After receiving any guests and meeting with the Dîvân, the grand vizier would make his way through the ornate **Gate of Felicity** ❸ into the Third Court, the palace's residential quarter. Here, he would brief the sultan on the deliberations and decisions of the Dîvân in the colonnaded **Audience Chamber** ❹.

Meanwhile, day-to-day domestic chores and intrigues would be underway in the **Harem** ❺ and servants would be preparing feasts in the massive **Palace Kitchens** ❻. Amid all this activity, the **Marble Terrace** ❼ was a tranquil retreat where the sultan would come to relax, look out over the city and perhaps regret his sequestered lifestyle.

DON'T MISS

There are spectacular views from the terrace above the Konyalı Restaurant and also from the Marble Terrace in the Fourth Court.

Harem
The sultan, his mother and the crown prince had sumptuously decorated private apartments in the Harem. The most beautiful of these are the Twin Kiosks (pictured), which were used by the crown prince.

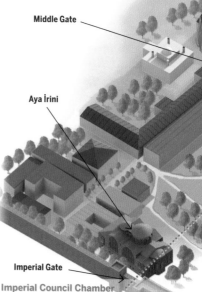

Harem Ticket Office

Middle Gate

Aya İrini

Imperial Gate

Imperial Council Chamber
This is where the Dîvân (Council) made laws, citizens presented petitions and foreign dignitaries were presented to the court. The sultan sometimes eavesdropped on proceedings through the window with the golden grille.

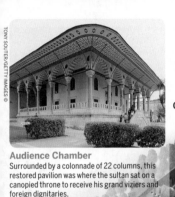

Audience Chamber
Surrounded by a colonnade of 22 columns, this restored pavilion was where the sultan sat on a canopied throne to receive his grand viziers and foreign dignitaries.

Marble Terrace
This gorgeous terrace is home to the Baghdad and Revan Kiosks, the tiled imperial circumcision room and the İftariye Kameriyesi, a viewing platform with a gilded canopy. During Ramazan, the sultan would enjoy his *iftar* (breaking of the fast) here.

Kiosk of Mustafa Pasha

Baghdad Kiosk

Revan Kiosk

Library of Ahmet III

Circumcision Room

Head Physician's Pavilion

⑦

Dormitory of the Privy Chamber (Royal Portraits)

Sacred Safekeeping Rooms

⑤

Outer Treasury (Arms & Armour)

④

②

①

③

⑥

Mecidiye Kiosk

Terrace

Dormitory of the Expeditionary Force (Costume Collection)

Ticket Office

Imperial Treasury
One of the highlights here is the famous Topkapı Dagger, which was commissioned in 1747 by Sultan Mahmut I as a lavish gift for Nadir Shah of Persia. The shah was assassinated before it could be given to him.

Gate of Felicity
This rococo-style gate was used for state ceremonies, including the sultan's accession and funeral. A 1789 work by court painter Kostantin Kapidagli records the enthronement ceremony of Sultan Selim III.

Palace Kitchens
Keeping the palace's 4000 residents fed was a huge task. Topkapı's kitchens occupied 10 domed buildings with 20 huge chimneys, and were workplace and home for 800 members of staff.

POMP AND CIRCUMSTANCE

During the great days of the empire, foreign ambassadors were received at Topkapı on days when the janissaries (the sultan's personal bodyguards) were scheduled to receive their pay. Huge sacks of silver coins were brought to the Imperial Council Chamber in the Second Court and court officers would dispense the coins to long lines of the tough, impeccably costumed and faultlessly disciplined troops as the ambassadors looked on in admiration.

Sultan İbrahim I (r 1640–48), known as 'İbrahim the Crazy', spent his early life imprisoned in the *kafes* before succeeding his brother Murat IV in 1640. His reign was marked by extravagance and instability, and he was deposed and strangled in 1648.

SPOONMAKER'S DIAMOND

The Spoonmaker's Diamond in the Topkapı collection is one of the largest diamonds in the world. According to legend, it was found in a rubbish dump in Eğrıkapı and purchased by a wily street peddler for three spoons before eventually being purchased by a grand vizier and becoming part of the Imperial Treasury.

Gate of Felicity

would be schooled in Islam and in Turkish culture and language, as well as the arts of make-up, dress, comportment, music, reading, writing, embroidery and dancing. They then entered a meritocracy, first as ladies-in-waiting to the sultan's concubines and children, then to the sultan's mother and finally – if they were particularly attractive and talented – to the sultan himself.

The sultan was allowed by Islamic law to have four legitimate wives, who received the title of *kadın* (wife). If a wife bore him a son she was called *haseki sultan;* if she bore him a daughter, *haseki kadın.*

Ruling the Harem was the *valide sultan* (mother of the reigning sultan), who often owned large landed estates in her own name and controlled them through black eunuch servants. Able to give orders directly to the grand vizier, her influence on the sultan, on his wives and concubines, and on matters of state was often profound.

The earliest of the 300-odd rooms in the Harem were constructed during the reign of Murat III (r 1574–95); the harems of previous sultans were at the now-demolished Eski Sarayı (Old Palace), near present-day Beyazıt Meydanı.

The Harem complex has six floors, but only one of these can be visited. This is approached via the **Carriage Gate**. Inside the gate is the **Dome with Cupboards**, the Harem treasury where financial records were kept. Beyond it is a room where the

Harem's eunuch guards were stationed. This is decorated with fine Kütahya tiles from the 17th century. Adjoining this is the **Mosque of the Black Eunuchs**, which features depictions of Mecca on its 17th-century tiles.

Beyond is the narrow **Courtyard of the Black Eunuchs**, also decorated with Kütahya tiles. Behind the marble colonnade on the left are the **Black Eunuchs' Dormitories**. In the early days white eunuchs were used, but black eunuchs sent as presents by the Ottoman governor of Egypt later took control. As many as 200 lived here, guarding the doors and waiting on the women of the Harem.

At the far end of the courtyard is the **Main Gate** into the Harem, as well as a guard room featuring two gigantic gilded mirrors. On the left, the **Concubines' Corridor**, with frescoes of the palace at the far end, leads to the **Courtyard of the Concubines and Sultan's Consorts**. This is surrounded by baths, a laundry fountain, a laundry, dormitories and private apartments.

Turn right at the end of the Concubines' Corridor for **Sultan Ahmet's Kiosk**, which is decorated with a tiled chimney, followed by the **Apartments of the Valide Sultan**, the centre of power in the Harem. From these ornate rooms the *valide sultan* oversaw and controlled her huge 'family'. Of particular note is the **Salon of the Valide Sultan** with its lovely 19th-century murals featuring bucolic views of İstanbul.

Past the **Courtyard of the Valide Sultan** is a splendid reception room with a large fireplace that leads to a vestibule covered in Kütahya and İznik tiles dating from the 17th century. This is where the princes, *valide sultan* and senior concubines waited before entering the handsome **Imperial Hall** for an audience with the sultan. Built during the reign of Murat III, the hall was redecorated in baroque style by order of Osman III (r 1754–57).

Nearby is the **Privy Chamber of Murat III**, one of the most sumptuous rooms in the palace. Dating from 1578, virtually all of its decoration is original and is thought to be the work of Sinan. The restored three-tiered marble fountain was designed to give the sound of cascading water and to make it difficult to eavesdrop on the sultan's conversations. The gilded canopied seating areas are later 18th-century additions.

Continue to the **Privy Chamber of Ahmet III** and peek into the adjoining dining room built in 1705. The latter is lined with wooden panels decorated with images of flowers and fruits painted in lacquer.

Back through the Privy Chamber of Murat III are two of the most beautiful rooms in the Harem – the **Twin Kiosk/Apartments of the Crown Prince**. These two rooms date from around 1600; note the painted canvas dome in the first room and the fine İznik tile panels above the fireplace in the second. The stained glass is also noteworthy.

Past these rooms is the **Courtyard of the Favourites**. Over the edge of the courtyard (really a terrace) you'll see a large empty pool. Overlooking the courtyard are the tiny windows of the many small dark rooms comprising the *kafes* (cage) where brothers or sons of the sultan were imprisoned. Adjoining it is the tiled **Harem Mosque** with its baroque *mihrab* (niche in a minaret indicating the direction of Mecca).

From here, you can follow the passage known as the Golden Road and exit into the palace's Third Court, or follow the corridor north and exit into the Fourth Court by the Circumcision Room.

Third Court

The Third Court is entered through the **Gate of Felicity**. The sultan's private domain, it was staffed and guarded by white eunuchs. Inside is the **Audience Chamber**, constructed in the 16th century but refurbished in the 18th century.

LIFE IN THE CAGE

In the early centuries of the empire, Ottoman princes were schooled as youths in combat and statecraft by direct experience. But as the Ottoman dynasty did not observe primogeniture (succession of the firstborn), the death of the sultan regularly resulted in a fratricidal bloodbath as his sons – often from different mothers – battled among themselves for the throne. This changed when Sultan Ahmet I (r 1603–20) couldn't bring himself to murder his brother Mustafa and decided instead to keep him imprisoned in Topkapı's Harem, so beginning the tradition of *kafes hayatı* (cage life). This house arrest, adopted in place of fratricide by succeeding sultans, meant the pampered princes were kept ignorant of war and statecraft and usually rendered unfit to rule if the occasion arose. The practice contributed to the decline of the empire's power and that of succeeding sultans, even though in later years the dynasty observed the custom of primogeniture.

Sultan Murat III (r 1574–95) had 112 children.

Important officials and foreign ambassadors were brought to this little kiosk to conduct the high business of state. The sultan, seated on a huge divan, inspected the ambassador's gifts and offerings as they were passed through the doorway on the left.

Right behind the Audience Chamber is the pretty **Library of Ahmet III**, built in 1719. Light-filled, it has comfortable reading areas and stunning inlaid woodwork.

On the eastern edge of the Third Court is the **Dormitory of the Expeditionary Force**, which now houses a rich collection of imperial robes, kaftans and uniforms worked in silver and gold thread. Also here is a fascinating collection of talismanic shirts, which were believed to protect the wearer from enemies and misfortunes of all kinds. Textile design reached its highest point during the reign of Süleyman the Magnificent, when the imperial workshops produced cloth of exquisite design and work. Don't miss Süleyman's gorgeous silk kaftan with its appliquéd tulip design.

On the other side of the Third Court are the **Sacred Safekeeping Rooms**. These rooms, sumptuously decorated with İznik tiles, house many relics of the Prophet. When the sultans lived here, the rooms were opened only once a year, for the imperial family to pay homage to the memory of the Prophet on the 15th day of the holy month of Ramazan. An imam sometimes sits near the exit and recites from the Koran.

Next to the sacred Safekeeping Rooms is the **Dormitory of the Privy Chamber**, which houses portraits of 36 sultans, from austere 17th- and 18th-century patriarchs to their later descendants. The highlight is Konstantin Kapidagli's wonderful painting of the **Enthronement Ceremony of Sultan Selim III** (1789) with its curving line of turbanned spectators.

En route to the Fourth Court you will pass the **Dormitory of the Treasury**, which accommodated the palace treasury's many staff, who numbered over 150 by the 18th century. This houses an exhibition of Ottoman calligraphy by Kazasker Mustafa İzzet Efendi (1801–76).

Imperial Treasury

Located on the eastern edge of the Third Court, Topkapı's Treasury features an incredible collection of objects made from or decorated with gold, silver, rubies, emeralds, jade, pearls and diamonds. The building itself was constructed during Mehmet the Conqueror's reign in 1460 and was used originally as reception rooms.

TOPKAPI PALACE HAREM

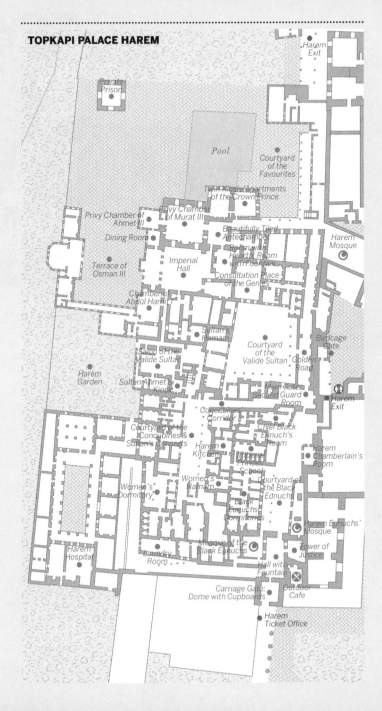

Harem Exit

Private Prison

Pool

Courtyard of the Favourites

Twin Kiosk/Apartments of the Crown Prince

Privy Chamber of Murat III

Privy Chamber of Ahmet III

Dining Room

Beautifully Tiled Antechamber

Room with Hearth

Room with Fountain

Harem Mosque

Terrace of Osman III

Imperial Hall

Consultation Place of the Genies

Chamber of Abdül Hamit

Sultan's Hamam

Courtyard of the Valide Sultan

Birdcage Gate

Salon of the Valide Sultan

Golden Road

Harem Garden

Sultan Ahmet's Kiosk

Main Gate; Second Guard Room

Harem Exit

Concubines' Corridor

Chief Black Eunuch's Room

Harem Chamberlain's Room

Courtyard of the Concubines & Sultan's Consorts

Harem Kitchen

Imperial Harem School

Women's Hamam

Courtyard of the Black Eunuchs

Women's Dormitory

Black Eunuchs' Dormitories

Harem Eunuchs' Mosque

Harem Hospital

Laundry Room

Mosque of the Black Eunuchs

Tower of Justice

Hall with Fountain

Outdoor Cafe

Carriage Gate; Dome with Cupboards

Harem Ticket Office

TULIP SULTAN

When he ascended the throne aged 29, Sultan Ahmet III (r 1703–30) introduced many changes at Topkapı. He extended the palace Harem and ordered the construction of several new structures – one of which was the elegant street fountain outside the Imperial Gate that is named in his honour. Ahmet is best known, however, for presiding over the Lâle Devri (Tulip Period), a peaceful era of modernisation that also saw a tulip craze in Ottoman court society. Ahmet even introduced an annual festival to celebrate the blooming of this prized flower. Held over the three days surrounding the first full moon in April, the fête was staged in the gardens of the palace's Fourth Court, which was specially decorated with vases of tulips and tiny coloured glass lamps. Trilling nightingales in cages provided entertainment, as did palace musicians. Today the annual İstanbul Tulip Festival in April continues the tradition across the city.

Looking over the Marble Terrace towards the Baghdad Kiosk

In the first room, look for the jewel-encrusted Sword of Süleyman the Magnificent and the Throne of Ahmed I (aka Arife Throne), which is inlaid with mother-of-pearl and was designed by Sedefhar Mehmet Ağa, architect of the Blue Mosque. It's one of four imperial thrones on display here. The second room exhibits non-Ottoman objects received as gifts or spoils of war, including a glittering zinc jug with golden adornments from Tabriz, Iran. The tiny Indian figures, mainly made from seed pearls, are also well worth seeking out.

After passing through the third room and admiring the 16th-century gold-plated Ottoman helmet encrusted with turquoise, rubies and emeralds, you will come to the last and most impressive room, which is home to the Treasury's most famous exhibit: the **Topkapı Dagger**. The object of the criminal heist in Jules Dassin's 1964 film *Topkapı*, the dagger features three enormous emeralds on the hilt and a watch set into the pommel. Also here is the **Kasıkçı (Spoonmaker's) Diamond**, a teardrop-shaped 86-carat rock surrounded by dozens of smaller stones. It was first worn by Mehmet IV at his accession to the throne in 1648.

Fourth Court

Pleasure pavilions occupy the palace's Fourth Court, also known as the Tulip Garden. These include the **Mecidiye Kiosk**, which was built by Abdül Mecit (r 1839–61) according to 19th-century European models. Beneath this is the Konyalı restaurant, which offers wonderful views from its terrace but is let down by the quality and price of its food; a çay will set you back ₺7, and a slice of gateau ₺22.

Up steps from the Mecidiye Kiosk is the **Head Physician's Pavilion**. Interestingly, the head physician was always one of the sultan's Jewish subjects. On this terrace you will also find the late-17th-century **Kiosk of Kara Mustafa Pasha** (Sofa Köşkü), with its gilded ceiling, painted walls and delicate stained-glass windows. During the reign of Ahmet III, the Tulip Garden outside the kiosk was filled with the latest varieties of the flower.

Up the stairs at the end of the Tulip Garden is the **Marble Terrace**, a platform with a decorative pool, three pavilions and the whimsical **İftariye Kameriyesi**, a small structure commissioned by İbrahim I in 1640 as a picturesque place to break the fast of Ramazan.

Murat IV built the **Revan Kiosk** in 1636 after reclaiming the city of Yerevan (now in Armenia) from Persia. The kiosk was also known as the Chamber of Turbans (Sarık Odası) because the sultans' turbans were kept there. In 1639 Murat IV constructed the **Baghdad Kiosk**, one of the last examples of classical palace architecture, to commemorate his victory over that city. Notice its superb İznik tiles, painted ceiling and mother-of-pearl and tortoiseshell inlay. The small **Circumcision Room** (Sünnet Odası) was used for the ritual that admits Muslim boys to manhood. Built by İbrahim in 1640, the outer walls of the chamber are graced by particularly beautiful tile panels.

TOP SIGHT
BLUE MOSQUE

İstanbul's most photogenic building was the grand project of Sultan Ahmet I (r 1603–17), whose *türbe* (tomb) is located on the north side of the site facing Sultanahmet Park. Officially known as the Sultanahmet Camii (Sultanahmet Mosque), its wonderfully curvaceous exterior features a cascade of domes and six slender minarets, while blue İznik tiles adorn the interior and give the building its unofficial but commonly used name.

Exterior

Ahmet set out to build a monument that would rival and even surpass the nearby Aya Sofya in grandeur and beauty. Indeed the young sultan was so enthusiastic about the project that he is said to have worked with the labourers and craftsmen on site, pushing them along and rewarding extra effort. Ahmet did in fact come close to his goal of rivalling Aya Sofya – and made future generations of local hoteliers happy: a 'Blue Mosque view' from the roof terrace is a top selling point of hotels in the area.

With the mosque's exterior, the architect, Sedefkâr Mehmet Ağa, managed to orchestrate a visual wham-bam effect similar to that of Aya Sofya's interior. Its curves are voluptuous; its courtyard is the biggest of all the Ottoman mosques; and it has more minarets than any other İstanbul mosque – a record only recently equalled by the colossal new Çamlıca Mosque on the city's Asian side. In fact, there was concern at the time of the Blue Mosque's construction that the sultan was being presumptuous in specifying six minarets, as the only equivalent was in Mecca.

In order to fully appreciate the mosque's design you should approach it via the middle of the Hippodrome rather than entering from Sultanahmet Park. When inside the courtyard, which is the same size as the mosque's interior, you'll be able to appreciate the

DON'T MISS

➡ The approach from the Hippodrome
➡ The İznik tiles
➡ The carved white marble *mimber*

PRACTICALITIES

➡ Map p240, D4
➡ ☎0545 577 1899
➡ www.bluemosque.co
➡ Hippodrome
➡ ⊘closed to non-worshippers during 6 daily prayer times
➡ 🚊Sultanahmet

perfect proportions of the building. Walk towards the mosque through the gate in the peripheral wall, noting on the way the small dome atop the next gate: this is the motif Sedefkâr Mehmet Ağa uses to lift your eyes to heaven. As you cross the outer courtyard, your eyes follow a flight of stairs up to yet more domes: that of the ablutions fountain in the centre of the mosque courtyard and, as you ascend the stairs, a semidome over the mosque's main door, then one above it, and another and another. Finally the main dome crowns the whole, and your attention is drawn to the sides, where forests of smaller domes reinforce the effect, completed by the minarets, which lift your eyes heavenward.

Interior

The mosque is such a popular tourist sight that admission is controlled in order to preserve its sacred atmosphere. Only worshippers are admitted through the main door; visitors must use the south door (follow the signs). You must remove your shoes, and women who haven't brought their own headscarf or are considered to be too scantily dressed will be loaned a headscarf and/or robe.

The interior is conceived on a grand scale: it features more than 21,000 İznik tiles, 260 windows and a huge central prayer space. The **stained-glass windows** and **İznik tiles** immediately attract attention. Though the windows are replacements, they still create the luminous effect of the originals, which came from Venice. Tiles line the walls with an explosion of flower motifs, particularly in the upstairs galleries (which are not open to the public).

Once inside, it's easy to see that the mosque, which was constructed between 1606 and 1616, more than 1000 years after nearby Aya Sofya, is not as architecturally daring as its predecessor. Four massive pillars hold up the less ambitious dome, a sturdier solution lacking the innovation and grace of the 'floating' dome in Justinian's cathedral.

The semidomes and the dome are painted with graceful **arabesques**. Of note in the main space are the **müezzin mahfili** (*müezzin's* lodge), a raised platform where the *müezzin* repeats the call to prayer at the start of each service; the **mihrab** (niche in a minaret indicating the direction of Mecca), which features a piece of the sacred Black Stone from the Kaaba in Mecca; and the high, elaborate **kursi** (chair) from which the imam gives the sermon on Fridays. The beautifully carved white marble **mimber** (pulpit), with its curtained doorway at floor level, features a flight of steps and a small kiosk topped by a spire.

SULTAN AHMET I

Designed by Sedefkâr Mehmet Ağa and built in 1616–19, Ahmet I's *türbe* (tomb) is on the north side of the mosque facing Sultanahmet Park. Ahmet, who had ascended the imperial throne aged 13, died at just 27, one year after construction of the mosque was completed. Buried with him are his wife, Kösem (strangled to death in the Topkapı Harem), and his sons, Sultan Osman II (r 1618–22), Sultan Murat IV (r 1623–40) and Prince Beyazıt (murdered by order of Murat). Like the mosque, the *türbe* features fine İznik tiles.

Mosques built by the great and powerful usually included numerous public-service institutions, including hospitals, soup kitchens and schools. Here, a large *medrese* (Islamic school of higher studies) on the northwestern side of the complex (closed to the public) and *arasta* (row of shops by a mosque; now the Arasta Bazaar, p88) remain.

TOP SIGHT
İSTANBUL ARCHAEOLOGY MUSEUMS

This superb museum showcases archaeological and artistic treasures from the Topkapı Palace collections formed during the late 19th century by museum director, artist and archaeologist Osman Hamdi Bey. Housed in three buildings – the Museum of the Ancient Orient (Eski Şark Eserler Müzesi), the Archaeology Museum (Arkeoloji Müzesi) and the Tiled Pavilion (Çinili Köşk) – its exhibits include ancient artefacts, classical statuary and an exhibition tracing İstanbul's history.

Museum of the Ancient Orient

Immediately on the left after you enter the complex, this 1883 building has a collection of pre-Islamic items gathered from the expanse of the Ottoman Empire. Its steps are flanked by two impressive late Hittite lions, dating to the 8th century BC. Inside, highlights include further late Hittite statues and reliefs, and a series of large blue-and-yellow glazed-brick panels that once lined the processional street and the Ishtar gate of ancient Babylon. The panels, which date from 604–562 BC, depict real and mythical animals such as lions, dragons and bulls.

Archaeology Museum

On the opposite side of the column-filled courtyard to the Museum of the Ancient Orient is this imposing neo-classical building, which was wrapped in scaffolding and tarpaulin and undergoing renovation when we visited. It houses an extensive collection of classical statuary and

DON'T MISS

➜ Royal Necropolis of Sidon sarcophagi

➜ Glazed panels from the processional street and Ishtar gate of ancient Babylon

➜ Late Hittite statues and reliefs

➜ Classical statuary

➜ İbrahim Bey İmâret *mihrab*

PRACTICALITIES

➜ İstanbul Arkeoloji Müzeleri

➜ Map p238, C3

➜ ☏0212-520 7740

➜ www.istanbularkeoloji. gov.tr

➜ Osman Hamdi Bey Yokuşu Sokak, Gülhane

➜ adult/child under 12yr ₺20/free

➜ ⊙9am-7pm, last entry 6pm

➜ 🚇Gülhane

sarcophagi plus a sprawling exhibit documenting İstanbul's history.

The museum's major treasures are sarcophagi from sites including the Royal Necropolis of Sidon (Side in modern-day Lebanon), unearthed in 1887 by Osman Hamdi Bey. The extraordinary *Alexander Sarcophagus* and *Mourning Women Sarcophagus* were not on display when we visited. However, some good pieces from the statuary collection are exhibited on the way into the museum, including a marble head of Alexander from Pergamum.

On the 1st floor, a fascinating albeit dusty, exhibition called **İstanbul Through the Ages** traces the city's history through its neighbourhoods during different periods: Archaic, Hellenistic, Roman, Byzantine and Ottoman. On the 2nd floor is the museum's 'Anatolia and Troy Through the Ages' exhibition; on the 3rd floor, the 'Neighbouring Cultures of Anatolia, Cyprus, Syria and Palestine' exhibition was closed at the time of research.

At the time of research, a separate entrance led to an impressive collection of ancient grave-cult sarcophagi from Syria, Lebanon, Thessalonica and Ephesus, including impressive **anthropoid sarcophagi** from Sidon. Three halls are filled with the amazingly detailed stelae and sarcophagi, most dating from between 140 and 270 AD. Many of the sarcophagi look like tiny temples or residential buildings; don't miss the **Sidamara Sarcophagus** from Konya with its interlocking horses' legs and playful cherubs. The last room in this section contains Roman floor mosaics and examples of Anatolian architecture from antiquity.

Tiled Pavilion

This handsome pavilion was constructed in 1472 by order of Mehmet the Conqueror. The portico, which has 14 marble columns, was constructed during the reign of Sultan Abdül Hamit I (1774–89) after the original burned down in 1737.

On display here are Seljuk, Anatolian and Ottoman tiles and ceramics dating from the end of the 12th century to the beginning of the 20th century. The collection includes İznik tiles from the period between the mid-14th and 17th centuries when that city produced the finest coloured tiles in the world. When you enter the central room you can't miss the stunning **mihrab** from the İbrahim Bey İmâret in Karaman, built in 1432.

ALEXANDER SARCOPHAGUS

This classical sculpture from the Royal Necropolis of Sidon is the Archaeology Museum's most significant possession – so named not because it belonged to the Macedonian general, but because it depicts him among his army battling the Persians, who were led by King Abdalonymos (whose sarcophagus it is). The sarcophagus is carved out of Pentelic marble and dates from the last quarter of the 4th century BC. Alexander, on horseback, has a lion's head as a headdress. The sculpture retains remnants of its original red-and-yellow paintwork.

The Tiled Pavilion in the museum compound was originally an outer pavilion of Topkapı Palace. The sultan used it to watch sporting events being staged in the palace grounds below (now Gülhane Park).

➡ Leave Gülhane Park to find Kybele Cafe (p88) in an eclectic hotel with hundreds of colourful glass lights hanging from the ceiling.

➡ Seek out Sefa Restaurant (p82) for an authentic taste of delicious Turkish *hazır yemek* (ready-made dishes).

TOP SIGHT
BASILICA CISTERN

This subterranean structure was commissioned by Emperor Justinian and built in 532. The largest surviving Byzantine cistern in İstanbul, it was constructed using 336 columns, many of which were salvaged from ruined temples and feature fine carved capitals. Its symmetry and sheer grandeur of conception are quite breathtaking, and its cavernous depths make a great retreat on summer days.

The cistern was originally designed to service the Great Palace and surrounding buildings, and was able to store up to 80,000 cu metres of water delivered via 20km of aqueducts from a reservoir near the Black Sea, but was closed when the Byzantine emperors relocated from the Great Palace. Forgotten by city authorities, it wasn't rediscovered until 1545, when scholar Petrus Gyllius found local residents were obtaining water by lowering buckets into a dark space below their basement floors. Some were even catching fish this way. Intrigued, Gyllius explored and accessed the cistern through one of the basements. After the discovery, the Ottomans used it as a dumping ground for all sorts of junk, including corpses.

Now cleaned and renovated, it still has bucketloads of atmosphere. Walking along the raised wooden platforms, you'll feel water dripping from the vaulted ceiling and see schools of ghostly carp patrolling the water.

DON'T MISS

➡ Upside-down head of Medusa used as a column base
➡ Teardrop column

PRACTICALITIES

➡ Yerebatan Sarnıçı
➡ Map p240, E1
➡ ☏0212-512 1570
➡ www.yerebatan.com
➡ Yerebatan Caddesi
➡ admission ₺20
➡ ⊙9am-6.30pm mid-Apr–Sep, to 5.30pm Nov–mid-Apr
➡ 🚇Sultanahmet

⊙ SIGHTS

AYA SOFYA   MUSEUM
See p54.

TOPKAPI PALACE   PALACE
See p109.

İSTANBUL ARCHAEOLOGY MUSEUMS
MUSEUM
See p74.

BLUE MOSQUE   MOSQUE
See p118.

BASILICA CISTERN   CISTERN
See p76.

★**MUSEUM OF TURKISH
& ISLAMIC ARTS**   MUSEUM
Map p240 (Türk ve Islam Eserleri Müzesi; www.
tiem.gov.tr; Atmeydanı Caddesi 46, Hippodrome;
adult/child under 12yr ₺25/free; ⊙9am-5pm, last
entry 4.30pm, end Oct–mid-Apr 9am-7pm, last
entry 6.30pm mid-Apr–end Oct; ⊟Sultanahmet)
This Ottoman palace was built in 1524 for
İbrahim Paşa, childhood friend, brother-
in-law and grand vizier of Süleyman the
Magnificent. Recently renovated, it has a
magnificent collection of artefacts, including exquisite calligraphy and one of the
world's most impressive antique carpet collections. Some large-scale carpets have been
moved to the Carpet Museum (p79) from
the upper rooms, but the collection remains
a knockout with its palace carpets, prayer
rugs and glittering artefacts such as a 17th-
century Ottoman incense burner.

Born in Greece, İbrahim Paşa was captured there as a child and sold as a slave
into the imperial household in İstanbul. He
worked as a page in Topkapı Palace, where
he became friendly with Süleyman, who
was the same age. When his friend became
sultan, İbrahim was made in turn chief fal-
coner, chief of the royal bedchamber and
grand vizier. This palace was bestowed on
him by Süleyman the year before he was
given the hand of Süleyman's sister, Hadice,
in marriage. Alas, the fairy tale was not to
last for poor İbrahim. His wealth, power
and influence on the monarch became so
great that others wishing to influence the
sultan became envious, chief among them
Süleyman's powerful wife, Haseki Hürrem
Sultan (Roxelana). After a rival accused
İbrahim of disloyalty, Roxelana convinced
her husband that İbrahim was a threat and
Süleyman had him strangled in 1536.

Artefacts in the museum's collection date
from the 8th to the 19th century and come
from across the Middle East. They include
müknames (scrolls outlining an imperial
decree) featuring the sultan's *tuğra* (calligraphic signature); Iranian book binding
from the Safavid period (1501–1722); 12th-
and 13th-century wooden columns and
doors from Damascus and Cizre; Holbein,
Lotto, Konya, Uşhak, Iran and Caucasia
carpets; and even a cutting of the Prophet's
beard. Sections of the Hippodrome walls
can be seen near the entrance.

HIPPODROME   PARK
Map p240 (Atmeydanı; Atmeydanı Caddesi; ⊟Sul-
tanahmet) The Byzantine Emperors loved
nothing more than an afternoon at the
chariot races, and this rectangular arena
alongside Sultanahmet Park was their venue of choice. In its heyday, it was decorated
by obelisks and statues, some of which remain in place today. Re-landscaped in more
recent years, it is one of the city's most popular meeting places and promenades.

Originally the arena consisted of two
levels of galleries, starting boxes and the
semicircular southern end known as the
Sphendone (Map p240; Nakilbent Sokak; ⊟Sul-
tanahmet), parts of which still stand. The galleries that once topped this stone structure
were damaged during the Fourth Crusade
and ended up being totally dismantled in
the Ottoman period – many of the original
columns were used in the construction of
the Süleymaniye Mosque.

The Hippodrome was the centre of Byzantium's life for 1000 years and of Ottoman
life for another 400 years, and has been
the scene of countless political dramas. In
Byzantine times, the rival chariot teams
of 'Greens' and 'Blues' had separate sectar-
ian connections. Support for a team was
akin to membership of a political party,
and a team victory had important effects
on policy. Occasionally, Greens and Blues
joined forces against the emperor, as was
the case in AD 532 when a chariot race was
disturbed by protests against Justinian's
high tax regime. This escalated into the
Nika riots (so called after the protesters'
cry of Nika!, or Victory!), which led to tens
of thousands of protesters being massacred
in the Hippodrome by imperial forces. Not
surprisingly, chariot races were banned for
some time afterwards.

Ottoman sultans also kept an eye on activities in the Hippodrome. If things were

SULTANAHMET & AROUND SIGHTS

going badly in the empire, a surly crowd gathering here could signal the start of a disturbance, then a riot, then a revolution. In 1826 the slaughter of the corrupt janissary corps (the sultan's personal bodyguards) was carried out here by the reformer Sultan Mahmut II. In 1909 there were riots here that caused the downfall of Abdül Hamit II.

Despite the ever-present threat of the Hippodrome being the scene of their downfall, emperors and sultans sought to outdo one another in beautifying it, and adorned the centre with statues from the far reaches of the empire. Unfortunately, many priceless statues carved by ancient masters have disappeared from their original homes here. Chief among those responsible for such thefts were the soldiers of the Fourth Crusade, who invaded Constantinople, a Christian ally city, in 1204.

Near the northern end of the Hippodrome, the little gazebo with beautiful stonework is known as **Kaiser Wilhelm's Fountain** (Map p240; Atmeydanı Caddesi; ⊟Sultanahmet). The German emperor paid a state visit to Sultan Abdül Hamit II in 1898 and presented this fountain to the sultan and his people as a token of friendship in 1901. The monograms on the dome's interior feature Abdül Hamit's *tuğra* (calligraphic signature) and the first letter of Wilhelm's name, representing their political union.

The immaculately preserved pink granite **Obelisk of Theodosius** (Map p240; Atmeydanı Caddesi; ⊟Sultanahmet) in the centre was carved in Egypt during the reign of Thutmose III (r 1549–1503 BC) and erected in the Amon-Re temple at Karnak. Theodosius the Great (r 379–95) had it brought from Egypt to Constantinople in AD 390. On the marble podium below the obelisk, look for the carvings of Theodosius, his wife, his sons, state officials and bodyguards watching the chariot-race action from the *kathisma* (imperial box).

South of the obelisk is a strange column coming up out of a hole in the ground. Known as the **Spiral Column** (Map p240; Atmeydanı Caddesi; ⊟Sultanahmet), it was once much taller and was topped by three serpents' heads. Originally cast to commemorate a victory of the Hellenic confederation over the Persians in the battle of Plataea, it stood in front of the Temple of Apollo at Delphi (Greece) from 478 BC until Constantine the Great had it brought to his new capital city around AD 330. Though badly damaged in Byzantine times, the ser-

pents' heads survived until the early 18th century. Now all that remains of them is one upper jaw, which was discovered in a basement of Aya Sofya and is housed in the İstanbul Archaeology Museums (p74).

After sacking Aya Sofya in 1204, the soldiers of the Fourth Crusade tore all the plates from the **Rough-Stone Obelisk** (Map p240; Atmeydanı Caddesi; ⊟Sultanahmet), at the Hippodrome's southern end, in the mistaken belief that they were solid gold (in fact, they were gold-covered bronze). The Crusaders also stole the famous Triumphal Quadriga (team of four horses cast in bronze) and placed it atop the main door of Venice's Basilica di San Marco; replicas are now located there, as the originals were moved into the basilica for safekeeping.

MUSEUM OF GREAT PALACE MOSAICS
MUSEUM

Map p240 (✆0212-518 1205; http://ayasofya muzesi.gov.tr/en/museum-great-palace-mosaics; Torun Sokak; admission ₺15; ⊙9am-7pm mid-Apr-Sep, to 5pm Oct–mid-Apr, last entry 30min before closing; ⊟Sultanahmet) When archaeologists from the University of Ankara and Scotland's University of St Andrews excavated around the nearby Arasta Bazaar in the 1930s and 1950s, they uncovered a stunning mosaic pavement featuring hunting and mythological scenes. Dating from early Byzantine times, it was restored between 1983 and 1997 and is now preserved in this museum.

Thought to have been added by Justinian to the Great Palace of Byzantium, the pavement is estimated to have measured from 3500 to 4000 sq metres in its original form. The 250 sq metres preserved here is the largest discovered remnant – the rest has been either destroyed or remains buried underneath the Blue Mosque and surrounding shops and hotels.

The pavement is filled with bucolic imagery and has a gorgeous ribbon border with heart-shaped leaves. In the last room is one of the most colourful and dramatic pictures, that of two men in leggings carrying spears and holding off a raging tiger.

The museum has informative panels documenting the floor's history, rescue and renovation.

AYA SOFYA TOMBS
TOMBS

Map p240 (Aya Sofya Müzesi Padişah Türbeleri; ✆0212-522 1750; http://ayasofyamuzesi.gov.tr/en; Babıhümayun Caddesi; ⊙9am-5pm; ⊟Sultanahmet) FREE Part of the Aya Sofya complex but entered via Babıhümayun Caddesi, these tombs are the final resting places of five 16th- and 17th-century sultans – Mehmet III, Selim II, Murat III, İbrahim I and Mustafa I – most of whom are buried with members of their families. The ornate interior decoration in the tombs features the very best Ottoman tile work, calligraphy and decorative paintwork.

Mehmet III's tomb dates from 1608 and Murat III's from 1599; both are adorned with particularly beautiful İznik tiles. Next to Murat's tomb is that of his five children, who died in a plague epidemic; this was designed by Sinan and has simple but beautiful painted decoration.

Selim II's tomb, which was designed by Sinan and built in 1577, is particularly poignant, as it houses the graves of five of his sons, murdered on the same night in December 1574 to ensure the peaceful succession of the oldest, Murat III. It also houses the graves of 19 of Murat's sons, murdered in January 1595 to ensure Mehmet III's succession. They were the last of the royal princes to be murdered by their siblings – after this, the younger brothers of succeeding sultans were confined to the *kafes* (cage) in Topkapı Palace instead.

The fifth tomb is Aya Sofya's original baptistry, converted to a mausoleum for sultans İbrahim I and Mustafa I during the 17th century.

CARPET MUSEUM
MUSEUM

Map p240 (Halı Müzesi; ☎0212-518 1330; www.halimuzesi.com; cnr Babıhümayun Caddesi & Soğukçeşme Sokak; admission ₺10; ⊙9am-6pm Tue-Sun mid-Apr–mid-Oct, to 4pm mid-Oct–mid-Apr; 🚇Sultanahmet or Gülhane) Housed in an *imaret* (soup kitchen) added to the Aya Sofya complex in the 18th century, this museum is entered through a spectacular baroque gate and gives the visitor an excellent overview of the history of Anatolian carpet making. The carpets, which have been sourced from mosques throughout the country, date from the 14th to 20th centuries.

There are three galleries, each entered through Tardis-like humidity-controlled entrances. The first, in the *me'kel* (dining hall), features early Anatolian-era carpets with geometric and abstract designs; these are sometimes called Holbein carpets in honour of Dutch artist Hans Holbein the Younger, who often depicted them in his paintings. Also here are examples of the best-known type of Turkish carpets: Uşak (Ushak) carpets of the 16th and 17th centuries.

The second gallery, in the *aşhane* (kitchen), displays rugs with Central and Eastern Anatolian motifs including star-shaped medallions and keyholes; the latter is said to have been inspired by the mosque *mihrab* (panels decode the many symbols' meanings). On the left at the end of the room, don't miss the particularly fine red-and-yellow 19th-century Hereke rug from the Mustafa Mosque in Sirkeci. The third gallery, in the *fodlahane* (bakery), is the most impressive, with huge 17th- and 18th-century Uşak carpets from the Süleymaniye Mosque and another 19th-century example from the Blue Mosque. The latter is also a late example of a *saf* prayer rug; several people could pray side by side in a *saf* (line) on its multiple *mihrab* decorations.

AYA İRİNİ
CHURCH

Map p238 (Hagia Eirene, Church of the Divine Peace; ☎0212-512 0480; http://topkapisarayi.gov.tr/en/hagia-irene-0; 1st Court, Topkapı Palace; adult/child under 6yr ₺20/free; ⊙9am-7pm Wed-Mon Apr–mid-Oct, to 5pm mid-Oct–Mar; 🚇Sultanahmet) Commissioned by Justinian in the 540s, this Byzantine church is almost exactly as old as its near neighbour, Aya Sofya. Used as an arsenal for centuries, it is now open to visitors but the entrance fee is exorbitant considering the fact that there are no exhibits inside. The serenely beautiful interior and superb acoustics make this one of the most sought-after venues for the İstanbul International Music Festival. To attend a festival event here try your luck online at Biletix (p40).

SOĞUKÇEŞME SOKAK
HISTORIC SITE

Map p238 (🚇Sultanahmet or Gülhane) Running between the Topkapı Palace walls and Aya Sofya, this cobbled street is named after the Soğuk Çeşme (Cold Fountain) at its southern end. It is home to the Carpet Museum, to a row of faux-Ottoman houses functioning as a hotel and to an undoubtedly authentic restored Byzantine cistern that now operates as the hotel restaurant.

In the 1980s the Turkish Touring & Automobile Association (Turing) acquired a row of buildings on this street and decided to demolish most of them in order to build nine re-creations of the prim Ottoman-style houses that had occupied the site in the previous two centuries. What ensued was a vitriolic battle played out on the pages of İstanbul's newspapers, with some experts arguing that the city would be left with a Disney-style

Neighbourhood Walk
Sultanahmet Saunter

START AYA SOFYA MEYDANI
END ARASTA BAZAAR
LENGTH 2.3KM; TWO HOURS

Set off from Aya Sofya Meydanı and turn left into Babıhümayun Caddesi to visit the **1 Aya Sofya Tombs** (p78). Then head towards the **2 Fountain of Sultan Ahmet III** outside Topkapı Palace. This kiosk once dispensed cold drinks of water or şerbet (sherbet) to thirsty Ottoman travellers.

Veer left into cobbled Soğukçeşme Sokak and then turn left into Caferiye Sokak to visit the **3 Caferağa Medresesi** (p88), where you can enjoy a glass of tea after admiring the elegant Sinan-designed building. Back on Caferiye Sokak, continue until you reach the busy thoroughfare of Alemdar Caddesi and then walk along Sultanhamet Park to the **4 Hippodrome** (p77), where in Byzantine times horse-drawn chariots stormed around the perimeter.

Walk down Şehit Mehmet Paşa Yokuşu and continue down Katip Sinan Camii Sokak. You will arrive at the **5 Sokullu Şehit Me-**hmet Paşa Mosque (p81) on the left-hand side of the street. After admiring its İznik tiles, veer left down Şehit Mehmet Paşa Sokak to the residential neighbourhood of Küçük Ayasofya. You will come to a busy but narrow road called Kadırga Limanı Caddesi. Veer left here and follow the road until you arrive at the sadly delapidated **6 Çardaklı Hamam**, built in 1503. Turn right and you will see **7 Little Aya Sofya** (p81), one of the most beautiful Byzantine buildings in the city.

Continue east along Küçük Ayasofya Caddesi and walk left up the hill at Aksakal Caddesi. At the crest is the **8 Sphendone** (p77), originally part of the Hippodrome's southern stadium. Opposite is a huge carpet shop called **9 Nakkaş** (p82). Pop in here and ask a staff member to show you the restored Byzantine cistern in its basement.

From here, continue along Nakilbent Sokak and veer right down Şifa Hamamı Sokak, turning left into Küçük Ayasofya Caddesi. Continue straight to the **10 Arasta Bazaar** (p88), Sultanahmet's pre-eminent shopping precinct.

architectural theme park rather than a legitimate exercise in conservation architecture. Turing eventually got the go-ahead (after the intervention of the Turkish president, no less) and in time opened all of the re-created buildings as Ayasofya Konakları, one of the city's first boutique heritage hotels. Conservation theory aside, the street is particularly attractive and worth a look.

GÜLHANE PARK
PARK

Map p238 (Gülhane Parkı; ⊘7am-10pm; 🚇Gülhane) Gülhane Park was once the outer garden of Topkapı Palace, accessible only to the royal court. These days crowds of locals come here to picnic under the many trees, promenade past the formally planted flowerbeds, and enjoy wonderful views of the Bosphorus, Sea of Marmara and Princes' Islands from the Set Üstü Çay Bahçesi on the park's northeastern edge. The park is especially lovely during the **İstanbul Tulip Festival** FREE, in April, when tulips are arranged to resemble *nazar boncuk* 'evil eye' charms.

Green-fingered beautification has brought improvements to walkways and amenities, and the park has seen the opening of the İstanbul Museum of the History of Science & Technology in Islam (p82).

Next to the southern entrance is the Alay Köşkü (Parade Kiosk), now open to the public as the Ahmet Hamdi Tanpınar Literature Museum Library (p81).

Across the street and 100m downhill from the park's main gate is an outrageously curvaceous rococo gate leading into the precincts of what was the grand vizierate, or Ottoman prime ministry, known in the West as the **Sublime Porte** (Map p238; Alemdar Caddesi; 🚇Gülhane) thanks to this entrance. Today the buildings beyond the gate hold various offices of the İstanbul provincial government (the Vilayeti).

LITTLE AYA SOFYA
MOSQUE

Map p240 (Küçük Aya Sofya Camii; SS Sergius & Bacchus Church; Küçük Ayasofya Caddesi; ⊘sunrise-sunset; 🚇Sultanahmet or Çemberlitaş) FREE Justinian and his wife Theodora built this little church sometime between 527 and 536, just before Justinian built Aya Sofya. You can still see their monogram worked into some of the frilly white capitals. The building is one of the most beautiful Byzantine structures in the city despite being converted into a mosque in the early 16th century and having many of its original features obscured during an extensive restoration in 2007.

Named after Sergius and Bacchus, the two patron saints of Christians in the Roman army, the building has been known as Little (Küçük in Turkish) Aya Sofya for much of its existence. Its dome is architecturally noteworthy and its plan – an irregular octagon – is quite unusual. Its interior was originally decorated with gold mosaics and featured columns made from fine green and red marble. The mosaics are long gone, but the impressive columns remain. The church was converted into a mosque by the chief white eunuch Hüseyin Ağa around 1500; his tomb is to the north of the building. The minaret and *medrese* (seminary) date from this time.

The *medrese* cells, arranged around the mosque's forecourt, are now used by secondhand booksellers and bookbinders. In the leafy forecourt is a tranquil *çay bahçesi* (tea garden) where you can relax over a glass of çay.

SOKULLU ŞEHIT MEHMET PAŞA MOSQUE
MOSQUE

Map p240 (Sokullu Mehmet Paşa Camii; cnr Şehit Mehmet Paşa & Özbekler Sokaks, Kadırga; ⊘sunrise-sunset; 🚇Sultanahmet or Çemberlitaş) Mimar Sinan designed this mosque in 1571 at the height of his architectural career. Besides its architectural harmony, the mosque is unusual because the *medrese* is not a separate building but part of the mosque structure, built around the forecourt. The interior walls and *mimber* are decorated with spectacular red-and-blue İznik tiles – some of the best ever made.

Though named after the grand vizier of the time, the mosque was actually sponsored by his wife Esmahan, daughter of Sultan Selim II. Inside are four fragments from the sacred Black Stone in the Kaaba at Mecca: one above the entrance framed in gold, two in the *mimber* and one in the *mihrab*.

AHMET HAMDI TANPINAR LITERATURE MUSEUM LIBRARY
LIBRARY

Map p238 (Ahmet Hamdi Tanpınar Edebiyat Müze Kütüphanesi; 📞0212-520 2081; Gülhane Park; ⊘10am-7pm Mon-Sat; 🚇Gülhane) FREE Built into the wall of Gülhane Park, the Alay Köşkü (Parade Kiosk) is where the sultan would sit and watch the periodic parades of troops and trade guilds that commemorated great holidays and military victories. It is now open to the public as a literature museum and library named in honour of novelist and essayist Ahmet Hamdi Tanpınar (1901–62).

Dating from the early 19th century, the kiosk is polygonal in shape and beautifully decorated inside, with painted walls, stained-glass windows, chandeliers and highly polished wooden floors. Inside are packed shelves of Turkish books and literary items such as pens belonging to Ayşe Kulin, author of *Last Train to Istanbul*.

İSTANBUL MUSEUM OF THE HISTORY OF SCIENCE & TECHNOLOGY IN ISLAM
MUSEUM

Map p238 (İstanbul İslam Bilim ve Teknoloji Tarihi Müzesi; ☑0212-528 8065; www.ibttm.org; Has Ahırlar Binaları, Gülhane Park; adult/child under 12yr ₺10/free; ☺9am-6.30pm Wed-Mon mid-Apr–Oct, to 4.30pm Nov–mid-Apr, last entry 30min before closing; ⬚Gülhane) Of interest to science buffs, the didactic exhibition in the museum argues that Islamic advances in science and technology preceded and greatly influenced those in Europe. Most of the exhibits are reconstructions of historical instruments and tools used by astronomers, seafarers and others. The physics room has some of the best contraptions, including a steam-powered turn-spit, built from notes left by a 16th-century Ottoman scholar, and an 11th-century entertainment machine, which operates a scene of moving figures using water power. Also look out for the models of trebuchet counterweight catapults in the military room, and those of İstanbul's great mosques.

MARMARA UNIVERSITY REPUBLICAN MUSEUM
MUSEUM

Map p240 (Üçler Sokak; ☺10am-5pm Tue-Sun; ⬚Sultanahmet) FREE Located at the southern end of the Hippodrome, this museum is housed in a handsome example of Ottoman Revivalism, a homegrown architectural style popular in the late 19th century. On display is the university's collection of original Turkish prints and etchings from the 1920s to the present day, including work by İhap Hulusi Görey, who introduced coloured posters to Turkey.

NAKKAŞ
MUSEUM

Map p240 (☑0212-516 5222; www.nakkasrug. com; Nakilbent Sokak 13; ☺9am-7pm; ⬚Sultanahmet) FREE This renovated 6th-century cistern houses exhibits of virtual and physical models that recreate the nearby Hippodrome as it was in its heyday. Also interesting is the bird's-eye view of Constantinople in 1200, when the Great Palace of Byzantium and the Hippodrome domi-

nated present-day Sultanahmet. When we visited, there were plans to make this informative exhibition permanent.

 EATING

Sultanahmet's lovely settings and great views are too often accompanied by disappointing meals. That said, we've eaten our way through the neighbourhood and, fortunately, there are a few gems to be found. If you're in the Sirkeci neighbourhood at lunchtime, join the locals in Hocapaşa Sokak, a pedestrianised street lined with cheap eateries. Here, *lokantas* offer *hazır yemek* (ready-made dishes), *köftecis* dish out flavoursome meatballs, *kebapçıs* grill meat to order and *pidecis* serve piping-hot pides (Turkish-style pizza). For more about eating in Sirkeci, check http://sirkecirestaurants. com. The Küçük Ayasofya neighbourhood is another good option for more authentic and affordable eateries.

SEFA RESTAURANT
TURKISH €

Map p238 (☑0212-520 0670; www.sefa restaurant.com.tr; Nuruosmaniye Caddesi 11, Cağaloğlu; portions ₺8-14, kebaps ₺20; ☺7am-5pm; ☑; ⬚Sultanahmet) Describing its cuisine as Ottoman, this popular place offers *hazır yemek* (ready-made dishes) and kebaps at reasonable prices. You can order from an English menu, but at busy times you may find it easier to just pick daily specials from the bain-marie. Try to arrive early-ish for lunch because many dishes run out by 1.30pm. No alcohol.

EROL LOKANTASI
TURKISH €

Map p240 (☑0212-511 0322; Çatal Çeşme Sokak 3, Cağaloğlu; portions ₺5.50-15.50; ☺11am-9pm Mon-Sat; ☑; ⬚Sultanahmet) One of Sultanahmet's last *lokantas* (eateries serving ready-made food), Erol wouldn't win any awards for its interior design but might for its warm welcome and food. The dishes in the bain-marie are made fresh daily using seasonal ingredients by the Erol family members, who have collectively put in several decades in the kitchen. English-speaking son and nephew Şenol will guide you through the meat and vegetable stews on offer.

ÇİĞDEM PASTANESI
CAFE €

Map p240 (Divan Yolu Caddesi 62a; pastries ₺1.50-7.50, cakes ₺3-10; ☺7.30am-11.30pm; ⬚Sultanahmet) Strategically located on the main drag between Aya Sofya Meydanı and the Grand Bazaar, Çiğdem has been tempting locals since 1961 with its mouthwatering window display of gateaux and pastries. Pop in for a quick tea (₺2.50) or coffee (flat white ₺7.50) accompanied by *börek* (filled pastries), baklava or *tavuk göğsü* (a dessert made from milk, rice and pounded chicken breast).

GÜLHANE KANDIL TESISLERI   TURKISH €

Map p238 (☑0212-444 6644; www.beltur.istanbul; Gülhane Park; sandwiches ₺6.50-16.50, all-day breakfast plates ₺22, mains ₺19; ☺11am-10pm; ⊠Gülhane) In spring, the perfume from a profusion of hyacinths blooming in Gülhane Park wafts over the outdoor tables of this garden cafe, which is built into the park's historic walls. It's a lovely spot, when the weather is kind, for breakfast, a light lunch or a coffee break (Turkish coffee ₺5, çay ₺2.50).

SEDEF İSKENDER   KEBAP €

Map p240 (☑0212-516 2420; www.sedefdoner. com; Divan Yolu Caddesi 21b; döner ₺13; ☺11am-10pm; ⊠Sultanahmet) Locals swear that Sedef serves Sultanahmet's best döner kebap, and keep the chef busy shaving thin slices of meat or chicken with his enormous knife. A portion stuffed into fresh bread *(yarım ekmek)* makes a great lunch, but the food is not fresh later in the day. Eat in the cafeteria at the back or order a cheaper *paket* (takeaway).

HOCAPAŞA PIDECISI   PIDE €

Map p238 (☑0212-512 0990; www.hocapasa. com.tr; Hocapaşa Sokak 19, Sirkeci; pides ₺8-20; ☺noon-8pm; ⊠Sirkeci) This much-loved place has been serving piping-hot pides straight from its oven since 1964. Accompanied by pickles, they can be eaten at one of the outdoor tables or ordered *paket* (to go).

KARADENIZ AILE PIDE
VE KEBAP SALONU   PIDE, KEBAP €

Map p240 (☑0212-522 9191; www.karadenizpide. net; Hacı Tahsinbey Sokak 7, off Divan Yolu Caddesi; pides ₺16-24, kebaps ₺18-32; ☺11am-10pm; ⊠Sultanahmet) Serving tasty pides and kebaps since 1985, the original Karadeniz (Black Sea)–style pide joint in this enclave is a hit with local shopkeepers. You can claim a table in the utilitarian interior (women usually sit upstairs) or on the lane. No alcohol. Make sure that you don't get this place confused with those nearby, which have cheekily used versions of its name but are nowhere near as good. This one is on the street corner.

TARIHI SULTANAHMET
KÖFTECISI SELIM USTA   KÖFTE €

Map p240 (☑0212-520 0566; www.sultanahmet koftesi.com; Divan Yolu Caddesi 12; köfte ₺16, beans ₺7, çorba ₺5; ☺11am-10pm; ⊠Sultanahmet) Not to be confused with the nearby Meşhur Sultanahmet Köftecisi, this no-frills place near the Sultanahmet tram stop is the most famous eatery in the Old City. It has been serving its slightly rubbery *ızgara köfte* (grilled meatballs) and bean salad to ultraloyal locals since 1920, and shows no sign of losing its custom – there's often a queue outside. Accompany your *köfte* with the green pickled chillies that are served on the side, or ask the waiter for some spicy red chilli sauce. No alcohol; ayran (yogurt drink) is the drink of choice.

HAFIZ MUSTAFA   SWEETS €

Map p238 (☑0212-527 6654; www.hafizmustafa. com; Muradiye Caddesi 51, Sirkeci; börek ₺5, baklava ₺6-7.50, puddings ₺6; ☺9am-6pm; 🖹; ⊠Sirkeci) Making locals happy since 1864, this *şekerlemeleri* (sweets shop) sells *lokum* (Turkish Delight), milk puddings and spinach or cheese *börek* (filled pastry). Put your sweet tooth to good use in the upstairs cafe, or choose a selection of indulgences to take home (you might want to avoid the baklava, though, which isn't the best).

There are **branches** on Divan Yolu Caddesi (Map p240; ☑0212-514 9068; Divan Yolu Caddesi 14; ☺9am-6pm; 🖹; ⊠Sultanahmet), in Sultanahmet, and Hamidiye Caddesi (p109), close to the Spice Bazaar.

TARIHI ÇEŞME RESTAURANT   TURKISH €€

Map p240 (☑0212-516 3580; www.tarihicesme restaurant.com; cnr Kadırga Liman Caddesi & Küçük Ayasofya Cami Sokak, Küçük Ayasofya; mezes ₺7, pides ₺13, mains ₺20; ☺11am-10pm; ⊠Sultanahmet or Çemberlitaş) Contrary to appearances, this no-frills eatery does serve beer and wine – both perfectly complemented by the outside terrace with its view of people ambling through this quiet neighbourhood. Kebaps, mixed grills and *güveç* (meat and vegetable stew) are all on the menu.

GÜVENÇ KONYALI   TURKISH €€

Map p238 (☑0212-527 5220; Hocapaşa Hamam Sokak 4, Sirkeci; soups ₺6-10, mains & pides ₺15-25; ☺11.30am-9pm; ⊠Sirkeci) Specialities from Konya in Central Anatolia are the draw at this bustling place just off the much-loved Hocapaşa Sokak food strip. Regulars come for the spicy *bamya çorbası* (sour soup with lamb and chickpeas), *etli ekmek* (flat bread with meat) and meltingly soft slow-cooked meats from the oven. No alcohol.

PALATIUM
PIDE, TURKISH €€

Map p240 (☎0543 844 5413; www.palatiumcafe andrestaurant.com; Kutlugün Sokak 33; mezes ₺11, pides ₺23, mains ₺30; ⊙11am-10pm; 🖥📶; 🚇Sultanahmet) Palatium is built atop part of the Great Palace of Byzantium, which you can see through its glass floor, between the rugs, beanbag seats at low tables and dangling lanterns. While the food is better than at many of the surrounding tourist haunts, the pide is probably the best choice, making Palatium better for lunch or a snack than dinner.

Dishes are cooked in traditional clay pots in a brick oven. Seafood, stews, pides and a wide range of kebaps are on offer. After you've eaten, follow the staircase at the rear to the palace below.

★DERALIYE
OTTOMAN €€€

Map p240 (☎0212-520 7778; www.deraliye restaurant.com; Ticarethane Sokak 10; mains ₺34-64; ⊙11am-10pm; 🖥📶; 🚇Sultanahmet) Starting with a complimentary glass of titillating pomegranate-flower juice, Deraliye offers a taste of the sumptuous dishes once served in the great Ottoman palaces. The menu gives a potted history of each dish, so you can live out your royal banquet fantasies by ordering the goose kebap served to Süleyman the Magnificent or Mehmet II's favourite lamb stew.

A good selection of Turkish wines complements the unusual historical dishes and old Turkish favourites such as *yaprak sarma* (stuffed vine leaves). Service is fast and efficient, and daily morning and afternoon cooking classes are offered.

★BALIKÇI SABAHATTIN
SEAFOOD €€€

Map p240 (☎0212-458 1824; www.balikci sabahattin.com; Şeyit Hasan Koyu Sokak 1, Cankurtaran; mezes ₺10-40, fish ₺40-60; ⊙11am-10pm; 🖥; 🚇Sultanahmet) Balıkçı Sabahattin is an enduring favourite with discerning Turks from near and far, who enjoy the limited menu of meze and seafood, including fish from red mullet to sole. This is Sultanahmet's most prestigious restaurant and its best food, although the service can be harried. You'll dine under a leafy canopy in the garden (one section smoking, the other nonsmoking).

Be sure to choose your fish from the display near the entrance; cold mezes are chosen from trays brought to your table. If

you have room at the end, the quince with cream is a delicious dessert.

★COOKING ALATURKA
TURKISH €€€

Map p240 (☎0212-458 5919; www.cookingalaturka. com; Akbıyık Caddesi 72a, Cankurtaran; set lunch or dinner ₺65; ⊙lunch 1-3pm & dinner 7-9pm by reservation Mon-Sat; 🖥📶; 🚇Sultanahmet) One of the Sultanahmet area's best dining experiences, this hybrid cooking-school–restaurant serves a set four- or five-course menu of Turkish home-cooking, regional Anatolian specialities and Ottoman classics. Sampling dishes such as *imam bayıldı* ('the imam fainted'; eggplant, onion, tomato and peppers slow-cooked in olive oil) with a glass of local wine is a wonderful way to experience authentic Turkish cuisine.

The menu can be tailored to suit vegetarians or those with food allergies (call ahead). No children under six years at dinner.

MATBAH
OTTOMAN €€€

Map p238 (☎0212-514 6151; www.matbah restaurant.com; Ottoman Hotel Imperial, Caferiye Sokak 6/1; mezes ₺15-23, mains ₺29-61; ⊙noon-10.30pm; 🖥📶; 🚇Sultanahmet) One of a growing number of İstanbul restaurants specialising in so-called Ottoman palace cuisine, Matbah offers dishes that were devised centuries ago in the royal kitchens of Constantinople. The menu changes with the season and features unusual ingredients such as goose, quail, quince and molasses. Try the sailor's roll starter (seven cheeses wrapped in filo, fried and drizzled with honey). The setting is attractive; the attentive staff is full of explanations about the historic dishes and there's live oud music on Friday and Saturday nights in summer.

AHIRKAPI BALIKÇISI
SEAFOOD €€€

Map p240 (☎0212-518 4988; Keresteci Hakkı Sokak 46, Cankurtaran; mezes ₺5-40, fish ₺35-80; ⊙noon-11pm; 🖥; 🚇Sultanahmet) Join the locals at this tiny and authentically Turkish neighbourhood fish restaurant where a seafood-packed fridge beckons to a quiet cobbled street. Get here early to score a table, especially at dinner.

DRINKING & NIGHTLIFE

Most **Sultanahmet restaurants are licensed**, while streets such as **Şeftali**

SULTANAHMET'S HIPPIE TRAIL

Plenty of monuments in Sultanahmet evoke the city's Byzantine and Ottoman past, but there are few traces of an equally colourful but much more recent period in the city's history – the hippie era of the 1960s and 1970s. Back then the first wave of Intrepids (young travellers following the overland trail from Europe to Asia) descended upon İstanbul and played a significant role in the Europeanisation of Turkey. The Intrepids didn't travel with itineraries, tour guides or North Face travel gear; their basic baggage embodied a rejection of materialism, a fervent belief in the power of love and a commitment to the journey rather than the destination. All that was leavened with liberal doses of sex, drugs and protest music, of course.

Sultanahmet had three central hippie hang-outs in those days: the Gülhane Hostel (now closed); a cafe run 'King of the Hippies' Sitki Yener (now a leather shop on İnciliçavuş Sokak); and the still-operating **Lâle Pastanesi** (Pudding Shop; Map p240; ☏0212-522 2970; www.puddingshop.com; Divan Yolu Caddesi 6; mains ₺25; ☺7am-11pm; 🚇Sultanahmet), known to hippie-trail veterans the world over as the Pudding Shop. Sadly, this retains few echoes of its countercultural past, substituting bland food in place of its former menu of psychedelic music and chillums of hash. Nonetheless, you may wish to turn on, tune in and drop by for a çay, to view the period photos on the tabletops, menus and walls recalling the eatery's halcyon days. Notes stuck in the window by enthusiastic tourists attempt to revive that spirit of old. To evoke those days, we highly recommend Rory Maclean's *Magic Bus: On the Hippie Trail from Istanbul to India*, a thought-provoking and wonderfully written history-travelogue.

Sokak (near the Basilica Cistern), the adjoining İncili Çavuş Sokak and, down in Cankurtaran, Akbıyık Caddesi are good hunting grounds for bars. Few are on a par with those in Beyoğlu, but do not despair. Why not substitute tobacco or caffeine for alcohol and visit one of the atmospheric *çay bahçesis* dotted around the neighbourhood?

DERVİŞ AİLE ÇAY BAHÇESİ   TEA GARDEN

Map p240 (cnr Dalbastı Sokak & Kabasakal Caddesi; ☺7am-midnight Apr-Oct; 🚇Sultanahmet) Superbly located directly opposite the Blue Mosque, the Derviş beckons patrons with its comfortable cane chairs and shady trees. Efficient service, reasonable prices and peerless people-watching opportunities make it a great place for a leisurely çay (₺3), nargile (₺22), *tost* (toasted sandwich; ₺7) and a game of backgammon.

CAFE MEŞALE   NARGILE CAFE

Map p240 (Arasta Bazaar, cnr Dalbastı & Torun Sokaks, Cankurtaran; ☺24hr; 🚇Sultanahmet) Located in a sunken courtyard behind the Blue Mosque, Meşale is a tourist trap *par excellence*, but still has loads of charm. Generations of backpackers have joined locals in claiming one of its cushioned benches and enjoying a tea and nargile. It has sporadic live Turkish music and a bustling vibe in the evening.

A'YA ROOFTOP LOUNGE   BAR

Map p240 (☏0212-402 3000; www.fourseasons. com/istanbul; Four Seasons Istanbul at Sultanahmet, Tevkifhane Sokak 1, Cankurtaran; ☺4pm-late; 🚇Sultanahmet) Open in summer, this rooftop bar has a full-on view of Aya Sofya, Ayasofya Hürrem Sultan Hamamı and the Bosphorus, while the Blue Mosque is only partially obscured. Cocktails (₺49), meze (₺30) and an impressive selection of spirits add to the appeal. In winter, sit downstairs in the lounge bar or courtyard garden.

CIHANNÜMA   BAR

Map p238 (☏0212-512 0207; www.cihannuma istanbul.com; And Hotel, Yerebatan Caddesi 18; ☺noon-midnight; 🚇Sultanahmet) We don't recommend eating at this rooftop hotel restaurant near Aya Sofya, but the view from its narrow balcony and glass-sheathed dining room is one of the Old City's best (spot Aya Sofya, Blue Mosque, Topkapı Palace, Galata Tower and the Bosphorus Bridge), so it's a great choice for a scenic afternoon drink or sundowner.

KYBELE CAFE   BAR, CAFE

Map p238 (☏0212-511 7766; www.kybelehotel. com; Yerebatan Caddesi 23; ☺7.30am-11.30pm; 🚇Sultanahmet) The hotel lounge bar–cafe close to the Basilica Cistern is chock-full of antique furniture, richly coloured rugs and old etchings and prints, but its signature

IHSAN GERCELMAN/SHUTTERSTOCK ©

1. Basilica Cistern (p76)
Dating to 532 AD, this is the largest surviving Byzantine cistern in İstanbul.

2. Aya Sofya (p54)
Part of the interior of the complex, showing mosaics on the walls and ceiling.

3. Topkapı Palace (p61)
Interior of the Baghdad Kiosk on the Marble Terrace of the Fourth Court.

4. İstanbul Archaeology Museums (p74)
Showcasing archaeological treasures including these brick panels from ancient Babylon.

style comes courtesy of the hundreds of colourful glass lights hanging from the ceiling.

CAFERAĞA MEDRESESI
ÇAY BAHÇESİ
TEA GARDEN

Map p238 (☑0212-513 3601; www.tkhv.org; Soğukkuyu Çıkmazı 5, off Caferiye Sokak; ◷9am-7pm Tue-Sun; 🚇Sultanahmet) On a fine day, sipping a çay in the gorgeous courtyard of this Sinan-designed *medrese* is a delight. Located close to both Aya Sofya and Topkapı Palace, it houses a craft centre and serves simple food at lunchtime.

HOTEL NOMADE TERRACE BAR
BAR

Map p240 (☑0212-513 8172; www.hotelnomade. com; Ticarethane Sokak 15, Alemdar; ◷2-11.30pm; 🚇Sultanahmet) The intimate terrace of this boutique hotel overlooks Aya Sofya and the Blue Mosque. Settle down in a comfortable chair to enjoy a glass of wine, beer or freshly squeezed fruit juice. The only music that will disturb your evening reverie is the Old City's signature sound of the call to prayer.

 # ENTERTAINMENT

LES ARTS TURCS
CULTURAL

Map p240 (☑0212-527 6859; www.lesartsturcs. com; 3rd fl, Incili Cavus Sokak 19, Alemdar; ₺70; 🚇Sultanahmet) This long-established cultural tourism outfit based near the Basilica Cistern offers twice-weekly opportunities to attend a *sema* (whirling-dervish ceremony) at the EMAV Silivrikapı Mevlana Cultural Center in Fatih on Thursdays at 8pm. The ticket cost includes a 15-minute Q&A session in English, a guide and minivan transfers to/from Sultanahmet.

The company also sometimes takes visitors to a Monday evening *sema* at a different *tekke* (Dervish lodge) in the same district. Other Les Arts Turcs offerings include religious tours and cultural workshops.

HODJAPASHA CULTURAL
CENTRE
PERFORMING ARTS

Map p238 (☑0212-511 4626; www.hodjapasha. com; Hocapaşa Hamamı Sokak 3b, Sirkeci; performances adult ₺70-80, child under 12yr ₺40-50; 🚇Sirkeci) Occupying a beautifully converted 550-year-old hamam, this cultural centre stages a one-hour whirling dervish performance at 7pm on Tuesday, Thursday and Saturday year-round, with additional performances in busy months (daily in April, May, September and October). Note that

children under seven are not admitted; and switch off your phone, as readers have reported draconian crowd-control here.

Also on offer are a 1¼-hour Turkish dance show (at 9pm on Tuesday, Thursday, Saturday and Sunday for most of the year) and a monthly 1¾-hour performance set in the Ottoman harem.

 # SHOPPING

The best shopping in Sultanahmet is found in and around the Arasta Bazaar, an historic arcade of shops that was once part of the *külliye* (mosque complex) of the Blue Mosque (Sultanahmet Camii). Some of Turkey's best-known rug and ceramics dealers have shops in the surrounding streets.

★JENNIFER'S
HAMAM
BATHWARES, HOMEWARES

Map p240 (☑0212-516 3022; www.jennifers hamam.com; Öğül Sokak 20; ◷8.30am-9pm Apr-Oct, to 7pm Nov-Mar; 🚇Sultanahmet) Owned by Canadian Jennifer Gaudet, this shop stocks top-quality hamam items, including towels, robes and *peştemals* (bath wraps) produced using certified organic cotton and silk on old-style shuttled looms. It also sells natural soaps and *keses* (coarse cloth mittens used for exfoliation). Prices are set; no bargaining. This is the main showroom; there are two further **branches** in the Arasta Bazaar (Map p240; Arasta Bazaar 125 and Arasta Bazaar 135; 🚇Sultanahmet).

★ÖZLEM TUNA
JEWELLERY, HOMEWARES

Map p238 (☑0212-527 9285; www.ozlemtuna. com; 5th fl, Nemlizade Han, Ankara Caddesi 65, Eminönü; ◷9am-6pm Mon-Fri; 🚇Sirkeci) A leader in Turkey's contemporary design movement, Özlem Tuna produces super-stylish jewellery and homewares and sells them from her atelier overlooking Sirkeci train station. Her pieces use forms and colours that reference İstanbul's history and culture (tulips, seagulls, Byzantine mosaics, *nazar boncuk* 'evil eye' charms) and include hamam bowls, coffee and teasets, coasters, rings, earrings, cufflinks and necklaces.

★GALERI KAYSERI
BOOKS

Map p240 (☑0212-516 3366; www.galeri kayseri.com; Divan Yolu Caddesi 11 & 58; ◷9am-8pm; 🚇Sultanahmet) Peddling literature since 1996, these twin shops stock a well-presented selection of English-language novels, history books, maps and coffee-table tomes on Turkey, and have knowledgable staff on hand to recommend a good holiday read. The second, smaller, shop is on the opposite side of the road half a block closer to Aya Sofya.

KHAFTAN ART, ANTIQUES

Map p240 (✆0212-458 5425; Nakilbent Sokak 16; ⊙9am-7pm; 🚇Sultanahmet) Gleaming Russian icons, delicate calligraphy (old and new), ceramics, *karagöz* (shadow-puppet theatre) puppets, Ottoman prints and contemporary paintings are on show in this attractive shop.

MEHMET ÇETINKAYA GALLERY CARPETS, JEWELLERY

Map p240 (✆0212-517 1603, 0212-517 6808; www.cetinkayagallery.com; Tavukhane Sokak 5-7; ⊙9am-8pm; 🚇Sultanahmet) Mehmet Çetinkaya is one of the country's foremost experts on antique oriental carpets and kilims. Built over a Byzantine well, his flagship store-cum-gallery stocks items of artistic and ethnographic significance, and is full of treasures including carpets, kilims, textiles and jewellery. A **branch** in the Arasta Bazaar (Map p240; Arasta Bazaar 58; ⊙9am-8pm; 🚇Sultanahmet) sells textiles and antique jewellery.

IZNIK CLASSICS CERAMICS

Map p240 (✆0212-516 8874; www.iznikclassics. com; Utangaç Sokak 17; ⊙9am-8pm, closes 6.30pm winter; 🚇Sultanahmet) İznik Classics is one of the best places in town to source hand-painted collector-item ceramics made with real quartz and using metal oxides for pigments. Admire the range here or at **branches** in the Arasta Bazaar (Map p240; ✆0212-517 3608; Arasta Bazaar 119; ⊙9am-8pm, closes 6.30pm winter; 🚇Sultanahmet) and Grand Bazaar (Map p85; ✆0212-520 2568; Şerifağa Sokak 188, İç Bedesten; ⊙8.30am-7pm Mon-Sat; 🚇Beyazıt-Kapalı Çarşı). The shop next door at number 13 sells Kütahya ceramics, including tiles, plates and bowls.

COCOON CARPETS, TEXTILES

Map p240 (✆0212-518 0338; www.yastk.com; Küçük Ayasofya Caddesi 17; ⊙9am-6pm; 🚇Sultanahmet) Sultanahmet is thickly carpeted with rug and textile shops but Cocoon is worth a look. Felt hats, felt-and-silk scarves, rugs, cushion covers and textiles from central Asia are artfully displayed. There's a second **branch** selling hamam items in the Arasta Bazaar (Map p240; Arasta Bazaar 93; ⊙9am-7pm; 🚇Sultanahmet).

YILMAZ IPEKÇILIK TEXTILES

Map p240 (✆0212-638 4579; www.yilmazipekcilik. com/en; Torun Sokak 3; ⊙9am-9pm Mon-Sat, to 7pm winter; 🚇Sultanahmet) The Büyükaşık family specialises in well-priced hand-loomed silk textiles made in Antakya. They have been at it for several generations, producing good-quality scarves, shawls and *peştemals* (bath wraps).

NAKKAŞ CARPETS

Map p240 (✆0212-516 5222; www.nakkasrug. com; Nakilbent Sokak 13; ⊙9am-7pm; 🚇Sultanahmet) Nakkaş sells carpets, textiles, ceramics and jewellery. Its varied collection of more than 20,000 carpets and kilims includes antique rugs, hand-woven pieces and traditional Anatolian carpets. A few have even won design awards.

SPORTS & ACTIVITIES

★İSTANBUL WALKS WALKING, CULINARY

Map p240 (✆0212-516 6300, 0554 335 6622; www.istanbulwalks.com; 1st fl, Şifa Hamamı Sokak 1; tours adult €35-75, child under 2/7yr free/30% discount; 🚇Sultanahmet) Specialising in cultural tourism, this company is run by history buffs and offers a large range of guided walking tours conducted by knowledgeable English-speaking guides. Tours concentrate on İstanbul's various neighbourhoods, but there are also tours of major monuments, a Turkish coffee trail, and a Bosphorus and Golden Horn cruise by private boat.

★İSTANBUL EATS WALKING

(http://istanbuleats.com; tours per person US$75-125) Full-day culinary walks around the Old City, Bazaar District, Beyoğlu, Kadıköy and the Bosphorus suburbs, as well as evenings spent sampling kebaps in Aksaray's 'Little Syria (p103)' district or visiting *meyhanes* (Turkish taverns) in Beyoğlu. All are conducted by the dedicated foodies who produce the excellent blog of the same name, and involve lots of eating.

COOKING ALATURKA COOKING

Map p240 (✆0212-458 5919; www.cookingala turka.com; Akbıyık Caddesi 72a, Cankurtaran; classes per person incl meal €65; ⊙10.30am &

4.30pm by reservation Mon-Sat; 🚇Sultanahmet) Established in 2002, this culinary school has changed hands but is still cooking up a storm under its Turkish-Italian ownership. Suitable for both novices and experienced cooks, its convivial 2½-hour classes give a great introduction to Turkish cuisine, from classic meze to Ottoman dishes such as Circassian chicken. The delicious results are enjoyed over a meal in the school's restaurant (p84).

URBAN ADVENTURES
WALKING TOUR, CULTURAL TOUR

(✆0532 641 2822; www.urbanadventures.com; tours adult €27-82, child €22-79) The international tour company Intrepid offers a program of city tours including a popular four-hour guided walk around Sultanahmet and the Bazaar District. Also on offer are the 'Picnic on Two Continents' and the 'Home Cooked İstanbul' tours, the latter including a no-frills dinner with a local family in their home and a visit to a neighbourhood teahouse.

AYASOFYA HÜRREM SULTAN HAMAMI
HAMAM

Map p240 (✆0212-517 3535; www.ayasofya hamami.com; Aya Sofya Meydanı 2; bath treatments €85-170, massages €40-75; ⏰8am-10pm; 🚇Sultanahmet) This meticulously restored twin hamam dating to 1556 offers the most luxurious traditional bath experience in the Old City. Designed by Mimar Sinan, it was built just across the road from Aya Sofya by order of Süleyman the Magnificent and named in honour of his wife Hürrem Sultan, commonly known as Roxelana.

The building's three-year, US$13 million restoration, completed in 2011, was closely monitored by heritage authorities and the end result is wonderful: it retains Sinan's austere design but endows it with an understated modern luxury. There are separate baths for males and females, both with a handsome *soğukluk* (entrance vestibule) surrounded by wooden change cubicles. Treatments are expert and the surrounds are exceptionally clean. The basic 35-minute bath treatment costs €85 and includes a scrub and soap massage, olive-oil soap and a personal *kese* (coarse cloth mitten used for exfoliation). Book ahead in high season. In warm weather, a cafe and restaurant operate on the outdoor terrace.

CRATUS TOUR
TOUR

(✆0212-235 1810; www.cratustour.com; up to 5 adults €180) Tayfun and team offer cultural tours focusing on topics such as İstanbul's Jewish heritage. The Istanbul Classics tour is their best, covering Sultanahmet's highlights and the Grand Bazaar, where Tayfun's father worked. The City Walls and Golden Horn tour covers the Western Districts including the Kariye Museum (Chora Church) and Eyüp.

CAFERAĞA MEDRESESI
COURSE

Map p238 (✆0212-513 3601; www.tkhv.org; Soğukkuyu Çıkmazı 5, off Caferiye Sokak; private 1hr classes ₺100; 🚇Sultanahmet) This 16th-century *medrese* (seminary) houses a a cultural organisation that teaches and promotes traditional Turkish handicrafts. Classes are available in calligraphy, marbling, glass painting, porcelain decoration and more. English is spoken.

CAĞALOĞLU HAMAMI
HAMAM

Map p238 (✆0212-522 2424; www.cagaloglu hamami.com.tr; Prof Kazım İsmail Gürkan Caddesi 24; bath, scrub & massage packages €40-120, self-service €30; ⏰8am-10pm; 🚇Sultanahmet) Built in 1741 by order of Sultan Mahmut I, this gorgeous hamam offers separate baths for men and women and a range of bath services that are – alas – overpriced considering how quick and rudimentary the wash, scrub and massage treatments are. Consider signing up for the self-service treatment (€30) only.

AMBASSADOR SPA
HAMAM

Map p240 (✆0212-512 0002; www.hotel ambassador.com; Ticarethane Sokak 3; Turkish bath treatments €30, massage treatments €25-60; ⏰9am-10pm; 🚇Sultanahmet) There's no Ottoman ambience on offer at the spa centre of this bland hotel just off Divan Yolu, but all treatments are private, meaning that you get the small hamam all to yourself. The signature 60- or 75-minute 'Oriental Massage' package (€50 to €60) includes a facial massage, hamam treatment and expert 30-minute oil massage.

The spa's massage therapist Zeki Ulusoy is trained in sports, remedial and aromatherapy massage and he really knows his stuff – you'll float out of here at the end of a session. The 50-minute 'Ottoman' package (€40) comprises a 20-minute body scrub and a 30-minute foam massage.

Bazaar District

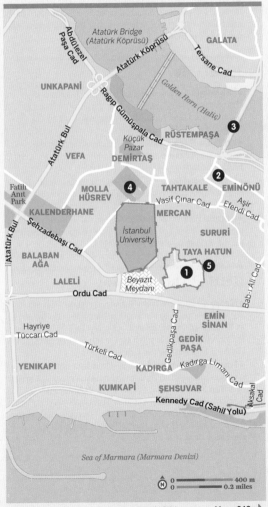

Neighbourhood Top Five

1 **Grand Bazaar** (p93) Enjoying getting lost in the labyrinthine lanes of the world's oldest shopping mall.

2 **Spice Bazaar** (p98) Shopping in and around this seductively scented market.

3 **Galata Bridge** (p101) Viewing the Old City's skyline while walking across this bridge at sunset.

4 **Süleymaniye Mosque** (p96) Visiting the remarkably intact *külliye* (mosque complex) of the greatest of İstanbul's Ottoman monuments.

5 **Grand Bazaar** (p102) Lunching with the locals in and around the bazaar.

For more detail of this area see Map p242

Lonely Planet's Top Tip

If you're walking to the Grand Bazaar from Sultanahmet, you can avoid the traffic and touts along Divan Yolu Caddesi by instead heading up Yerebatan Caddesi, left into Nuruosmaniye Caddesi, across Cağaloğlu Meydanı, along pedestrianised Nuruosmaniye Caddesi and across Vezir Han Caddesi towards the Nuruosmaniye Mosque.

Best Mosque Architecture

➡ Süleymaniye Mosque (p96)

➡ Rüstem Paşa Mosque (p99)

➡ Nuruosmaniye Mosque (p100)

For reviews, see p99.➡

Best Places to Eat

➡ Develi Baklava (p102)

➡ Fatih Damak Pide (p103)

➡ Little Urfa (p103)

➡ Hamdi Restaurant (p105)

➡ Siirt Şeref Büryan Kebap (p105)

For reviews, see p102.➡

Best Places to Shop

➡ Abdulla Natural Products (p108)

➡ Altan Şekerleme (p109)

➡ Derviş (p109)

➡ Epoque (p108)

➡ Necef Antik & Gold (p109)

For reviews, see p108.➡

Explore Bazaar District

There's loads to see in this district, so you'll need to plan your time to make the most of it. Ideally, you should dedicate a full day to the bazaars, starting at the Grand Bazaar in the morning, having lunch and then walking down Mahmutpaşa Yokuşu to the Spice Bazaar and Eminönü.

Another day could be spent following our walking tour (p104). On this you'll visit two important Ottoman mosques and get a taste of local life while lunching at a regional eatery in the Kadınlar Pazarı (Women's Market) near the Roman-era Aqueduct of Valens.

Nothing much is open in this district on Sunday, so visit Monday to Saturday only. And try to avoid the mosques at prayer times and from late morning to early afternoon on Friday, when weekly group prayers and sermons are held.

Local Life

➡**Tahtakale** Locals shop in the streets between the Grand and Spice Bazaars rather than in the bazaars themselves. Head to Mahmutpaşa Yokuşu and Hasırcılar Caddesi to join them.

➡**Kadınlar Pazarı** This atmospheric square in the Zeyrek neighbourhood is full of regional eateries and produce shops.

➡**Fish sandwiches** The city's signature fast-food treat is best enjoyed with crowds of locals at the Eminönü ferry docks.

➡**Nargile** Follow the evocative scent of apple tobacco to discover busy nargile (water pipe) cafes underneath Galata Bridge or along Divan Yolu Caddesi.

Getting There & Away

➡**Metro** To get here from Taksim Meydanı (Taksim Sq) or Şişhane, take the Yenikapı service and alight at Vezneciler. From the exit, walk left (east) along Şehzadebaşı Caddesi until you reach Beyazıt Meydanı (Beyazıt Sq), next to the Grand Bazaar.

➡**Tram** The neighbourhood is sliced into north and south areas by Ordu Caddesi, the western continuation of Divan Yolu Caddesi. Trams from Bağcılar and Cevizlıbağ to Kabataş run along this major road, passing through Aksaray, past the Grand Bazaar, across Sultanahmet and then down the hill to Eminönü, where the Spice Bazaar is located.

TOP SIGHT
GRAND BAZAAR

This colourful and chaotic bazaar is the heart of the Old City and has been for centuries. Starting as a small vaulted *bedesten* (warehouse) built on the order of Mehmet the Conqueror in 1461, it grew to cover a vast area as lanes between the *bedesten*, neighbouring shops and *hans* (caravanserais) were roofed and the market assumed the sprawling, labyrinthine form it retains today.

Exploring the Bazaar

When here, be sure to peep through doorways to discover hidden *hans*, veer down narrow lanes to watch artisans at work and wander the main thoroughfares to differentiate treasures from tourist tat. It's obligatory to drink lots of tea, compare price after price and try your hand at the art of bargaining.

Allow at least three hours for your visit; some travellers spend three days!

A Tour of the Bazaar

There are thousands of shops in the bazaar, and this can be overwhelming for the first-time visitor. By following this suggested itinerary, you should be able to develop an understanding of the bazaar's history, its layout and its important position as the hub of the surrounding retail precinct.

Start at the tram stop next to the tall column known as Çemberlitaş (p101). From here, walk down Vezir Han Caddesi and you will soon come to the entrance to the Vezir Han, a *han* (caravanserai) built between 1659 and 1660 by the Köprülüs, a distinguished

DON'T MISS

➡ İç (Inner) Bedesten
➡ Halıcılar Çarşısı Sokak
➡ Kuyumcular Caddesi
➡ Takkeciler Sokak
➡ Sahaflar Çarşısı

PRACTICALITIES

➡ Kapalı Çarşı, Covered Market
➡ Map p242, D5
➡ ⊘8.30am-7pm Mon-Sat, final entry 6pm
➡ ⓜBeyazıt-Kapalı Çarşı

MAHMUTPAŞA YOKUŞU

This busy thoroughfare links the Grand Bazaar with the Spice Bazaar at Eminönü. From the Grand Bazaar, leave the Mahmutpaşa Kapısı (Mahmutpaşa Gate; Gate 18) and walk downhill. Along the way you will pass one of the oldest hamams in the city: the **Mahmutpaşa Hamamı** (Map p242; Mahmutpaşa Yokuşu; 🚇Çemberlitaş), now a run-down shopping centre. If you veer left onto Tarakçılar Caddesi before the hamam and walk to Çakmakçılar Yokuşu, you will see the historic **Büyük Valide Han** (Map p242; 🚇Beyazıt-Kapalı Çarşı), a huge and sadly dilapidated caravanserai built by order of Murat IV's mother in 1651.

DID YOU KNOW?

Over the bazaar's history, most silversmiths who have worked here have been of Armenian descent and most goldsmiths have been of Arabic or Aramaic descent – this is still true today.

Ottoman family. Five of its members served as grand vizier (*vezir*) to the sultan, hence its name. In Ottoman times, this *han* would have offered travelling merchants accommodation and a place to do business. Though gold manufacturers still work here, the *han* is in a sadly dilapidated state. Look for the *tuğra* (monogram or crest) of the sultan over the main gateway.

Continue walking down Vezir Han Caddesi until you come to a cobbled pedestrianised street on your left. Walk along this until you reach the baroque-style Nuruosmaniye Mosque (p100). Next to it is one of the major entrances to the Grand Bazaar, the Nuruosmaniye Kapısı (Nuruosmaniye Gate; Gate 1), which is adorned by an imperial *tuğra*.

Head into brightly lit Kalpakçılar Caddesi, the busiest street in the bazaar. Originally named after the makers of fur hats (*kalpakçılars*) who had their stores here, it's now full of jewellers. Walk a short distance and then turn right into Sandal Bedestenı Sokak before veering left into Ağa Sokak, which takes you into the oldest part of the bazaar, the **İç (Inner) Bedesten**, where most of the bazaar's antique stores are located.

Exiting the İç Bedesten from its north door, head to the first cross street, **Halıcılar Sokak**, where popular bath ware and textile shops are located.

Walking east (right) you will come to Kuyumcular Caddesi (Street of the Jewellers). Turn left and walk past the little kiosk in the middle of the street. Built in the 19th century and known as the Oriental Kiosk, this was once home to the most famous *muhallebici* (milk-pudding shop) in the district. A little further down, on the right-hand side of the street, is the pretty **Zincirli (Chain) Han**.

From Kuyumcular Caddesi, turn sharp left into Perdahçılar Sokak (Street of the Polishers) and left again into Tekkeçiler Sokak (Street of the Skullcap Makers), home to marble *sebils* (public drinking fountains).

Turn right into Zenneciler Sokak (Street of the Clothing Sellers) and you will soon come to a junc-

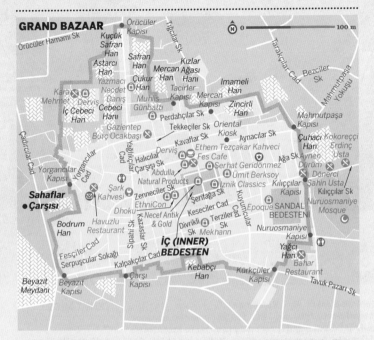

tion with another of the bazaar's major thoroughfares: Sipahi Sokak (Street of the Cavalry Soldiers). Şark Kahvesi (p108), a traditional coffeehouse, is on the corner.

Turn left into Sipahi Sokak and walk until you return to Kalpakçılar Caddesi. Turn right and exit the bazaar from the Beyazıt Kapısı (Beyazıt Gate; Gate 7). Turn right again and then left into the first passage on the left, where you'll find the **Sahaflar Çarşısı** (Old Book Bazaar; Map p95; Çadırcılar Caddesi, btwn Grand Bazaar & Beyazıt Mosque; ⌂Beyazıt-Kapalı Çarşı), a book and paper market established in Byzantine times. At the centre of its shady courtyard is a bust of İbrahim Müteferrika (1674–1745), who printed the first book in Turkey in 1732.

To learn more about day-to-day life in the bazaar, go to www.mygrandbazaar.com, which profiles some of the people who work here.

TOP SIGHT
SÜLEYMANIYE MOSQUE

Commissioned by Süleyman I, known as the Magnificent, this was the fourth imperial mosque built in İstanbul and it certainly lives up to its patron's nickname. Crowning one of İstanbul's seven hills, the mosque and its surrounding *külliye* (mosque complex) was designed by Mimar Sinan, the most famous and talented of all imperial architects.

The Mosque

The mosque was built between 1550 and 1557. Though it's seen some hard times, having been damaged by fire in 1660 and then having its wonderful columns covered by cement and oil paint at some point after this, restorations in 1956 and 2010 mean that it's now in great shape. It's also one of the most popular mosques in the city, with its worshippers rivalling those of the Blue and New Mosques in number.

The building's setting and plan are particularly pleasing, featuring gardens and a three-sided forecourt with a central domed ablutions fountain. The four minarets with their 10 beautiful şerefes (balconies) are said to represent the fact that Süleyman was the fourth of the Osmanlı sultans to rule the city and the 10th sultan after the establishment of the empire.

In the garden behind the mosque is a terrace offering lovely views of the Golden Horn and Bosphorus. The street underneath once housed the külliye's arasta (row of shops), which was built into the retaining wall of the terrace. Close by was a five-level *mülazim* (preparatory school).

Inside, the building is breathtaking in its size and pleasing in its simplicity. Sinan incorporated the four buttresses into the walls of the building – the result is wonderfully 'transparent' (ie open and airy) and highly reminiscent of Aya Sofya, especially as the dome is nearly as large as the one that crowns the Byzantine basilica.

DON'T MISS

➡ Mosque
➡ *Türbes* (tombs)
➡ *Külliye* (mosque complex)
➡ View from terrace

PRACTICALITIES

➡ Map p242, C3
➡ Professor Sıddık Sami Onar Caddesi
➡ Ⓜ Vezneciler

The *mihrab* (niche in a minaret indicating the direction of Mecca) is covered in fine İznik tiles. Other interior decoration includes window shutters inlaid with mother-of-pearl, gorgeous stained-glass windows, painted *muqarnas* (corbels with honeycomb detail), a spectacular persimmon-coloured floor carpet, painted pendentives and medallions featuring fine calligraphy.

The Külliye

Süleyman specified that his mosque should have the full complement of public service, including: *imaret* (soup kitchen), *medrese* (Islamic school of higher studies), hamam, caravanserai and *darüşşifa* (hospital). Today the imaret, with its charming garden courtyard, houses the Darüzziyafe (p108) cafe and is a lovely place to enjoy a çay. On its right-hand side (north) is a tabhane (inn for travelling dervishes) that was being restored at the time of research, and on its left-hand side (south) is Lale Bahçesi (p108), a popular tea garden set in a sunken courtyard.

The main entrance to the mosque is accessed from Professor Sıddık Sami Onar Caddesi, formerly known as Tiryaki Çarşışı (Market of the Addicts). The buildings here once housed three medreses and a primary school; they're now home to the Süleymaniye Library and a raft of popular streetside fasülye (bean) restaurants that were formerly teahouses selling opium (hence the street's former name). On the corner of Professor Sıddık Sami Onar Caddesi and Şifahane Sokak is the darüşşifa, also under restoration.

The still-functioning Süleymaniye Hamamı is on the eastern side of the mosque.

Türbes

To the right (southeast) of the main entrance is the cemetery, home to the tombs of Süleyman and his wife Haseki Hürrem Sultan (Roxelana). The tile work surrounding the entrances to both is superb and the ivory-inlaid panels in Süleyman's tomb are lovely.

SURROUNDING STREETS

The streets surrounding the mosque are home to what may well be the most extensive concentration of Ottoman timber houses on the Historic Peninsula, many of which are currently being restored as part of an urban regeneration project. To see some, head down Fetva Yokuşu (between the *tabhane* and Sinan's tomb) and veer right into Namahrem Sokak and Ayrancı Sokak. One of the many Ottoman-era houses here was once occupied by Mimar Sinan; it now houses a cafe. To see other timber houses, take a walk down Kayserili Ahmetpaşa Sokak, behind the bean restaurants and souvenir shops on Professor Sıddık Sami Onar Caddesi.

Although Sinan described the smaller Selimiye Mosque in Edirne as his best work, he chose to be buried in the Süleymaniye complex, probably knowing that this would be the achievement for which he would be best remembered. His *türbe* (tomb) is just outside the mosque's walled garden, next to a disused *medrese* (seminary) building.

TOP SIGHT
SPICE BAZAAR

Vividly coloured spices are displayed alongside jewel-like *lokum* **(Turkish Delight) at this Ottoman-era marketplace, providing eye candy for the thousands of tourists and locals who visit each day. Stalls also sell dried herbs, caviar, nuts, honey in the comb, dried fruits and** *pestil* **(fruit pressed into sheets and dried). It's a great place to stock up on edible souvenirs.**

The market was constructed in the 1660s as part of the New Mosque (p99), with rent from the shops supporting the upkeep of the mosque as well as its charitable activities, which included a school, hamam and hospital. The name Mısır Çarşısı (Egyptian Market) comes from the fact that the building was initially endowed with taxes levied on goods imported from Egypt. In its heyday the bazaar was the last stop for the camel caravans that travelled the Silk Road from China, India and Persia.

On the west side of the market, there are outdoor produce stalls selling fresh foodstuff from all over Anatolia, including a wonderful selection of cheeses. Also here is the most famous coffee supplier in İstanbul, Kurukahveci Mehmet Efendi (p111), established over 100 years ago. This is located on the corner of Hasırcılar Caddesi, which is full of shops selling foodstuffs and kitchenware.

DID YOU KNOW?

➡ Leeches are still used for traditional medical treatments in Turkey. You'll see them being offered for sale in the outdoor market on the eastern side of the Spice Bazaar, alongside poultry and pot plants.

PRACTICALITIES

➡ Mısır Çarşısı, Egyptian Market

➡ Map p242, E2

➡ ☎212-513 6597

➡ www.misircarsisi.org

➡ ⊙8am-7.30pm

➡ Ⓜ️Eminönü

SIGHTS

GRAND BAZAAR   MARKET
See p93.

SÜLEYMANIYE MOSQUE   MOSQUE
See p96.

SPICE BAZAAR   MARKET
See p98.

RÜSTEM PAŞA MOSQUE   MOSQUE
Map p242 (Rüstem Paşa Camii; Hasırcılar Caddesi, Rüstem Paşa; ⍟Eminönü) Nestled in the middle of the busy Tahtakale shopping district, this diminutive mosque is a gem. Dating from 1560, it was designed by Sinan for Rüstem Paşa, son-in-law and grand vizier of Süleyman the Magnificent. A showpiece of the best Ottoman architecture and tile work, it is thought to have been the prototype for Sinan's greatest work, the Selimiye Camii in Edirne.

The mosque is easy to miss because it's not at street level. There's a set of access stairs on Hasırcılar Caddesi and another on the small street that runs right (north) off Hasırcılar Caddesi towards the Golden Horn. At the top of the stairs, there's a terrace and the mosque's colonnaded porch. You'll immediately notice the exquisite panels of İznik tiles set into the mosque's facade. The interior is covered in more tiles and features a lovely dome, supported by four tiled pillars.

The preponderance of tiles was Rüstem Paşa's way of signalling his wealth and influence, with İznik tiles being particularly expensive and desirable. It may not have assisted his passage into the higher realm though, because by all accounts he was a loathsome character. His contemporaries dubbed him Kehle-i-Ikbal (the Louse of Fortune) because he was found to be infected with lice on the eve of his marriage to Mihrimah, Süleyman's favourite daughter. He is best remembered for plotting with Roxelana to turn Süleyman against his favourite son, Mustafa. They were successful and Mustafa was strangled in 1553 on his father's orders.

HÜNKÂR KASRI   MUSEUM
Map p242 (Hünkâr Mahfili; Arpacılar Caddesi 29, Eminönü; ⍟9am-5pm Mon-Sat during exhibitions; ⍟Eminönü) FREE Built over a grand archway attached to the New Mosque, this small *kasrı* (pavilion) or *mahfili* (loge), dates from the same period and functioned as a waiting area and retreat for the sultans. It comprises a salon, bedchamber and toilet and is decorated with exquisite İznik tiles throughout. Entry is via an extremely long and wide staircase that is now ulitised by the İstanbul Ticaret Odası (Chamber of Commerce) as a temporary exhibition space.

The *kasrı* opens when exhibitions are being staged. These tend to open on the second Thursday of each month and have a life of two weeks. Check the Yeni Cami Hünkâr Kasrı Sergi Salonu Facebook page for details.

NEW MOSQUE   MOSQUE
Map p242 (Yeni Camii; Yenicamii Meydanı Sokak, Eminönü; ⍟Eminönü) Only in İstanbul would a 400-year-old mosque be called 'new'. Constructed between 1597 and 1665, its design references both the Blue Mosque and the Süleymaniye Mosque, with a large forecourt and a square sanctuary surmounted by a series of semidomes crowned by a grand dome. The interior is richly decorated with gold leaf, İznik tiles and carved marble.

Originally commissioned by Valide Sultan Safiye, mother of Sultan Mehmet III, the mosque was completed six sultans later by order of Valide Sultan Turhan Hadice, mother of Sultan Mehmet IV.

The site had earlier been occupied by a community of Karaite Jews, radical dissenters from Orthodox Judaism. When the *valide sultan* decided to build her grand mosque here, the Karaites were moved to Hasköy, a district further up the Golden Horn that still bears traces of their presence.

The mosque's proportions aren't as pleasing as the city's other imperial mosques and neither are its tiles. This reflects the fact that there was a diminution in the quality of the products coming out of the İznik workshops in the second half of the 17th century. Compare the tiles here with the exquisite examples found in the nearby Rüstem Paşa Mosque, which are from the high period of İznik tile work, and this will immediately become apparent. Nonetheless, the mosque is a popular place of worship and a much-loved adornment to the city skyline. Note that it is closed to visitors during prayer times and on Fridays before 2.30pm.

Across the road from the mosque is the *türbe* (tomb) of Valide Sultan Turhan Hadice. Buried with her are no fewer than six sultans, including her son Mehmet IV, plus dozens of imperial princes and princesses. Her *türbe* was closed for restoration at the time of research.

If it is open, be sure to visit the Hünkar Kasrı (p99), once the sultan's waiting room, located above the grand archway on the eastern side of the mosque.

NURUOSMANIYE MOSQUE   MOSQUE

Map p242 (Nuruosmaniye Camii, Light of Osman Mosque; Vezir Han Caddesi, Beyazıt; ⓂÇemberlitaş) Facing one of the major gateways into the Grand Bazaar, this large mosque complex was built in Ottoman baroque style between 1748 and 1755. Construction was started by order of Mahmut I and finished during the reign of his successor, Osman III. Meticulously restored in recent years, it has a central prayer hall topped by one of the largest domes ever built in an Ottoman mosque, a unique polygonal rear courtyard and a *külliye* comprising *medrese, imaret, kütüphane* and *türbe*.

Though designed in the then highly fashionable and modern baroque style, the mosque has very strong echoes of Aya Sofya – specifically the lofty dome, colonnaded mezzanine galleries, broad band of calligraphy around the interior (in this case a marble relief of the Sura Al-Fath) and 174 windows topped with Roman arches. Despite its prominent position on the busy pedestrian route from Cağaloğlu Meydanı and Nuruosmaniye Caddesi to the bazaar, it is surprisingly peaceful and contemplative inside. The *türbe* contains Şehsuvar Sultan, mother of Osman III, and the library (being restored at the time of research) is home to more than 5000 handwritten and printed manuscripts. Visitor entry to the mosque is via the rear courtyard.

ŞEHZADE MEHMET MOSQUE   MOSQUE

Map p242 (Şehzade Mehmet Camii, Mosque of the Prince; Şehzadebaşı Caddesi, Kalenderhane; ⓂVezneciler) Süleyman the Magnificent built this square-shaped mosque between 1543 and 1548 as a memorial to his son Mehmet, who died of smallpox in 1543 at the age of 22. It was the first important mosque to be designed by Mimar Sinan and has a lovely garden setting, two double-balconied minarets and attractive exterior decoration. Inside, the central dome is supported by four semidomes (one on each side of the square).

Among the many important people buried in tile-encrusted tombs on the mosque's eastern side are Prince Mehmet, his brothers and sisters and two of Süleyman's grand *vezirs*: Rüstem Paşa and İbrahim Paşa. Other still-surviving parts of the *külliye* include a partially demolished *medrese* and a *tabhane* (inn for travelling dervishes) that is now used as a laboratory by the neighbouring Vefa Lycée.

WOMEN'S BAZAAR   MARKET

(Kadınlar Pazarı; İtfaiye Caddesi, Fatih; ⓂVezneciler) Though it's a wonderful spot to observe local life, the vibrant Women's Bazaar isn't for the faint-hearted. Freshly slaughtered sheep carcasses swing in the wind and shops sell dried sheep heads, pungent *tulum* cheese and other unusual produce. Most shopkeepers are from the southeastern corner of Turkey – specifically Siirt – and the tasty food served at the bazaar's eateries reflects this.

AQUEDUCT OF VALENS   LANDMARK

Map p242 (Atatürk Bulvarı, Zeyrek; ⓂVezneciler) Rising majestically over the traffic on busy Atatürk Bulvarı, this limestone aqueduct is one of the city's most distinctive landmarks. Commissioned by the Emperor Valens and completed in AD 378, it linked the third and fourth hills and carried water to a cistern at Beyazıt Meydanı before finally ending up at the Great Palace of Byzantium.

The aqueduct was part of an elaborate system sourcing water from the north of the city and linking more than 250km of water channels, some 30 bridges and more than 100 cisterns within the city walls, making it one of the greatest hydraulic engineering achievements of ancient times. After the Conquest, it supplied the Eski (Old) and Topkapı Palaces with water.

CHURCH OF THE MONASTERY OF CHRIST PANTOKRATOR   MONASTERY

Map p242 (Molla Zeyrek Camii; İbadethane Sokak, Zeyrek; ⓂVezneciler) This church and a series of cisterns are the only remaining structures of an important Byzantine monastery complex that also included a library, hospital and chapel. One of the finest examples of Byzantine architecture in İstanbul, it is the second-largest surviving Byzantine church in the city after Aya Sofya. Sorely neglected for centuries, it is currently undergoing a controversial restoration.

The monastery was commissioned in 1118 by Empress Eirene (she features in a mosaic at Aya Sofya with her husband, Emperor John II Comnenus), who wanted to give succour to 'poor, sick, and suffering souls'. Building works were completed after her death. The north and south churches, dedicated to Christ Pantokrator and the Archangel St Michael, were connected by an imperial chapel that was used as a mausoleum for the Komnenos and Palaiologos dynasties.

After the Conquest, the church was converted into a mosque named in honour of Molla Zeyrek, a well-known scholar who lived during the reign of Sultan Mehmed II. The cisterns were in use until the end of the 18th century and have recently been restored. Sadly, they are not open to the public.

Until recently, the church building was included on the World Monument Fund's (WMF) list of the world's 100 most endangered cultural heritage sites. It is now undergoing an excruciatingly slow restoration that was instigated and initially funded by the WMF, but has since been tended out to private contractors, who are applying liberal amounts of ugly pink concrete to the stone walls. The interior of the northern section of the church has been unsympathetically (we would say incompetently) stabilised with ugly metal braces and decorated with dreadful faux-marble painted walls. It is now functioning as a mosque.

GALATA BRIDGE   BRIDGE
Map p242 (Galata Köprüsü; 🚇Eminönü, Karaköy) To experience İstanbul at its most magical, walk across the Galata Bridge at sunset. At this time, the historic Galata Tower is surrounded by shrieking seagulls, the mosques atop the seven hills of the city are silhouetted against a soft red-pink sky and the evocative scent of apple tobacco wafts out of the nargile cafes under the bridge.

During the day, the bridge carries a constant flow of İstanbullus crossing to and from Beyoğlu and Eminönü, a handful or two of hopeful anglers trailing their lines into the waters below and a constantly changing procession of street vendors hawking everything from fresh-baked *simits* (sesame-encrusted bread rings) to Rolex rip-offs. Underneath, restaurants and cafes serve drinks and food all day and night.

Come here to enjoy a beer and nargile while watching the ferries making their way to and from the Eminönü and Karaköy ferry docks.

The present, quite ugly bridge was built in 1992 to replace an iron structure dating from 1909 to 1912, which in turn had replaced two earlier structures. The iron bridge was famous for the ramshackle fish restaurants, teahouses and nargile joints that occupied the dark recesses beneath its roadway. However, it had a major flaw: it floated on pontoons that blocked the natural flow of water and kept the Golden Horn from flushing itself free of pollution. In the late 1980s, the municipality started to draw up plans to replace it with a new bridge that would allow the water to flow. A fire expedited these plans in the early 1990s and the new bridge was built a short time afterwards. The remains of the old, much-loved bridge were moved further up the Golden Horn near Hasköy.

COLUMN OF CONSTANTINE   MONUMENT
Map p242 (Hooped Column; Divan Yolu Caddesi, Çemberlitaş; 🚇Çemberlitaş) Erected by order of the Emperor Constantine to celebrate the dedication of New Rome (Constantinople) as capital of the Roman Empire in 330, this column is one of the city's most ancient monuments. Located in a pigeon-packed plaza next to the Çemberlitaş tram stop, it once stood in the grand Forum of Constantine and was topped by a statue of the great emperor himself in the guise of Apollo.

The column was damaged by an earthquake in 416 and iron bands were secured around it to ensure that it remained upright (*cemberlitaş* means 'hooped stone'). The column lost its crowning statue of Constantine in 1106 and was damaged in the 1779 fire that ravaged the nearby Grand Bazaar. It has recently been restored.

BEYAZIT SQUARE   SQUARE
Map p242 (Beyazıt Meydanı, Hürriyet – Freedom – Meydanı; 🚇Beyazıt-Kapalı Çarşı) In Byzantine times, this public square was called the Forum of Theodosius. Today it's home to street vendors, students from the adjoining İstanbul University and plenty of pigeons. The main building here is the Beyazıt Mosque (p102), and there are also various buildings that originally formed part of its *külliye*. These include a *medrese* that now houses a Museum of Calligraphy (currently closed for restoration); an *imaret* (soup

kitchen) and *kervansaray* (caravanserai) complex now functioning as the magnificent Beyazıt State Library; and a disused double hamam.

After the Conquest, Mehmet the Conqueror built his first palace here, a wooden structure called the Eski Sarayı (Old Seraglio). After Topkapı was built, the Eski Sarayı became home to women when they were pensioned out of the main palace – this is where *valide sultans* (mothers of the reigning sultans) came when their sultan sons died and they lost their powerful position as head of the harem. The original building was demolished in the 19th century to make way for a grandiose Ministry of War complex designed by Auguste Bourgeois; this now houses the university.

The 85m-tall Beyazıt Tower in its grounds sits on top of one of the seven hills on which Constantine the Great built the city, following the model of Rome. Commissioned by Mahmut II, the stone tower was designed by Senekerim Balyan and built in 1828 in the same location as a previous wooden tower. The tower was used by the İstanbul Fire Department to spot fires until 1993. The coloured lights on it indicate weather conditions – blue for clear and sunny, green for rain, yellow for fog and red for snow.

Both the university and tower are off limits to travellers.

BEYAZIT STATE LIBRARY · LIBRARY

Map p242 (Beyazıt Devlet Kütüphanesi; ☏0212-522 3167; www.beyazitkutup.gov.tr; Turan Emeksiz Sokak 6, Beyazıt; ⊙8.30am-5pm Mon-Fri; 🚇Beyazıt-Kapalı Çarşı) Occupying the former *imaret* (soup kitchen) and *kervansaray* (caravanserai) of the Beyazıt Mosque's *külliye*, this library has recently been the subject of a splendid 'minimal intervention' restoration and extension by local architectural firm Tabanlıoğlu Partnership. The multidomed building dates from 1884 and houses a notable rare-book collection.

BEYAZIT MOSQUE · MOSQUE

Map p242 (Beyazıt Camii, Mosque of Sultan Beyazıt II; Beyazıt Meydanı, Beyazıt; 🚇Beyazıt-Kapalı Çarşı) The second imperial mosque built in İstanbul (after the Fatih Camii), Beyazıt Camii was built between 1501 and 1506 by order of Beyazıt II, son of Mehmet the Conqueror. Architecturally, it links Aya Sofya, which obviously inspired its design, with great mosques such as the Süleyman-

iye, which are realisations of Aya Sofya's design fully adapted to Muslim worship. It was undergoing a major and long-overdue restoration at the time of research.

The mosque's exceptional use of fine stone is noteworthy, with marble, porphyry, verd antique and rare granite featuring. The mihrab is simple, except for the rich stone columns framing it. The enclosed courtyard features 24 small domes and a central ablutions fountain. Beyazıt's *türbe* (tomb) is behind the mosque.

LALELI MOSQUE · MOSQUE

Map p242 (cnr Divan Yolu & Fethi Bey Caddesis, Laleli; 🚇Laleli-Üniversite, Aksaray) A baroque-style Imperial mosque commissioned by Sultan Mustafa III and built between 1759 and 1763, the Laleli ('with Tulips') Camii is a short walk from the Grand Bazaar in a district of clothing stores. The mosque has pretty stained-glass windows, and a shop selling olive-oil products now occupies its lovely street-level *sebil* (kiosk that once dispensed water or *şerbet*, or sherbet).

✕ EATING

Generations of shoppers have worked up an appetite around the Grand Bazaar. Fortunately there have always been eateries to meet this need, including a range of good *lokantas* (eateries serving ready-made food) and fast-food stands. Down near the water, there aren't too many choices – a fish sandwich on the quay at Eminönü, a döner kebap at Bereket Döner in the Küçük Pazar, or a more formal meal at Hamdi Restaurant are your best bets.

★DEVELI BAKLAVA · SWEETS €

Map p242 (☏0212-512 1261; Hasırcılar Caddesi 89, Eminönü; portions ₺10-12; ⊙7am-7pm Mon-Sat; 🚇Eminönü) As with many things Turkish, there's a ritual associated with eating baklava. Afficionados don't use a knife and fork. Instead, they turn their baklava upside down with the help of an index finger and thumb, and pop it into the mouth. To emulate them, head to this famous shop close to the Spice Bazaar, one of the city's best *baklavacıs*.

The baklava here is made with butter and real sugar (inferior products use glucose) and it's absolutely delicious. Try the

WORTH A DETOUR

LITTLE SYRIA

In recent decades, the Laleli and Aksaray neighbourhoods west of the Bazaar District have developed a reputation as the centre of İstanbul's main red-light district, home to seedy nightclubs, petty crims and sex workers from Eastern Europe. It's a sad fate for areas where *valide sultans* (mothers of the reigning sultans) once commissioned ornate imperial mosques.

However, these neighbourhoods now possess another, much more interesting claim to fame. For decades Aksaray has been home to a large concentration of immigrants from the southeast of Turkey. These residents opened food stands and restaurants serving dishes popular in their home region, and the streets immediately north of the Aksaray metro station became known as Little Urfa after the city on the Turkish–Syrian border. More recently, nearby neighbourhoods have become a haven for the many Syrian refugees who have fled the troubles in their homeland, and a number of eateries serving Syrian cuisine now enrich the culinary landscape. To hear some of these refugees' stories and sample Syrian home cooking, consider signing up for a dinnertime visit to **Small Projects İstanbul** (www.smallprojectsistanbul.org), an NGO based in the neighbouring suburb of Çapa. The tour is run by **Urban Adventures** (☑0535 022 2003; www.urbanadventures.com; tours from €27) and all funds raised go to support services for the refugees.

Every adventurous foodie should be sure to eat in this part of town at least once during their time in the city. Head to the streets around Sofular Caddesi and enjoy a sit-down Syrian-influenced feast at **Hatay Haskral Sofrası** (☑0210-534 9707; www.hatayhaskralsofrasi.com; Ragıb Bey Sokak 25, Aksaray; mezes ₺6-25, mains ₺22-45; ◐9am-midnight; 🚇Aksaray) or **Akdenıs Hatay Sofrası** (☑0212-444 7247; www.akdenizhataysofrasi.com.tr; Ahmediye Caddesi 44, Aksaray; mezes ₺8-10, mains ₺20-40; ◐9am-midnight; ☑; 🚇Aksaray). Alternatively pop into **Şanlı Urfa Zaman** (☑0212-521 2206; Simitçi Şakir Sokak 38, Aksaray; kebaps ₺16-22, dürum kebaps ₺11-13; 🚇Aksaray) for a *ciğer* (liver) kebap, **Ehli Kebap** (☑0212-631 3700; www.ehlikebap.com.tr; Simitçi Şakır Sokak 32, Aksaray; soups ₺5-10, kebaps ₺15-20; ◐10am-3pm Mon-Sat; 🚇Aksaray) for a delicious and filling bowl of *bayran çorbasi* (spicy lamb-based soup), or **Altın Pide ve Lahmacun** (Ragıp Bey Sokak 33, Aksaray; lahmacun ₺3-4, pide ₺7.50-8.50; ◐10am-10pm; 🚇Aksaray) for crispy *lahmacun* (thin pizza) straight from the traditional tiled oven. As a finale, make the short trek to **Salloura Oğlu** (☑0212-542 5661; Turgut Özal Millet Caddesi 60, Fındıkzade; sweets ₺5-10; ◐10am-10pm; 🚇Haseki), a historic Aleppo business that moved here from its war-torn home in 2014 and has since built a fanatical local following for its sweet cheese desserts.

classic with your choice of nut filling, or try the indulgent *bülbül yuvası* (nightingale's nest), a pastry filled with *kaymak* (clotted cream) and pistachio. Those in the know (and with a big appetite) tend to order Develi's Gaziantep-style *katmer* (flaky pastry stuffed with pistachio and *kaymak,* ₺25), which takes around 15 minutes to cook and comes to your table piping hot. Bliss!

★**FATIH DAMAK PIDE**   PIDE €
(☑0212-521 5057; www.fatihdamakpide.com; Büyük Karaman Caddesi 48, Fatih; pides ₺17-25; ◐7am-11pm; 🚇Vezneciler) It's worth mak-

ing the trek to this *pideci* overlooking the Fatih İtfaiye Park near the Aqueduct of Valens. Its reputation for making the best Karadeniz (Black Sea)–style pide on the Historic Peninsula is well deserved and the pots of tea served with meals are a nice touch (the first pot is free, subsequent pots are charged).

Toppings are mostly standard – the *sucuklu-peynirli* (sausage and cheese) option is particularly tasty – but there's also an unusual *bafra pidesi* (rolled-up pide, ₺18) and a *kapalı kavurmalı pide* (roasted meat calzone, ₺20). It's best for lunch; no alcohol.

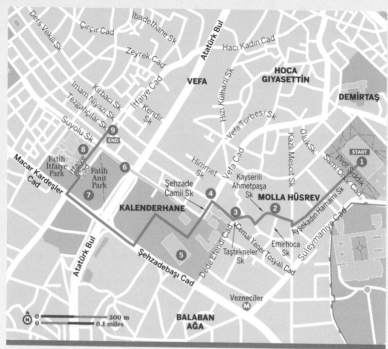

⚡ Neighbourhood Walk
Ottoman Heartland

START SÜLEYMANIYE MOSQUE
END WOMEN'S BAZAAR
LENGTH 2KM; TWO HOURS

Start at the magnificent **①Süleymaniye Mosque** (p96), cross Professor Sıddık Sami Onar Caddesi and enter narrow Ayşekadın Hamamı Sokak (opposite the mosque's main gate). Follow it and Kayserili Ahmetpaşa Sokak through the Molla Hüsrev district, which is slowly being restored as part of the Süleymaniye Urban Regeneration Project. Kayserili Ahmetpaşa Sokak is home to a number of pretty timber houses built in the late 19th and early 20th centuries, including the **②Kayserili Ahmet Paşa Konağı**, a three-storey mansion once home to an Ottoman navy minister and now headquarters of the city's Directorate of Inspection of Conservation Implementation. Follow the street and veer right until you come to the **③Ekmekçizade Ahmetpaşa Medresesi**, built between 1603 and 1617 by the son of a baker from Edirne who rose up the ranks of Ottoman society to become a *defterder* (first

lord of the treasury). Turn right and follow Cemal Yener Tosyalı Caddesi until you come to a junction with Vefa Caddesi. The famous **④Vefa Bozacısı** (p106) is close by – consider stopping for a glass of *boza*. Back on Cemal Yener Tosyalı Caddesi, turn left into Şehzade Camii Sokak and go under the stone arch to reach the rear gate of **⑤Şehzade Mehmet Mosque** (p100). If the gate is closed, you will need to backtrack along Cemal Yener Tosyalı Caddesi and turn right into Dede Efedi Caddesi to access the main entrance on Şehzadebaşı Caddesi. After the mosque, head west and you'll see remnants of the majestic Byzantine **⑥Aqueduct of Valens** (p100). Cross Atatürk Bulvarı and head to the aqueduct through **⑦Fatih Anıt (Monument) Park**. The huge monument shows Mehmet the Conqueror (Fatih) astride his horse. Passing a handsome Ottoman Revivalist building housing the **⑧Fatih İtfaiye (Fire Station)** on your left, head under the aqueduct and into the **⑨Women's Bazaar** (p100) on İtfaiye Caddesi, a vibrant local shopping precinct where there are a number of excellent eateries.

⭐**BEREKET DÖNER**   KEBAP €

Map p242 (Hacı Kadın Caddesi, cnr Tavanlı Çeşme Sokak, Küçük Pazar; döner sandwich from ₺3.50; ⏱11am-8pm Mon-Sat; MHaliç) The best döner *ekmek* (sandwich) in the district – maybe even the city – can be found at this local eatery in the run-down Küçük Pazar shopping strip between Eminönü and Atatürk Bulvarı. Definitely worth the trek.

SIIRT ŞEREF BÜRYAN KEBAP   ANATOLIAN €

(✆0212-635 8085; http://serefburyan.org; İtfaye Caddesi 4, Kadınlar Pazarı, Fatih; büryan ₺15, perde pilavi ₺15, kebaps ₺13-32; ⏱9.30am-10pm Sep-May, till midnight Jun-Aug; P❄👶; MVezneciler) Those who enjoy investigating regional cuisines should head to this four-storey eatery in the Women's Bazaar (p100) near the Aqueduct of Valens. It specialises in two dishes that are a speciality of the southeastern city of Siirt: *büryan* (lamb slow-cooked in a pit) and *perde pilavi* (chicken and rice cooked in pastry). Both are totally delicious.

The *büryan* here is cooked in pits at the rear of the restaurant and is meltingly tender. It's served on flat bread with crispy bits of lamb fat and a dusting of salt. *Perde pilavi* is made with rice, chicken, almonds and currants that are encased in a thin pastry shell and then baked until the exterior turns golden and flaky. Order either with a glass of frothy homemade *ayran* (salty yogurt drink) and you'll be happy indeed. Note that on weekends the food tends to run out by 9pm. No alcohol.

KURU FASÜLYECI
ERZINCANLI ALI BABA   TURKISH €

Map p242 (✆0212-514 5878; www.kuru fasulyeci.com; Professor Sıddık Sami Onar Caddesi 11, Süleymaniye; beans with pilaf & pickles ₺17; ⏱8am-9pm; 🚫; MVezneciler) Join the crowds of hungry locals at this long-time *fasülyeci* (restaurant specialising in beans) opposite the Süleymaniye Mosque. It's been dishing up its signature *kuru fasülye* (white beans cooked in a spicy tomato sauce) accompanied by pilaf (rice) and *turşu* (pickles) since 1924. The next-door *fasülyeci* is nearly as old and serves up more of the same. No alcohol.

MAVI HALIÇ PIDECISI   PIDE €

Map p242 (✆0212-513 6304; Kutucular Caddesi 28, Eminönü; pides ₺10-15; ⏱11am-6pm; 🚇Eminönü) Fight your way through the crowds of shoppers that jam Hasırcılar Caddesi and you'll eventually come to this tiny *pideci*

on the corner of Limoncu Sokak, which is known for its *kıymalı* (ground beef and tomato) pide.

BAHAR RESTAURANT   TURKISH €

Map p95 (Yağcı Han 13, off Nuruosmaniye Sokak, Nuruosmaniye; soup ₺6, portions ₺10-16; ⏱noon-4pm Mon-Sat; 🚇Çemberlitaş) Tiny Bahar ('Spring') is popular with local shopkeepers and is always full, so arrive early to score a table. Dishes change daily and with the season – try the flavourful soups and tasty meat dishes. No alcohol.

HAMDI RESTAURANT   KEBAP €€

Map p242 (✆0212-444 6463; www.hamdi restorant.com.tr; Kalçın Sokak 11, Eminönü; mezes ₺11.50-26, kebaps ₺28-50; ⏱noon-midnight; P❄👶; 🚇Eminönü) One of the city's best-loved restaurants, this place near the Spice Bazaar is owned by Hamdi Arpacı, who started out as a street-food vendor in the 1960s. His tasty Urfa-style kebaps were so popular that he soon graduated from his modest stand to this building, which has views of the Old City, Golden Horn and Galata from its top-floor terrace.

The food is excellent. Try the *yoğurtlu şakşuka* (yoghurt meze with fried eggplant, peppers and potato), the *içli köfte* (meatballs rolled in bulgur) and the *lahmacun* (thin, meat-topped pizza) followed by any of the kebaps and you'll leave replete and happy – extremely replete if you finish with the house-made baklava, *katmer* or *künefe*. Any place this good is always going to be busy, so make sure you book, and don't forget to request a rooftop table with a view (outside if the weather is hot).

One slight caveat: staff work hard and are clearly encouraged to turn tables over as fast as possible. Don't expect much personal service, and be prepared for little time between courses.

There's another **branch** on the rooftop of the Radisson Blu Hotel in Beyoğlu (Map p248; ✆0212-377 2500; http://hamdi.com.tr/en/pera; Radisson Blu Hotel, Refik Saydam Caddesi 19, Tepebaşı; mezes ₺11.50-26, kebaps ₺28-50; ❄👶; MŞişhane, ⊗Tünel).

SUR OCAKBAŞI   KEBAP €€

(✆0212-533 8088; www.surocakbasi.com; İtfaye Caddesi 27, Fatih; kebaps ₺15-30; ⏱11am-1am; MVezneciler) Indulge in some peerless people watching while enjoying the grilled meats at this popular place in the Women's Bazaar (p100). The square is always full of locals shopping or enjoying a gossip, and tourists were a rare sight before Anthony Bourdain filmed a segment of *No Reservations* here and blew Sur's cover.

There are plenty of options on offer: consider the mixed Sur kebap plate (₺30), *içli köfte* (deep-fried lamb and onion meatballs with a bulgur coating, ₺4), *çiğ köfte* (meat pounded with spices and eaten raw, ₺10) and *lahmacun* (₺5). There's no alcohol, but there's homemade *ayran*.

FES CAFE
CAFE ₺₺

Map p95 (📞0212-528 1613; www.fescafe.com; Halıcılar Caddesi 62, Grand Bazaar; sandwiches ₺15-18, salads ₺20-25; ◷9.30am-6pm Mon-Sat; 🚇Beyazıt-Kapalı Çarşı) After a morning spent trading repartee with the Grand Bazaar's many touts, you'll be in need of respite. Those who want a cafe with a Western-style ambience and menu are sure to be happy with this stylish cafe at the centre of the bazaar action. Sandwiches and salads feature on the menu, along with good espresso and Turkish coffee.

There's another **branch** (Ali Baba Türbe Sokak 25) in nearby Nuruosmaniye, but this was closed for renovation at the time of research.

FISH SANDWICHES

The city's favourite fast food is undoubtedly the *balık ekmek* (fish sandwich), and the most atmospheric place to try one of these is at the Eminönü end of the Galata Bridge (p101). Here, in front of fishing boats tied to the quay, are a number of stands where mackerel fillets are grilled, crammed into fresh bread and served with salad. A generous squeeze of bottled lemon juice is optional but recommended. A sandwich will set you back a mere ₺8, and is delicious accompanied by a glass of the *şalgam* (sour turnip juice, ₺2) sold by nearby pickle vendors.

There are plenty of other places around town to try a *balık ekmek* – head to any *iskele* (ferry dock) and there's bound to be a stand nearby. For an upmarket version (₺30), head to stylish eatery Karaköy Gümrük (p133) near the derköy docks.

HAVUZLU RESTAURANT
TURKISH ₺₺

Map p95 (📞0212-527 3346; www.havuzlu restaurant.com; Gani Çelebi Sokak 3, Grand Bazaar; portions ₺17-30; ◷9am-7pm Mon-Sat; ✴🚻; 🚇Beyazıt-Kapalı Çarşı) After a morning spent in the Grand Bazaar, many visitors choose to park their shopping bags at this well-known *lokanta*. A lovely space with a vaulted ceiling, Havuzlu (named after the small fountain at its entrance) serves up simple but tasty fare to hungry hordes of tourists and shopkeepers – go early when the food is freshest. No alcohol.

DRINKING & NIGHTLIFE

Like most parts of the Old City, the area around the Grand Bazaar is conservative and there are few places serving alcohol. There are loads of *çay bahçesis* (tea gardens), nargile cafes and *kahvehanesis* (coffeehouses) to visit, though.

★MIMAR SINAN TERAS CAFE
NARGILE CAFE

Map p242 (📞0212-514 4414; Mimar Sinan Han, Fetva Yokuşu 34-35, Süleymaniye; ◷8am-1am; 📶; Ⓜ Vezneciler) A magnificent panorama of the city can be enjoyed from the spacious outdoor terrace of this popular student cafe in a ramshackle building located in the shadow of Süleymaniye Mosque. Head here during the day or in the evening to admire the view over a coffee, unwind with a nargile or enjoy a glass of *çay* and game of backgammon.

★ERENLER NARGILE VE ÇAY BAHÇESİ
TEA GARDEN

Map p242 (Yeniçeriler Caddesi 35, Beyazıt; ◷7am-midnight; 🚇Beyazıt-Kapalı Çarşı) Set in the vine-covered courtyard of the Çorlulu Ali Paşa Medrese, this nargile cafe near the Grand Bazaar is the most atmospheric in the Old City.

VEFA BOZACISI
BOZA BAR

Map p242 (📞0212-519 4922; www.vefa.com.tr; 66 Vefa Caddesi, Molla Hüsrev; boza ₺3; ◷8am-midnight; Ⓜ Vezneciler) This famous *boza* bar was established in 1876 and locals still flock here to drink the viscous tonic, which is made from water, sugar and fermented barley and has a slight lemony tang. Topped

CHEAP EATS: THE GRAND BAZAAR

Lunch is an important part of the day for the shopkeepers, artisans and porters who work in and around the Grand Bazaar. As well as providing an excuse for a break, it's also a chance to chat with fellow workers and catch up with the local gossip. Of the hundreds of food stands in the streets and lanes in and around the bazaar, the following are our favourites. Most have a few stools for customers; a few are takeaway only.

Note that when ordering döner or kokoreç in ekmek (bread), you will usually have to choose from three sizes: çeyrek (a quarter of a loaf), yarım (half a loaf) or bütün (a whole loaf). The term dürüm, which means wrapped, applies when meat is served in thin lavaş bread.

Gazientep Burç Ocakbaşı (Map p95; Parçacılar Sokak 12, off Yağlıkçılar Caddesi; kebaps ₺15-20; ⊙noon-4pm Mon-Sat; ☒Beyazıt-Kapalı Çarşı) The usta (master chef) at this simple place presides over a charcoal grill where choice cuts of meats are cooked to perfection. We particularly recommend the spicy Adana kebap and the delectable dolma (eggplant and red peppers stuffed with rice and herbs).

Dönerci Şahin Usta (Map p95; ☎0212-526 5297; www.donercisahinusta.com; Kılıçcılar Sokak 9, Nuruosmaniye; döner kebap from ₺9; ⊙11am-3pm Mon-Sat; ☒Çemberlitaş) Ask any shopkeeper in the Grand Bazaar about who makes the best döner in the immediate area, and you will likely get the same answer: 'Şahin Usta, of course!'

Pak Pide & Pizza Salonu (Map p242; ☎0212-513 7664; Paşa Camii Sokak 16, Mercan; pides ₺9-14; ⊙11am-3pm Mon-Sat; ☒Eminönü) Finding this worker's pideci is an adventure in itself (it's hidden in the steep narrow lanes behind the Büyük Valide Han), but your quest will pay off when you try the fabulous pides, which are served straight from the oven.

Aynen Dürüm (Map p95; Muhafazacılar Sokak 29; dürüm kebap ₺9-12; ⊙7am-6pm Mon-Sat; ☒Çemberlitaş) You'll find this perennially busy place just inside the Grand Bazaar's Kılıçcılar Kapısı (Kılıçcılar Gate), near where the currency dealers ply their noisy trade. Patrons are free to doctor their choice of grilled meat (we like the chicken) with pickled cucumber, grilled and pickled green chillies, parsley, sumac and other accompaniments that are laid out on the communal bench.

Dürümcü Raif Usta (Map p242; ☎0212-528 4910; Küçük Yıldız Han Sokak 6, Mahmutpaşa; dürüm kebap ₺10-12; ⊙11.30am-6pm Mon-Sat; ☒Çemberlitaş) The assembly line of staff assisting the usta at this place attests to the excellence and popularity of its speciality: Adana and Urfa kebaps served with raw onion and parsley and wrapped in lavaş bread. Note that the Adana is spicy; Urfa isn't.

Kokoreçci Erdinç Usta (Map p95; ☎0212-514 6029; Kılıçcılar Sokak 33, Nuruosmaniye; kokoreç from ₺5; ⊙9am-6pm Mon-Sat; ☒Çemberlitaş) Devotees of offal flock here for the kokoreç (seasoned lamb intestines stuffed with sweetbreads or other offal, seasoned with red pepper and oregano, wrapped around a skewer and grilled over charcoal).

Meşhur Dönerci Hacı Osman'ın Yeri (Map p242; Fuat Paşa Caddesi 16, Mercan; döner kebap from ₺4.50; ⊙11am-5pm Mon-Sat; ☒Beyazıt-Kapalı Çarşı) This döner stand occupying an elegant Ottoman sebil (fountain) outside the Ali Paşa Camii is very popular with local shopkeepers and shoppers as well as students from nearby İstanbul University.

Bena Dondurmaları (Map p242; ☎0212-520 5440; Gazı Atik Ali Paşa Camii 12b, Çemberlitaş; ice cream ₺1 per scoop, desserts ₺3-5; ⊙10am-6pm Mon-Sat; ☒Çemberlitaş) There's inevitably an afternoon queue in front of this tiny dondurma (Turkish ice cream) shop in the courtyard of the Atik Ali Paşa Camii. Though the dondurma is an undeniable draw, we tend to opt for the fırın sütlaç (rice pudding) or decadent trileçe (cream-soaked sponge cake with a caramel topping).

with dried chickpeas and a sprinkle of cinnamon, it has a reputation for building up strength and virility, and tends to be an acquired taste.

In summer, the bar also serves şıra, a fermented grape juice.

BAZAAR DISTRICT SHOPPING

PANDELI
CAFE

Map p242 (☑0212-527 3909; www.pandeli.com.tr; Spice Bazaar, Eminönü; ⊙9am-7pm Mon-Sat; ⌂Eminönü) Dating from 1901, Pandeli has three salons that are encrusted with stunning turquoise-coloured İznik tiles and also feature painted ceilings and chandeliers. Though its location above the main entrance to the Spice Bazaar makes it a popular lunch spot for tourists (most locals wouldn't dream of eating here), we suggest visiting for tea or coffee after lunch instead.

DARÜZZIYAFE (FORMER SOUP KITCHEN)
CAFE

Map p242 (☑0212-511 8414; www.daruzziyafe.com.tr; ⊙11am-11pm; Ⓜ︎Vezneciler) Set in the former *imaret* (soup kitchen) of the Süleymaniye Mosque, this cafe has a gorgeous courtyard, so is an excellent tea or coffee stop. The food is mediocre and not recommended.

LALE BAHÇESI
TEA GARDEN

Map p242 (Şifahane Caddesi 2, Süleymaniye; ⊙9am-11pm; Ⓜ︎Vezneciler) Make your way down the stairs into the sunken courtyard opposite the Süleymaniye Mosque to discover this outdoor teahouse, which is popular with students from the nearby theological college and İstanbul University, who head here to enjoy çay and nargiles.

KAHVE DÜNYASI
CAFE

Map p242 (☑0212-527 3282; Nuruosmaniye Caddesi 79; ⊙7.30am-9.30pm; ☎; ⌂Çemberlitaş) The name means 'Coffee World', and this coffee chain has the local world at its feet. The secret of its success lies in the huge coffee menu, reasonable prices, delicious chocolate spoons (yes, you read that correctly), comfortable seating and free wi-fi. The filter coffee is better than its espresso-based alternatives. There's another **branch** near the Spice Bazaar in Eminönü (☑0212-520 0204; Kızıl Han Sokak 18; ⌂Eminönü).

ETHEM TEZÇAKAR KAHVECI
CAFE

Map p95 (☑0212-513 2133; Halıcılar Çarşışı Sokak 61-63, Grand Bazaar; ⊙8.30am-6pm Mon-Sat; ⌂Beyazıt-Kapalı Çarşı) Bekir Tezçakar's family has been at the helm of this tiny coffee shop for four generations. Smack bang in the middle of the bazaar's most glamorous retail strip, its traditional brass-tray tables and wooden stools are a good spot to enjoy a break and watch the passing parade of shoppers.

ŞARK KAHVESI
CAFE

Map p95 (Oriental Coffee Shop; ☑0212-512 1144; Yağlıkçılar Caddesi 134, Grand Bazaar; ⊙8.30am-7pm Mon-Sat; ⌂Beyazıt-Kapalı Çarşı) The Şark's arched ceiling betrays its former existence as part of a bazaar street – years ago some enterprising *kahveci* (coffeehouse owner) walled up several sides and turned it into a cafe. Located on one of the bazaar's major thoroughfares, it's popular with both stallholders and tourists, who enjoy tea, coffee (Turkish, espresso and filter) or a cold drink.

🔒 SHOPPING

The city's two most famous shopping destinations – the Grand and Spice Bazaars – are in this district. In between the two is the vibrant local shopping neighbourhood of Tahtakale.

⭐ABDULLA NATURAL PRODUCTS
TEXTILES, BATHWARE

Map p95 (☑0212-527 3684; www.abdulla.com; Halıcılar Sokak 60, Grand Bazaar; ⊙8.30am-7pm Mon-Sat; ⌂Beyazıt-Kapalı Çarşı) The first of the Western-style designer stores to appear in this ancient marketplace, Abdulla sells top-quality cotton bed linen and towels, hand-spun woollen throws from eastern Turkey, cotton *peştemals* (bath wraps) and pure olive-oil soap.

⭐EPOQUE
ANTIQUES

Map p95 (☑0212-527 7865; Sandal Bedesten Sokak 38, Grand Bazaar; ⊙8.30am-7pm Mon-Sat; ⌂Beyazıt-Kapalı Çarşı) Serious antique shoppers should make their way to this old-fashioned business near the bazaar's Nuruosmaniye Gate. Silver candlesticks and trays, enamelled cigarette cases, jewellery, watches and an extraordinary range of icons are on offer in the elegant shop. The elderly owner and sales members are happy to welcome browsers.

⭐NECEF ANTIK & GOLD
JEWELLERY

Map p95 (☑0212-513 0372; necefantik@outlook.com; Şerifağa Sokak 123, İç Bedesten, Grand Bazaar; ⊙8.30am-7pm Mon-Sat; ⌂Beyazıt-Kapalı Çarşı) Owner Haluk Botasun has been handcrafting 24-carat gold jewellery in his tiny İç Bedesten store for decades, producing attractive pieces in Byzantine and Ottoman styles. The earings and cufflinks featuring delicate mosaics are particularly desirable.

★**ALTAN ŞEKERLEME** FOOD & DRINKS
Map p242 (☎0212-522 5909; Kıble Çeşme Caddesi 68, Eminönü; ☺8am-7pm Mon-Sat, 9am-6pm Sun; Ⓜ Haliç) Kids aren't the only ones who like candy stores. İstanbullus of every age have been coming to this shop in the Küçük Pazar (Little Bazaar) precinct below the Süleymaniye Mosque since 1865, lured by its cheap and delectable *lokum* (Turkish Delight), *helva* (sweet made from sesame seeds) and *akide* (hard candy).

MEKHANN TEXTILES
Map p95 (☎0212-519 9444; www.mekhann.com; Divrikli Sokak 49, Grand Bazaar; ☺8.30am-7pm Mon-Sat; Ⓖ Beyazıt-Kapalı Çarşı) Bolts of richly coloured, hand-woven silk from Uzbekistan and a range of finely woven shawls join finely embroidered bedspreads and pillow slips on the crowded shelves of this Grand Bazaar store, which sets the bar high when it comes to quality and price. There's another branch near the tram stop in Tophane.

DERVIŞ TEXTILES
Map p95 (☎0212-528 7883; www.dervis.com; Halıcılar Sokak 51, Grand Bazaar; ☺8.30am-7pm Mon-Sat; Ⓖ Beyazıt-Kapalı Çarşı) Raw cotton and silk *peştemals* (bath wraps) share shelf space here with traditional Turkish dowry vests and engagement dresses. If these don't take your fancy, the pure olive-oil soaps and old hamam bowls are sure to step into the breach. There's another **branch** (Map p95; Cebeci Han 10) in the Grand Bazaar, off Yağlıçılar Caddesi.

ÜMIT BERKSOY JEWELLERY
Map p95 (☎0212-522 3391; İnciler Sokak 2-6, Grand Bazaar; ☺8.30am-7pm Mon-Sat; Ⓜ Vezneciler, Ⓖ Beyazıt-Kapalı Çarşı) Jeweller Ümit Berksoy handcrafts gorgeous Byzantine-style rings, earings and necklaces using gold and old coins at his tiny atelier just outside the İç Bedesten. He also creates contemporary pieces.

YAZMACI NECDET DANIŞ TEXTILES
Map p95 (Yağlıçılar Caddesi 57, Grand Bazaar; ☺8.30am-7pm Mon-Sat; Ⓖ Beyazıt-Kapalı Çarşı) Fashion designers and buyers from every corner of the globe know that, when in İstanbul, this is where to come to source top-quality textiles. It's crammed with bolts of fabric of every description – shiny,

simple, sheer and sophisticated – as well as *peştemals*, scarves and clothes. Murat Danış next door is part of the same operation.

SILK & CASHMERE CLOTHING
Map p242 (☎0212-528 5286; www.silkcashmere.com; Nuruosmaniye Caddesi 38, Nuruosmaniye; ☺9.30am-7pm Mon-Sat; Ⓖ Çemberlitaş) The Nuruosmaniye branch of this popular chain sells cashmere and silk-cashmere-blend cardigans, jumpers, tops and shawls. All are remarkably well priced considering their quality.

SOFA ART, JEWELLERY
Map p242 (☎0212-520 2850; www.kashifsofa.com; Nuruosmaniye Caddesi 53, Nuruosmaniye; ☺9.30am-6.30pm Mon-Sat; Ⓖ Çemberlitaş) Investigation of Sofa's three floors of artfully arranged clutter reveals an eclectic range of pricey jewellery, prints, textiles, calligraphy, Ottoman miniatures and contemporary Turkish art.

ALI MUHIDDIN HACI BEKIR FOOD
Map p242 (☎0212-522 8543; www.hacibekir.com.tr; Hamidiye Caddesi 33, Eminönü; ☺9am-7.30pm; Ⓖ Eminönü) Many people think that this historic shop, which has been operated by members of the same family for over 200 years, is the best place in the city to buy *lokum* (Turkish Delight). Choose from *sade* (plain), *cevizli* (walnut), *fıstıklı* (pistachio), *badem* (almond) or *roze* (rose water). There are other **branches** in Beyoğlu (p145) and Kadıköy (p160).

HAFIZ MUSTAFA FOOD
Map p242 (☎0212-513 3610; www.hafizmustafa.com; Hamidiye Caddesi 84, Eminönü; ☺8am-8pm Mon-Sat, 9am-8pm Sun; Ⓖ Eminönü) 🖋 Located opposite Ali Muhıddin Hacı Bekir, Hafız Mustafa sells excellent *lokum*. You can buy a small bag of freshly made treats to sample, plus gift boxes to take home. Best of all, staff are happy to let you taste before buying (within reason, of course). There are other **branches** in Sirkeci (p83) and Sultanahmet (p83).

NIL BAHARAT SPICES
Map p242 (☎0212-527 0187; www.nilbaharat.com; Asmaaltı Büyükbaş Sokak 1, Eminönü; ☺7am-6pm Mon-Sat; Ⓖ Eminönü) There are plenty of spices sold in the nearby Mısır Çarşısı (Spice Bazaar), but those sold at this shop on the western side of the bazaar tend to be both cheaper and fresher.

MUHLIS GÜNBATTI
TEXTILES

Map p95 (☎0212-511 6562; www.muhlis gunbatti.com.tr; Perdahçılar Sokak 48, Grand Bazaar; ⊗8.30am-7pm Mon-Sat; 🚇Beyazıt-Kapalı Çarşı) One of the most famous stores in the Grand Bazaar, Muhlis Günbattı specialises in *suzani* fabrics from Uzbekistan. These beautiful bedspreads, tablecloths and wall hangings are made from fine cotton embroidered with silk. As well as the textiles, it stocks a small range of antique Ottoman fabrics and clothing richly embroidered with gold.

ETHNICON
CARPETS

Map p95 (☎0212-527 6841; www.ethnicon. com; Tekkeçiler Sokak 58-60, Grand Bazaar; ⊗8.30am-7pm Mon-Sat; 🚇Beyazıt-Kapalı Çarşı) The name is a shortening of 'Ethnic' and 'Contemporary' and that, in a nutshell, is the type of rug that this fashionable shop produces. EthniCon can be said to have started the current craze in contemporary kilims (pileless woven rugs).

DHOKU
CARPETS

Map p95 (☎0212-527 6841; www.dhoku.com; Tekkeçiler Sokak 58-60, Grand Bazaar; ⊗8.30am-7pm Mon-Sat; 🚇Beyazıt-Kapalı Çarşı) One of the new generation of rug stores opening in the bazaar, Dhoku (meaning 'texture') sells artfully designed wool kilims in resolutely modernist designs. Its sister store, EthniCon, opposite Dhoku, sells similarly stylish rugs in vivid colours.

SERHAT GERIDÖNMEZ
JEWELLERY

Map p95 (☎0212-519 8017; Şerifağa Sokak 69, İç Bedesten, Grand Bazaar; ⊗8.30am-7pm Mon-Sat; 🚇Beyazıt-Kapalı Çarşı) There are plenty of jewellers in the Grand Bazaar, but few sell objects as gorgeous as the expertly crafted copies of Hellenistic, Roman and Byzantine pieces on offer at this tiny store.

SEVAN BIÇAKÇI
JEWELLERY

Map p242 (☎0212-520 4516; www.sevanbicakci. com; Gazi Sinan Paşa Sokak 16, Nuruosmaniye; ⊗10am-6pm Mon-Sat; 🚇Çemberlitaş) Inspired by the monuments and history of his much-loved İstanbul, flamboyant jeweller Sevan Bıçakçı creates wearable art that aims to impress. His flagship store is near the Grand Bazaar's Nuruosmaniye Gate.

KOÇ DERI LEATHER
CLOTHING

Map p242 (☎0212-527 5553; http://kocderi. com/en/; Kürkçüler Çarşısı 22-46, Grand Bazaar; ⊗8.30am-7pm Mon-Sat; 🚇Beyazıt-Kapalı Çarşı) If you fancy a leather jacket or coat, Koç is bound to have something that suits. It's one of the bazaar's busiest stores and certainly the most stylish of the leather outlets here.

CANKURTARAN GIDA
FOOD

Map p242 (Cankurtaran Food Center; ☎0212-520 2937; www.eng.cankurtarangida.com.tr; Spice Bazaar 33, Eminönü; ⊗8am-7.30pm; 🚇Eminönü) Supplying locals with amber-hued honey from Hakkari and Siirt, pungent pastrami from Kayseri and cheeses from every corner of the country since 1946, Cankurtaran Gıda is the best deli in the Spice Bazaar and a great spot to visit if you're after picnic provisions.

ARIFOĞLU
SPICES

Map p242 (☎0212-522 6612; www.arifoglu. com; Spice Bazaar 31, Eminönü; ⊗8am-7.30pm; 🚇Eminönü) Well-priced Iranian saffron joins honey, perfumed oils and spices of every imaginable colour and aroma on the shelves of this reliable store in the Spice Bazaar. There's another branch at number 59.

UCUZCULAR BAHARAT
SPICES

Map p242 (☎0212-528 2895; www.ucuzcular. com.tr; Spice Bazaar 51, Eminönü; ⊗8am-7.30pm; 🚇Eminönü) A showcase of colourful and fragrant spices, Ucuzcular concocts its own blends and will vacuum pack them for travellers who are keen to add them to their luggage.

MALATYA PAZARI
FOOD

Map p242 (☎0212-520 0440; www.malatya pazari.com.tr; Spice Bazaar 44, Eminönü; ⊗8am-7.30pm; 🚇Eminönü) The city of Malatya in central-eastern Turkey is famous for its apricots, and this shop with two branches near the Spice Bazaar's Tahmis Caddesi doorway stocks the cream of the crop, dried both naturally and chemically. Its other quality dried fruit and nuts eclipse all others in this bazaar.

MEHMET KALMAZ BAHARATÇI
BEAUTY

Map p242 (☎0212-522 6604; Spice Bazaar 41, Eminönü; ⊗8am-7.30pm; 🚇Eminönü) Members of the Kalmaz family have been concocting remedies based on Ottoman-era recipes at this old-fashioned shop since 1950. Customers come here to source potions, lotions, teas and medicinal herbs, enabling them to look younger, feel stronger and overcome ailments.

KURUKAHVECI MEHMET EFENDI COFFEE

Map p242 (✆0212-511 4262; www.mehmet efendi.com; Tahmis Sokak 66, Eminönü; ☺8am-8pm Mon-Sat; 🚇Eminönü) Caffeine addicts are regularly spotted queuing outside this flagship store of İstanbul's most famous coffee purveyor. Housed on the ground floor of an art-deco building next to the Spice Bazaar, it is best known for its Turkish-style grind, which it has been producing since 1871.

VAKKO İNDIRIM FASHION & ACCESSORIES

Map p242 (Vakko Sale Store; Sultan Hamamı Caddesi 8a, Eminönü; ☺10am-6.30pm Mon-Sat; 🚇Eminönü) This remainder outlet of İstanbul's famous fashion store should be on the itinerary of all bargain hunters. Top-quality men's and women's clothing – often stuff that's been designed and made in Italy – is sold here for a fraction of its original price.

ARMINE CLOTHING

Map p242 (✆0212-511 2211; www.armine.com; Mahmutpaşa Yokuşu 135, Eminönü; ☺10am-6pm Mon-Sat; 🚇Eminönü) İstanbul is a fashionable city with a highly idiosyncratic style. In Bebek and Beyoğlu the fashion might be for tight jeans, revealing jackets and chunky jewellery, but in the city's conservative neighbourhoods, there's little make-up and even less flesh on show. Wildly popular Armine is where Zara style meets the headscarf, and it's an exemplar of affordable Islamic chic.

🏃 SPORTS & ACTIVITIES

★ALTERNATIVE CITY TOURS TOUR

(www.alternativecitytours.com; tour per group of up to 6 people €150 plus lunch) Having lived in İstanbul for many years, New York–born photographer Monica Fritz recently made the decision to share some of the many secrets she has learned about the city with fellow shutterbugs. Her informed and enjoyable tour portfolio covers the European and Asian shores and beyond, and she provides plenty of cultural and historical context.

Tours include one of the Grand Bazaar that introduces participants to hidden *hans* (caravanserais) and passageways, as well as taking to the roof à la James Bond in *Skyfall*. Other unique offerings include a Grand Bazaar scavenger hunt for kids, a tour of the city's hidden synagogues and a cruise on a private yacht going to the Princes' Islands or other interesting places along the Bosphorus (the latter costs €350 for up to seven people).

ÇEMBERLITAŞ HAMAMI HAMAM

Map p242 (✆0212-522 7974; www.cemberlitas hamami.com; Vezir Han Caddesi 8, Çemberlitaş; self-service ₺70, bath, scrub & soap massage ₺115; ☺6am-midnight; 🚇Çemberlitaş) There won't be too many times in your life when you'll get the opportunity to have a Turkish bath in a building dating back to 1584, so now might well be the time to do it – particularly as this twin hamam was designed by the great architect Sinan and is among the most beautiful in the city.

The building was commissioned by Nurbanu Sultan, wife of Selim II and mother of Murat III. Both of its bath chambers have a huge marble *sıcaklık* (circular marble heat platform) and a gorgeous dome with glass apertures. The *camekan* (entrance hall) for men is original, but the women's version is new.

It costs ₺75 to add an oil massage to the standard bath package, but all massages and treatments here are perfunctory, so we'd suggest giving this a miss and opting for the cheaper self-serve option. Tips are meant to be covered in the treatment price and there's a 20% discount for ISIC-student-card holders.

GEDIKPAŞA HAMAMI HAMAM

Map p242 (✆0212-517 8956; www.gedikpasa hamami.com; Emin Sinan Hamamı Sokak 61, Gedikpaşa; bath, scrub & soap massage ₺80; ☺6am-midnight; 🚇Çemberlitaş) This Ottoman-era hamam has been operating since 1475. Its shabby interior isn't as beautiful as those at Çemberlitaş (p111) and Cağaloğlu (p90), but services are cheaper and there are separate hamams, small dipping pools and saunas for both sexes. The operators will sometimes transport guests to and from Sultanahmet hotels at no charge – ask your hotel to investigate this option.

Western Districts

Neighbourhood Top Five

❶ Kariye Museum (p114) Admiring the mosaics and frescoes adorning the interior of one of İstanbul's Byzantine treasures.

❷ Eyüp (p119) Taking a ferry up the Golden Horn to visit the Eyüp Sultan Mosque and enjoy the hilltop view from the terrace of Pierre Loti Café.

❸ Patriarchal Church of St George (p117) Visiting this church, one of Turkey's major pilgrimage destinations, and wandering up nearby Vodina Caddesi for a glimpse of Fener and Balat's neighbourhood life.

❹ Asitane (p122) Sampling dishes such as stuffed quince, goose kebap and 'fatty apron' kebap, once enjoyed by Süleyman the Magnificent and other sultans.

❺ Yavuz Sultan Selim Mosque (p118) Exploring the streets around this historic mosque in the fascinating Çarşamba district.

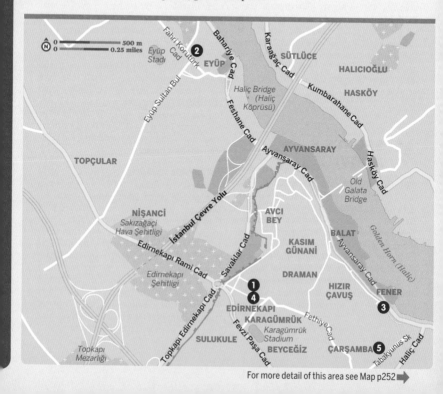

For more detail of this area see Map p252 ➡

Explore Western Districts

It's a great shame that so few visitors head to this fascinating part of town. Try to dedicate at least one day of your stay to exploring the area; two would be better.

Spend the first of these taking the Golden Horn ferry trip from Eminönü, first alighting at Ayvansaray to visit the Kariye Museum (Chora Church) and then continuing to Eyüp. Either on the same day or the next, try to incorporate a wander along Vodina Caddesi to experience the eclectic, bohemian and multicultural Fener and Balat neighbourhoods and to see the Patriarchal Church of St George's ornate interior. If you are able to spend a second day here, we recommend starting in the Bazaar District and then continuing uphill towards the Fatih and Yavuz Sultan Selim Mosques. A good day for this is Wednesday, when the weekly market takes place in the streets around Fatih Mosque. Note that these districts are quiet at night and on Sundays, so you're best off exploring during the day on weekdays or Saturdays.

Local Life

➜ **Produce shopping** Locals shop along Fevzi Paşa Caddesi and at the Çarşamba Pazarı, aka Wednesday Market (p118) in Fatih, on Murat Molla Caddesi in Çarşamba and along Vodina Caddesi in Balat.

➜ **Gathering spots** Popular local gathering spots include the terrace of the Yavuz Sultan Selim Mosque (p118) and the forecourts of the Eyüp Sultan Mosque (p118) and Fatih Mosque (p118).

➜ **Cultural hub** Vodina Caddesi has several antique shops and regular antique auctions, along with little stores selling vintage clothing, handmade shoes, ceramics and more. With artists moving into the area, galleries and studios are likely to spring up in the coming years.

Getting There & Away

➜ **Ferry** The most enjoyable way to access the neighbourhood, the Haliç (Golden Horn) ferry from Eminönü stops at Ayvansaray near Edirnekapı and at Eyüp, with a new stop in Balat set to be added.

➜ **Bus** Regular services (99, 99A and 99Y) travel from Eminönü up the Golden Horn on the main shore road. Bus 55T links Fener and Balat with Taksim. En route back to Eminönü, 99Y detours to Karaköy via the Atatürk Bridge, before recrossing the Golden Horn on the Galata Bridge.

➜ **Taxi** From Taksim to Fener costs around ₺15; Sultanahmet to Edirnekapı about ₺20.

Lonely Planet's Top Tip

Much of this area's appeal lies in its neighbourhood charms. Especially around Vodina Caddesi, you can enjoy the contrasts between tumbledown late-Ottoman houses and graffiti murals, İstanbullu hipsters and conservative Islamic folk, chic cafes and locals selling fresh veg from vans on back lanes. Rather than rushing through, factor in time to walk the streets – preferably on a Wednesday, when the Çarşamba Pazarı (Wednesday Market; p118) is held around the Fatih Mosque.

◉ **Best Churches**

➜ Patriarchal Church of St George (p117)

➜ Church of St Mary of the Mongols (p120)

➜ Church of St Stephen of the Bulgars (p121)

For reviews, see p117.➡

◉ **Best Byzantine Mosaics**

➜ Kariye Museum (p114)

➜ Fethiye Museum (p117)

For reviews, see p117➡

✕ **Best Cafes**

➜ Coffee Department (p122)

➜ Pierre Loti Café (p122)

➜ Aziz Cafe (p122)

For reviews, see p121.➡

WESTERN DISTRICTS

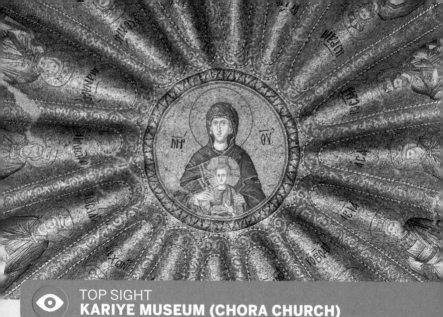

TOP SIGHT
KARIYE MUSEUM (CHORA CHURCH)

İstanbul has more than its fair share of Byzantine monuments, but few are as drop-dead gorgeous as this mosaic-laden church. Nestled in the shadow of Theodosius II's monumental land walls and now a museum overseen by the curators of Aya Sofya, it receives a fraction of the visitor numbers that its big sister attracts but offers an equally fascinating insight into Byzantine art.

Origins of the Church

The building was originally known as the Church of the Holy Saviour Outside the Walls (Chora literally means 'country' and Kariye is the Turkish version of the ancient Greek word Khora, which means the same thing), reflecting its original location outside the city walls built by Constantine the Great. Within a century, the church and the monastery complex in which it was located were engulfed by Byzantine urban sprawl and enclosed within a new set of walls built by Emperor Theodosius II. Around AD 500, Emperor Anastasius and his court moved from the Great Palace of Byzantium in Sultanahmet to the Palace of Blachernae, a new complex built close to the point where Theodosius' land walls met the old sea walls on the Golden Horn. Its proximity to the Chora Monastery led to the monastery expanding and being rebuilt in 536 during the rule of Justinian.

What you see today isn't Justinian's church, though. That building was destroyed during the Iconoclastic period (711–843) and reconstructed at least five times, most significantly in the 11th, 12th and 14th centuries. Today the

DON'T MISS

⇒ *Khalke Jesus*
⇒ *The Genealogy of Christ*
⇒ *Mary and the Baby Jesus*
⇒ Frescoes in the parecclesion

PRACTICALITIES

⇒ Kariye Müzesi
⇒ Map p172, A3; p254
⇒ ☎0212-631 9241
⇒ www.choramuseum.com
⇒ Kariye Camii Sokak 18, Edirnekapı
⇒ adult/child ₺30/free
⇒ ◷9am-7pm mid-Apr–late Oct, to 5pm late Oct–mid-Apr, last entry 30min before closing
⇒ 🚌28 from Eminönü, 87 from Taksim, 🚊Ayvansaray

Chora consists of five main architectural units: the nave, the two-storied structure (annexe) added to the north, the inner and outer narthexes, and the chapel for tombs (pareecclesion) to the south.

Virtually all of the interior decoration – the famous mosaics and the less renowned but equally striking frescoes – dates from c 1320 and was funded by court treasurer Theodore Metochites. One of the museum's most wonderful mosaics, found above the door to the nave in the inner narthex, depicts Theodore offering the church to Christ (item 48).

Metochites also established a very large and rich library inside the monastery; unfortunately, no traces of this or the other monastery buildings have survived. The structure and environs of the church weren't the only thing to change over the years: after centuries of use as a church, the building became a mosque during the reign of Beyazıt II (1481–1512), and the 14th-century belfry was replaced by a minaret. The church was converted into a museum in 1945.

Mosaics

Most of the interior is covered with mosaics depicting the lives of Christ and the Virgin Mary. Look out for the **Khalke Jesus** (item 33), under the right dome in the inner narthex, which shows Christ and Mary with two donors – Prince Isaac Comnenos and Melane, daughter of Byzantine emperor Michael VIII Palaiologos. Sadly, only scant remains exist. On the dome itself is a stunning depiction of **Jesus and his ancestors** (*The Genealogy of Christ*; item 27). On the narthex' left dome is a serenely beautiful mosaic of **Mary and the Baby Jesus surrounded by her ancestors** (item 34).

In the *naos* (nave) are three mosaics: of **Christ** (item 50c), of **Mary and the Baby Jesus** (item 50b) and of the **Assumption of the Virgin** (item 50a). Turn around to see the latter, as it's above the main door you just entered. The 'infant' being held by Jesus is actually Mary's soul.

Frescoes

To the right of the nave is the parecclesion, a side chapel built to hold the tombs of the church's founder and his relatives, close friends and associates. This is decorated with frescoes that deal with the themes of death and resurrection, depicting scenes taken from the Old Testament. The striking painting in the apse known as the **Anastasis** (item 51) shows a powerful Christ raising Adam and Eve out of their sarcophagi, with saints and kings in attendance. The gates of hell are shown under Christ's feet. Less majestic but no less beautiful are the frescoes

THE CHORA'S PATRON

Theodore Metochites was born in Constantinople in 1270, the son of a senior official in the court of Michael VIII Palaiologos. In 1290 he was accepted into the court of Andronikos II and was appointed logothetes, official responsible for the treasury, making him the highest Byzantine official after the emperor. In 1316 Metochites was appointed by the emperor as *ktetor* (donor) for the restoration of the Chora Monastery. When the restoration of the monastery was completed in 1321, he was granted the title of grand logothetes. Metochites lost his position in 1328 when Emperor Andronikos II was dethroned, and he was banished from Constantinople. He was allowed to return in 1330 and chose to become a priest in the monastery that he had so generously endowed. He died in 1332 and is buried in a grave niche.

The building originally had a belltower, constructed in the southwest corner and later replaced by the present minaret. Most of İstanbul's Byzantine belfries disappeared with Ottoman restrictions on the use of bells and the conversion of churches into mosques.

adorning the dome, which show **Mary and 12 attendant angels** (item 65). The **Last Judgement** (item 56) strikingly depicts this scene from the Book of Revelation in dazzling white with gilt accents, with the rolling up of heaven represented by a coiling motif surrounded by the choirs of heaven.

Though no one knows for certain, it is thought that the frescoes were painted by the same masters who created the mosaics. Theirs is an extraordinary accomplishment, as the paintings, with their sophisticated use of perspective and exquisitely portrayed facial expressions, are reminiscent of those painted by the Italian master Giotto (c 1266–1337), the painter who more than any other ushered in the Italian Renaissance and who was painting at around the same time.

The message behind the perspective is important: the objects at the back are as big as those at the front, because the artists were giving the impression that the picture ends in the viewer. Such artistic sophistication has led historians to speculate that the Byzantines would have started the Renaissance had the Ottomans not taken İstanbul. Indeed, Byzantine artists who fled Constantinople to Europe did have some influence on Early Renaissance art.

Marble

The nave and the narthexes feature very fine, multicoloured marble work. The marble door in the north axis of the nave is an imitation of the bronze-and-wood doors of the 6th century, and is one of the few surviving examples of its kind.

Restoration

Between 1948 and 1958, the church's interior decoration was carefully restored under the auspices of the Byzantine Society of America. Plaster and whitewash that covered the mosaics and frescoes was removed and everything was cleaned. In 2013 a second major restoration commenced. This ongoing process is happening in stages, and involves closure of parts of the museum; first the nave and the two-storey annexes on the northern side of the building, followed by the inner narthex, and finally the outer narthex and parecclesion. As the parecclesion has the finest frescoes, it may not be worth visiting the church during the final stage.

Despite signs clearly prohibiting the use of camera flashes in the museum, many visitors ignore this rule, endangering these wonderful mosaics and frescoes. Please don't be one of them.

Getting to the Museum

The best way to get to this part of town is to catch the Haliç (Golden Horn) ferry from Eminönü to Ayvansaray and walk up the hill along Dervişzade Sokak, turn right into Eğrikapı Mumhane Caddesi and then almost immediately left into Şişhane Caddesi. From here you can follow the remnants of Theodosius II's land walls, passing the Palace of Constantine Porphyrogenitus on your way. From Hoca Çakır Caddesi, veer left into Vaiz Sokak just before you reach the steep stairs leading up to the ramparts of the wall, then turn sharp left into Kariye Sokak and you'll come to the museum.

Buses including 28 from Eminönü and 87 from Taksim stop near the museum at the Edirnekapı stop on Fevzi Paşa Caddesi. From Sultanahmet, you can also catch the tram to Aksaray followed by the metro to Topkapı-Ulubatlı and finally the tram again to Edirnekapı.

⊙ SIGHTS

KARIYE MUSEUM
(CHORA CHURCH)   MUSEUM
See p114.

MIHRIMAH SULTAN MOSQUE   MOSQUE
Map p252 (Mihrimah Sultan Camii; Ali Kuşçu Sokak, Edirnekapı; 🚌28 from Eminönü, 87 from Taksim) The great Sinan put his stamp on the entire city and this mosque, constructed in the 1560s next to the Edirnekapı section of the historic land walls, is one of his best works. Commissioned by Süleyman the Magnificent's favourite daughter, Mihrimah, it features a wonderfully light and airy interior with delicate stained-glass windows and an unusual 'bird cage' chandelier.

Occupying the highest point in the city, the mosque's dome and one slender minaret are major adornments to the skyline; they are particularly prominent on the road from Edirne. Sinan was in love with Mihrimah, who was married to grand vizier Rüstem Paşa, and he symbolised his frustrated affection in the symmetry between this mosque and its identically named counterpart in Üsküdar. As the sun sets behind this mosque, the moon rises behind the other – a reference to Mihrimah's name, which means 'sun and moon' in Farsi.

Remnants of the *külliye* (mosque complex) include a still-functioning hamam (p122).

FETHIYE MUSEUM   MUSEUM
Map p252 (Fethiye Müzesi, Church of Pammakaristos; ☎0212-635 1273; http://ayasofyamuzesi.gov.tr/en; Fethiye Caddesi, Çarşamba; ₺5; ⊙9am-7pm mid-Apr–late Oct, to 5pm late Oct–mid-Apr; 🚌99, 99A, 99Y from Eminönü, 55T from Taksim) Not long after the Conquest, Mehmet the Conqueror visited this 13th-century church to discuss theological questions with the Patriarch of the Orthodox Church. They talked in the southern side chapel known as the parecclesion, which is decorated with gold mosaics and is now open as a small museum.

The church was endowed by a nephew of Emperor Michael VIII Palaeologos and built between 1292 and 1294. The chapel was endowed by the benefactor's wife (the inscription around Christ's head at the base of the half dome reads 'The nun Maria gave the promise of salvation in the name of her husband, the victorious and deserving protostrator Michael Glabas Ducas') and dates from 1315. It was the seat of the Christian Orthodox Patriarchate from 1455 to 1587, after which time it was converted into a mosque and named Fethiye (Conquest) to commemorate Sultan Murat III's victories in Georgia and Azerbaijan. Part of the building still functions as a mosque, while this part is a deconsecrated museum.

In the paracclesion, the most impressive of the mosaics are the Pantokrator and 12 Prophets adorning the dome, and the Deesis (Christ with the Virgin and St John the Baptist) in the apse.

PATRIARCHAL CHURCH
OF ST GEORGE   CHURCH
Map p252 (St George in the Phanar; ☎0212-531 9670; www.ec-patr.org; Sadrazam Ali Paşa Caddesi, Fener; ⊙8.30am-4.30pm; 🚌99, 99A, 99Y from Eminönü, 55T from Taksim) Dating from 1836, this church is part of the Greek Patriarchate (p121) compound. Inside the church are artefacts including Byzantine mosaics, religious relics and a wood-and-inlay patriarchal throne. The most eye-catching feature is an ornately carved wooden iconostasis (screen of icons) that was restored and lavishly gilded in 1994.

The patriarchal throne is in the middle of the nave. Made of walnut inlaid with ivory, mother-of-pearl and coloured wood, it is thought to date from the last years of Byzantium.

Other treasures include the 11th-century mosaic icon that is on the south wall to the right of the iconostasis. This shows the Virgin Mary holding and pointing to the Christ Child, and was originally created for the Byzantine church of Pammakaristos (now the Fethiye Museum).

Look for the Column of Christ's Flagellation in the southern corner of the nave. The church claims that this is a portion of the column to which Jesus Christ was bound and whipped by Roman soldiers before the Crucifixion. It was supposedly brought to Constantinople by St Helen, mother of the first Christian emperor, Constantine.

Note that the church is closed between 9.15am and 12.20pm for Sunday service when the Patriarch is in residence (usually once per month).

Coming from Eminönü, get off the bus at the Fener stop, just after passing the Haliç Kebap restaurant on the left, and walk inland to find the church.

WESTERN DISTRICTS SIGHTS

YAVUZ SULTAN SELIM MOSQUE MOSQUE

Map p172 (Sultan Selim Camii, Mosque of Yavuz Selim; Yavuz Selim Caddesi, Çarşamba; ⊘tomb 9am-5pm; ⬚99, 99A, 99Y from Eminönü, 55T from Taksim) The sultan to whom this mosque was dedicated (Süleyman the Magnificent's father, Selim I, known as the Grim) is famous for having killed two of his brothers, six of his nephews and three of his own sons in order to assure his succession and that of Süleyman. He did, however, lay the groundwork for his son's imperial success and, to this day, İstanbullus love his mosque.

The reason for this ongoing adulation is the 'Tough' Sultan Selim Mosque's position atop the Old City's fifth hill. Its terrace has panoramic views over the Golden Horn (the mosque you see on the right is Süleymaniye Mosque) and is a popular picnic and relaxation spot. Selim's *türbe* (tomb) is in the garden behind the mosque.

The mosque is located in the fascinating Çarşamba district, one of the city's most conservative enclaves. Women in black chadors and men with long beards and traditional clothing are seen everywhere, often hurrying to prayers at the İsmail Ağa Mosque, headquarters of the Nakşibendi Tarikatı, a Sufi sect. The huge sunken park next door was originally a 5th-century open Roman cistern; it's now home to playing fields, basketball courts and an excellent children's playground.

The building itself, constructed between 1522 and 1529, has a simple but elegant design. Inside, its mother-of-pearl inlay and painted woodwork provide the most distinctive features.

PHANAR GREEK ORTHODOX COLLEGE HISTORIC BUILDING

Map p172 (Megali School, Great School, Kırmızı Mektep; Sancaktar Caddesi, Fener; ⬚99, 99A, 99Y from Eminönü, 55T from Taksim) Rising Hogwarts-like from the urban jumble, this Fener landmark, known locally as *kırmızı kale* (the red castle) for its castellated red-brick facade, still functions as a Greek school. A small student body of some 50 pupils studies here. Built in the early 1880s, it was designed by Ottoman Greek architect Konstantinos Dimadis, who is known for his European chateaux. The institution within predates the Ottoman arrival in Constantinople, making it Turkey's oldest educational body.

For more information on the college and the area's many intriguing piles, pick up a copy of tour guide Ahmet Faik Ozbilge's fascinating historical tome, *Nooks and Crannies of Old Istanbul: Fener, Balat, Ayvansaray.*

FATIH MOSQUE MOSQUE

(Fatih Camii, Mosque of the Conqueror; Fevzi Paşa Caddesi, Fatih; ⬚28 from Eminönü, 87 from Taksim) The Fatih was the first great imperial mosque built in İstanbul following the Conquest. Mehmet the Conqueror chose to locate it on the hilltop site of the ruined Church of the Apostles, burial place of Constantine and other Byzantine emperors. Mehmet decided to be buried here as well; his tomb is behind the mosque and is inevitably filled with worshippers.

The original *külliye* (mosque complex), finished in 1470, was enormous. Set in extensive grounds, it included 15 charitable establishments such as *medreses* (Islamic schools of higher studies), a hospice for travellers and a caravanserai. Many of these still stand; the most interesting is the multidomed *tabhane* (inn for travelling dervishes) to the southeast of the mosque. Its columns are said to have been originally used in the Church of the Apostles.

Unfortunately the mosque you see today is not the one Mehmet built. The original stood for nearly 300 years before toppling in an earthquake in 1766. The current baroque-style mosque was constructed between 1767 and 1771.

The front courtyard of the mosque is a favourite place for locals to congregate. On Wednesday the streets behind and to the north of the mosque host the **Çarşamba Pazarı** (Wednesday Market; Fatih Pazarı; Fatih; ⬚28 from Eminönü, 87 from Taksim), selling food, clothing and household goods.

EYÜP SULTAN MOSQUE MOSQUE

Map p172 (Eyüp Sultan Camii, Mosque of the Great Eyüp; Camii Kebir Sokak, Eyüp; ⊘tomb 9.30am-4.30pm; ⬚99, 99A, 99Y from Eminönü, 55T from Taksim, ⊛Eyüp) This important complex marks the supposed burial place of Ebu Eyüp el-Ensari, a friend of the Prophet who fell in battle outside the walls of Constantinople while carrying the banner of Islam during the Arab assault and siege of the city (AD 674 to 678). His tomb is İstanbul's most important Islamic shrine.

Eyüp's grave was identified in a location outside the city walls immediately after the

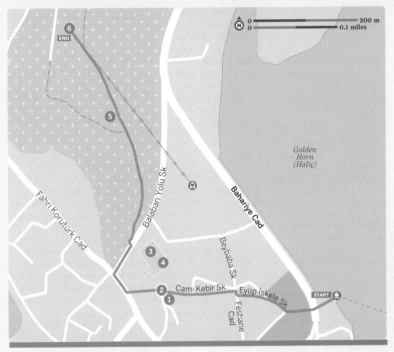

Neighbourhood Walk
Exploring Eyüp

START EYÜP İSKELESI
END PIERRE LOTI CAFÉ
LENGTH 1KM; ONE HOUR

Take the Golden Horn ferry from Karaköy or Eminönü and disembark at Eyüp. Cross busy Bahariye Caddesi; walk through the park and veer slightly right into Eyüp İskele Sokak, following it to pedestrian-only Cami Kebir Sokak, which is lined with stalls selling religious souvenirs and tourist tat. At the top of the street is the ❶ **Tomb of Sokullu Mehmet Paşa** (p120), an Ottoman grand vizier. The tomb is next to ❷ **Eyüp Meydanı**, where pilgrims and family groups congregate around the fountain and where street vendors sell fairy floss, *macun* (luridly coloured twisted candy on a stick), *kağıt helvas* (wafers filled with sweet sesame paste), *kestane* (roasted chestnuts) and *mısır* (grilled corn on the cob). Often the family groups include young boys dressed up in white satin suits with spangled caps and coloured sashes emblazoned with the word 'Maşallah' (May God Protect Him). These lads are on the way to their *sünnet*

(circumcision) and have made a stop beforehand in this holy area.

On the northern edge of the square is the ❸ **Eyüp Sultan Mosque** (p118) and the ❹ **Tomb of Ebu Eyüp el-Ensari**, the most important religious site in İstanbul. Enter the mosque's courtyard, which is shaded by a huge plane tree; the mosque is to your right and the tomb, rich with silver, gold and crystal chandeliers and coloured İznik tiles, is to your left.

After visiting both, walk out of the main gate and turn right into Balaban Yolu Sokak. Walk around the mosque complex (keeping it to your right) until you see a set of stairs and a cobbled path going uphill into the ❺ **Eyüp Sultan Mezarlığı** (Cemetery of the Great Eyüp), where many important Ottomans are buried. It is worth wandering off the path and through the cemetery, as many of the headstones and tombs feature fine calligraphy and statuary. Walk uphill for approximately 15 minutes to reach your final destination, the ❻ **Pierre Loti Café** (p122), from where you can admire a panoramic view of the Golden Horn.

Conquest, and Sultan Mehmet II decided to build a grand tomb to mark its location. The mosque complex that he commissioned became the place where the Ottoman princes came for the Turkish equivalent of a coronation ceremony: girding the Sword of Osman to signify their power and their title as *padişah* (king of kings) or sultan. In 1766 Mehmet's building was levelled by an earthquake; a new mosque was built on the site by Sultan Selim III in 1800.

Be careful to observe Islamic proprieties when visiting, as this is an extremely sacred place for Muslims, ranking fourth after the big three: Mecca, Medina and Jerusalem. It's always busy on weekends and religious holidays.

TOMB OF SOKULLU
MEHMET PAŞA   TOMB
(Sokullu Mehmed Paşa Türbe; Cami Kebir Sokak, Eyüp; 🚌99, 99A, 99Y from Eminönü, 55T from Taksim, 🚢Eyüp) Designed by Mimar Sinan and constructed around 1572, this *türbe* was part of a *külliye* (mosque complex) commissioned by Ottoman statesman Sokullu Mehmet Paşa (c 1506–79). Assassinated after 14 years as grand vizier, he was buried here next to his wife Ismihan, the daughter of Sultan Selim II. Inside, the stained glass is particularly noteworthy. The *külliye* also includes a *medrese* (seminary).

Sokullu Mehmet Paşa's life story is fascinating. Born in Bosnia, he was captured by Ottoman troops and recruited into the *devşirme*, the annual intake of Christian youths into the janissaries (this also happened to Sinan). After converting to Islam, he rose through the ranks, holding important positions such as high admiral of the fleet, before becoming a vizier and then grand vizier for a total of 24 years under three sultans: Süleyman the Magnificent, Selim II and Murat III. During his time in office, he amassed a great fortune and commissioned religious buildings including the Sokullu Şehit Mehmet Paşa Mosque (p81) in Sultanahmet.

GÜL MOSQUE   MOSQUE
Map p252 (Gül Camii; cnr Gül Camii & Şerefiye Sokaks, Fener; 🚌99, 99A, 99Y from Eminönü, 55T from Taksim) This mosque started life as the 11th-century Church of St Theodosia. Legend has it that one day before the Conquest, worshippers filled the church with rose petals in St Theodosia's honour and prayed for her intervention against the

Ottomans. Their prayers went unanswered, but the invaders renamed the building Gül (Rose) Mosque after the petals they found on entering.

But legends, however appealing, are rarely true. In reality, the building was used as a shipyard warehouse after the Conquest and wasn't converted into a mosque until the reign of Beyazıt II (r 1481–1512). The extremely high central dome is an Ottoman addition and the pretty minaret dates from the rule of Selim I (r 1512–20).

PALACE OF CONSTANTINE
PORPHYROGENITUS   HISTORIC BUILDING
Map p252 (Palace of the Sovereign, Tekfur Sarayı; Hoca Çakır Caddesi, Edirnekapı; 🚌99, 99A, 99Y, 28 from Eminönü, 55T, 87 from Taksim, 🚢Ayvansaray) Though only a shell these days, the remnants of this Byzantine palace give a good idea of how it would have looked in its heyday. Built in the late 13th or early 14th century, the large three-storied structure may have been an annexe of the nearby imperial Palace of Blachernae, of which few traces exist today.

The building's later uses were not so regal: after the Conquest it functioned in turn as a menagerie for exotic wild animals, a brothel, a poorhouse for destitute Jews, a pottery and finally a car park.

When we visited, restoration of the palace's remaining sections had finished, but it was closed to the public with no opening date forthcoming.

CHURCH OF ST
MARY OF THE MONGOLS   CHURCH
Map p252 (Church of Theotokos Panaghiotissa, Kanlı Kilise; Tevkii Cafer Mektebi Sokak, Fener; ⊙9am-5pm Sat & Sun; 🚌99, 99A, 99Y from Eminönü, 55T from Taksim) Consecrated in the 13th century and saved from conversion into a mosque by the personal decree of Mehmet the Conqueror, this is the only church in İstanbul to remain in Greek hands ever since Byzantine times. It was named after Princess Maria Paleologina, an illegitimate daughter of Emperor Michael VIII Paleologos.

Maria was sent from Byzantium to marry Hulagu, the Great Khan of the Mongols, in 1265. By the time she arrived in his kingdom, he had died, so she was forced to marry his son Abagu instead. On Abagu's death, she returned to Byzantium and retired to a convent attached to this church.

THE ECUMENICAL PATRIARCHATE

The **Ecumenical Patriarchate of Constantinople** (Rum Ortodoks Patrikhanesi; Map p252; ☑0212-531 9670; www.ec-patr.org; Sadrazam Ali Paşa Caddesi, Fener; ☐99, 99A, 99Y from Eminönü, 55T from Taksim) is the symbolic headquarters of the Greek Orthodox Church, and one of the most significant sites in the larger Eastern Orthodox Church. It has been led by 270 Ecumenical Patriarchs since its establishment in 330 AD.

To the Turkish government, the Ecumenical Patriarch is a Turkish citizen of Greek descent nominated by the church and appointed by the government as an official in the Directorate of Religious Affairs. In this capacity the patriarch is the religious leader of the country's Orthodox citizens and is known officially as the Greek Patriarch of Fener (Fener Rum Patriği).

The Patriarchate has been based in a series of churches over its history, including Hagia Eirene (Aya İrini; 272–398), Hagia Sofya (Aya Sofya; 398–1453) and the Church of Pammakaristos (Fethiye Museum; 1456–1587). It moved to its current location in Fener in 1601.

The relationship between the Patriarchate and the wider Turkish community has been strained in the past, no more so than when Patriarch Gregory V was hanged for treason after inciting Greeks to overthrow Ottoman rule at the start of the Greek War of Independence (1821–32).

Current tensions are focused on the Turkish government's refusal to allow the the Patriarchate to reopen the Orthodox Theological School of Halki, located on Heybeliada in the Princes' Islands. Opened in 1844, the school was closed by government order in 1971. The US Commission on International Religious Freedom (USCIRF) is one of the organisations calling on Turkey to reopen the seminary.

The church is usually open on weekends. If the doors aren't open, ring the bell on the outside gate to attract the attention of the caretaker.

CHURCH OF ST STEPHEN OF THE BULGARS
CHURCH

Map p172 (Sveti Stefan Church; Mürsel Paşa Caddesi 85, Fener; ☐99, 99A, 99Y from Eminönü, 55T from Taksim) These days we're accustomed to kit homes and we self-assemble furniture from Ikea but, back in 1871, when this Gothic Revival–style church was constructed from cast-iron pieces shipped down the Danube and across the Black Sea from Vienna on 100 barges, the idea was extremely novel.

The building's interior features screens, a balcony and columns all cast from iron. It is extremely beautiful, with the gilded iron glinting in the hazy light that filters in through stained-glass windows.

The congregation comprises members of the Bulgarian Orthodox Exarchate (Bulgarian Orthodox Church), which broke away from the Greek Ecumenical Orthodox Patriarchate in 1872. This is the church's İstanbul base. The building was closed for restoration at the time of research.

EATING

Head to the Vodina Caddesi area for a mix of hip cafes, excellent restaurants neighbourhood bakeries and supermarkets catering to locals.

KÖMÜR TURK MUTFAĞI
TURKISH €

(☑0212-521 9999; www.komurturkmutfagi.com; Fevzi Paşa Caddesi 18, Fatih; veg portion ₺7-8, meat portion ₺10-15, grills ₺13-32; ⊙5am-11pm; ☑; ☐28 from Eminönü, 87 from Taksim) Located amid the wedding-dress shops on Fatih's main drag is this five-floor Türk *mutfağı* (Turkish kitchen) where brides-to-be join businesspeople and worshippers from the nearby Fatih Mosque for lunch. The gleaming ground-floor space has a huge counter where ready-made dishes are displayed and where fresh meat and fish can be cooked to order.

AGORA MEYHANESI
TURKISH €€

Map p252 (☑0212-631 2136; www.agora meyhanesi.com; Mürselpaşa Caddesi 185, Balat; ⊙11am-midnight; ☎; ☐99, 99A, 99Y from Eminönü, 55T from Taksim) Dating from 1890, this city institution has recently changed hands but its new owner, Turkish film actor and director Ezel Akay, has worked hard to retain its traditional rakı-soaked atmosphere. The mezes are so so, but the menu comes into its own with the seafood mains (₺25), which are excellent. Enter from either Mürselpaşa Caddesi or Leblebiciler Sokak.

FORNO
PIDE, BREAKFAST €€

Map p252 (☑0212-521 2900; www.fornobalat. com; Fener Kireçhane Sokak 13, Fener; pides & pizza ₺16-21; ☉10am-8.30pm Tue-Fri, from 9.30am Sat & Sun; ☐99, 99A, 99Y from Eminönü, 55T from Taksim) In a bright and informal space dominated by a long kitchen table, Forno serves delicious pide, pizza and *lahmacun* (Arabic-style pizza). The weekend breakfast buffet (₺35) is a rich spread replete with towers of bread and mini vegetable kebaps, and the organic apricot soufflé and frozen chocolate cake are delectable.

AZIZ CAFE
CAFE €€

Map p252 (☑0539 280 3749; Yıldırım Caddesi 23, Fener; mains ₺15; ☉8am-7pm; ☎; ☐99, 99A, 99Y from Eminönü, 55T from Taksim) Expats eagerly consume the wi-fi, excellent chocolate brownies (₺8) and less impressive coffee (₺7) at this friendly neighbourhood spot, which fills with İstanbullus on sunny weekends. The limited menu includes *mantı* (Turkish ravioli), chicken or haleoumi salad and a breakfast platter (₺20). The mellow and welcoming atmosphere also makes it a great place for a drink and people watching.

★ASITANE
OTTOMAN €€€

Map p252 (☑0212-635 7997; www.asitane restaurant.com; Kariye Oteli, Kariye Camii Sokak 6, Edirnekapı; starters ₺18-28, mains ₺58; ☉noon-10.30pm; ☑; ☐28 from Eminönü, 87 from Taksim, ☮Ayvansaray) This elegant restaurant next to the Kariye Museum serves Ottoman dishes devised for the palace kitchens at Topkapı, Edirne and Dolmabahçe. Its chefs have been tracking down historic recipes for years, and the menu is full of versions that will tempt most modern palates, including vegetarian.

In the pretty outdoor courtyard or somewhat bland interior, try dishes such as stuffed quince, goose kebap or the 'fatty apron' kebap, featuring lamb and beef wrapped in caul (stomach lining) fat.

DRINKING & NIGHTLIFE

Vodina Caddesi offers the best selection of cafes. Much of the Golden Horn (Haliç) hinterland is conservative Islamic territory and the whole area is quiet after dark.

PIERRE LOTI CAFÉ
CAFE

Map p172 (Gümüşsuyu Balmumcu Sokak 1, Eyüp; ☉8am-midnight; ☮Eyüp) Many visitors head to this hilltop cafe after visiting the Eyüp Sultan Mosque (p118). Named for the famous French novelist who is said to have come here for inspiration, it offers lovely views across the Golden Horn and is a popular weekend destination for locals, who relax over tea, coffee, ice cream and nargiles (water pipes). A cable car (one way ₺4.00; cheaper on an Istanbulkart) to the cafe leaves from near the mosque.

COFFEE DEPARTMENT
COFFEE

Map p252 (☑0532 441 6663; http://coffee department.co; Kürçü Çeşmesi Sokak 5a, Balat; ☉10am-8pm; ☐99, 99A, 99Y from Eminönü, 55T from Taksim) Decked out with big sacks of coffee and wood-and-metal seating, this caffeine-besotted cafe roasts its own beans, and sells bags of coffee and filterdrip coffee-making kits. Kenyan, Ethiopian and Costa Rican beans are on offer, with the Latin American selection set to increase. The Costa Rican makes a smooth flat white (₺9) with apple-pie and milk-chocoloate tastes.

SPORTS & ACTIVITIES

MIHRIMAH SULTAN HAMAMI
HAMAM

Map p252 (☑0212-523 0487; www.mihrimah sultanhamami.com; Fevzi Paşa Caddesi 333, Edirnekapı; bath ₺25, incl scrub & massage ₺45; ☉men 7am-11pm, women 9am-8pm; ☐28 from Eminönü, 87 from Taksim) Visit this restored hamam for an affordable and authentic experience. It lacks the architectural beauty of its counterparts in Sultanahmet, but is satisfyingly clean and has a friendly neighbourhood atmosphere. There are separate sections for men and women.

Beyoğlu

GALATA, TOPHANE & KARAKÖY | İSTIKLAL & AROUND | ÇUKURCUMA & CIHANGIR

Neighbourhood Top Five

❶ ARTER (p129) Visiting cultural institutions such as this art gallery to see why İstanbul is now acknowledged as having one of the world's most exciting visual-art scenes.

❷ Galata Mevlevi Museum (p143) Seeing dervishes whirl in a 15th-century *semahane* (whirling-dervish hall).

❸ Museum of Innocence (p131) Admiring Orhan Pamuk's ambitious and thought-provoking conceptual art project.

❹ Kılıç Ali Paşa Hamamı (p146) Indulging in a traditional hamam treatment in this magnificently restored 16th-century Turkish bath.

❺ Balık Pazarı (p128) Sampling the sights, smells and flavours in this historic market.

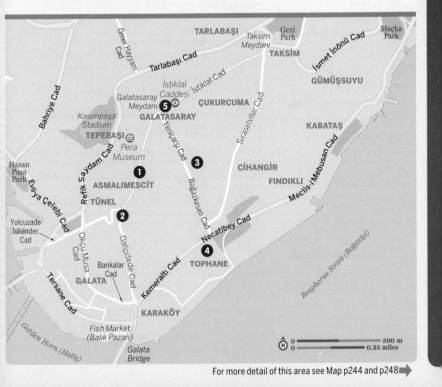

For more detail of this area see Map p244 and p248 ➡

Lonely Planet's Top Tip

The neighbourhoods within Beyoğlu all have distinct and fascinating characters. Be sure to veer off İstiklal Caddesi and explore districts such as Cihangir, Çukurcuma, Tophane, Asmalımescit and Galata.

✕ Best Places to Eat

➡ Antiochia (p134)
➡ Cuma (p140)
➡ Eleos (p135)
➡ Hayvore (p134)
➡ Karaköy Lokantası (p133)
➡ Neolokal (p133)

For reviews, see p131. ➡

🍷 Best Cafes

➡ Dem (p140)
➡ Federal Coffee Company (p137)
➡ Fil (p137)
➡ Karabatak (p137)
➡ Kronotrop (p137)

For reviews, see p137. ➡

🍷 Best Bars & Clubs

➡ 360 (p141)
➡ CUE İstiklal (p142)
➡ Geyik (p137)
➡ Indigo (p141)
➡ Kloster (p142)
➡ Unter (p140)

For reviews, see p140. ➡

BEYOĞLU

Explore Beyoğlu

If you have the time, it makes sense to spread your exploration of this neighbourhood over two days. The first day could be spent in Tophane, Karaköy, Galata and Tünel, visiting sights such as the İstanbul Modern and wandering around the fascinating streets. The second day could be spent walking from Taksim Meydanı (Taksim Sq) along İstiklal Caddesi, veering off into the districts of Cihangir, Çukurcuma, Asmalımescit and Tepebaşı.

If you only have one day, start in Taksim Meydanı and work your way down İstiklal Caddesi, exploring the Balık Pazarı, heading into Tepebaşı to visit the Pera Museum and then making your way through Galata and down to Karaköy. Even if you're staying in another neighbourhood, it makes sense to follow the lead of locals and head here every night for dinner, bar-hopping and clubbing.

Local Life

➡**Streetside cafes** Take a break and enjoy a glass of tea at old-fashioned outdoor cafes such as Cafe Grand Boulevard (p141) off İstiklal Caddesi, Kardeşler Cafe in Cihangir and Cafe Gündoğdu in the square below Galata Tower.

➡**Sugar hits** During the afternoon, recharge with a sweet treat at local institutions İnci Pastanesi (p134) and Karaköy Güllüoğlu (p131).

➡**Tea by the Bosphorus** To enjoy a million-dollar view with a cheap glass of tea, try the ramshackle *çay bahçesi* (tea gardens) at the edge of the Bosphorus, opposite the Fındıklı tram stop. There's even a kids' playground nearby to make toddlers happy.

Getting There & Away

➡**Tram** A tram runs from either Cevizlibağ or Bağcılar in the city's west to Kabataş, near Taksim Meydanı in Beyoğlu, stopping at Sultanahmet, Eminönü, Karaköy and Tophane en route.

➡**Funicular** It's a steep uphill walk from all tram stops to İstiklal, so most commuters use the funiculars that link Karaköy with Tünel Meydanı and Kabataş with Taksim Meydanı.

➡**Metro** Trains travel between Yenikapı on the Sea of Marmara and Taksim Meydanı, stopping at Vezneciler in the Old City, on a bridge over the Golden Horn and in Şişhane (near Tünel Meydanı) en route. From Taksim, the metro continues to Nişantaşı and the ritzy residential and commercial suburbs to its north.

➡**Bus** Buses to every part of the city leave from the bus interchanges underneath Taksim Meydanı and near the tram stop at Kabataş.

 TOP SIGHT
İSTIKLAL CADDESI

Once called the Grand Rue de Pera but renamed İstiklal (Independence) in the early years of the Republic, Beyoğlu's premier boulevard is a perfect metaphor for 21st-century Turkey. A long pedestrianised strip crammed with shops, cafes and cultural centres, it showcases İstanbul's Janus-like personality, embracing modernity one minute and happily bowing to tradition the next.

At İstiklal's northern end is **Taksim Meydanı** (Map p244; Ⓜ Taksim), the symbolic heart of the modern city. At its southern end is the relatively tranquil district of Galata, home to crooked lanes and traces of a fortified settlement built by Genoese merchants in the 13th century.

In the 19th century, new ideas brought from Europe by traders and diplomats walked into Ottoman daily life down the streets of Pera (as Beyoğlu was originally called). Today, the area remains European in flavour and contains most of the city's cultural and entertainment venues. Huge crowds of İstanbullus head here in the early evening and on weekends to promenade the length of İstiklal, shop in the multinational chain stores, visit galleries and cultural centres, listen to street buskers, drink coffee and party in *meyhanes* (taverns). We highly recommend you join them.

DON'T MISS

➡ ARTER (p129)
➡ Balık Pazarı (p128)
➡ Çiçek Pasajı (p129)

PRACTICALITIES

➡ Independence Ave
➡ Map p244, C5
➡ Ⓜ Taksim, Şişhane

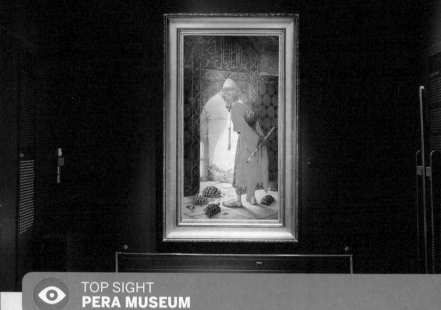

TOP SIGHT
PERA MUSEUM

There's plenty to see at this impressive museum, but the major drawcard is its wonderful exhibition of paintings featuring Turkish Orientalist themes. Drawn from the world-class Kıraç collection, the works provide fascinating glimpses into the Ottoman world from the 17th to 20th centuries and include the most beloved painting in the Turkish canon – Osman Hamdı Bey's *The Tortoise Trainer* (1906; pictured).

As well as opulent portraits of sultans, courtiers and ambassadors, there are quaint scenes of old Stamboul and plenty of depictions of life in the Ottoman harem. After enjoying these, you can choose to head to the upper floors to see high-profile temporary exhibitions (past exhibitions have showcased Warhol, de Chirico, Picasso and Botero), or make your way downstairs to the permanent exhibits on Kütahya tiles and ceramics, as well as Anatolian weights and measures.

Students are given free entry to the museum every Wednesday, and all visitors are given free entry from 6pm to 10pm on Friday. Many museum-goers pop in to the comfortable Pera Café (p134) on the ground floor for coffee and cake, a light lunch or a glass of wine during or after their visit.

DON'T MISS

- ➡ Suna and İnan Kıraç Foundation Collection
- ➡ Temporary exhibitions on the upper floors
- ➡ Kütahya tiles and ceramics on the 1st floor

PRACTICALITIES

- ➡ Pera Müzesi
- ➡ Map p244, A6
- ➡ ☑0212-334 9900
- ➡ www.peramuseum.org
- ➡ Meşrutiyet Caddesi 65, Tepebaşı
- ➡ adult/student/child under 12yr ₺20/10/free
- ➡ ⊙10am-7pm Tue-Thu & Sat, to 10pm Fri, noon-6pm Sun
- ➡ Ⓜ Şişhane, ⓠTünel

⊙ SIGHTS

⊙ Galata, Tophane & Karaköy

İSTANBUL MODERN   GALLERY

Map p248 (İstanbul Modern Sanat Müzesi; ☑0212-334 7300; www.istanbulmodern.org; Meclis-i Mebusan Caddesi, Tophane; adult/student/child under 12yr ₺25/14/free; ☉10am-6pm Tue, Wed & Fri-Sun, to 8pm Thu; 🚋Tophane) This large, lavishly funded and innovative museum has an extensive collection of Turkish art and also stages a constantly changing and uniformly excellent program of mixed-media exhibitions by high-profile local and international artists. Its permanent home is next to the Bosphorus in Tophane, but the massive Galataport redevelopment project currently under way means that it will temporarily relocate to another site in Beyoğlu some time in 2016/17.

MUSEUM OF TURKISH JEWS   MUSEUM

Map p248 (500 Yil Vakfi Türk Musevileri, The Quincentennial Foundation Museum of Turkish Jews; ☑0212-292 6333; www.muze500.com; Büyük Hendek Caddesi 39, Şişhane; adult/child under 12yr ₺20/free; ☉10am-4pm Mon-Thu, to 1pm Fri, to 2pm Sun; Ⓜ Şişhane, 🚋Tünel) Housed in a building attached to the Neve Shalom synagogue near the Galata Tower, this museum was established in 2001 to commemorate the 500th anniversary of the arrival of the Sephardic Jews in the Ottoman Empire, and moved to its current location in 2014. The imaginatively curated and chronologically arranged interactive collection comprises photographs, video, sound recordings and objects that document the history of the Jewish people in Turkey. Visitors must have photo ID with them to enter.

The history of Jews in İstanbul is as long as it is fascinating. Jews were granted freedom of religion and worship in Anatolia by the Seljuks (1077–1308), but weren't treated as liberally by the Byzantines in Constantinople. This led many of them to view the Ottomans as saviours, particularly when Mehmet II made the following offer to Jews fleeing Spain in 1492: 'The God has presented me with many lands and ordered me to take care of the dynasty of his servants Abraham and Jacob...Who, amongst you, with the consent of God, would like to settle in İstanbul, live in peace in the shade of the figs

and vineyards, trade freely and own property?' By the end of the Ottoman Empire, there were tens of thousands of Jews living in the city (10,000 in the neighbourhood of Balat alone, and nearly as many in Hasköy).

Alas, this enlightened state didn't last through the centuries, and Jewish Turks were made to feel considerably less welcome when racially motivated 'wealth taxes' were introduced in 1942; these applied until 1944. Many members of the community emigrated to the newly established nation of Israel between 1947 and 1949 and others left when violence against Jews and other minorities was unleashed in the 1950s. More recently Islamist terrorists have bombed synagogues on a number of occasions, including here at the Neve Shalom and at Şişli's Bet Israel synagogue on 15 November 2003. Twenty-four people (six Jews and 18 Muslims) died as a result of these bombings. Fascinating objects in the museum's collection include an array of Jewish ceremonial regalia with Turkish Ottoman influence, including a 19th-century *hanukkiah* (menorah made just for Hanukkah) in the shape of a minaret. Other highlights include a section about the Ladino language that includes musical recordings.

The Neve Shalom synagogue was built in 1951 and has the largest congregation in the city. It is possible to order kosher food packages to collect from the museum (call at least one day ahead); you can also enjoy a kosher meal in the museum's cafe.

Approximately 17,000 Jews currently live in Turkey, with 1700 residing in İstanbul (most in the suburbs of Nişantaşı, Etiler, Kemerburguz and Gayrettepe). Sephardic Jews make up around 96% of this number, while the rest are primarily Ashkenazic. There are a total of 19 functioning synagogues in the city. For a list of these, and for information about how to visit them, see www.jewish-europe.net/turkey/en/synagogue. To visit decommissioned synagogues in the city, contact the Chief Rabbinate at tjc@tjcomm.org.

GALATA MEVLEVI MUSEUM   MUSEUM

Map p248 (Galata Mevlevihanesi Müzesi; www.galatamevlevihanesimuzesi.gov.tr; Galipdede Caddesi 15, Tünel; admission ₺10; ☉9am-4pm Tue-Sun; Ⓜ Şişhane, 🚋Tünel) The *semahane* (whirling-dervish hall) at the centre of this *tekke* (dervish lodge) was erected in 1491 and renovated in 1608 and 2009. It's part of a complex including a *meydan-ı şerif* (courtyard), *çeşme* (drinking fountain), *türbesi* (tomb) and *hamuşan* (cemetery). The oldest of six historic

BALIK PAZARI

Opposite the grandiose entrance to the 1868 **Galatasaray Lycée** (Galatasaray Lisesi, High School; Map p244; ⓂTaksim), one of the city's most prestigious educational institutions, is the much-loved **Balık Pazarı** (Fish Market; Map p248; Şahne Sokak, off İstiklal Caddesi, Galatasaray; ⓂTaksim). At its entrance are stands selling *midye tava* (skewered mussels fried in hot oil), *kokoreç* (seasoned lamb or mutton intestines wrapped around a skewer and grilled over charcoal) and other snacks. Further inside are shops selling fish, caviar, fruit, vegetables and other produce; most of these are in Duduodaları Sokak on the left (southern) side of the market.

Many of the shops have been here for close on a century and have extremely loyal clienteles. Check out **Sütte Şarküteri** (Map p244; ☑0212-293 9292; Duduodaları Sokak 13; ⊗8am-10pm; ⓂTaksim) for its delicious charcuterie, *kaymak* (clotted cream) and takeaway sandwiches; **Üç Yıldız Şekerleme** (Map p244; ☑0212-293 8170; www.ucyildiz sekerleme.com; Duduodaları Sokak 7; ⊗7am-8.30pm Mon-Sat, 9am-6pm Sun; ⓂŞişhane, 🚠Tünel) for jams, *lokum* (Turkish Delight) and sweets; **Petek Turşuları** (Map p244; ☑0212-249 1324; Duduodaları Sokak; ⊗8.30am-8pm Mon-Sat; 🚠Kabataş, then funicular to Taksim) for pickles; and **Reşat Balık Market** (Map p244; ☑0212-293 6091; www.resatbalikmarket.com; Sahne Sokak 8b; ⓂTaksim) for caviar and the city's best *lakerda* (strongly flavoured salted bonito).

At 24a Şahne Sokak, look for the gigantic black doors to the courtyard of the **Üç Horan Ermeni Kilisesi** (Armenian Church of Three Altars; Map p244; Sahne Sokak 24a; 🚠Kabataş, then funicular to Taksim), an Armenian church dating from 1838. Visitors can enter providing the doors are open. On the opposite side of the street is the neoclassical **Avrupa Pasajı** (European Passage; Map p244; ⓂTaksim), an attractive arcade full of shops that once sold antiques, but now seem to stock little except tourist tat.

Mevlevihaneleri (Mevlevi *tekkes*) remaining in İstanbul, the complex was converted into a museum in 1946.

The Mevlevi *tarika* (order), founded in the central Anatolian city of Konya during the 13th century, flourished throughout the Ottoman Empire. Like several other orders, the Mevlevis stressed the unity of humankind before God, regardless of creed. Taking their name from the great Sufi mystic and poet Celaleddin Rumi (1207–73), called Mevlana (Our Leader) by his disciples, Mevlevis seek to achieve mystical communion with God through a *sema* (ceremony) involving chants, prayers, music and a whirling dance. This *tekke's* first *şeyh* (sheikh) was Şemaî Mehmed Çelebi, a grandson of the great Mevlana.

Dervish orders were banned in the early days of the Turkish Republic because of their ultraconservative religious politics. Although the ban has been lifted, only a handful of functioning *tekkes* remain in İstanbul, including this one and the İstanbul Bilim Sanat Kültür ve Eğitim Derneği in Fatih. Konya remains the heart of the Mevlevi order.

Beneath the *semahane* is an interesting exhibit that includes displays of Mevlevi clothing, turbans and accessories. The *mahfiller* (upstairs floor) houses the *tekke's* collection of traditional musical instruments, calligraphy and *ebru* (paper marbling). The *hamuşan* is full of stones with graceful Ottoman inscriptions, including the tomb of Galip Dede, the 17th-century Sufi poet whom the street is named after. The shapes atop the stones reflect the headgear of the deceased, each hat denoting a different religious rank.

GALATA TOWER
TOWER

Map p248 (Galata Kulesi; www.galatakulesi.org; Galata Meydanı, Galata; adult/child under 12yr ₺25/5; ⊗9am-8.30pm; 🚠Karaköy, 🚠Tünel) The cylindrical Galata Tower stands sentry over the approach to 'new' İstanbul. Constructed in 1348 it was the tallest structure in the city for centuries and it still dominates the skyline north of the Golden Horn. Its vertiginous upper balcony offers 360-degree views of the city, but we're not convinced that the view (though spectacular) justifies the steep admission cost. Be warned that queues can be long and the viewing balcony can get horribly overcrowded. An elevator goes most of the way to the top, but there is one flight of stairs to climb.

CHRIST CHURCH
CHURCH

Map p248 (Crimean Memorial Church; Serdar-i Ekrem Sokak 52, Galata; donation requested; ⊗services 10am Sun; 🚠Tophane) The cornerstone of this Gothic-style Anglican church was laid in 1858 by Lord Stratford de Redcliffe, known as 'The Great Elchi' (*elçi* meaning ambassador) because of his paramount influence in mid-19th-century Ottoman affairs. The largest of the city's Protestant churches, it was dedicated in 1868 as the Crimean Memorial Church and restored and renamed in the mid-1990s.

Inside, there is a painted rood screen by Scottish artist Mungo McCosh that depicts notable İstanbul residents (mainly expats). Services are so wonderfully High that they would almost be at home at St Peter's.

AZAPKAPI SOKOLLU
MEHMET PAŞA MOSQUE
MOSQUE

Map p248 (Tersane Caddesi; MHaliç) This pretty mosque, designed by Sinan and built in 1577, is unusual in that it, and the minaret, are raised on a platform. It was commissioned by Sokollu Mehmet Paşa, a grand *vezir* of Süleyman the Magnificent. Today it's totally overshadowed by the approach to Atatürk/Unkapanı Bridge. Still it's well worth a visit, particularly for its fine marble *mihrab* (niche in a minaret indicating the direction of Mecca) and *mimber* (pulpit in a mosque).

The nearby rococo fountain was built by Saliha Valide Hatun, mother of Mahmut I.

In 2016 the İstanbul Metropolitan Municipality announced a plan to demolish Atatürk Bridge and replace it with a US$34-million tunnel under the Golden Horn connecting the Unkapanı and Kasımpaşa districts. The project's estimated completion date is 2018. If this does eventuate, the mosque will reclaim its grand setting and once again be listed among the city's most impressive imperial mosques.

ARAB MOSQUE
MOSQUE

Map p248 (Arap Camıı; Galata Mahkemesi Sokak, Galata; MKaraköy) Built by the Genoese in 1337, this fortress-like mosque was the largest of İstanbul's Latin churches. Converted to a mosque after the Conquest, it was given to the recently arrived community of Spanish Muslims after their expulsion from Spain in the late 15th century. Notable features include the stone exterior and a magnificent wooden ceiling.

SALT GALATA
CULTURAL CENTRE

Map p248 (☑0212-334 2200; www.saltonline. org/en; Bankalar Caddesi 11, Karaköy; ☑noon-8pm Tue-Sat, to 6pm Sun; MKaraköy) FREE The descriptor 'cultural centre' is used a lot in

İstanbul, but is often a misnomer. Here at SALT Galata it really does apply. Housed in a magnificent 1892 bank building designed by Alexandre Vallaury and cleverly adapted by local architectural firm Mimarlar Tasarım, the cutting-edge institution offers an exhibition space, auditorium, arts research library, cafe and glamorous restaurant.

Funded by the Garanti Bank, SALT aims to be a centre of learning and debate in the city and hosts regular conferences, lectures and workshops. The building also houses a small Ottoman Bank Museum.

DEPO
CULTURAL CENTRE

Map p248 (☑0212-292 3956; www.depoistanbul. net; Lüleci Hendek Caddesi 12, Tophane; ☑11am-7pm Tue-Sun; MTophane) FREE Occupying a former tobacco warehouse, this alternative space is operated by Anadolu Kültür (www. anadolukultur.org), a not-for-profit organisation that facilitates artistic collaboration, promotes cultural exchange and stimulates debates on social and political issues relevant to Turkey, the South Caucasus, the Middle East and the Balkans. It hosts talks, art exhibitions and film screenings.

◉ İstiklal & Around

İSTIKLAL CADDESI
STREET

See p125.

PERA MUSEUM
MUSEUM

See p126.

ARTER
GALLERY

Map p248 (☑0212-708 5800; www.arter.org.tr; İstiklal Caddesi 211; ☑11am-7pm Tue-Thu, noon-8pm Fri-Sun; MŞişhane, ☑Tünel) FREE A stunning marble spiral staircase, prominent location on İstiklal Caddesi and an international exhibition program featuring the likes of Mona Hatoum, Sarkis, Marc Quinn, Patricia Piccinini and Sophia Pompéry make this four-floor art space one of the most prestigious art venues in town.

ÇIÇEK PASAJI
HISTORIC BUILDING

Map p244 (Flower Passage; İstiklal Caddesi; MTaksim) Back when promenading down the Grand Rue de Pera (now İstiklal Caddesi) was the height of fashion, the Cité de Pera building was İstanbul's most glamorous address. Built in 1876 and decorated in Second Empire style, it housed a shopping arcade and apartments. The arcade is now known as the Çiçek Pasajı and is full of *meyhanes* (taverns) serving mediocre food.

As Pera declined in the mid-20th century, so too did this building. Its once-stylish shops gave way to rough *meyhanes* where beer barrels were rolled out onto the pavement, wooden stools were arranged and enthusiastic revellers caroused the night away. It continued in this vein until the late 1970s, when parts of the building collapsed. When it was reconstructed, the arcade acquired a glass canopy to protect pedestrians from bad weather, its makeshift barrels and stools were replaced with solid wooden tables and benches, and its broken pavement was covered with smooth tiles. These days its raffish charm is nearly gone and most locals bypass the touts and the mediocre food on offer and instead make their way behind the passage to the bars and *meyhanes* on or around Nevizade Sokak.

PERA PALACE HOTEL
HISTORIC BUILDING

Map p248 (Pera Palas Oteli; ☎0212-377 4000; www.perapalace.com; Meşrutiyet Caddesi 52, Tepebaşı; Ⓜ Şişhane, 🚇Tünel) The Pera Palace was a project of Georges Nagelmackers, the Belgian entrepreneur who linked Paris and Constantinople with his famous *Orient Express* train service. The 1892 building has undergone a €23-million restoration in recent years and claims to have regained its position as İstanbul's most glamorous hotel (p184). Its bar, tea lounge, patisserie and restaurant are open to the public.

Nagelmackers founded the Compagnie Internationale des Wagons-Lits et Grands Express Européens in 1868. The *Orient Express* service first operated in 1883 and the entrepreneur soon realised that İstanbul had no suitably luxurious hotels where his esteemed passengers could stay. His solution was to build one himself and he commissioned the fashionable İstanbul-born but French-trained architect Alexandre Vallaury to design it.

On opening, the hotel advertised itself as having 'a thoroughly healthy situation, being high up and isolated on all four sides', and 'overlooking the Golden Horn and the whole panorama of Stamboul'. Its guests included Agatha Christie, who supposedly wrote *Murder on the Orient Express* in room 411; Mata Hari, who no doubt frequented the elegant bar with its lovely stained-glass windows and excellent eavesdropping opportunities; and Greta Garbo, who probably enjoyed her own company in one of the spacious suites.

AYA TRIADA
CHURCH

Map p244 (Hagia Triada; Meşelik Sokak, Taksim; ⊘8.30am-6pm; Ⓜ Taksim) Built in 1880, this is İstanbul's largest Greek Orthodox church and has a small but loyal congregation. Attacked during the appalling anti-minority events of 6–7 September 1955, it was extensively damaged and pillaged but managed to survive an arson attempt. Finally restored in the first years of the new millennium, it was re-inaugurated in 2003.

İSTANBUL ARAŞTIRMALARI ENSTİTÜSÜ
CULTURAL CENTRE

Map p244 (İstanbul Research Institute; ☎0212-334 0900; http://en.iae.org.tr; Meşrutiyet Caddesi 47, Tepebaşı; ⊘10am-7pm Mon-Sat; Ⓜ Şişhane, 🚇Tünel) FREE Associated with the nearby Pera Museum, this institution incorporates a publicly accessible research library focusing on the cultural and social history of İstanbul during the Byzantine, Ottoman and Republican periods. It also stages temporary exhibitions, conferences and seminars dealing with this subject.

GALERI NEV
GALLERY

Map p244 (☎0212-252 1525; www.galerinevistanbul.com; 4th fl, Mısır Apt, İstiklal Caddesi 163; ⊘11am-6.30pm Tue-Sat, closed Sat Jul & Aug; Ⓜ Şişhane, 🚇Tünel) One of the city's oldest and most impressive commercial galleries, Nev numbers many of the country's best-known modernists among its stable of artists.

GALERIST
GALLERY

Map p248 (☎0212-252 1896; www.galerist.com.tr; 1st fl, Meşrutiyet Caddesi 67, Tepebaşı; ⊘11am-7pm Tue-Sat; Ⓜ Şişhane, 🚇Tünel) Located in one of the city's most fashionable enclaves, this highly regarded commercial gallery shows Turkish and international artists working in a variety of media. It has a second space in the rapidly gentrifying Golden Horn suburb of Hasköy.

MIXER
GALLERY

Map p244 (☎0212-243 5443; www.mixerarts.com; basement, Sıraselvıler Caddesi 35, Taksim; ⊘11am-7pm Tue-Sat; Ⓜ Taksim) Its avowed purpose is to discover emerging artists and make unique artworks accessible to all, and since opening in Tophane in 2012 Mixer has done a good job in both areas. This new space in Taksim opened in late 2015 and has hosted a number of exciting group shows. Its 'Mixer Editions' program offers original artworks at affordable prices.

AKBANK ART CULTURAL CENTRE

Map p244 (Akbank Sanat; ☑0212-252 3500; www.
akbanksanat.com; İstiklal Caddesi 8; ☉10.30am-
7.30pm Tue-Sat; ⓂTaksim) **FREE** Turkey's big
banks and philanthropic trusts vie to be seen
as the greatest sponsor of the arts. İstiklal
is a showcase for their generosity, and with
this venue Akbank joins ARTER in offering
a stage for the city's thriving arts scene. It
has an art gallery, performance hall, dance
studio and arts library. The centre is the venue for the Akbank-sponsored **İstanbul Jazz**
(http://caz.iksv.org/en) and **Akbank Short Film**
(Akbank Kısa Film Festivali; www.akbanksanat.com)
festivals as well as for performances by the
Akbank Chamber Orchestra. It also pub-
lishes the *Contemporary Art Map İstanbul,* a
handy bi-monthly guide to art events around
town. This is available at cafes, design shops
and galleries, or online through its website.

⊙ Çukurcuma & Cihangir

⭐**MUSEUM OF INNOCENCE** MUSEUM

Map p248 (Masumiyet Müzesi; ☑0212-252 9738;
www.masumiyetmuzesi.org; Çukurcuma Caddesi,
Dalgıç Çıkmazı 2; adult/student ₺25/10; ☉10am-
6pm Tue-Sun, to 9pm Thu; 🚈Tophane) The painstaking attention to detail in this fascinating
museum/piece of conceptual art will certainly provide every amateur psychologist
with a theory or two about its creator, Nobel
Prize–winning novelist Orhan Pamuk. Vit-
rines display a quirky collection of objects
that evoke the minutiae of İstanbullu life in
the mid- to late 20th century, when Pamuk's
novel of the same name is set.

Occupying a modest 19th-century timber house, the museum relies on its vit-
rines, which are reminiscent of the work of
American artist Joseph Cornell, to retell the
story of the love affair of Kemal and Füsun,
the novel's protagonists. These displays are
both beautiful and moving. Some, such as
the installation using 4213 cigarette butts,
are as strange as they are powerful.

Pamuk's 'Modest Manifesto for Museums' is reproduced on a panel on the ground
floor. In it he asserts: 'The resources that
are channeled into monumental, symbolic
museums should be diverted to smaller museums that tell the stories of individuals'.
The individuals in this case are fictional, of
course, and their story is evoked in a highly
nostalgic fashion, but in creating this museum Pamuk has put his money where his

mouth is and come out triumphant. Hiring
an audio guide (₺5) provides an invaluable
commentary and is highly recommended.

THE EMPIRE PROJECT GALLERY

Map p248 (☑0212-292 5968; www.theempire
project.com; Defterdar Yokuşu 35, Cihangir;
☉11am-6.30pm Tue-Sat; 🚈Tophane) Operating
since 2011, The Empire Project is one of the
most interesting commercial galleries in the
city. Curatorially its focus is on artists whose
influences lie in the Mediterranean, Arabian
Peninsula, Eastern Europe and Central Asia
rather than Western Europe. Buzz for entry
and then head to the upstairs gallery spaces.

EATING

As is the case in all big international
cities, the dining scene in İstanbul
can change at a fast and furious pace,
meaning that what's hot one month
can be closed due to lack of patrons
the next. What can be relied on are the
many eateries in this part of town that
take pride in serving traditional Turkish
regional food, and the growing number
of casual places delivering clever modern
rifts on old-fashioned favourites using
locally sourced, seasonal produce.

✖ Galata, Tophane & Karaköy

⭐**KARAKÖY GÜLLÜOĞLU** SWEETS, BÖREK €

Map p248 (☑0212-293 0910; www.karakoy
gulluoglu.com; Katlı Otopark, Kemankeş Caddesi, Karaköy; portion baklava ₺8-17, portion börek
₺7.50-8; ☉7am-11pm Sun-Thu, 8am-11.30pm
Fri & Sat; 🚈; 🚈Karaköy) This much-loved
baklavacı (baklava shop) opened in 1949
and was the first İstanbul branch of a business established in Gaziantep in the 1820s.
A family feud has since led to the opening
of other Güllüoğlu offshoots around town,
but this remains the best. Pay for a *porsiyon*
(portion) of whatever takes your fancy at the
register, then order at the counter.

The most popular baklava flavours are
fıstıklı (pistachio) and *cevizli* (walnut), and
many regulars order a serve of *kaymak*
(clotted cream) on the side. A glass of tea
will take the edge off the sweetness. Note
that the *börek* (filled pastry) here is good,
too.

Neighbourhood Walk
Galatasaray to Galata

START GALATASARAY MEYDANI
END SALT GALATA
LENGTH 1.4KM; TWO HOURS

Start this walk in front of the ❶ **Galat-asaray Lycée** (p128), a prestigious public school located on the corner of İstiklal and Yeniçarşı Caddesis. Established in 1868 by Sultan Abdül Aziz, it educates the sons of İstanbul's elite. Walk south down İstiklal and you'll pass the neo-Gothic ❷ **St Anthony's Cathedral** on your left. Built between 1906 and 1911, it is one of two churches fronting the street in this stretch. Further south is the ❸ **Netherlands Consulate General**, a handsome building renovated in 1854 by the Swiss-born Fossati brothers, who designed many buildings for Sultan Abdülmecit I.

Crossing Postacılar Sokak, you'll see ❹ **ARTER** (p129), one of the city's most exciting cultural centres. Continuing down İstiklal, the next major building is the ❺ **Russian Consulate**, a grand building designed by the Fossati brothers and built in 1837. From here, veer left down steep Kumbaracı Yokuşu and then into the first street on your right. Walk up the hill past ❻ **Christ Church** (p128) and then veer right and sharp left into one of Beyoğlu's most interesting shopping streets, Serdar-ı Ekrem Caddesi. One of İstanbul's most desired residential addresses, the historic ❼ **Doğan Apartments**, is on the left. Home to artists, writers, celebrities and expats, the 1895 complex has a beautiful central garden and a handsome entrance featuring stained-glass panels.

Continue straight ahead to ❽ **Galata Tower** (p128) and then head down winding Camekan and Bereketzade Medresesi Sokaks. You'll eventually come to the sculptural ❾ **Camondo Stairs**, commissioned and paid for by the famous Jewish banking family of the same name. At the bottom is Bankalar Caddesi, centre of the city's prosperous banking industry in the 19th century. It's now home to the ❿ **SALT Galata** (p129) cultural centre, a former bank building that now hosts a library, Ottoman banking museum, temporary exhibition space, cafe and restaurant.

MAVRA
CAFE €

Map p248 (✐0212-252 7488; Serdar-ı Ekrem Caddesi 31, Galata; breakfast ₺16-32, sandwiches ₺12-24, pastas ₺18-22; ⊙9.30am-1am; 🛜✐; Ⓜ Şişhane, ⛟Tünel) Serdar-ı Ekrem Caddesi is one of the most interesting streets in Galata, full of ornate 19th-century apartment blocks and avant-garde boutiques. Mavra was the first of the cafes to open on the strip, and remains one of the best, offering simple food and drinks amid thrift-shop chic decor.

NAMLI GURME
DELI €

Map p248 (✐0212-293 6880; http://namligurme. com.t/; Rıhtım Caddesi 1, Karaköy; breakfast plate ₺19.50, sandwiches ₺6-14, mezes ₺38 per 1kg; ⊙7am-10pm; ✳🛜✐; ⛟Karaköy) As well as being one of the best delicatessens in the city, Namlı offers a tempting sit-down or takeaway selection of breakfast dishes, sandwiches, salad and mezes. Its weekend brunch is justly famous (expect to queue for a table), with patrons choosing from the meze array and paying by the weight of their plate.

★KARAKÖY LOKANTASI
TURKISH €€

Map p248 (✐0212-292 4455; www.karakoy lokantasi.com; Kemankeş Caddesi 37a, Karaköy; mezes ₺10-24, lunch portions ₺13-25, mains ₺28-55; ⊙noon-4pm & 6pm-midnight Mon-Sat, 6pm-midnight Sun; ✳🛜; ⛟Karaköy) Known for its gorgeous tiled interior, genial owner and bustling vibe, Karaköy Lokantası serves tasty and well-priced food to its loyal local clientele. It functions as a *lokanta* (eatery serving ready-made food) during the day, but at night it morphs into a *meyhane* (tavern), with slightly higher prices. Bookings are essential for dinner.

KARAKÖY GÜMRÜK
MODERN TURKISH €€

Map p248 (✐0212-244 2252; http://karakoy gumruk.com.tr; Gümrük Sokak 4, Karaköy; snacks & small plates ₺22-45, mains ₺23-52; ⊙10am-midnight Mon-Sat; ✳🛜; ⛟Karaköy) An exemplar of the casually stylish restaurant model that has been trending in İstanbul for a few years now, Gümrük has a menu that changes each day according to what's fresh at the market. Dishes are often clever twists on classic Turkish street food – think beautifully presented pilafs, flavourful offal dishes and a delectable *balık ekmek* (fish sandwich).

DANDIN
CAFE €€

Map p248 (✐0212-245 3369; www.dandin.co; Kılıçalipaşa Mescidi Sokak 17a, Karaköy; sandwiches ₺21-26, cakes ₺8-15; ⊙10am-11pm Sun-Thu, to midnight Fri & Sat; ✳🛜✐; ⛟Tophane) A decadent array of cakes and pastries provide the headline act at this happening cafe, with savoury treats, including pizzas and sandwiches, supplying a trusty backup. The loft-like white space, with its hanging brass lamps and huge tiled counter, is a lovely environment in which to enjoy them accompanied by fresh juice, good espresso coffee or herbal tea.

GÜNEY
TURKISH €€

Map p248 (✐0212-249 0393; www.guney restaurant.com; Galata Kulesı Meydanı 2, Galata; mezes ₺8-24, grills ₺21-44; ⊙8am-1am; ✐🔧; ⛟Karaköy, ⛟Tünel) Once a reliable but no-frills *lokanta,* Güney has been spruced up recently but has retained its loyal local following. The outdoor tables are popular with smokers and beer drinkers, but it's more demure inside. Diners can choose from the offerings in the bain-marie or order pizza, pasta, sandwiches and grills from the friendly waiters.

CAFE PRIVATO
CAFE €€

Map p248 (✐0212-293 2055; Tımarcı Sokak 3b, Galata; breakfast ₺40; ⊙9am-10.30pm; 🛜✐; Ⓜ Şişhane, ⛟Tünel) The enclave off Galipdede Caddesi in Galata has been reinvented in the past couple of years, trading in its rough-and-ready heritage for hipster credentials. Privato is one of the best-loved of the recent cafe arrivals and is well worth visiting for its *köy kahvaltası* (village breakfast) or for a drink (espresso and Turkish coffee, range of herbal teas, house-made *limonata* – lemonade).

★NEOLOKAL
MODERN TURKISH €€€

Map p248 (✐0212-244 0016; www.neolokal. com; 1st fl, SALT Galata, Bankalar Caddesi 11, Karaköy; mains ₺42-62; ⊙6-11pm Tue-Sun; ✳🛜; ⛟Karaköy) Chef Maksut Aşkar opened this swish eatery in late 2014 and has been wowing local and international diners with his exciting twists on traditional Turkish food ever since. Utilising ingredients listed on the Slow Food Foundation's Ark of Taste, his refined and delicious dishes are enjoyed alongside the spectacular Old City views offered from both the dining room and terrace. The restaurant is accessed via a staircase in the ground-floor cafe – sadly, the food served there is nowhere near as impressive as its upstairs counterpart.

✖ İstiklal & Around

★HAYVORE
LOKANTA €

Map p244 (✐0212-245 7501; www.hayvore.com; Turnacıbaşı Sokak 4, Galatasaray; soups ₺6-10, pides ₺16-23, portions ₺10-20; ⏰11.30am-11pm; ❄️📶♿; 🚇Taksim) Notable *lokantas* (traditional eateries serving ready-made dishes) are few and far between in modern-day Beyoğlu, so the existence of this bustling place next to the Galatasaray Lycée is to be wholeheartedly celebrated. Specialising in Black Sea cuisine, its delicious leafy greens, pilafs, *hamsi* (fresh anchovy) dishes, soups and pides (Turkish-style pizza) are best enjoyed at lunch – go early to score a table.

HELVETIA LOKANTA   TURKISH €

Map p248 (📞0212-245 8780; General Yazgan Sokak 8a, Tünel; mixed plate ₺12.50-15; ⏰noon-10pm Mon-Sat; 🖊️; 🚇Şişhane, 🚇Tünel) This tiny *lokanta* with its open kitchen is popular with locals, who head here to enjoy the freshly prepared, vegetarian-friendly fare. Choose up to five of the home-style dishes for your plate and enjoy them in the relaxed dining space. No alcohol, and cash only.

İNCI PASTANESI   DESSERTS €

Map p244 (Mis Sokak 18; profiteroles ₺7; ⏰7am-midnight; ❄️; 🚇Taksim) A Beyoğlu institution, İnci was forced out of its historic İstiklal Caddesi premises in 2012, but has reopened here and continues to delight devotees with its profiteroles covered in chocolate sauce. We're also particularly partial to the moist chocolate cake filled with candied fruit, but usually ask the staff to hold the chocolate topping.

ÇUKUR MEYHANE   TURKISH €

Map p244 (📞0212-244 5575; basement, Kartal Sokak 1a, Galatasaray; mezes ₺7-10, mains ₺15-20; ⏰6pm-1am Mon-Sat; ❄️; 🚇Taksim) Despite their long and much-vaunted tradition in the city, it is becoming increasingly difficult to find *meyhanes* (taverns) serving good food. Standards have dropped in many of our old favourites (sob!), and we're constantly on the search for replacements. Fortunately, Çukur fits the bill. On offer are a convivial cafeteria-style atmosphere, great food and relatively cheap prices. No English spoken.

PERA CAFÉ   CAFE €

Map p244 (www.peramuseum.org; Pera Museum, Meşrutiyet Caddesi 65, Tepebaşı; sandwiches ₺15-16, pastas ₺18-20, cakes ₺7-12; ⏰10am-7pm Tue-Thu & Sat, to 10pm Fri, noon-6pm Sun; ❄️🛜; 🚇Şişhane, 🚇Tünel) Decorated in art deco style (as befits its location in a building that originally housed the swish Bristol Hotel), this ground-floor cafe in the Pera Museum is a comfortable and extremely convenient pit stop for art-goers. Pop in for coffee and cake, or opt for something more substantial – it serves pastas, sandwiches and salads and even has an alcohol licence.

ASMALI CANIM CIĞERIM   ANATOLIAN €

Map p248 (Minare Sokak 1, Asmalımescit; portion ₺26, half portion ₺18, dürüm ₺14; 🚇Şişhane, 🚇Tünel) The name means 'my soul, my liver', and this small place behind the Ali Hoca Türbesi specialises in grilled liver served with herbs, *ezme* (spicy tomato sauce) and grilled vegetables. If you can't bring yourself to eat offal, fear not – you can substitute the liver with lamb. No alcohol, but *ayran* (yogurt drink) is the perfect accompaniment.

ZENCEFIL   VEGETARIAN €

Map p244 (📞0212-243 8234; Kurabiye Sokak 8; soup ₺9, mains ₺15-21; ⏰10am-11pm Mon-Sat, noon-10pm Sun; 🛜🖊️; 🚇Taksim) We're not surprised this vegetarian cafe has a loyal following. Its interior is comfortable and stylish, with a glassed courtyard and bright colour scheme, and its food is 100% homemade, fresh and varied. Dishes are either vegetarian or vegan and are available in small and large sizes. There's a small cover charge for the home-baked bread and herb butter. 'Zencefil' means 'ginger' in Turkish, and the cafe makes its own ginger beer and ginger ale. You can order wine by the glass and fresh *limonata* (lemonade) served with vodka.

★ANTIOCHIA   SOUTHEASTERN ANATOLIA €€

Map p248 (📞0212-244 0820; www.antiochiaconcept.com; General Yazgan Sokak 3, Tünel; mezes & salads ₺13-18, pides ₺21-22, kebaps ₺24-52; ⏰noon-midnight Mon-Sat; ❄️🛜♿; 🚇Tünel) Dishes from the southeastern city of Antakya (Hatay) are the speciality here. Cold mezes feature olives and wild herbs, and hot choices include delicious *içli köfte* (ground lamb and onion with a bulgar coating)and *özel peyniri* (special fried cheese). Kebaps are exceptional – try the succulent *şiş et* (grilled lamb). Set dinner meals offer excellent value and there's a 20% discount at lunch, when pides reign supreme.

★ZÜBEYIR OCAKBAŞI   KEBAP €€

Map p244 (📞0212-293 3951; Bekar Sokak 28; mezes ₺10, kebaps ₺28-38; ⏰noon-midnight; ❄️🛜; 🚇Taksim) Every morning the chefs at this popular *ocakbaşı* (grill house) prepare the fresh, top-quality meats – spicy chicken wings and Adana kebaps, flavoursome ribs, pungent liver kebaps and well-marinated lamb *şiş* kebaps – to be grilled over handsome copper-hooded barbecues that night. Their offerings are famous throughout the city, so booking a table is essential.

SOFYALI 9
TURKISH €€

Map p248 (📞0212-252 3810; www.sofyali.com.tr; Sofyalı Sokak 9, Asmalımescit; mezes ₺5.50-26, mains ₺26-52; ⏱1pm-midnight Sun-Thu, to 2am Fri & Sat; ❄️🖊️📶; Ⓜ️Taksim, 🚇Tünel) Tables at this *meyhane* are hot property on a Friday or Saturday night, when locals flock here to enjoy the tasty food and convivial atmosphere. Regulars tend to stick to mezes, choosing cold dishes from the waiter's tray and ordering *kalamar tava* (fried calamari), *folyoda ahtapot* (grilled octopus in foil) and *Anavut ciğeri* (Albanian fried liver) from the menu.

KAFE ARA
CAFE €€

Map p244 (📞0212-245 4105; http://kafeara.com; Tosbağ Sokak 2, Galatasaray; sandwiches ₺24-34, pastas ₺26-28, mains ₺26-40; ⏱7.30am-11pm Mon-Thu, to 1am Fri, 10.30am-1am Sat, 10am-11pm Sun; 📶🖊️; Ⓜ️Şişhane, 🚇Tünel) This casual cafe occupies a converted garage in a lane opposite the Galatasaray Lycée and is named after legendary local photographer Ara Güler, whose photographs of the city adorn the walls. It serves an array of well-priced salads, sandwiches and Turkish comfort food. Enjoying Sunday brunch (₺35) at one of the lane tables is particularly pleasant. No alcohol.

KLEMURI
ANATOLIAN €€

Map p244 (📞0212-292 3272; www.klemuri.com; 1st fl, Büyük Parmakkapı Sokak 2; soup ₺6-7, mains ₺15-26; ⏱noon-11pm Mon-Sat; 📶🖊️; Ⓜ️Taksim) The Laz people hail from the Black Sea region, and their cuisine relies heavily on fish, kale and dairy products. One of only a few Laz restaurants in the city, Klemuri serves home-style cooking in bohemian surrounds. There are plenty of choices for vegetarians and vegans and a dessert (Laz *böreği*; ₺10) that has attained a cult following.

HACI ABDULLAH
LOKANTA €€

Map p244 (📞0212-293 8561; www.haciabdullah. com.tr; Sakız Ağacı Caddesi 9a; veg portions ₺14-25, meat portions ₺32-37; ⏱11.30am-10.30pm; ❄️📶🖊️; Ⓜ️Taksim) This upmarket İstanbul institution (it was established in 1888) serves a good, albeit pricey, range of *hazır yemek* (ready-made food). There's no alcohol, but the range of delicious desserts well and truly compensates (try the quince dessert with clotted cream). Come for lunch rather than dinner and be prepared for the double whammy of cover and service charges.

★ELEOS
MEYHANE €€€

Map p248 (📞0212-244 9090; www.eleos restaurant.com; 2nd fl, İstiklal Caddesi 231, Tünel; mezes ₺10-30, mains from ₺30; ⏱2.30pm-midnight; ❄️📶🖊️; Ⓜ️Şişhane, 🚇Tünel) Hidden upstairs in the shabby Hıdivyal Palas building, Eleos transports its diners from Beyoğlu to the Greek islands. A stylish blue-and-white decor and fabulous Bosphorus view set the scene, and the food seals the deal – colourful mezes featuring plenty of herbs and garlic, tender octopus and calamari, perfectly grilled fish and fresh fruit to finish. Advance bookings essential.

MEZE BY LEMON TREE
MODERN TURKISH €€€

Map p248 (📞0212-252 8302; www.mezze.com. tr; Meşrutiyet Caddesi 83b, Tepebaşı; mezes ₺14-39, mains ₺40-56, 4-course degustation menu for 2 ₺196; ⏱6pm-midnight; ❄️🖊️; Ⓜ️Şişhane, 🚇Tünel) Chef Gençay Üçok creates some of the most interesting and delicious modern Turkish food seen in the city and serves it in an intimate restaurant opposite the Pera Palace Hotel. Regulars tend to opt for the degustation menu, or choose from the wonderful array of hot and cold mezes rather than ordering mains. Bookings essential.

SAHRAP
MODERN TURKISH €€€

Map p248 (📞0212-243 1616; www.sahrap restaurant.com; General Yazgan Sokak 13a, Asmalımescit; mezes ₺12-22, mains ₺28-42; ⏱noon-11pm Mon-Sat, 6-11pm Sun; ❄️🖊️📶; Ⓜ️Şişhane, 🚇Tünel) Popular cookbook writer and TV chef Sahrap Soysal oversees the menu here, and the result is a tasty and well-priced introduction to modern Turkish cuisine. The two-level dining space is attractively decorated and Sahrap's food is fresh and full of flavour, with an emphasis on legumes, seasonal vegetables and seafood.

ASMALI CAVIT
TURKISH €€€

Map p248 (Asmalı Meyhane; 📞0212-292 4950; Asmalımescit Sokak 16, Asmalımescit; mezes ₺10-25, kebabs ₺30-45; ⏱10.30am-1.30am Mon-Sat; Ⓜ️Şişhane, 🚇Tünel) Cavit Saatcı's place is an old-style *meyhane* (tavern) that, like other old-timers on this street, has stood the test of time and retained a loyal local following. The menu offers all the usual dishes (mezes, fried calamari, *börek* stuffed with meat, fried liver, kebaps). Tables are spread over two floors and are almost always full, so bookings are essential.

AHESTE
MODERN TURKISH €€€

Map p248 (☏0212-243 2633; www.aheste restaurant.com; Meşrutiyet Caddesi 107, Asmalımescit; breakfast plate ₺36, mezes ₺13-31, mains ₺38-67; ◷6pm-midnight Mon-Fri, 9am-3pm & 6pm-midnight Sat & Sun; ❄ ✐; Ⓜ Şişhane, 🚇 Tünel) A perfect example of the design-driven eatery that has been trending in İstanbul over the past few years, Aheste is known for its attractive, mood-lit interior and excellent weekend breakfast/brunch. Dinners can be uneven in quality – we've enjoyed delicious mezes here, but have been disappointed with our main courses.

MIKLA
MODERN TURKISH €€€

Map p248 (☏0212-293 5656; www.miklarestaurant.com; Marmara Pera Hotel, Meşrutiyet Caddesi 15, Tepebaşı; 3-course set menu ₺185, 7-course tasting menu ₺265, wine match ₺165; ◷6pm-1am Mon-Sat; ❄; Ⓜ Şişhane, 🚇 Tünel) The only Turkish restaurant to feature on San Pellegrino's 'World's 100 Best Restaurants' list, Mikla is fronted by local celebrity chef Mehmet Gürs. Sadly, we've found our recent meals here disappointingly executed, lacking both flavour and innovation. At these prices, diners should be delivered more than extraordinary views and luxe surrounds. Vegetarians should steer clear, as meat and fish dominate.

✗ Çukurcuma & Cihangir

SAVOY PASTANESI
CAFE €

Map p244 (☏0212-249 1818; www.savoypastanesi.com; Sıraselviler Caddesi 91a, Cihangir; börek ₺7, millefeuille ₺7.50; ◷7am-11pm Mon-Sat; 🛜 🚹; Ⓜ Taksim) İstanbul has many businesses that have attained iconic status and Savoy is undoubtedly one of them. Down the hill from Taksim Meydanı, it was established in 1950 and is known for its delicious cakes (especially the decadently creamy *millefeuille*), milk puddings, biscuits and *börek*. Sit upstairs or on the streetside terrace.

DATLI MAYA
BAKERY €

Map p248 (☏0212-292 9057; www.datlimaya.com; Türkgücü Caddesi 59, Cihangir; breakfast dishes ₺10-35, pides ₺10-22, lahmacuns ₺5-7, cakes & pastries ₺5-10; ◷9am-10pm Tue-Sun; 🛜 ✐; Ⓜ Taksim) A tiny cafe-bakery located behind the Firuz Ağa Mosque in Cihangir, Datlı Maya is particularly popular with vegetarians, vegans and the gluten-free. The old

wood-fired oven produces vegetable *güveç*s (stews), *lahmacun*s (Arabic pizzas) and pides (Turkish-style pizza), all of which can be taken away or enjoyed in the tiny upstairs dining area.

JOURNEY
CAFE €€

Map p248 (☏0212-244 8989; www.journeycihangir.com; Akarsu Yokuşu 21a, Cihangir; sandwiches ₺19-22, salads ₺19-24, mains ₺18-44; ◷9am-2am Tue-Sun, to 1am Mon; 🛜 ✐ 🚹; Ⓜ Taksim) This laid-back lounge cafe located in the expat enclave of Cihangir serves a great range of Mediterranean comfort foods, including sandwiches, soups, pizzas and pastas. Many of the dishes use organic produce and vegetarian, vegan and gluten-free options are on offer. Locals have been known to claim the front couch for breakfast and stay put until closing time.

ÇUKURCUMA 49
PIZZA €€

Map p244 (☏0212-249 0048; Turnacıbaşı Caddesi 49, Çukurcuma; pizzas ₺18-40; ◷10.30am-10.30pm; ❄ 🛜 ✐ 🚹; Ⓜ Taksim) A hipster vibe, mellow jazz soundtrack and Italian-style pizzas are the drawcards at this neighbourhood favourite. We're fans of the cheap 'desperate house wine' (an extremely quaffable red from Yunatçılar winery on the Aegean island of Bozcaada) and also of the pizza with thyme, mozzarella and *pastırma* (pressed beef preserved in spices). Check the Facebook feed for details of weekly live jazz sessions.

JASH
ANATOLIAN €€

Map p248 (☏0212-244 3042; www.jashistanbul.com; Cihangir Caddesi 9, Cihangir; mezes ₺8-28, mains ₺24-50; ◷noon-2am; ❄; Ⓜ Taksim) Armenian specialities such as *topik* (a cold meze made with chickpeas, pistachios, onion, flour, currants, cumin and salt) make an appearance on the menu of this bijou *meyhane* in trendy Cihangir. Come on the weekend, when there's live music and unusual dishes including *harisa* (chicken with a hand-forged wheat and butter sauce) are on offer.

KAHVE 6
CAFE €€

Map p248 (☏0212-293 0849; Anahtar Sokak 13, Cihangir; breakfast dishes ₺16-23, sandwiches ₺12-23, pastas ₺18-22; ◷9am-10pm; 🛜 ✐; Ⓜ Taksim) An expat haven in Cihangir, Kahve Altı (Coffee 6) has a pretty interior salon and a sunny rear courtyard. The menu is simple, but deserves kudos for emphasising local, natural and seasonal (often organic) produce. No alcohol.

COFFEE CRAZE

Coffee has traditionally played a minor role in the lives of İstanbullus. For the vast majority of locals, çay was the hot beverage of choice and the viscous brew known as *Türk khavesi* (Turkish coffee) was drunk only occasionally. However, all this has changed in recent years and it is safe to say that espresso and other Western-style brews have taken the city by storm. The best cafes in the city are located in Beyoğlu and are popular as meeting points and informal workplaces (the vast majority offer free wi-fi). Others are little more than bars supplying rapid caffeine refuels. The following are our favourites:

Coffee Sapiens (Map p248; ⏎www.coffeesapiens.com; 0212-244 1296; Kılıç Ali Paşa Mescidi 10, Karaköy; ⊙8.30am-11.30pm; 🖰; 🚊Tophane) Serving coffee home-roasted at their facility in Hasköy, these sapiens have well and truly wised up to the science behind the brew. Choose from Aeropress, Chemex, cold brew, French press, espresso or siphon and drink it takeaway, standing at the bar or at an outdoor table overlooking goings-on in Karaköy's hippest lane.

Federal Coffee Company (Map p248; ⏎0212-245 0903; www.federal.coffee; Küçük Hendek Caddesi 7, Galata; ⊙8am-midnight; 🖰; Ⓜ Şişhane, 🚊Tünel) This place advertises itself as an 'Australian Coffee Roaster' and visitors from Down Under will certainly feel at home when sipping a perfectly executed espresso-style coffee in its stylish surrounds. Couches, reading material and wi-fi make it a perfect caffeine-fuelled workspace.

Fil (Map p248; ⏎0212-243 1994; www.filbooks.net; Ali Paşa Değirmeni Sokak 1, Karaköy; ⊙10am-10pm Tue-Sun; 🚊Karaköy) Dedicated to photography books, creative workshops and coffee, this bookshop-cafe in Karaköy is crammed into two floors of a small space that has been stylishly fitted out with a marble bar, comfortable banquettes and upstairs work desks.

Geyik (Map p248; ⏎0532 773 0013; Akarsu Yokuşu 22, Cihangir; ⊙10am-2am; Ⓜ Taksim) Hybrid coffee roastery and cocktail bar? Yep, you read that correctly. Run by one-time Turkish barista champion Serkan İpekli and mixologist Yağmur Engin, this fashionable place is popular with coffee aficionados during the day and barflies at night.

Karabatak (Map p248; ⏎0212-243 6993; www.karabatak.com; Kara Ali Kaptan Sokak 7, Karaköy; ⊙8.30am-10pm Mon-Fri, 9.30am-10pm Sat & Sun; 🖰; 🚊Tophane) Importing dark-roasted Julius Meinl coffee from Vienna, Karabatak's baristas use it to conjure up some of Karaköy's best brews. The outside seating is hotly contested, but the quiet tables inside can be just as alluring. Choose from filter, espresso or Turkish brews.

Kronotrop (Map p248; ⏎0212-249 9271; www.kronotrop.com.tr/en; Firuzağa Cami Sokak 2b, Cihangir; ⊙7.30am-9pm Mon-Fri, 10am-10pm Sat, 10am-9pm Sun; 🖰; Ⓜ Taksim) This hip place opposite the Firuz Ağa Mosque in Cihangir helped spearhead İstanbul's boom in speciality coffee bars. Owned by noted restaurateur Mehmet Gürs, it sources beans from across the globe and roasts them in a purpose-built facility in nearby Maslak. Choose from espresso, cold-drip, filtered, Aeropress, Chemex and traditional Turkish varieties.

Old Java (Map p248; ⏎0212-243 9455; Tartar Beyi Sokak 8, Galata; ⊙10.30am-8pm; 🖰; Ⓜ Şişhane, 🚊Tünel) It's all about the beans. Here they roast their own, make a good brew and offer it in stylish surrounds where 'bean raves', hipster beards, tats and DJ sets are par for the course.

For those wanting to sample Turkish coffee, there's only one possible recommendation: tiny and old-fashioned **Manda Batmaz** (p140), off İstiklal Caddesi.

★**CUMA**　　　　MODERN TURKISH €€€
Map p244 (⏎0212-293 2062; www.cuma.cc; Çukurcuma Caddesi 53a, Çukurcuma; breakfast plate ₺42, lunch dishes ₺19-34, dinner mains ₺30-36; ⊙9am-11pm Mon-Sat, to 8pm Sun; 🖰🍴🆓;

Ⓜ Taksim) Banu Tiryakioğulları's laid-back foodie oasis in the heart of Çukurcuma has one of the most devoted customer bases in the city. Tables are on the leafy terrace or in the atmospheric upstairs dining space,

BYGURZOGLU/SHUTTERSTOCK ©

1. Whirling dervishes (p39)

By whirling, chanting and praying adherents believe they are attaining a higher union with God.

2. Galata Tower (p128)

For centuries after it was built in 1348, Galata Tower was the tallest structure in İstanbul.

3. Balık Pazarı (p128)

As well as fish and caviar, the Fish Market sells a range of other fresh produce, with some stalls residing here for more than a century.

4. Beyoğlu (p131)

The distinct neighbourhoods of this district offer a variety of eating, drinking and relaxation options for any occasion.

MARTINA I. MEYER/SHUTTERSTOCK ©

and the healthy, seasonally driven menu is heavy on flavour and light on fuss – breakfast is particularly delicious (we love the fruit smoothies and house-baked bread).

DEMETI
TURKISH €€€

Map p248 (📞0212-244 0628; www.demeti.com.tr; 1st fl, Şimşirci Sokak 6, Cihangir; mezes ₺10-34, mains ₺34-42; ⏲4pm-2am; 🕿🖋; MTaksim) This neighbourhood *meyhane* (tavern) has a friendly feel and simple but stylish decor. Reservations are a must if you want one of the four tables on the terrace, which have an unimpeded Bosphorus view. There's occasional live music (cover charge applies).

🍷 DRINKING & NIGHTLIFE

There are hundreds of bars in Beyoğlu, with the major bar strips being Balo, Nevizade, Gönül and Sofyalı Sokaks. As a rule, drinks are much cheaper at street-level venues than at rooftop bars. Note that many of the Beyoğlu clubs close over the warmer months (June to September), when the party crowd moves down to Turkey's southern coasts.

🍷 Galata, Tophane & Karaköy

★UNTER
BAR

Map p248 (📞0212-244-5151; www.unter.com.tr; Kara Ali Kaptan Sokak 4, Karaköy; ⏲9am-midnight Tue-Thu & Sun, to 2am Fri & Sat; 🕿; 🚋Tophane) This scenester-free zone epitomises the new Karaköy style: it's glam without trying too hard, and has a vaguely arty vibe. Ground-floor windows open to the street in fine weather, allowing the action to spill outside during busy periods. Good cocktails and decent wine by the glass are major draws, as is the varied food menu (breakfast ₺18 to ₺32, mains ₺27 to ₺48).

DEM
TEAHOUSE

Map p248 (📞0212-293 9792; www.demkarakoy.com; Hoca Tahsin Sokak 17, Karaköy; ⏲10am-11pm; 🚋Tophane) As far from a traditional *çay bahçesi* as one can imagine, Dem serves 60 types of freshly brewed tea in fine china cups and with milk on request. A selection of panini, wraps, cakes and scones is also on offer, and everything is served on street-

side tables or under the ultra-chic Zettel'z 5 light fitting in the main space.

RITIM GALATA
BAR, CAFE

Map p248 (📞0212-292 4929; www.ritimgalata.com; Galata Kulesi Sokak 3, Galata; ⏲11am-11pm, later on Fri & Sat; 🕿; MŞişhane, 🚋Tünel) Weekdays are relatively quiet at this friendly neighbourhood cafe/bar nestled in the shadow of the Galata Tower, but the action heats up when the DJ spins everything from house to pop on Friday and Saturday nights from 9pm. The menu is geared towards drinkers, being filled with cheap comfort food (burgers, pastas, fries).

SENSUS WINE BAR
WINE BAR

Map p248 (📞0212-245 5657; www.sensuswine.com; Büyük Hendek Sokak 5, Galata; ⏲1-11pm; 🕿; MŞişhane, 🚋Tünel) Set in a stone basement lined with wine bottles, this bar beneath the Anemon Galata Hotel has a great concept, but needs to work on its customer service. There are close to 300 bottles of local wine on the shelves, and you can enjoy your choice with a cheese or *şarkuterı* (charcuterie) plate (₺26 to ₺44).

🍷 İstiklal & Around

★MIKLA
BAR

Map p248 (📞0212-2935656; www.miklarestaurant.com; Marmara Pera Hotel, Meşrutiyet Caddesi 15, Tepebaşı; ⏲from 6pm Mon-Sat summer only; MŞişhane, ⊖Tünel) It's worth overlooking the occasional bit of uppity service at this stylish rooftop bar to enjoy excellent cocktails and what could be the best view in İstanbul. In winter the drinking action moves to the bar in the upmarket restaurant one floor down.

★MANDA BATMAZ
COFFEE

Map p244 (Olivia Geçidi 1a, off İstiklal Caddesi; ⏲10am-11pm; MŞişhane, 🚋Tünel) Bored with the brouhaha over modern-day coffee culture? Don't care where your beans have been roasted, or whether your barista's tattoos are on show? If so, this tiny coffee shop is for you. Serving Beyoğlu's best Turkish coffee for over two decades, its cups of ultra-thick aromatic coffee are much cheaper than the indifferently made lattes ubiquitous elsewhere.

SOLERA
WINE BAR

Map p244 (📞0212-252 2719; Yeniçarşı Caddesi 44, Galatasaray; ⏲11am-2am; 🕿; MŞişhane, 🚋Tünel) Stocking more than 300 Turkish wines and pouring an extraordinary 100 by the glass, this atmospherically lit wine cavern is the city's best wine bar. Regulars tend to head here after work for a glass of wine accompanied by a cheese plate (₺22); many stay on for a perfectly cooked steak (₺35). Bookings are essential on Friday and Saturday night.

ALEX'S PLACE   BAR

Map p248 (Gönül Sokak 7, Asmalımescit; ◷6pm-1am Tue-Sat; ⓂŞişhane, ⒻTünel) A hole-in-the-wall speakeasy in the heart of the Asmalımescit entertainment precinct, this place is beloved of local bohemians who work in the arts and cultural sectors. American owner Alex Waldman is passionate about cocktails and his craft creations have been known to convert beer and wine drinkers alike.

CAFE GRAND BOULEVARD   TEA GARDEN

Map p244 (Hazzo Pulo Pasajı; ◷8am-3am; ⓂŞişhane, ⒻTünel) There aren't as many traditional teahouses in Beyoğlu as on the Historic Peninsula, so this *çay bahçesi* (tea garden) in a picturesque cobbled courtyard fringed by secondhand bookshops and vintage boutiques is beloved of locals. To access it from İstiklal Caddesi, head through the narrow passage full of tacky jewellery stands.

360   BAR

Map p244 (☏0533 691 0360; www.360istanbul.com; 8th fl, İstiklal Caddesi 163; ◷noon-2am Sun-Thu, to 4am Fri & Sat; ⛶; ⓂŞişhane, ⒻTünel) İstanbul's most famous bar, and deservedly so. If you can score one of the bar stools on the terrace you'll be happy indeed – the view is truly extraordinary. It morphs into a club after midnight on Friday and Saturday, when a cover charge of ₺50 applies (this includes one drink). The food is overpriced and underwhelming – don't bother with dinner.

PARANTEZ   BAR

Map p248 (☏0212-245 7513; www.parantezbistro.com; Sofyalı Sokak 20, Asmalımescit; ◷10am-3am; ⓂŞişhane, ⒻTünel) Asmalımescit's most popular bar is tiny, so on weekend evenings the action spills out into Jurnal Sokak and a party atmosphere ensues. Fight your way to the bar to order a cocktail or bottled beer – if it's too crowded there are plenty of other bars in the immediate vicinity.

INDIGO   CLUB

Map p244 (☏0212-244 8567; http://indigo-istanbul.com; 1st-5th fl, 309 Akarsu Sokak, Galatasaray; cover varies; ◷11.30pm-5am Fri & Sat, closed

summer; ⓂŞişhane, ⒻTünel) Its popularity has waxed and waned over the years, but Beyoğlu's four-floor electronic music temple is back in big-time favour with the city's dance-music enthusiasts. The program spotlights top-notch local and visiting DJs or live acts, focusing on house, tech house and tech disco, with an occasional electro-rock number thrown into the mix. Smokers congregate on the upstairs terrace.

LEB-I DERYA   BAR

Map p248 (☏0212-293 4989; www.lebiderya.com; 6th fl, Kumbaracı İş Hanı, Kumbaracı Yokuşu 57, Galata; ◷4pm-2am Mon-Thu, to 3am Fri, 10am-3am Sat, to 2am Sun; ⛶; ⓂŞişhane, ⒻTünel) On the top floor of a dishevelled building off İstiklal, Leb-i Derya has wonderful views across to the Old City and down the Bosphorus, meaning that seats on the small outdoor terrace or at the bar are highly prized. Many people enjoy the pricey modern Mediterranean food on offer, but we aren't impressed, so only recommend it as a bar.

RAVOUNA 1906   BAR

Map p248 (☏0212-924 8760; www.cafe.ravouna1906.com; 7th fl, İstiklal Caddesi 201; ◷noon-midnight Mon-Sat, 10am-midnight Sun; ⓂŞişhane, ⒻTünel) A glass eyrie on the roof of a charming art nouveau building on Beyoğlu's major boulevard, this comfortable bar/restaurant commands a panoramic view of the Historical Peninsula and Bosphorus and is a fabulous perch for those wanting to enjoy a sunset drink. It also offers a menu of international dishes, including burgers (₺39), steaks (₺65) and salads (₺25 to ₺30). To access the rooftop, enter the ground-floor cafe, head to the rear and continue up one set of stairs. An elevator will then take you the rest of the way.

CUE İSTIKLAL   CLUB

Map p244 (☏0536 460 7137; 5th fl, Yenıçarşı Caddesi 38, Galatasaray; cover varies; ◷10pm-4am Tue-Sat; ⓂŞişhane, ⒻTünel) A magnificent view, large dance floor, decent sound system and well-made cocktails are the draws at this popular temple to electronica. Check its Twitter and Facebook feeds for who is playing/spinning the deep house, techno and tech house soundtrack.

KLOSTER   CLUB

Map p244 (☏0533 258 9393; http://kloster.com.tr; Kamer Hatun Caddesi 10; cover varies; ◷10pm-6am Wed-Sat; ⓂTaksim) Three floors, three different stages and a famous rooftop

BEYOĞLU DRINKING & NIGHTLIFE

terrace make this temple to electronica the largest club in the city. There are regular appearances by European DJs – check the Facebook feed for details.

TOPLESS TERAS
BAR, CLUB

Map p244 (☑0532 384 1054; www.topless.com.tr; 6th fl, İstiklal Caddesi 12; ☺7pm-2am; Ⓜ Taksim) Amazing views and a deep house soundtrack are the draws at this rooftop venue above the Fitaş Cinema.

HASPA
GAY

Map p244 (☑0212-243 8601; 2nd fl, İpek Sokak 16, Taksim; ☺8pm-2am; Ⓜ Taksim) In an area with a few popular gay bars (including one on the floor above and another in nearby Büyük Parmakappı Sokak), this casual bar hosts live Turkish pop acts and the occasional male belly dancer.

URBAN
BAR, CAFE

Map p244 (☑0212-252 1325; Kartal Sokak 6a, Galatasaray; ☺11am-1am; 🛜; Ⓜ Taksim) A tranquil bolt hole in the midst of İstiklal's mayhem, Urban is where the preclub crowd congregates at night and where many of them can be found kicking back over a coffee during the day. The vaguely Parisian interior is a clever balance of grunge and glamour.

TEK YÖN
GAY

Map p244 (http://clubtekyon.com; 1st fl, Siraselviler Caddesi 63, Taksim; ☺10pm-5am; Ⓜ Taksim) This sleek dance premises features the city's largest gay dance floor as well as a garden popular with smokers and cruisers. The core clientele is hirsute and fashion-challenged (and that includes the drag queens). Cuddly bears abound. To find it, look for the 'İstanbul Club' sign.

OFF PERA
CLUB

Map p248 (☑0212-249 2697; Gönül Sokak 14a, Asmalımescit; no cover; ☺10pm-4am Tue-Sat; Ⓜ Şişhane, 🚡 Tünel) You'll need to squeeze your way into this tiny club, but once inside your persistence is sure to pay off. The DJs perch on a balcony over the bar and the multi-aged crowd spills out onto the street to smoke and catch its breath. Go on a Tuesday night, when Turkish pop dominates the sound system after midnight.

ARAF
CLUB

Map p244 (☑0212-244 8301; www.araf.com.tr; 5th fl, Balo Sokak 32; ☺5pm-4am Tue-Sun; Ⓜ Taksim) Grungy English teachers, Erasmus exchange students and Turkish-language students have long claimed this as their favoured destination, listening to world music and swilling some of the cheapest club beer in the city. No cover.

MINIMÜZIKHOL
CLUB

Map p244 (MMH; ☑0212-245 1718; www.minimuzikhol.com; Soğancı Sokak 7, Cihangir; no cover; ☺10pm-late Fri & Sat; Ⓜ Taksim) Once the mother ship for inner-city hipsters, this small, slightly grungy venue near Taksim isn't the hotspot it once was, but retains a crew of devoted regulars. It's best after 1am.

🍸 Çukurcuma & Cihangir

SMYRNA
BAR

Map p248 (☑0212-244 2466; Akarsu Yokuşu 29, Cihangir; ☺10am-midnight; 🛜; Ⓜ Taksim) The original boho bar on Cihangir's main entertainment strip, Smyrna has a relaxed atmosphere, retro decor and a self-consciously liter-arty clientele. If you decide to make a night of it here, there's simple food available.

CIHANGIR 21
BAR

Map p248 (☑0212-251 1626; Coşkun Sokak 21, Cihangir; ☺9.30am-2.30am; 🛜; Ⓜ Taksim) The great thing about this neighbourhood place is its inclusiveness – the regulars include black-clad boho types, besuited professionals, expat loafers and quite a few characters who defy categorisation. There's beer on tap (Efes and Miller), a smokers' section and a bustling feel after work hours; it's quite laid-back during the day.

5 KAT
BAR

Map p244 (☑0212-293 3774; www.5kat.com; 5th fl, Soğancı Sokak 7, Cihangir; ☺5pm-2am Mon-Fri, 10am-2am Sat, 11am-2am Sun; 🛜; Ⓜ Taksim) This İstanbul institution has been around for over two decades and is a great alternative for those who can't stomach the style overload at many of the high-profile Beyoğlu bars. In winter drinks are served in the boudoir-style bar on the 5th floor; in summer action moves to the outdoor roof terrace. Both have great Bosphorus views.

⭐ ENTERTAINMENT

GALATA MEVLEVI MUSEUM
PERFORMING ARTS

Map p248 (Galata Mevlevihanesi Müzesi; www.galatamevlevihanesimuzesi.gov.tr; Galipdede Caddesi 15, Tünel; ₺70; ⊘performances 5pm Sun; ⓂŞişhane, ☖Tünel) The 15th-century *semahane* (whirling-dervish hall) at this *tekke* (dervish lodge) is the venue for a one-hour *sema* (ceremony) held on Sundays throughout the year. Come early to buy your ticket.

SALON
LIVE MUSIC

Map p248 (✉0212-334 0700; www.saloniksv. com; ground fl, İstanbul Foundation for Culture & Arts, Sadi Konuralp Caddesi 5, Şişhane; ⊘Oct-May; ⓂŞişhane, ☖Tünel) This intimate performance space in the İstanbul Foundation for Culture & Arts (İKSV) building hosts live contemporary music (classical, jazz, rock and world music) as well as theatrical and dance performances. Check its Facebook and Twitter feeds for program details and book through Biletix (p40) or the venue's box office.

NARDIS JAZZ CLUB
JAZZ

Map p248 (✉0212-244 6327; www.nardisjazz. com; Kuledibi Sokak 14, Galata; cover varies; ⊘9.30pm-12.30am Mon-Thu, 10.30pm-1.30am Fri & Sat, closed Jul & Aug; ⓂŞişhane, ☖Tünel) Named after a Miles Davis track, this intimate venue near the Galata Tower is run by jazz guitarist Önder Focan and his wife Zuhal. Performers include gifted amateurs, local jazz luminaries and visiting international artists. It's small, so you'll need to book if you want a decent table. There's a limited dinner/snack menu.

GARAJİSTANBUL
CULTURAL CENTRE

Map p244 (✉0212-244 4499; www.garajistanbul. org; Kaymakem Reşat Bey Sokak 11a, Galatasaray; ⓂŞişhane, ☖Tünel) This performance space occupies a former car garage in a narrow street behind İstiklal Caddesi and is about as edgy as the city's performance scene gets. It hosts contemporary dance performances, poetry readings, theatrical performances and live music (especially jazz).

BORUSAN ART
PERFORMING ARTS

Map p248 (Borusan Sanat; ✉0212-705 8700; www.borusansanat.com/en; İstiklal Caddesi 160a; ⓂŞişhane, ☖Tünel) An exciting privately funded cultural centre on İstiklal, Borusan is housed in a handsome building and hosts classical, jazz, world and new music concerts in its music hall. The occasional dance performance is included in its schedule.

BAŞKA SINEMA
CINEMA

Map p244 (www.baskasinema.com; Halep Pasajı, İstiklal Caddesi 62; ⓂTaksim) Art-house opera-tion screening classic, alternative and experimental films in the Beyoğlu Cinema.

MUNZUR CAFE & BAR
LIVE MUSIC

Map p244 (✉0212-245 4669; www.munzur cafebar.com; Hasnun Galip Sokak 17, Galatasaray; ⊘1pm-4am, music from 9pm; ⓂTaksim) Hasnun Galip Sokak is home to a number of Türkü *evleri*, Kurdish-owned bars where musicians perform live, emotion-charged *halk meziği* (folk music). This simple place, which is two decades old, has a regular line-up of singers and expert *bağlama* (lute) players.

JOLLY JOKER
LIVE MUSIC

Map p244 (✉0212-249 0749; www.jjistanbul. com; Balo Sokak 22; ⊘from 10pm Wed-Sat, closed summer; ⓂTaksim) The gig-goers among the lively multinational crowd here gravitate towards the upstairs bi-level performance hall, which hosts Turkish rock, alternative and pop outfits. Check the website for schedules and cover charges.

🛍 SHOPPING

İstiklal Caddesi has a long history as the city's most glamorous shopping strip, but has lost its sheen in recent years, probably due to the phenomenal popularity of the sleek shopping malls opening in the affluent suburbs north of Beyoğlu. You'll find the city's best book and music shops here, but not much else worthy of comment. Next to the Flower Passage (Çiçek Pasajı; p129), along Şahne Sokak, is Beyoğlu's Fish Market (Balık Pazarı; p128), with stalls selling fruit, vegetables, caviar, pickles and other produce. Leading off the Fish Market is the neoclassical European Passage (Avrupa Pasajı; p128), a pretty passageway with a handful of shops selling tourist wares and antique prints. Aslıhan Pasajı, nearby, is a two-storey arcade bursting with secondhand books. The streets around Tünel Meydanı and Galata Kulesi Meydanı are being colonised by avant-garde fashion and homeware designers and make for exciting shopping. Between the two squares is Galipdede Caddesi, home to a major concentration of musical-instrument shops. Antique stores can be found dotting the narrow winding streets of Çukurcuma, and small fashion ateliers are scattered across Tophane and the

expat enclave of Cihangir. **All three areas are well worth a wander.**

🏠 Galata, Tophane & Karaköy

★ HIÇ
HOMEWARES, HANDICRAFTS

Map p248 (📞0212-251 9973; www.hiccrafts.com; Lüleci Hendek Caddesi 35, Tophane; ⏰10.30am-7pm Mon-Sat; 🚋Tophane) Interior designer Emel Güntaş is one of İstanbul's style icons and this recently opened contemporary crafts shop in Tophane is a favourite destination for the city's design mavens. The stock includes cushions, carpets, kilims (pileless woven rugs), silk scarves, lamps, furniture, glassware, porcelain and felt crafts. Everything here is artisan-made and absolutely gorgeous.

★ NYKS
HOMEWARES

Map p248 (📞0212-252 6957; www.nyks.com.tr; Serdar-ı Ekrem Sokak 49/1a, Galata; Ⓜ Şişhane, 🚋Tünel) Olive-oil candles scented with mint, thyme, bay leaf, pine, lavender, cedar, bergamot, rosemary and green mandarin are presented in gorgeous copper, marble, glass and ceramic containers and offered at this cute shop on one of the city's most attractive shopping streets. Well priced and unusual, they are excellent souvenirs to take home or give to friends and family.

ARTRIUM
ART, JEWELLERY

Map p248 (📞0212-251 4302; www.artrium.com. tr; Müellif Sokak 12, Tünel; ⏰9am-7pm Mon-Sat; Ⓜ Şişhane, 🚋Tünel) Crammed with antique ceramics, calligraphy, maps, prints and jewellery, this Aladdin's cave of a shop is most notable for its exquisite miniatures.

HAMM
HOMEWARES

Map p248 (📞0533 234 1122; www.hamm.com. tr; Boğazkesen Caddesi 71a, Tophane; ⏰10am-7pm Mon-Sat, 11am-5pm Sun; 🚋Tophane) Its location on Boğazkesen Caddesi, near the Tophane tram stop, is one of Beyoğlu's style hubs, and Hamm is a great place to garner an understanding of contemporary Turkish style. It showcases furniture, lighting and homewares designed and made in İstanbul.

MABEL ÇIKOLATA
FOOD

Map p248 (📞0212-244 3462; www.mabel.com. tr; Gümrük Sokak 11, Karaköy; ⏰9am-7pm Mon-Fri, to 4pm Sat; 🚋Karaköy) The city's most beloved chocolate company started trading in 1947 and neither its logo nor this flagship store have changed much since that time. The milk, dark and flavoured varieties are equally delicious, and retro treats such as the chocolate umbrellas are perennially popular. There's another branch in Nişantaşı.

EYÜP SABRI TUNCER
BEAUTY

Map p248 (📞0212-244 0098; www.eyupsabri tuncer.com; Mumhane Caddesi 10, Karaköy; ⏰10am-7pm; 🚋Karaköy) Turks of every age adore the colognes and beauty products produced by this local company, established in 1923. Its *doğal zeytinyağlı* (natural olive oil) body balms and soaps are wonderfully inexpensive considering their quality.

SELDA OKUTAN
JEWELLERY

Map p248 (📞0212-514 1164; www.seldaokutan. com; Ali Paşa Değirmeni Sokak 10a, Tophane; ⏰10am-7pm Mon-Sat; 🚋Tophane) Selda Okutan's sculptural pieces featuring tiny naked figures have the local fashion industry all aflutter. Come to her design studio in Tophane to see what all the fuss is about.

BOU ART & DESIGN
HOMEWARES

Map p248 (📞0212-243 7555; www.bou.com. tr; Mumhane Caddesi 57, Karaköy; 🚋Tophane) Aiming to 'present contemporary pieces and limited designs that add value to daily life', Bou stocks furniture and lighting, as well as glass, metalwork and ceramic objects made by local artisans.

İRONI
HOMEWARES

Map p248 (📞0212-245 7803; www.ironi.com. tr; Camekan Sokak 4e, Galata; ⏰10.30am-8pm; Ⓜ Şişhane, 🚋Tünel) Güney İnan's range of silver-plated Turkish-style homewares includes plenty of options for those wanting to take home a souvenir of their trip. The tea sets (tray, glasses with holders, sugar bowls) are extremely attractive, as are the light fittings.

ARZU KAPROL
CLOTHING

Map p248 (📞0212-252 7571; www.arzukaprol. net; Serdar-ı Ekrem Sokak 22, Galata; Ⓜ Şişhane, 🚋Tünel) Arzu Kaprol is Parisian-trained and lauded throughout Turkey for her exciting designs. Her collections of women's clothing and accessories feature in Paris Fashion Week and are stocked by international retailers, including Harrods in London. This store showcases her sleek prêt-à-porter range.

🏠 İstiklal & Around

⭐**NAHIL** HANDICRAFTS, BATHWARE
Map p244 (📞0212-251 9085; www.nahil.com.tr;
Bekar Sokak 17, Taksim; ⊘10am-7pm Mon-Sat;
ⓂTaksim) The felting, lacework, embroidery,
all-natural soaps and soft toys in this lovely
shop are made by economically disadvantaged women in Turkey's rural areas. All
profits are returned to them, ensuring that
they and their families have better lives.

DENIZLER KITABEVI MAPS
Map p248 (📞0212-249 8893; www.denizler
kitabevi.com; İstiklal Caddesi 199a; ⊘10am-8pm
Mon-Sat, noon-8pm Sun; ⓂŞişhane, 🚇Tünel)
One of the few interesting shops remaining on İstiklal, Denizler Kitabevi sells
antique maps, books, prints, photographs
and postcards.

MEPHISTO MUSIC
Map p244 (📞0212-249 0696; www.mephisto.
com.tr; İstiklal Caddesi 125; ⊘9am-midnight;
ⓂTaksim) If you develop a taste for local music while you're in town, this popular store
is the place to indulge it. As well as a huge
CD collection of Turkish popular music,
there's a select range of Turkish folk, jazz
and classical music. It also stocks DVDs
and has an upstairs cafe. There are other
branches in Kadıköy (p160) and Beşiktaş.

LALE PLAK MUSIC
Map p248 (📞0212-293 7739; Galipdede Caddesi
1, Tünel; ⊘9am-7.30pm; ⓂŞişhane, 🚇Tünel)
This small shop is crammed with CDs,
including a fine selection of Turkish classical, jazz and folk music. It's a popular
hang-out for local musicians.

MISELA FASHION & ACCESSORIES
Map p248 (📞0212-243 5300; www.misela
istanbul.com; Meşrutiyet Caddesi 107e, Tepebaşı;
⊘11am-7pm Mon-Thu, to 8pm Fri, noon-8pm Sat;
ⓂŞişhane, 🚇Tünel) No self-respecting local
fashionista would be without a chic handbag designed by local Serra Türker. Quality
materials and workmanship are the hallmarks, for which you will pay accordingly.

ANTIJEN DESIGN CLOTHING
Map p244 (📞0212-251 8614; www.niluferkaraca.
com.tr; Yenicarşı Caddesi 9, Galatasaray; ⊘10am-
7pm Mon-Sat; ⓂTaksim) Local designer
Nilüfer Karaca creates sculptural pieces in
muted tones that customers can purchase

off the rack or have made to measure in
two or three days. Her form-hugging frocks
and statement winter coats are particularly
desirable.

SEYAHAN JEWELLERY
Map p244 (📞0212-243 6016; www.seyahan.com;
Hazzo Pulo Pasajı; ⊘10am-7pm, to 9pm Jun-Aug;
ⓂŞişhane, 🚇Tünel) Established by American-
German couple Matthias Weimer and
Laura Parker, Seyahan works with Turkish
artisans and two women's cooperatives to
produce handcrafted silver jewellery. There
are two stores in the city – this boutique inside the Meşrutiyet Caddesi entrance to the
Hazzo Pulo Pasajı and another in Galata
(Map p248; Camekan Sokak 4j).

ALI MUHIDDIN HACI BEKIR FOOD
Map p244 (📞0212-244 2804; www.hacibekir.com.
tr; İstiklal Caddesi 83; ⓂTaksim) The Beyoğlu
branch of the famous *lokum* (Turkish
Delight) shop.

PANDORA BOOKS
Map p244 (📞0212-243 3503; www.pandora.com.
tr; Büyük Parmakkapı Sokak 3, Taksim; ⊘10am-
8pm Mon-Wed, to 9pm Thu-Sat, 1-8pm Sun;
ⓂTaksim) A long-standing business with
three floors of books – head to the 3rd floor
for English-language titles.

TEZGAH ALLEY CLOTHING
Map p248 (Terkoz Pasajı; Terkoz Cikmazı, off
İstiklal Caddesi; ⊘Mon-Sat; ⓂŞişhane, 🚇Tünel)
Put your elbows to work fighting your way
to the front of the *tezgah* (stalls) in this alleyway, which is heaped with clothing for
under ₺20 per piece. Turkey is a major centre
of European clothing manufacture, and
the items here are sometimes factory runs
from designer or major chain-store
orders. The 'Terkos Pasajı' sign marks the
spot.

HAFIZ MUSTAFA SWEETS
Map p244 (İstiklal Caddesi 35, Taksim; ⊘8am-
1am; ⓂTaksim) The Beyoğlu branch of this
much-loved sweets store, signed as 'Hakkı
Zade', is close to Taksim Meydanı.

🏠 Çukurcuma & Cihangir

OPUS3A MUSIC
Map p248 (📞0212-251 8405; www.opus3a.com;
Cihangir Caddesi 3a, Cihangir; ⊘11am-8.30pm,
to 9.30pm Jun-Aug; ⓂTaksim) Those keen to

supplement their CD or vinyl collections with some Turkish music should head to this large shop in Cihangir, where knowledgeable, English-speaking staff can steer you towards the best local classical, jazz, alternative and pop recordings.

A LA TURCA
CARPETS, ANTIQUES

Map p244 (⯑0212-245 2933; www.alaturca house.com; Faikpaşa Sokak 4, Çukurcuma; ⏰10.30am-7.30pm Mon-Sat; ⓂTaksim) Antique Anatolian kilims and textiles are stacked alongside top-drawer Ottoman antiques in this fabulous shop in Çukurcuma. This is the best area in the city to browse for antiques and curios, and A La Turca is probably the most interesting of its retail outlets. Ring the doorbell to gain entrance.

MEKHANN
TEXTILES

Map p248 (⯑0212-249 7849; www.mekhann.com; Boğazkesen Caddesi 32a, Tophane; 🚃Tophane) The Beyoğlu branch of the well-known Grand Bazaar shop is located close to the Tophane tram stop.

MARIPOSA
CLOTHING

Map p248 (⯑0212-249 0483; www.atolye mariposa.com; Şimşirci Sokak 11a, Cihangir; ⏰10am-8pm Mon-Fri, 11am-8.30pm Sat & Sun; ⓂTaksim) Designer Banu One turns out a particularly fetching line in floral frocks at her Cihangir atelier. Fashionistas will adore the fact that she not only makes to order, but also designs and tailors unique ensembles. As well as the dresses, coats and jackets on the racks, the shop sells pretty bedspreads and pillowslips. There's another branch in Teşvikiye.

LA CAVE WINE SHOP
FOOD & DRINKS

Map p248 (La Cave Şarap Evi; ⯑0212-243 2405; Sıraselviler Caddesi 109, Cihangir; ⏰9.30am-8pm; ⓂTaksim) Its enormous selection of local and imported wine makes La Cave a good stop for tipplers. The staff can differentiate a Chablis from a Chardonnay, and though they don't speak much English, they are always happy to give advice on the best Turkish bottles to add to your cellar.

🏃 SPORTS & ACTIVITIES

⭐KILIÇ ALI PAŞA HAMAMI
HAMAM

Map p248 (⯑0212-393 8010; http://kilicalipasa hamami.com; Hamam Sokak 1, off Kemeraltı Caddesi, Tophane; ⏰women 8am-4pm, men 4.30-11.30pm; 🚃Tophane) It took seven years to develop a conservation plan for this 1580 Sinan-designed building and complete the meticulous restoration. Fortunately, the result was well worth waiting for. The hamam's interior is simply stunning and the place is run with total professionalism, ensuring a clean and enjoyable Turkish bath experience. Services include a traditional hamam ritual (₺170) and massage (from ₺140).

ARTWALK ISTANBUL
WALKING

(⯑0537 797 7525; www.artwalkistanbul.com; group tours ₺75-100 per person, private tours by negotiation; ⏰Apr-Dec) Saliha Yavuz and her small team of curators, artists and critics offer guided English-language visits to commercial and artist-run galleries, as well as artists' studios, providing an excellent introduction to the city's vibrant contemporary-art scene. Tours concentrate on neighbourhoods, with gallery walks in Galata, Tophane, Taksim and Nişantaşı, and a tour of artists' studios in Kadıköy.

The gallery walks cover seven or eight spaces, and the studio walk visits four or five artist workspaces; all take approximately three hours. Participant numbers are limited to 15 and tours can also be run in Italian and German.

İSTANBUL ON FOOD
WALKING

(⯑0538 966 7671; http://istanbulonfood.com; tour US$100) New to the city's increasingly cluttered food-tour scene, this small outfit offers a popular four-hour 'Twilight at Taksim' tour with a maximum of seven participants. You'll wander through the side streets on either side of İstiklal Caddesi sampling plenty of street food and kebaps before popping into a *meyhane* (tavern) for a rakı and finishing with baklava at Karaköy Güllüoğlu.

Other offerings include 'Flavours of the Old City' and 'Taste of Two Continents', both of which are similar to tours devised by İstanbul Eats (p89) and Turkish Flavours (p160).

Beşiktaş, Nişantaşı & Ortaköy

Neighbourhood Top Five

❶ Dolmabahçe Palace
(p149) Getting a glimpse
into the public and private
lives of the last Ottoman
sultans in their supremely
ornate pad.

❷ Ortaköy (p51) Wandering the streets surround-
ing the waterside *meydan*
(square) of this former
fishing village and admiring

its spectacular view of the
Bosphorus Bridge.

**❸ İstanbul Naval
Museum** (p150) Admiring
the fleet of 19th-century
imperial *caïques* (ornately
decorated wooden row-
boats) in the copper-clad
exhibition hall.

**❹ Palace Collections
Museum** (p150) Gaining

an insight into life in the
royal palaces and pavilions
through this collection of
some 5000 items in the
former Dolmabahçe Palace
kitchens.

**❺ National Palaces
Painting Museum** (p150)
Viewing 19th-century
Ottoman paintings in a
crown prince's residence.

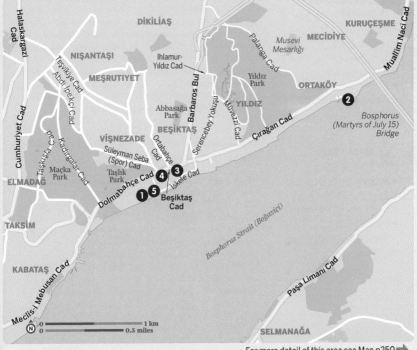

For more detail of this area see Map p250 ➡

Lonely Planet's Top Tip

It can be difficult to get past the door staff at the super-clubs on the Golden Mile if you're not a celebrity or socialite. If you're keen to party with the glitterati, consider making a booking at one of the club restaurants, which should ensure you get automatic entrance.

Best Museums

➡ İstanbul Naval Museum (p150)
➡ Palace Collections Museum (p150)
➡ National Palaces Painting Museum (p150)
➡ Askeri Müze (p151)

For reviews, see p150. ➡

Best Places to Eat

➡ Kantın (p152)
➡ Hünkar (p152)
➡ Alancha (p152)
➡ Banyan (p152)
➡ Vogue (p153)
➡ Pare Baklava Bar (p152)

For reviews, see p152. ➡

☆ Best Places to Party

➡ Babylon Bomonti (p154)
➡ Klein (p153)
➡ Love Dance Point (p153)
➡ Reina (p153)

For reviews, see p154. ➡

Explore Beşiktaş, Nişantaşi & Ortaköy

This part of town has the largest concentration of Ottoman palaces and pavilions in İstanbul. Start by walking to Dolmabahçe Palace from the tram stop at Kabataş, and then walk or bus your way down to the Palace Collections Museum, İstanbul Naval Museum and Yıldız Park. At present, constant traffic jams along the main coast road, which is variously called Dolmabahçe, Beşiktaş, Çırağan, Muallim Naci and Kuruçeşme Caddesi, make car and bus trips slow. Aim to stop for lunch and perhaps a spot of shopping in the upmarket suburb of Nişantaşı, which is located approximately 2km north of Dolmabahçe Palace. It's a steep walk to get here, so consider hailing a taxi for the short trip. Most of its cafes, restaurants and shops are found on Teşvikiye Caddesi, Abdi İpekçi Caddesi and Akkavak Sokak. In the evening, consider a sundowner in Ortaköy, where restaurants on the waterside main square near the pretty baroque mosque are popular. It's a good place to kick off an evening of clubbing at the venues along the Golden Mile.

Local Life

➡**Picnic in the park** You don't need to organise a portable barbecue or furniture to enjoy an alfresco lunch in popular Yıldız Park (p151); although many locals do.

➡**İskele idling** Watch the ferries head in and out of dock while lingering in cafes and bars on pedestrianised promenade İskele Yolu, behind Bahçeşehir University and next to the Beşiktaş İskelesi (Beşiktaş Ferry Dock).

➡**Kümpir** Join the crowds tucking into *kümpir* (stuffed baked potato) and sweet waffles from the stands (Map p250; Mecidiye Köprüsü Sokak, Ortaköy; ☺11am-10pm; *kümpir* or waffles ₺15; 🚌Kabataş Lisesi) behind the Ortaköy Mosque.

Getting There & Away

➡**Bus** Lines including 22 and 25E travel along the coast road to/from Kabataş tram and funicular terminals. There are also numerous buses including 40, 40T and 42T to/from Taksim.

➡**Ferry** Regular services connect Beşiktaş with Kadıköy and Üsküdar on the Asian shore. There are also commuter services between Eminönü and Beşiktaş and Eminönü and Ortaköy, leaving Beşiktaş and Ortaköy in the morning and Eminönü in the late afternoon.

➡**Metro** Osmanbey, one stop north of Taksim, is convenient for Nişantaşı. A new metro line linking Kabataş and Mahmutbey is scheduled to open in 2017 and will include a stop in Beşiktaş.

TOP SIGHT
DOLMABAHÇE PALACE

This 19th-century residence with its formal garden and waterside location marks a final flourish of the imperial dynasty and is a clear crowd favourite.

Entered via an ornate imperial gate, the palace is divided into three sections: the over-the-top Selâmlık (Ceremonial Quarters), the slightly more restrained Harem and the Veliaht Dairesi (Apartments of the Crown Prince), now home to the National Palaces Painting Museum (p150). The Selâmlık and Harem are visited on a compulsory – and dreadfully rushed – combined guided tour; the Veliaht Dairesi can be visited independently.

The tourist entrance to the palace is near the ornate Clock Tower, built between 1890 and 1894. There's an outdoor cafe nearby with premium Bosphorus views and reasonable prices.

Note that visitors to the palace are limited to 3000 per day and this ceiling is often reached on weekends and holidays. Come midweek if possible, and even then be prepared to queue (often for long periods and in full sun). If arriving before 3pm, you must buy a joint ticket for the Selâmlık and Harem; after 3pm you can visit only one. The Selâmlık, with its huge chandeliers and crystal staircase made by Baccarat, is the more impressive of the two.

Note that admission to the palace is not covered by the Museum Pass İstanbul.

DON'T MISS

➡ Selâmlık
➡ Harem
➡ National Palaces Painting Museum

PRACTICALITIES

➡ Dolmabahçe Sarayı
➡ Map p162, A5
➡ ☏ 0212-327 2626
➡ www.millisaraylar.gov.tr
➡ Dolmabahçe Caddesi, Beşiktaş
➡ adult Selâmlık ₺30, Harem ₺20, joint ticket ₺40
➡ ⊙ 9am-4pm Tue, Wed & Fri-Sun
➡ 🚋 Kabataş

◉ SIGHTS

DOLMABAHÇE PALACE   PALACE
See p149.

NATIONAL PALACES
PAINTING MUSEUM   GALLERY
Map p250 (Milli Saraylar Resim Müzesi; ☏0212-236 9000; www.millisaraylar.gov.tr; Dolmabahçe Caddesi, Beşiktaş; admission ₺20; ☺9am-4pm Tue, Wed & Fri-Sun; 🚌Akaretler, 🚌Kabataş) Reopened in 2014 after a long restoration, the Veliaht Dairesi (Apartments of the Crown Prince) in Dolmabahçe Palace now showcase the palace's collection of paintings. Highlights include the downstairs 'Turkish Painters 1870–1890' room, which includes two Osman Hamdi Bey works, and the upstairs 'İstanbul views' room, which is home to 19th-century street scenes by Germain Fabius Brest. The gallery is included in the Dolmabahçe ticket price and can be accessed from the palace grounds.

PALACE COLLECTIONS
MUSEUM   MUSEUM
Map p250 (Saray Koleksiyonları Müzesi; ☏0212-236 9000; www.millisaraylar.gov.tr; Beşiktaş Caddesi, Beşiktaş; adult/child ₺5/2; ☺9am-5pm Tue-Sun; 🚌Akaretler, 🚌Kabataş) Occupying the warehouse-like Dolmabahçe Palace kitchens, this museum exhibits items used in the royal palaces and pavilions during the late Ottoman Empire and early Turkish Republic. It is a fascinating hotchpotch of some 5000 objects, including palace portraits and photos, teasets, tiled Islamic wall inscriptions, prayer rugs and embroidery. Hereke carpets and Yıldız Porselen Fabrikası (p151) porcelain are also here.

Entrance is free with the Dolmabahçe Palace Selâmlık and Harem joint ticket.

YILDIZ ŞALE   MUSEUM
Map p250 (Yıldız Chalet Museum; ☏0212-327 2626; www.millisaraylar.gov.tr) Originally an imperial hunting lodge, this oft-extended Ottoman guesthouse has hosted royalty galore. Built for Sultan Abdül Hamit II in 1880, the şale (chalet) was closed to the public at the time of research, but is well worth a visit should it reopen.

The building is at the top of the hill in Yıldız Park, enclosed by a wall. After being expanded and renovated for the use of Kaiser Wilhelm II of Germany in 1889, it underwent a second extension in 1898 to accommodate a huge ceremonial hall.

After his imperial guest departed, Abdül Hamit became quite attached to his 'rustic' creation and decided to live here himself, forsaking the palaces of Dolmabahçe and Çırağan on the Bosphorus shore.

İSTANBUL NAVAL MUSEUM   MUSEUM
Map p250 (İstanbul Deniz Müzesi; ☏0212-327 4345; www.denizmuzeleri.tsk.tr; Beşiktaş Caddesi 6, Beşiktaş; adult/student & child ₺6.50/free; ☺9am-5pm Mon-Fri, 10am-6pm Sat & Sun mid-May–mid-Oct, 9am-5pm Tue-Sun mid-Oct–mid-May; 🚌Bahçeşehir Ünv.) Established over a century ago to celebrate and commemorate Turkish naval history, this museum has been undergoing a prolonged and major renovation. Its architecturally noteworthy copper-clad exhibition hall opened in 2013 and showcases a spectacular collection of 19th-century imperial caïques, ornately decorated wooden rowboats used by the royal household. Temporary exhibitions take place in the downstairs gallery.

The next stage of the renovation will see the museum's original building reopened with exhibits including 'The Navy in the Turkish Republic' and 'Cartography and Navigational Instruments'; the latter is likely to focus on the achievements of the 16th-century cartographer Piri Reis.

In the square opposite the museum is the Sinan-designed tomb of the admiral of Süleyman the Magnificent's fleet, Barbaros Heyrettin Paşa (1483–1546), better known as Barbarossa. The museum is located on the Bosphorus shore close to the Beşiktaş bus station and ferry dock. Across Beşiktaş Caddesi, dolmuşes (minibuses) run from outside Akbank up to Taksim Meydanı (Taksim Sq; ₺2.50) and to Harbiye, where Turkey's major military museum, the Askeri Müze (p151), is located. The Ottoman military band known as the Mehter performs there most days at 3pm and 4pm.

ORTAKÖY MOSQUE   MOSQUE
Map p162 (Ortaköy Camii, Büyük Mecidiye Camii; İskele Meydanı, Ortaköy; 🚌Ortaköy) This elegant baroque-style structure was designed by Nikoğos Balyan, one of the architects of Dolmabahçe Palace, and built for Sultan Abdül Mecit I between 1853 and 1855. The modern Bosphorus Bridge) looms behind the recently restored mosque, providing a fabulous photo opportunity for those wanting to illustrate İstanbul's 'old meets new' character.

Beneath the mosque's ornate ceiling hang several masterful examples of Arabic calligraphy executed by Abdül Mecit, who was an accomplished calligrapher.

The mosque fronts onto İskele Meydanı, the hub of this former fishing village and home to a pretty fountain and waterfront cafes. On weekends the square and surrounding streets host an unremarkable but popular street market.

ASKERİ MÜZE   MUSEUM

Map p250 (Military Museum; ☑0212-233 2720; www.askerimuze.tsk.tr; Vali Konağı Caddesi, Harbiye; adult/student & child ₺10/free; ⊘9am-5pm; ⬚Cumhuriyet Cad) For a rousing museum experience, present yourself at this little-visited military museum 1km north of Taksim to view the militaria dating from Ottoman to recent times. Try to visit in the afternoon so that you can enjoy a concert by the Mehter military band, which plays most days between 3pm and 4pm.

The large museum is spread over two floors. On the ground floor are displays of weapons and Turkish military uniforms through the ages, as well as glass cases holding battle standards, both Turkish and captured, including Byzantine, Greek, British, Austro-Hungarian, Italian and imperial Russian standards.

Also on show is an old-fashioned diorama of the Conquest, and a tapestry woven by Ottoman sailors (who must have had lots of time on their hands) shows the flags of important maritime nations from around the world.

The upper floor has a Çanakkale (Gallipoli) diorama and a room devoted to Atatürk, who was a famous Ottoman general before he became founder and commander-in-chief of the republican army and first president of the Turkish Republic.

Perhaps the best reason to visit this museum is to view the short concert by the Mehter. Turkish historians argue that the Mehter was the world's first true military band. Its purpose was not to make pretty music for dancing, but to precede the conquering Ottoman *paşas* (governors or generals) into vanquished towns, impressing upon the defeated populace their new, subordinate status. Children in particular will love watching the band members march with their steady, measured pace, turning in unison to face first the left side of the line of march, then the right.

The easiest way to get to the museum is to walk up Cumhuriyet Caddesi from Taksim Meydanı. This will take around 20 minutes. Alternatively, take any bus heading up Cumhuriyet Caddesi from Taksim Meydanı.

YILDIZ PARK   PARK

Map p250 (Yıldız Parkı; Çırağan Caddesi, Yıldız; ⬚Çırağan) This large and leafy retreat is alive with birds, picnicking families and young couples strolling hand in hand. The best time to visit is in April, when the spring flowers (including thousands of tulips) are in bloom. At the park's highest point is Yıldız Şale (p150), built as a hunting lodge for Sultan Abdül Hamit II in 1880.

Around 500m past the turn-off to Yıldız Şale, you'll come to the Malta Köşkü (p153), now an unlicensed restaurant and function centre. Built in 1870, this was where Abdül Hamit imprisoned his brother Murat V, whom he had deposed in 1876. The terrace has Bosphorus views, as does the upstairs dining room with its ornate ceiling and chandelier.

If you continue walking past the Malta Köşkü for 10 minutes, you'll arrive at the **Yıldız Porselen Fabrikası** (Yıldız Porcelain Factory; Map p250; ☑0212-260 2370; www.millisaraylar.gov.tr; Yıldız Parkı, Yıldız; adult/child & student ₺5/1; ⊘9am-6pm Mon-Fri; ⬚Kabataş Lisesi). This factory occupies a wonderful building designed by Italian architect Raimondo D'Aronco, who introduced the art nouveau style to İstanbul. You can visit the workshop inside. The showroom at the gate sells porcelain made here, including cups and saucers, whirling dervish figures and fun mugs depicting the Ottoman sultans.

The steep walk uphill from Çırağan Caddesi to the *şale* takes 15 to 20 minutes. If you come to the park by taxi, have it take you up the slope to the *şale*.

ÇIRAĞAN PALACE   PALACE

Map p162 (Çırağan Sarayı; Çırağan Caddesi 84, Ortaköy; ⬚Çırağan) Not satisfied with the architectural exertions of his predecessor at Dolmabahçe Palace, Sultan Abdül Aziz (r 1861–76) built his own grand residence at Çırağan, only 1.5km away. Here, architect Nikoğos Balyan, who had also worked on Dolmabahçe, created an interesting building melding European neoclassical with Ottoman and Moorish styles. The Çırağan Palace Kempinski Hotel (p153) now occupies part of the palace.

BEŞİKTAŞ, NİŞANTAŞI & ORTAKÖY SIGHTS

EATING

The student and professional population ensures plenty of eateries in Beşiktaş and Ortaköy. On weekends in Ortaköy, locals flock to the *kümpir* (stuffed baked potatoes) and waffle stands behind Ortaköy Mosque or to branches of the chains Kitchenette and House Cafe. Inland from the main square, *kebapçıs* (kebap restaurants) and other affordable eateries are found in the lanes and Muallim Naci Caddesi. Likewise in Beşiktaş, affordable seafood restaurants, attracting students and middle-class locals, sit near the fish market between Ortabahçe Caddesi and the streets leading east to Barbaros Bulvarı. Head to affluent Nişantaşı to sample the finest contemporary Turkish cuisine.

PARE BAKLAVA BAR
SWEETS €

Map p250 (🖉0212-236 5920; www.parebaklava bar.com; Şakayık Sokak 32, Nişantaşı; ⊙8am-10pm Mon-Sat, 10am-4pm Sun; ❄🛜; MOsmanbey) Billing itself as Turkey's first-ever baklava bar, this bijou business flies in top-grade baklava and *katmer* (flaky pastry stuffed with pistachios and clotted cream) from Gaziantep every day. Make your choice and settle back to enjoy a few pieces with a glass of tea or a well-made coffee.

FOODIE
BAKERY €

Map p250 (🖉0212-231 5113; www.foodie.com. tr; Güzelbahçe Sokak 23, Nişantaşı; cakes from ₺10; ⊙9am-6pm Mon-Fri; MOsmanbey) Try the eclairs at this tiny artisan cake shop, which also makes brownies, cheesecakes and other treats.

SAAT KULE CAFE
CAFE €

Map p250 (Dolmabahçe Caddesi, Beşiktaş; tost ₺5, mains ₺10; ⊙8.30am-10pm; 🚈Kabataş) If the onslaught of late Ottoman decadence at Dolmabahçe Palace makes you feel faint, head to its Clock Tower Cafe to recover over a drink or snack. The windows overlook the Bosphorus, and prices are reasonable for a museum cafe (çay ₺2.50; cappuccino ₺7).

KANTIN
MODERN ANATOLIAN €€

Map p250 (🖉0212-219 3114; www.kantin.biz; Maçka Caddesi 35a, Milli Reasürans Pasajı 16 ve 60, Nişantaşı; mains ₺15-44; ⊙11am-5pm Mon, 11am-11.30pm Tue-Sat; MOsmanbey) An early and much-loved adopter of the Slow Food philosophy, 'Canteen' remains one of

İstanbul's best bistros (and high-end takeaways). Chef-owner Semsa Denizsel, a pioneer of the farm-to-table approach in Turkey, serves 'new İstanbul cuisine', reflecting the city's melting-pot heritage of Turkish, Greek, Armenian and Jewish home-cooking. Only local and seasonal produce is used and the menu changes regularly.

HÜNKAR
ANATOLIAN €€

Map p250 (🖉0212-225 4665; www.hunkar lokantasi.com; Mim Kemal Öke Caddesi 21, Nişantaşı; meze ₺10, mains ₺35; ⊙noon-10.30pm; 🅿; MOsmanbey) If you decide to spend a half-day shopping in Nişantaşı, consider taking a break and eating at Hünkar, one of the city's best *lokantas* (eateries serving ready-made food). In business since 1950, it serves all the classic mezes and grilled meat dishes.

AŞŞK KAHVE
CAFE €€

(🖉0212-265 4734; www.asskkahve.com; Muallim Naci Caddesi 64b, Kuruçeşme; brunch ₺20-40; ⊙9am-midnight, closed Mon winter; 🅿; 🚈Kuruçeşme) Aşk means 'love' in Turkish; the extra ş creates something similar to 'loove' in English. Semantics aside, Aşşk serves İstanbullus their beloved leisurely Turkish breakfast by the Bosphorus. Go early to snaffle a table by the water, preferably on a weekend. Sandwiches, pizza and cocktails make a visit later in the day also worthwhile. Access is via the stairs behind the Macrocenter.

ALANCHA
MODERN TURKISH €€€

Map p250 (🖉0212-261 3535; http://en.alancha. com; Maçka Kempinski Residence, Şehit Mehmet Sokak 9, Maçka; menu ₺240; ⊙7.30-10pm; MOsmanbey) Alancha's designer decor is as striking as its colourful and artfully arranged dinner dishes, which include servings of wild sea bass to filet mignon. Go for the Anatolian tasting menu, which features a dozen courses prepared with artisan ingredients from the seven regions of Anatolia, starting with stuffed mussels and continuing through pistachio kebap to baklava and *lokum* (Turkish Delight). Wine pairing costs ₺160.

BANYAN
ASIAN €€€

Map p250 (🖉0212-259 9060; www.banyan restaurant.com; 2nd fl, Salhane Sokak 3, Ortaköy; sushi ₺40, mains ₺80; ⊙noon-midnight; 🅿; 🚈Kabataş Lisesi) The menu here travels around Asia, featuring Thai, Japanese, Indian, Vietnamese and Chinese dishes, and including soups, sushi, satays and salads. Banyan claims to serve food for the soul, and you can enjoy it with exceptional views of the Ortaköy Mosque and Bosphorus Bridge, or linger over a sunset cocktail (₺60) at the open-fronted terrace bar.

VOGUE
INTERNATIONAL €€€

Map p250 (✆0212-227 4404; www.vogue restaurant.com; 13th fl, A Blok, BJK Plaza, Spor Caddesi 92, Akaretler, Beşiktaş; starters ₺26-50, mains ₺30-75; ⊙noon-2am; ✎; 🚊Akaretler) This sophisticated bar-restaurant in a Beşiktaş office block opened in 1997, and feels like it has been going strong since Atatürk was lodging in the nearby Dolmabahçe Palace. A menu of pasta, seafood, sushi, lamb shanks and roast duck, the panoramic Bosphorus views and its various molecular cocktails make Vogue a favourite haunt of the Nişantaşı powerbroker set.

🍷 DRINKING & 🍸 NIGHTLIFE

The stretch of Bosphorus shoreline between Ortaköy and Kuruçeşme is often referred to as the Golden Mile, a reference to its string of high-profile waterfront nightclubs. Clubs are best visited during summer, when they open nightly and their waterside terraces are truly magical party venues. A night here won't suit everyone, though: drinks are pricey, club restaurants poor quality and pricey, entrance policies inconsistent, and door staff notoriously rude and tip-hungry. There's usually a cover charge Friday and Saturday nights, but you can often avoid this with a restaurant booking.

MALTA KÖŞKÜ
CAFE

Map p250 (✆0216-413 9253; www.beltur. istanbul/malta-kosku.asp; Yıldız Parkı; çay ₺2.50, mains ₺20-30; 🚊Çırağan) Built in 1870, this unlicensed restaurant and function centre was where Sultan Abdül Hamit II imprisoned his brother Murat V, having deposed him in 1876. The terrace has Bosphorus views, as does the upstairs dining room with its ornate ceiling and chandelier. Food is available, but we recommend sticking to tea or coffee, as the service can be slow and unfriendly.

ÇIRAĞAN PALACE KEMPINSKI HOTEL
BAR

Map p250 (✆0212-326 4646; www.kempinski. com; Çırağan Caddesi 32, Beşiktaş; 🚊Çırağan) Nursing a mega-pricey çay (₺18), coffee (₺20) or beer (₺20) at one of the Çırağan's terrace tables and watching the scene around İstanbul's best swimming pool, which is right on the Bosphorus, lets you sample the lifestyle of the city's rich and famous. The hotel occupies part of the 19th-century Çırağan Palace (p151); look out for the photos of celebrity guests.

LOVE DANCE POINT
GAY

Map p250 (✆0212-232 5683; www.lovedp.net; Cumhuriyet Caddesi 349, Harbiye; ⊙11.30pm-5am Fri & Sat; 🚇Taksim or Osmanbey) Well into its second decade, LDP is the most Europhile of the local gay venues, hosting gay musical icons and international circuit parties. Hard-cutting techno is thrown in with gay anthems and Turkish pop. The place attracts the well travelled and the unimpressionable, as well as some straight hipsters from nearby Nişantaşı.

REINA
CLUB

Map p250 (✆0212-259 5919; www.reina.com.tr; Muallim Naci Caddesi 44, Ortaköy; ⊙7pm-5am; 🚊Ortaköy) Gazing up at the Bosphorus Bridge from the waterfront, Reina claims it is 'a meeting point for international statesmen, a location where businessmen sign agreements worth billions of dollars and where world stars enjoy their meals'. In reality, it's where İstanbul's C-list celebrities congregate, its nouveaux riches flock and where an occasional tourist gets past the doorperson to ogle the spectacle.

SORTIE
CLUB

Map p250 (✆0212-327 8585; www.sortie.com. tr; Muallim Naci Caddesi 54, Kuruçeşme; ⊙7pm-late; 🚊Şifa Yurdu) Behind its high walls, Sortie has long vied for the title of reigning queen of the Golden Mile, nipping at the heels of its rival dowager Reina. It pulls in the city's glamour pusses and poseurs, all of whom are on the lookout for the odd celebrity guest. Its six restaurants open in summer give extra reasons to sortie.

KLEIN
CLUB

Map p250 (✆0212-291 8440; Cebel Topu Sokak 4, Harbiye; cover ₺50; ⊙11pm-4am Fri & Sat; 🚇Taksim) A subterranean space with a huge dance floor and top-notch sound

BEŞİKTAŞ, NİŞANTAŞI & ORTAKÖY DRINKING & NIGHTLIFE

system, Klein has DJs who spin techno and electronica, two bars and a dance-focused crowd. Check the Facebook feed for events.

 SHOPPING

Serious shoppers, visiting celebs, public-relations professionals and the city's gilded youth gravitate towards upmarket **Nişantaşı**, which is located about 2km north of Taksim Meydanı and accessed via the metro (Osmanbey stop). International fashion and design shops are found in the streets surrounding the main artery, Teşvikiye Caddesi, which prompts some locals to refer to that area as Teşvikiye. Nişantaşı is one of İstanbul's major fashion hubs, especially Abdi İpekçi Caddesi, where Turkish and international designers can be found.

LOKUM ISTANBUL   FOOD

(✆0212-257 1052; www.lokumistanbul.com; Kuruçeşme Caddesi 19, Kuruçeşme; ⊕9am-8pm Mon-Fri, from 10am Sat & Sun; 🚌Kuruçeşme) *Lokum* (Turkish Delight) is elevated to the status of artwork at this boutique. Owner and creator Zeynep Keyman brings back the delights, flavours, knowledge and beauty of Ottoman-Turkish products, including colourful and chunky pomegranate and pistachio *lokum* (a small box for ₺65), *akide* candies (traditional boiled lollies), cologne water and scented candles. The gorgeous packaging makes these treats perfect gifts.

GÖNÜL PAKSOY   CLOTHING

Map p250 (✆0212-236 0209; gonulpaksoy@gmail.com; Demet Apt 4a, Akkavak Sokak, Nişantaşı; ⊕10am-7pm Tue-Sat, from 1pm Mon; 🚇Osmanbey) Paksoy creates and sells pieces that transcend fashion and step into art. Her work – distinctive handmade clothing using naturally dyed fabrics including silk, linen, cotton, cashmere, goat hair and wool, and often decorated with vintage beads – was once the subject of an exhibition at İstanbul's Rezan Haş Gallery. She also creates and sells delicate silk and cotton knits and exquisite jewellery based on traditional Ottoman designs.

WORTH A DETOUR

BABYLON BOMONTI

İstanbul's pre-eminent live-music venue, **Babylon Bomonti** (✆0212-334 0190; www.babylon.com.tr; Tarihi Bomonti Bira Fabrikası, Birahane Sokak 1, Bomonti; 🚇Osmanbey) FREE has been packing the crowds in since 1999 and shows no sign of losing its mojo, especially now that it has moved to a larger space in an atmospheric old beer factory in the upmarket arts enclave of Bomonti, reasonably close to the Osmanbey metro stop in Nişantaşı. In summer the action moves to the club's beach clubs in the Black Sea resort of Kilyos and in Çeşme on the North Aegean coast.

CITY'S NISANTASI   SHOPPING CENTRE

Map p250 (✆0212-373 3535; http://citysnisantasi.com/tr/sinema; Teşvikiye Caddesi 162, Nişantaşı; ⊕10am-10.30pm Sun-Thu, to 12.30am Fri & Sat; 🚇Osmanbey) This shopping mall includes a food court and seven-screen multiplex cinema.

KANYON   SHOPPING CENTRE

(✆0212-317 5300; www.kanyon.com.tr; Büyükdere Caddesi 185, Levent; ⊕10am-10pm; 🚇Levent) This upmarket shopping mall includes a nine-screen multiplex cinema.

 SPORTS & ACTIVITIES

FOUR SEASONS ISTANBUL
AT THE BOSPHORUS   SPA

Map p250 (✆0212-381 4000; www.fourseasons.com/bosphorus; Çırağan Caddesi 28, Beşiktaş; 30/45/60min hamam experience €125/155/185; ⊕9am-9pm; 🚌Bahçeşehir Ünv. or Çırağan) With its luxury-hotel setting, this spa has wow-factor in spades, including a stunning indoor pool area, steam room, sauna and relaxation lounge. Facials and massages, from deep tissue to hot stone, are available and the gorgeous marble hamam is perfect if you're looking for an indulgent Turkish bath experience. The hamam and treatment packages include full access to the spa facilities.

Kadıköy

Neighbourhood Top Five

1 **Kadıköy Produce Market** (p103) Signing up for a culinary walk through the city's best street market.

2 **Yeldeğirmeni** Checking out the vibrant and always changing street-art scene.

3 **Meshur Dondurmacı Ali Usta** (p158) Enjoying an ice cream from a master ice-cream maker.

4 **Fazıl Bey** (p159) Following the aroma of freshly roasted coffee beans to this much-loved coffeeshop.

5 **Kadife Sokak** Kicking back after sunset at one of the grunge bars.

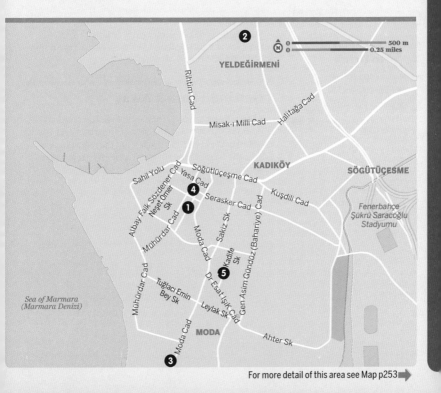

For more detail of this area see Map p253 ➡

Lonely Planet's Top Tip

Females should bring a scarf or shawl to use as a head covering if they are planning to visit Üsküdar's impressive array of imperial mosques, and all visitors should dress appropriately (ie no shorts, short skirts or skimpy tops).

⊙ Best Detour

➡ Üsküdar (p160)

For reviews, see p158.➡

✕ Best Places to Eat

➡ Baylan Pastanesi (p158)
➡ Cibalikapı (p159)
➡ Çiya Sofrası (p158)

For reviews, see p158.➡

🍷 Best Places to Drink

➡ Arkaoda (p159)
➡ Fazıl Bey (p159)
➡ Karga Bar (p159)

For reviews, see p159.➡

Explore Kadıköy

Located on the Anatolian (Asian) side of the city, Kadıköy is a short but atmospheric ferry ride from the European shore and offers a very different – and authentically local – experience for those travellers who are keen to cross continents.

İstanbullus come here from every corner of the city to stock up on speciality food items, fresh-from-the-farm produce and kitchenware. To join them and see the suburb at its bustling best, you should head here on a morning any day except Sunday.

We suggest catching the ferry here, exploring the market and then enjoying lunch before heading back to the *iskele* (ferry dock) for your return trip, or making your way to nearby Üsküdar to visit its imperial mosques.

Local Life

➡**Coffee culture** Locals love to catch up over cups of sugar-sweetened *Türk kahve* (Turkish coffee) in the Seraskar Caddesi *khavehanis* (coffeehouses).

➡**Beer and backgammon** Enjoying a late-afternoon beer and game of *tavla* (backgammon) is a popular pastime at the Kadife Sokak bars.

➡**Football** Ultra-loyal Canary fans flock to Fenerbahçe's Şükrü Saracoğlu Stadium for home matches and can be found in the suburb's restaurants and bars before and after games.

Getting There & Away

➡**Ferry** Boats travel to/from Eminönü, Karaköy and Beşiktaş, occasionally stopping at Haydarpaşa en route.

➡**Metro** A branch line travels from the metro station near the İskele Camii to Ayrılık Çeşmesi, from where the Marmaray metro travels to Üsküdar, Sirkeci, Yenikapı and Kazlıçeşme.

TOP SIGHT
KADIKÖY PRODUCE MARKET

An aromatic and alluring showcase of the best fresh produce in the city, the Kadıköy Pazarı (Market) is foodie central for locals and is becoming an increasingly popular destination for tourists. Equally rewarding to explore independently or on a guided culinary walk, it's small enough to retain a local feel yet large enough to support a variety of specialist traders.

Getting here involves crossing from Europe to Asia and is best achieved on a ferry – from the deck you'll be able to admire the domes and minarets studding the skylines of both shores and watch seagulls swooping overhead. Once arrived, cross Rihtim Caddesi in front of the *iskele* (ferry dock), head right (south) across Söğütlüçeşme Caddesi and then walk up either Yasa or Muvakkithane Caddesis to reach the centre of the action.

The best produce shops are in Güneşlibahçe Sokak – you'll see fish glistening on beds of crushed ice, displays of seasonal fruits and vegetables, combs of amber-hued honey, tubs of tangy pickles, bins of freshly roasted nuts and much, much more.

Eating and drinking opportunities are plentiful: creamy yogurt and honey at Honeyci (p158), regional Anatolian specialities at Çiya Sofrasi (p158), the catch of the day at Kadı Nımet Balıkçılık (p159) and the city's best Turkish coffee at Fazıl Bey (p159). For gifts to take home, consider *lokum* (Turkish Delight) from Ali Muhıddın Hacı Bekir (p160), coffee from Fazıl Bey or olive-oil soap from one of the herbalists in Güneşlibahçe Sokak.

DON'T MISS

➡ The Serasker Caddesi *khavehanis* (coffeeshops)
➡ Çiya Sofrasi

PRACTICALITIES

➡ Map p253, A4
➡ streets around Güneşlibahçe Sokak
➡ ⊙Mon-Sat
➡ 🚇Kadıköy

⊙ SIGHTS

KADIKÖY PRODUCE MARKET MARKET
See p103.

AYA EFIMIA RUM
ORTODOKS KILISESI CHURCH
Map p253 (Hagia Euphemia; cnr Mühürdar & Yasa Caddesi; 🚊Kadıköy) This Greek Orthodox church dates from 1830, although there had been a previous church on the same site from the late 17th century. Legend tells us that St Euphemia was a local Christian who, in the 3rd century AD, was tortured and murdered for refusing to pray to a pagan god.

SURP TAKAVOR ERMENI KILISESI CHURCH
Map p253 (Church of Christ the King; cnr Mukkadderhane & Mühürdar Caddesi; 🚊Kadıköy) This Armenian church in the centre of the bazaar was built in the late 19th century, although an Armenian church in one form or another has occupied this site since the 17th century.

HAYDARPAŞA RAILWAY
STATION LANDMARK
Map p253 (🚊Haydarpaşa) Funded by the German government, this railway station was built in the first decade of the 20th century as the İstanbul stop for a planned Berlin to Baghdad railway service. The station building was designed by German architects, but the lovely tile-adorned station *iskele* (ferry dock) was designed by noted Turkish architect Vedat Tek.

STREET ART

Kadıköy is the centre of the city's street art scene, and the Yeldeğirmeni district (Karakolhane Sokak near the railway tracks, Misak-ı Milli Sokak, İzzettin Sokak and Macit Erbudak Sokak) near the *iskele* (ferry dock) is where many local and visiting artists hang out. Other examples are on or near Moda Caddesi – look for murals by Adekan next to the Gerekli Şeyler bookshop and on the side of the tennis courts in Hüseyin Bey Sokak off Osman Yeki Üngör Sokak; for the mural by Canavar in the square next to the Mopaş supermarket on Dr Esat Işık Caddesi; and for the mural by Yabancı on the side of the Greek school in Neşe Sokağı. When wandering through the streets you'll also see interesting tagging by Yok ('nothing' in Turkish).

The station opened in 1908 and functioned as the main terminus for Asian railway services until it was badly damaged by fire in 2011. Left to deteriorate, it was placed on the World Monument Fund's international watch list of endangered buildings and many locals feared that it would be demolished or unsympathetically redeveloped. In 2016, after much public discussion of its future, the İstanbul Metropolitan Municipality announced that the building would be restored and remain a train station, becoming the terminus of the İstanbul–Ankara fast-train line.

✖ EATING

BAYLAN PASTANESI SWEETS €
Map p253 (📞0216-336 2881; www.baylan pastanesi.com.tr; Muvakkithane Caddesi 9; parfaits ₺16-19, cakes ₺16; ⊙7am-10pm; 🚊Kadıköy) The front window and interior of this Kadıköy cake shop, which opened in 1961, have stood the test of time and so too has its popularity. Regulars tend to order a decadent ice-cream sundae or a pile of chocolate and caramel profiteroles, but an espresso coffee and plate of house-made macaroons (₺14) is a tempting alternative.

MESHUR DONDURMACI
ALI USTA ICE CREAM €
(Moda Caddesi 176, Moda; dondurma from ₺4 per cone, milk puddings ₺8-9; ⊙11am-2am; 🏮; 🚊Kadıköy) Weekend and summer-night saunters down Moda Caddesi wouldn't be the same without a cone of the *dondurma* (ice cream) produced by master ice-cream maker Ali Usta. There are more than 40 flavours on offer – we like the *fıstıklı* (pistachio). In winter, a cup of *sahlep* (hot milky drink made from crushed orchid-root extract) with a milk pudding hits the spot.

HONEYCI SWEETS €
Map p253 (📞0533 515 8888; www.honeyci.com. tr; Güneşli Bahçe Sokak 28; yogurt & honey tub ₺5; ⊙9am-10pm; 🥄; 🚊Kadıköy) To sample one of the market's greatest treats, stop at this honey shop and ask for a yogurt with a generous swirl of honey from the comb on top.

★ÇIYA SOFRASI ANATOLIAN €€
Map p253 (📞0216-330 3190; www.ciya.com. tr; Güneşlibahçe Sokak 43; portions ₺12-30; ⊙11.30am-10pm; ❄️🥄🏮; 🚊Kadıköy) Known throughout the culinary world, Musa

Dağdeviren's *lokanta* (eatery serving ready-made food) showcases dishes from regional Turkey and is a wonderful place to sample treats such as *lahmacun* (Arabic-style pizza), *içli köfte* (meatballs rolled in bulgar and fried) and *perde pılavı* (chicken and rice in pastry casing). No alcohol, but the homemade *şerbet* (sweet fruit drink) is a delicious accompaniment. Vegetarians are very well catered for here, but should avoid Çiya's adjoining *kebapçı* (kebaps ₺18 to ₺40), which sells a huge variety of tasty meat dishes.

KADI NIMET BALIKÇILIK
SEAFOOD €€

Map p253 (📞0216-348 7389; www.kadinimet. com; Serasker Caddesi 10a; mezes ₺9-25; ⊘11am-11pm; ✳️🅿️; 🚇Kadıköy) Tucked in behind one of the market's best fish stalls, with the same owners, this much-loved restaurant is a good place to enjoy the daily catch. Make your choice from the cold mezes on display, choose your fish (daily price by weight) and let the waiters do the rest. Cold beer or rakı (aniseed brandy) are the usual accompaniments.

CIBALIKAPI
SEAFOOD €€€

(📞0216-348 9363; www.cibalikapibalikcisi.com; Moda Caddesi 163a, Moda; mezes ₺8-20, fish mains from ₺24; ⊘noon-midnight; ✳️; 🚇Kadıköy) Generally acknowledged as one of the city's best fish restaurants, Cibalikapı has two branches – one on the Golden Horn and the other here in Moda. Super-fresh mezes and seafood are enjoyed in the pleasant dining room or on the garden terrace. If you go with a large appetite the daily degustation (₺180 for two persons) is good value. The other branch is next to Kadir Has University in Fener on the Golden Horn.

 DRINKING & NIGHTLIFE

★FAZIL BEY
COFFEE

Map p253 (📞0216-450 2870; www.fazilbey.com; Serasker Caddesi 1; ⊘8am-11pm; 🚇Kadıköy) Making the call as to who makes the best Turkish coffee in İstanbul is no easy task, but our vote goes to Fazıl Bey, the best-loved *khavehan* (coffeeshop) on Serasker Caddesi. Enjoying a cup while watching the passing parade of shoppers has kept locals entertained for decades. There are other, less atmospheric, branches in Tavus Sokak and Bağdat Caddesi.

ARKAODA
BAR, CAFE

Map p253 (📞0216-418 0277; www.arkaoda.com; Kadife Sokak 18; ⊘noon-2am; 🛜; 🚇Kadıköy) A hub of indie music and art, this relaxed place hosts concerts, DJ sets, festivals, parties, themed markets and film screenings. The comfortable couches in the upstairs lounge are a great spot to while away the daytime hours with a coffee or tea; evening action moves to the rear courtyard, which is covered in winter.

KARGA BAR
BAR

Map p253 (📞0216-449 1725; www.karga.com. tr; Kadife Sokak 16; ⊘11am-2am; 🛜; 🚇Kadıköy) Multi-storey Karga is one of the most famous bars in the city, offering cheap drinks, alternative music (DJs and live acts) and avant-garde art on its walls. It's not signed well – look for the small black bird.

ARTHERE
CAFE

Map p253 (📞05380867691; www.arthereistanbul. com; Beydağı (Ferit Bey) Sokak 3, Rasimpaşa; ⊘10am-10pm; 🚇Kadıköy) Run by an artist collective, this hybrid cafe, art gallery and performance space is dedicated to artistic creation and hosts arty happenings, including films, installations, performances, workshops and exhibitions. The cafe serves coffee, fresh fruit juices and homemade pastries.

WALTER'S COFFEE ROASTERY
CAFE

Map p253 (📞0532 200 9892; http://walters coffeeroastery.com; Badem Altı Sokak 21b, Moda; ⊘10am-midnight; 🛜; 🚇Kadıköy) Describing itself as the 'world's first coffee lab' (a claim we repeat with a degree of scepticism), this designer roastery and cafe takes its coffee making seriously and serves espresso, Aeropress, chemex, cold brew and drip versions in its spacious Moda premises. It's popular at breakfast (pancakes ₺16, bagels ₺6 to ₺16).

 ENTERTAINMENT

SÜREYYA OPERA HOUSE
CLASSICAL MUSIC

Map p253 (📞0216-346 1531; www.sureyya operasi.org; Gen Asim Gündüz (Bahariye) Caddesi 29; 🚇Kadıköy) Built in 1927 and used for many years as a cinema, this bijou building was restored and opened as an opera house in 2007. It is the base of the İstanbul State Opera and Ballet.

WORTH A DETOUR

ÜSKÜDAR

A working-class suburb with a conservative population, Üsküdar isn't blessed with the restaurants, bars and cafes that give Kadıköy such a vibrant and inclusive edge, but it does have one very big asset – an array of magnificent imperial mosques. Foremost among these is the **Atik Valide Mosque** (Atik Valide Camii; Valide Imaret Sokak), designed by Sinan for the Valide Sultan Nurbanu, wife of Selim II (the Sot) and mother of Murat III. Dating from 1583, it has retained most of the buildings in its original *külliye* (mosque complex) and has a commanding location on Üsküdar's highest hill. The nearby **Çinili Mosque** (Çinili Camii, Tiled Mosque; Çinili Hamam Sokak) is dwarfed in comparison, but is notable for the multicoloured İznik tiles that adorn its interior. Slightly further up the hill is one of the few architecturally notable modern mosques in the city, the **Şakirin Mosque** (cnr Huhkuyusu Caddesi & Dr Burhanettin Üstünel Sokak; 6, 9A, 11P, 11V, 12A, 12C). Designed by Hüsrev Tayla and featuring an interior by Zeynap Fadıllıoğlu, it is located opposite the Zeynep Kamil Hospital on the road to Kadıköy.

Down by the *iskele* (ferry dock) are the **Mihrimah Sultan Mosque** (Mihrimah Sultan Camii; Paşa Limanı Caddesi), a Sinan design from 1547–48 that was commissioned by the daughter of Süleyman the Magnificent; and the **Yeni Valide Mosque** (Yeni Valide Camii, New Queen Mother's Mosque; Demokrasi Meydanı), commissioned by Ahmet III for his mother. South of the *iskele* is yet another Sinan design: the diminutive 1580 **Şemsi Ahmed Paşa Mosque** (Şemsi Paşa Camii, Kuskonmaz Camii; Paşa Limanı Caddesi). Next to this is the popular **Mistanbul Hancı Cafe** (Sahil Yolu 12; 9am-midnight), a waterside *çay bahçesi* (tea garden) where you can enjoy a tea, coffee or soft drink while admiring the view and watching the ever-present group of anglers trying their luck in the choppy waters below. Before leaving the suburb, consider purchasing some of the unusual and delicious *lokum* (Turkish Delight) sold at **Şekerci Aytekin Erol Caferzade** (0216-337 1337; www.caferzade.com.tr; Atlas Sokak 21; 8am-9pm) in the Balıkçılar Çarşısı (Fish Market) off Hakimiyeti Milliye Caddesi.

To get here from Kadıköy, take bus 12 or 12A from the bus station in front of the Turyol *iskele*, or one of the many dolmuşes (minibuses that stop anywhere along their prescribed routes) picking up passengers nearby. From Üsküdar, ferries travel back to Eminönü, Karaköy, Kabataş and Beşiktaş. Use the Üsküdar ferry and metro stations.

 SHOPPING

MESUT GÜNEŞ TEXTILES
Map p253 (0216-337 6215; www.mesutgunes.com.tr; Yasa Caddesi 44-46; 8.30am-6pm Mon-Sat; Kadıköy) It may not look like much from the front, but this shop often sells top-quality towels and sheets manufactured in Turkey for major international brands such as Frette for a fraction of their usual price.

ALI MUHIDDIN HACI BEKIR FOOD & DRINKS
Map p253 (0216-336 1519; Muvakkithane Caddesi 6; 8am-8pm; Kadıköy) This Kadıköy branch of İstanbul's most famous purveyors of *lokum* (Turkish Delight) has a small cafe at the rear of the shop.

MEPHISTO MUSIC
Map p253 (0216-414 3519; www.mephisto.com.tr; Muvakkithane Caddesi 15; 9am-10pm; Kadıköy) The Kadıköy branch of the city's best-known music store also has a cafe on its 1st floor.

 SPORTS & ACTIVITIES

TURKISH FLAVOURS WALKING
(0532 218 0653; www.turkishflavours.com; tours per person US$80-125) A well-regarded outfit offering foodie walks and cooking classes, Turkish Flavours runs a five-hour 'Market Tour' that starts at Eminönü's Spice Bazaar and then takes a ferry to Kadıköy, where it tours the produce market and finishes with a lavish lunch at Çiya Sofrası (p158). Other tours include a 'Meyhane Experience' and a vegetarian food tour through Karaköy and Kadıköy.

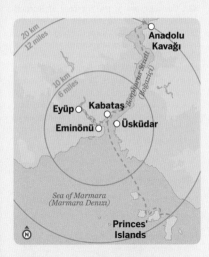

Day Trips

The Bosphorus p162

Running from the Galata Bridge all the way to the Black Sea (Karadeniz), 32km northeast, the mighty Bosphorus Strait has been İstanbul's major thoroughfare ever since classical times.

The Golden Horn p170

This stretch of water to the northwest of the Galata Bridge offers visitors a glimpse into the suburbs and lifestyles of working-class İstanbul. Get here before it gentrifies.

Princes' Islands p173

A favourite day-trip destination for İstanbullus, the Adalar Islands lie in the Sea of Marmara, about 20km southeast of the city. Come here to escape the sensory overload of the big smoke.

The Bosphorus

Explore

The Bosphorus deserves at least one day of your time; two days (one for each shore) is even better.

To spend a day exploring the European shore, purchase a one-way ticket for the Long Bosphorus Tour ferry trip leaving from Eminönü, alight at Sarıyer and work your way back to Kabataş or Taksim by bus, stopping at the Sadberk Hanım Museum, the Sakıp Sabancı Museum, Boru-san Contemporary, the fortress at Rumeli Hisarı, the waterside suburbs of Bebek, Arnavutköy and Ortaköy on the way.

To spend a day exploring the Asian shore, purchase a one-way ticket for the Long Bosphorus Tour ferry trip leaving from Eminönü, alight at Anadolu Kavağı and work your way back along that shore by bus, stopping to visit Hıdiv Kasrı, Küçüksu Kasrı and Beylerbeyi Palace before getting off the bus at Üsküdar and catching a ferry or the metro back to town.

Bosphorus Cruise

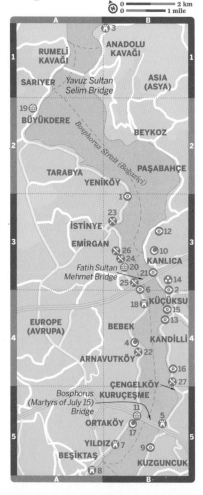

Bosphorus Cruise

Bosphorus Cruise

The Best...

➡**Sight** Beylerbeyi Palace (p164)
➡**Place to Eat** Kiyi (p170)
➡**Place to Drink** On the ferry

Top Tip

If you buy a return ticket on the Long Bosphorus Tour, you'll be forced to spend three hours in the tourist-trap village of Anadolu Kavağı. It's much better to buy a one-way ticket and alight there, at Sarıyer or at Kanlıca and make your way back to İstanbul by bus. Alternatively, take the Dentur Avraysa hop-on, hop-off tour from Kabataş.

Getting There & Away

➡**Long Bosphorus Tour (Uzun Boğaz Turu)** Most day-trippers take this ferry operated by İstanbul Şehir Hatları. It travels the entire length of the strait in a 95-minute one-way trip and departs from the *iskele* (ferry dock) at Eminönü daily at 10.35am, returning from Anadolu Kavağı at 3pm. A return (*çift*) ticket costs ₺25/free/12.50 per adult/child under six years/child six to 11 years; a one-way (*tek yön*) ticket costs ₺15/free/7.50. The ferry stops at Beşiktaş, Kanlıca, Sarıyer, Rumeli Kavağı and Anadolu Kavağı. It's not possible to get on and off the ferry at stops along the way using the same ticket.

➡**Short Bosphorus Tour (Kısa Boğaz Turu)** From early March to May and from mid-September to October, İstanbul Şehir Hatları offers a two-hour tour leaving Eminönü daily at 2.30pm, picking up passengers in Ortaköy 20 minutes later. It travels as far as the Fatih Sultan Mehmet Bridge before returning to Eminönü. Tickets cost ₺12/free/6 per adult/child under six years/ child six to 11 years. From November to early March the service is limited to Saturdays, Sundays and holidays.

➡**Hop-on, Hop-off Palace Tour** Departing from the *iskele* behind the petrol station at Kabataş, this tour operated by Dentur Avrasya costs ₺15, leaves four times daily at 12.45pm, 1.45pm, 2.45pm and 3.45pm, and allows passengers to alight at Emirgan, Küçüksu Kasrı and Beylerbeyi Palace and reboard on the same ticket. It would be very rushed to make three stops in one afternoon but two stops is achievable. Be aware that Küçüksu Kasrı and Beylerbeyi Palace close at 3.30pm in winter and 4.30pm in summer. Dentur Avrasya also operates one long and short tour each day from Kabataş; check website for details.

➡**Excursion Tours** A number of companies offer short tours from Eminönü to Anadolu Hisarı and back without stopping. Turyol is probably the most reputable. Its boats leave from the dock on the western side of the Galata Bridge (hourly, 10am to 6pm). Boats operated by other companies leave from near the Boğaz İskelesi and from near the Haliç İskelesi. The entire trip takes about 90 minutes and tickets usually cost ₺12.

Getting Around

All bus tickets and commuter ferry trips cost ₺4 (₺2.30 with an İstanbulkart).

➡**From Sarıyer** Buses 25E and 40 head south to Emirgan.

➡**From Emirgan** Buses 22, 22RE and 25E head to Kabataş, and 40, 40T and 42T go to Taksim. All travel via Rumeli Hisarı, Bebek, Ortaköy, Yıldız and Beşiktaş.

➡**From Anadolu Kavağı** Bus15A leaves from the square straight ahead from the ferry terminal en route to Kavacık. Get off at Kanlıca to visit Hıdiv Kasrı or transfer to bus 15 at Beykoz, which will take you south to Üsküdar via Çengelköy, the Küçüksu stop (for Küçüksu Kasrı) and the Beylerbeyi Sarayı stop (for Beylerbeyi Palace). Bus 15F and 15BK take the same route but continue to Kadıköy.

Need to Know

➡**Area Code** ☑0212 (European shore), 0216 (Asian shore)

◎ SIGHTS

The tour below follows the route of the Long Bosphorus Ferry Tour.

◎ Eminönü to Beşiktaş

Board the boat at the Boğaz İskelesi (Bosphorus Ferry Dock) on the Eminönü quay near the Galata Bridge. It's always a good idea to arrive 30 minutes or so before the scheduled departure time and manoeuvre your way to the front of the queue that builds near the doors leading to the dock. When these open and the boat can be boarded, you'll need to move fast to score a good seat. The best spots are on the sides of the upper deck at the bow or stern.

The Asian shore is to the right as the ferry cruises up the strait; Europe is to the left. When you start your trip, watch out for the small island of **Kız Kulesi**, just off the Asian shore near Üsküdar. One of the city's most distinctive landmarks, this 18th-century structure has functioned as a lighthouse, quarantine station and restaurant. It also featured in the 1999 James Bond film *The World Is Not Enough*. Just before the first stop at Beşiktaş, you'll pass the grandiose Dolmabahçe Palace (p149), built on the European shore of the Bosphorus by Sultan Abdül Mecit between 1843 and 1854.

◉ Beşiktaş to Kanlıca

After a brief stop at Beşiktaş, Çırağan Palace (p151), once home to Sultan Abdül Aziz and now a luxury hotel, looms up on the left. Next to it on the left is the Four Seasons Hotel; on the right is the long yellow building occupied by the prestigious Galatasaray University. Across the strait on the Asian shore is the **Fethi Ahmed Paşa Yalı** (Map p162; Kuzguncuk; 🚌15 from Üsküdar), a wide white building with a red-tiled roof that was built in the pretty suburb of Kuzguncuk in the late 18th century. The word *yalı* comes from the Greek word for 'coast', and describes the summer residences along the Bosphorus built by Ottoman aristocracy and foreign ambassadors in the 17th, 18th and 19th centuries, now all protected by the country's heritage laws.

A little further along on your left is the recently restored Ortaköy Mosque (p150). The mosque's dome and two minarets are dwarfed by the adjacent **Bosphorus Bridge**, opened in 1973 on the 50th anniversary of the founding of the Turkish Republic. The bridge acquired its now-official name of the **Martyrs of July 15 Bridge** after the unsuccessful military coup in July 2016.

Under the bridge on the European shore are two huge *yalıs:* the red-roofed **Hatice Sultan Yalı** (Map p250; Ortaköy; 🚌22 & 25E from Kabataş, 22RE & 40 from Beşiktaş, 40, 40T & 42T from Taksim), once the home of Sultan Murad V's daughter, Hatice; and the **Fehime Sultan Yalı** (Map p250; Ortaköy; 🚌22 & 25E from Kabataş, 22RE & 40 from Beşiktaş, 40, 40T & 42T from Taksim), home to Hatice's sister Fehime. Both are undergoing massive restorations and will be transformed into luxury hotels.

On the Asian side is the ornate **Beylerbeyi Palace** (Beylerbeyi Sarayı; Map p162; ☎0212-327 2626; www.millisaraylar.gov.tr; Abdullah Ağa Caddesi, Beylerbeyi; adult//student/child under 7yr ₺20/₺5/free; ⊙9am-4.30pm Tue, Wed & Fri-Sun Apr-Oct, to 3.30pm Nov-Mar; 🚌15 from Üsküdar), a 26-room waterside getaway built in 1865 for Abdül Aziz I (r 1861–76). Designed by Sarkis Balyan, brother of Nikoğos (architect of Dolmabahçe Palace), the baroque-style building delighted both Abdül Aziz and the foreign dignitaries who visited. The palace's last imperial 'guest' was the former sultan Abdül Hamit II, who spent the last years of his life (1913–18) under house arrest here. The palace interior features a grand *selamlik* (ceremonial quarters) and a small but opulent harem. Highlights include a hall featuring a huge marble pool used for cooling during summer, the elaborately painted and gilded sultan's apartment, the pretty sea-facing reception rooms of the *valide sultan* (mother of the sultan), the lavishly decorated blue hall in the *selamlik* and the dining room with chairs covered in gazelle skin. On the shoreline, look for its whimsical marble bathing pavilions on the shore; one was for men, the other for the women of the harem.

Further along on the Asian side, past the small village of Çengelköy, is the imposing **Kuleli Military School** (Map p162; Çengelköy; 🚌15, 15E, 15H, 15KÇ, 15M, 15N, 15P, 15ŞN, 15T, 15U from Üsküdar, 15F from Kadıköy), built in 1860 and immortalised in İrfan Orga's wonderful memoir *Portrait of a Turkish Family*. Look out for its two 'witch hat' towers.

Almost opposite Kuleli on the European shore is **Arnavutköy** (Albanian Village), which boasts a number of gabled Ottoman-era wooden houses and Greek Orthodox churches. On the hill above it are buildings formerly occupied by the American College for Girls. Its most famous alumni was Halide Edib Adıvar, who wrote about the years she spent here in her 1926 work *The Memoir of Halide Edib*. The building is now part of the prestigious Robert College.

Arnavutköy runs straight into the glamorous suburb of **Bebek**, known for its shopping and chic cafe-bars such as Lucca (p170). It also has the most glamorous Starbucks in the city, right on the water, with a lovely terrace. Bebek's shops surround a small park and the Ottoman Revivalist–style **Bebek Mosque** (Map p162; 🚌22, 22B & 25E from Kabataş, 22RE & 40 from Beşiktaş, 40, 40T & 42T from Taksim). To the east of these is the ferry dock; to the south is the **Egyptian consulate building** (Map p162; Bebek; 🚌22 & 25E from Kabataş, 22RE & 40 from Beşiktaş, 40, 40T & 42T from Taksim), thought by some to be the work of Italian architect Raimondo D'Aronco. This gorgeous art-nouveau mini-palace was built for Emine

Hanım, mother of the last khedive (viceroy) of Egypt, Abbas Hilmi II. It's the white building with two mansard towers and a wrought-iron fence.

Opposite Bebek on the Asian shore is **Kandilli**, the Place of Lamps, named after the lamps that were lit here to warn ships of the particularly treacherous currents at the headland. Among the many *yalıs* here is the huge red **Kont Ostrorog Yalı** (Map p162; Kandilli; 🚌15, 15F & 15T from Üsküdar), built in the 19th century by Count Leon Ostorog, a Polish adviser to the Ottoman court; Pierre Loti visited here when he was in İstanbul in the 1890s. A bit further on, past Kandilli, is the long white **Kıbrıslı (Cypriot) Yalı** (Map p162; Kandilli; 🚌15, 15E, 15H, 15KÇ, 15M, 15N, 15P, 15ŞN, 15T, 15U from Üsküdar, 14R & 15YK from Kadıköy), which dates from 1760.

Next to the Kıbrıslı are the **Büyük Göksu Deresi** (Great Heavenly Stream) and **Küçük Göksu Deresi** (Small Heavenly Stream), two brooks that descend from the Asian hills into the Bosphorus. Between them is a fertile delta, grassy and shady, which the Ottoman elite thought perfect for picnics. Foreign residents referred to it as the Sweet Waters of Asia. If the weather was good, the sultan joined the picnic, and did so in style. Sultan Abdül Mecit's answer to a simple picnic blanket was **Küçüksu Kasrı** (Map p162; ☎0216-332 3303; Küçüksu Caddesi, Küçüksu; adult/student/child under 7yr ₺5/1/free; ⊙9am-4.30pm Tue, Wed & Fri-Sun Apr-Oct, to 3.30pm Nov-Mar; 🚌15, 15E, 15H, 15KÇ, 15M, 15N, 15P, 15ŞN, 15T, 15U from Üsküdar, 14R & 15YK from Kadıköy, ⛴Kabataş), an ornate hunting lodge built in 1856–57. Earlier sultans had wooden kiosks here, but architect Nikoğos Balyan designed a rococo gem in marble for his monarch. You'll see its ornate cast-iron fence, boat dock and wedding-cake exterior from the ferry.

Close to the Fatih Sultan Mehmet Bridge are the majestic fortress structures of **Rumeli Hisarı** (Fortress of Europe; Map p162; ☎0212-263 5305; Yahya Kemal Caddesi 42; ₺10; ⊙9am-noon & 12.30-4pm Thu-Tue; 🚌22 & 25E from Kabataş, 22RE & 40 from Beşiktaş, 40, 40T & 42T from Taksim) and **Anadolu Hisarı** (Fortress of Anatolia; Map p162; 🚌15, 15KÇ & 15ŞN from Üsküdar, 15F from Kadıköy). Mehmet the Conqueror had Rumeli Hisarı built in a mere four months in 1452, in preparation for his siege of Byzantine Constantinople. For its location, he chose the narrowest point of the Bosphorus, opposite Anadolu Hisarı, which Sultan Beyazıt I had built in 1394. By doing so, Mehmet was able to control all traffic on the strait, cutting the city off from resupply by sea.

To speed up Rumeli Hisarı's completion, Mehmet ordered each of his three viziers to take responsibility for one of the three main towers. If his tower's construction was not completed on schedule, the vizier would pay with his life. Not surprisingly, the work was completed on time. The useful military life of the mighty fortress lasted less than one year. After the conquest of Constantinople, it was used as a glorified Bosphorus toll booth for a while, then as a barracks, a prison and finally as an open-air theatre. Within Rumeli Hisarı's walls are park-like grounds, an open-air theatre and the minaret of a ruined mosque. Steep stairs (with no barriers, so beware!) lead up to the ramparts and towers; the views of the Bosphorus are magnificent. Just next to the fortress is a clutch of cafes and restaurants, the most popular of which are Sade Kahve (p169) and Lokma (p170).

Between Rumeli Hisarı and the **Fatih Sultan Mehmet Bridge** is an eccentric-looking turreted building known locally as the Perili Köşk (Haunted Mansion). Properly referred to as the Yusuf Ziya Pasha mansion, the building's construction kicked off around 1910 but was halted in 1914 when the Ottoman Empire was drawn into WWI and all of its construction workers were forced to quit their jobs and enlist in the army. Work on the 10-storey building came to a standstill and it remained empty, leading to its 'haunted mansion' tag. Eighty years later, work finally resumed and the finished building became the home of **Borusan Contemporary** (Map p162; ☎0212-393 5200; www.borusancontemporary.com; Perili Köşk, Baltalimanı Hisar Caddesi 5, Rumeli Hisarı; adult/student/child under 12yr ₺10/5/free; ⊙10am-8pm Sat & Sun; 🚌22 & 25E from Kabataş, 22RE & 40 from Beşiktaş, 40, 40T & 42T from Taksim), a cultural centre.

The ferry doesn't stop at Rumeli Hisarı; you can either leave the ferry at Kanlıca and catch a taxi across the Fatih Bridge (this will cost around ₺25 including the bridge toll) or you can visit on your way back to town from Sarıyer. Though it's not open as a museum, visitors are free to wander about Anadolu Hisarı's ruined walls.

There are many architecturally and historically important *yalıs* in and around Anadolu Hisarı. These include the **Köprülü Amcazade Hüseyin Paşa Yalı** (Map p162; Anadolu Hisarı; 🚌15, 15KÇ & 15ŞN from Üsküdar, 15F from Kadıköy), a cantilevered box-like structure built for one of Mustafa II's grand viziers

1. Ortaköy Mosque (p150) & the Bosphorus (Martyrs of July 15) Bridge (p164)

Viewed from the water between Beşiktaş and Kanlıca, this location offers a fabulous photo opportunity.

2. *Faytons* (horse-drawn carriages; p174)

One of the main forms of transport on Büyükada island, the largest of the Princes' Islands.

3. Rumeli Hisarı (p165)

The Fortress of Europe, located on the European side of the Bosphorus, was built by Mehmet the Conqueror in just four months.

in 1698. The oldest *yalı* on the Bosphorus, it is currently undergoing a major renovation. Next door, the **Zarif Mustafa Paşa Yalı** (Map p162; Anadolu Hisarı; ⬚15, 15KÇ & 15ŞN from Üsküdar, 15F from Kadıköy) was built in the early 19th century by the official barista to Sultan Mahmut II. Look for its upstairs salon, which juts out over the water and is supported by unusual curved timber struts.

Almost directly under the Fatih Bridge on the European shore is the huge stone four-storey **Tophane Müşiri Zeki Paşa Yalı** (Map p162; Rumeli Hisarı; ⬚22 & 25E from Kabataş, 22RE & 40 from Beşiktaş, 40, 40T & 42T from Taksim), a mansion built in the early 20th century for a field marshall in the Ottoman army. Later, it was sold to Sabiha Sultan, daughter of Mehmet VI, the last of the Ottoman sultans, and her husband İmer Faruk Efendi, grandson of Sultan Abdül Aziz. When the sultanate was abolished in 1922, Mehmet walked from this palace onto a British warship, never to return to Turkey.

Past the bridge on the Asian side is **Kanlıca**, the ferry's next stop. This charming village is famous for the rich and delicious yoghurt produced here, which is sold on the ferry and in two cafes on the shady waterfront square. The small **Gâzi İskender Paşa Mosque** (Map p162; Kanlıca; ⬚Kanlıca) in the square dates from 1560 and was designed by Mimar Sinan. There are excellent views of a number of *yalıs* as the ferry arrives and departs here.

High on a promontory above Kanlıca is **Hıdiv Kasrı** (Khedive's Villa; Map p162; www.beltur.com.tr; Çubuklu Yolu 32, Çubuklu; ☉9am-10pm; ⬚Kanlıca) FREE, a palatial art-nouveau villa built in 1906. You can see its square white tower (often flying a Turkish flag) from the ferry. The property is known as the Khedive's Villa (Hıdiv Kasrı) in reference to the man who commissioned it, Khedive Abbas Hilmi II, *hıdiv* (khedive or viceroy) of Egypt. The khedives maintained close ties with the Ottoman Empire and many spent summers in İstanbul to escape the debilitating Egyptian heat. This villa functioned as one of their summer residences until the 1930s. Restored after decades of neglect, the villa now functions as a restaurant and cafe. The building is an architectural gem and the garden is superb, especially during the İstanbul International Tulip Festival in April. The villa is a 20-minute walk from the *iskele* (ferry dock) at Kanlıca. Head left (north) up Halide Edip Adivar Caddesi and turn right into the second street (Kafadar Sokak). Turn left into Hacı Muhittin Sokağı and walk up the hill until you come to a fork in the road. Take the left fork and follow the 'Hadiv Kasrı' signs to the villa's car park and garden.

⊙ Kanlıca to Sarıyer

On the shore opposite Kanlıca is the wealthy suburb of Emirgan, home to the impressive **Sakıp Sabancı Museum** (Map p162; ☎0212-277 2200; www.sakipsabancimuzesi.org; Sakıp Sabancı Caddesi 42, Emirgan; adult/student/child under 14yr ₺20/10/free, Wed free; ☉10am-5.30pm Tue, Thu & Fri-Sun, to 7.30pm Wed; ⬚22 & 25E from Kabataş, 22RE & 40 from Beşiktaş, 40, 40T & 42T from Taksim). This museum has a permanent collection showcasing Ottoman manuscripts and calligraphy, but is best known for its blockbuster temporary exhibitions. The permanent collection occupies a 1925 mansion designed by Italian architect Edouard De Nari for the Egyptian Prince Mehmed Ali Hasan and the temporary exhibitions are staged in an impressive modern extension designed by local firm Savaş, Erkel and Çırakoğlu.

On the hill above Emirgan is **Emirgan Korusu (Woods)**, a huge public reserve that is particularly beautiful in April, when it is carpeted with thousands of tulips.

North of Emirgan, there's a ferry dock near the small yacht-lined cove of **İstinye**. Nearby, on a point jutting out from the European shore, is the suburb of **Yeniköy**. This was a favourite summer resort for the Ottomans, as indicated by the cluster of lavish 18th- and 19th-century *yalıs* around the ferry dock. The most notable of these is the frilly white **Ahmed Afif Paşa Yalı** (Map p162; Yeniköy; ⬚25E from Kabataş, 40B from Beşiktaş, 40T & 42T from Taksim), designed by Alexandre Vallaury, architect of the Pera Palas Hotel in Beyoğlu, and built in the late 19th century.

On the opposite shore is the village of **Paşabahçe**, famous for its glassware factory. A bit further on is the fishing village of **Beykoz**, which has a graceful ablutions fountain, the **İshak Ağa Çeşmesi**, dating from 1746, near the village square. Much of the land along the Bosphorus shore north of Beykoz is a military zone.

Originally called Therapia for its healthy climate, the little cove of **Tarabya** on the European shore has been a favourite summer watering place for İstanbul's well-to-do for centuries, though modern developments such as the multistorey Grand Hotel Tarabya right on the promontory have poisoned much of its charm. For an account of Therapia in its heyday, read Harold Nicolson's 1921 novel *Sweet Waters*. Nicolson, who is best known as Vita Sackville-West's husband, served as the third Secretary in the British embassy in Constantinople between 1912 and 1914, the years of the Balkan wars, and clearly knew Therapia well. In the novel, the main character, Eirene, who was based on Vita, spent her summers here.

North of the village are some of the old summer embassies of foreign powers. When the heat and fear of disease increased in the warm months, foreign ambassadors would retire to palatial residences, complete with lush gardens, on this shore. The region for such embassy residences extended north to the village of Büyükdere, notable for its churches, summer embassies and the **Sadberk Hanım Museum** (Map p162; ☏0212-242 3813; www.sadberkhanimmuzesi.org.tr; Piyasa Caddesi 27-29, Büyükdere; adult/student ₺7/2; ⊙10am-4.30pm Thu-Tue; ℙ; ⊕Sarıyer). Named after the wife of the late Vehbi Koç, founder of Turkey's foremost commercial empire, this museum is housed in two late 19th-century *yalıs* and is a showcase of both Turkish-Islamic artefacts collected by Mrs Koç and antiquities from the noted Hüseyin Kocabaş collection. Objects include İznik and Kütahya ceramics, Ottoman silk textiles and needlework, and an exquisite collection of diadems from the Mycenaean, Archaic and classical periods. Labels are in English and Turkish, and there's an excellent gift shop. To get here, alight from the ferry at Sarıyer and walk left (south) from the ferry dock for approximately 10 minutes.

The residents of **Sarıyer**, the next village up from Büyükdere on the European shore, have traditionally made a living by fishing and it is still possible to see fisherfolk mending their nets and selling their catch north of the dock.

◉ Sarıyer to Anadolu Kavaği

From Sarıyer, it's a short trip to **Rumeli Kavağı**, a sleepy place where the only excitement comes courtesy of the arrival and departure of the ferry. South of the town lies the shrine of the Muslim saint Telli Baba, reputed to be able to find suitable husbands for young women who pray there. **Anadolu Kavağı**, on the opposite shore, is where the Long Bosphorus Ferry Tour finishes its journey. Once a fishing village, its local economy now relies on the tourism trade and its main square is full of mediocre fish restaurants and their touts.

Perched above the village are the ruins of **Anadolu Kavağı Kalesi** (Yoros Kalesi; Map p162; Anadolu Kavağı; ⊕Anadolu Kavağı), a medieval castle overlooking the Black Sea and the Bosphorus. The castle originally had eight massive towers in its walls, but little of the original structure has survived. First built by the Byzantines, it was restored and reinforced by the Genoese in the 1300s, and later by the Ottomans. An archaeological excavation is underway and, as a result, access is limited. There are, however, great views of the recently opened Yavuz Sultan Selim (Third) Bridge. It takes 30 to 50 minutes to walk up to the fortress from the town. Alternatively, taxis wait near the fountain in the town square just east of the ferry dock; they charge around ₺20 for the return trip with 30 minutes waiting time. Restaurants and *çay bahçesis* (tea gardens) along the walking route serve overpriced food and drink.

EATING & DRINKING

There are places to suit every taste and budget along the shores of the Bosphorus. Many day-trippers choose to organise an itinerary around their choice of lunch venue, and there's a lot to be said for following this example.

HIDIV KASRI GARDEN CAFE
CAFE €

Map p162 (☏0216-413 9253; www.beltur.com.tr; Çubuklu Yolu 32, Çubuklu; sandwiches ₺6.20-9.50, cakes ₺8.50; ⊙from 9am; ℙ⊕; ⊕Kanlıca) Occupying the conservatory and garden terrace of art-nouveau villa Hıdiv Kasrı, this cafe is an excellent choice on a sunny day. A toasted sandwich or cake is the most popular choice, but there are burgers, pastas and salads on offer, too.

SADE KAHVE
TURKISH €

Map p162 (☏0212-263 8800; www.sadekahve.com.tr; Yahya Kemal Caddesi 20a, Rumeli Hisarı; breakfast plates ₺5-12, gözleme & börek ₺14-15; ⊙7am-midnight; 🚌22 & 25E from Kabataş, 22RE & 40 from Beşiktaş, 40, 40T & 42T from Taksim) Seats on the outdoor terrace are hotly contested on sunny weekends at this İstanbul institution, where the all-day breakfasts are both cheap and tasty.

SÜTIŞ
CAFE €

Map p162 (📞0212-323 5030; www.sutis.com.tr; Sakıp Sabancı Caddesi 1, Emirgan; breakfast dishes ₺5-26, milk puddings ₺10; ⏰6am-2am; 🅿✳🛜♿; 🚌22 & 25E from Kabataş, 22RE & 40 from Beşiktaş, 40, 40T & 42T from Taksim) The Bosphorus branch of this popular chain has an expansive and comfortable terrace overlooking the water. It's known for all-day breakfasts and its huge range of sweet treats. We recommend a *simit* (sesame-encrusted bread ring) with *bal kaymak* (honey and clotted cream; ₺10) in the morning and a *muhallebisi* (milk pudding) in the afternoon. Watching the valet parking ritual on weekends is hilarious.

LOKMA
INTERNATIONAL €€

Map p162 (📞0212-265 7171; www.lokma.com.tr; Yahya Kemal Caddesi 18, Rumeli Hisarı; breakfast dishes ₺6.50-14.50, pizzas ₺17.50-27, burgers ₺18-28; ⏰6am-midnight; 🛜♿; 🚌22 & 25E from Kabataş, 22RE & 40 from Beşiktaş, 40, 40T & 42T from Taksim) Enjoying brunch in Rumeli Hisarı is a popular pastime, so this newcomer to the main drag has no problems filling its 300-odd seats on weekends. The huge terrace (glassed-in during the winter months) with its Bosphorus view is a great spot to enjoy *börek* or eggs at breakfast; pizzas and burgers are the rule at lunch. No alcohol.

KIYI
SEAFOOD €€€

Map p162 (📞0212-262 0002; Haydar Aliyev Caddesi 186, Tarabya; mezes ₺12-30, mains from ₺40; ⏰midday-midnight; 🚌22, 25E & 29C from Kabataş, 22RE & 40 from Beşiktaş, 40, 40T & 42T from Taksim) Named after a species of freshwater whitefish, this large and often boisterous restaurant has been serving excellent seafood to locals since the 1960s and remains popular with many of the city's movers and shakers. In summer, the upstairs terrace is the place to be; during winter the action moves into the art-adorned dining room. Menu items are standard but delicious.

ANTICA LOCANDA
ITALIAN €€€

Map p162 (📞0212-287 9745; www.anticalocanda.com.tr; Satış Meydanı 12, Arnavutköy; starters ₺20-40, mains ₺36-70; ⏰6.30-10pm Tue, noon-2pm & 6.30-10pm Wed-Sat, noon-2pm Sun; 🅿✳🛜♿; 🚌22, 22RE & 25E from Kabataş, 40, 40T & 42T from Taksim) Milanese-born chef Gian Carlo Talerico and his Turkish wife Beldan Erkkul converted this former residence of the Aya Strati Taksiarhi Greek Orthodox Church complex into an elegant trattoria in 2011. They keep a loyal coterie of locals happy with takes on classic Italian dishes including grills, pastas and pizzas.

TAPASUMA
MODERN TURKISH €€€

Map p162 (📞0216-401 1333; www.tapasuma.com; Kuleli Caddesi 43, Çengelköy; mezes ₺14-35, mains ₺49-85; ⏰11.30am-midnight; ✳; 🚌15, 15E, 15H, 15KÇ, 15M, 15N, 15P, 15ŞN, 15T, 15U from Üsküdar) Set in a restored 19th-century rakı distillery (*suma* is a Turkish word meaning 'unadulterated spirit'), this stylish restaurant is attached to the luxury Sumahan on the Water hotel and has a stunning waterside location. The menu features Turkish mezes with a modern twist, as well as fresh seafood mains. Sadly, service standards don't match the hefty prices.

MÜZEDECHANGA
MODERN TURKISH €€€

Map p162 (📞0212-323 0901; www.changa-istanbul.com; Sakıp Sabancı Müzesi, Sakıp Sabancı Caddesi 42, Emirgan; starters ₺35-48, mains ₺65-85; ⏰10.30am-midnight Tue-Sun; ✳🛜♿; 🚌22 & 25E from Kabataş, 22RE & 40 from Beşiktaş, 40, 40T & 42T from Taksim) A glamorous terrace with Bosphorus views is the main draw of this design-driven restaurant at the Sakıp Sabancı Museum. Sadly, the overpriced menu offerings look better than they taste. If you don't feel like visiting the museum, door staff will waive the entry fee and point you towards the restaurant.

LUCCA
BAR

Map p162 (📞0212-257 1255; www.luccastyle.com; Cevdetpaşa Caddesi 51b, Bebek; ⏰10am-2am; 🚌22, 22B & 25E from Kabataş, 22RE & 40 from Beşiktaş, 40, 40T & 42T from Taksim) Embraced by the in-crowd since 2005, Lucca's star shows no sign of waning. Glam young things flock here on Friday and Saturday nights to see and be seen, but the mood is more relaxed during the week. Food choices are global; coffee reigns supreme during the day; and cocktails claim the spotlight at night.

The Golden Horn

Explore

You can explore the Haliç (Golden Horn) in half a day by boarding the commuter ferry in Karaköy or Eminönü, alighting once at either Hasköy (for the Rahmi M Koç Museum) or Eyüp (for the Eyüp Sultan Mosque) and then reboarding a ferry for the return trip. If you have a full day, you could visit both of these sights and also visit Aynalıkavak Kasrı before or after visiting the Rahmi M Koç Museum. Another good option is to alight at Ayvansaray on your return trip, follow the historic land walls up the hill and visit the Kariye Museum (Chora Church).

The Best...

⇒ **Sight** Rahmi M Koç Museum (p172)
⇒ **Local Life** Eyüp Medanı
⇒ **Place to Drink** Pierre Loti Café (p122)

Top Tip

If visiting the Eyüp Sultan Mosque (p118), dress appropriately (no shorts or skimpy skirts and tops). Females should bring a scarf or shawl to use as a head covering.

Getting There & Around

Ferry

⇒ **İstanbul Şehir Hatları** (İstanbul City Routes; ☏153; www.sehirhatlari.com.tr) Operates the commuter Haliç ferry service. Departs Üsküdar hourly from 7.30am to 8.45pm and travels up the Golden Horn to Eyüp, picking up most passengers in Karaköy and Eminönü; the last ferry returns from Eyüp at 7.45pm (8.45pm on Sunday). The trip takes 55 minutes (35 minutes from Eminönü) and tickets cost ₺4 (₺2.30 with an İstanbulkart). If you alight, you'll need to pay a new fare for the next leg. Note that all passengers must alight at Eyüp. Check online for timetable and fare updates.

⇒ **Dentur Avraysa** (☏444 6336; www.denturavrasya.com) Offers a hop-on, hop-off tour (₺15) departing from Beşiktaş at 10am, noon, 2pm, 4pm and 6pm, stopping at Kabataş (where most people board), Hasköy, Eyüp and the Miniatürk theme park in Sütlüce before making the return trip. Check online for schedule updates.

Bus

All bus tickets cost ₺4 (₺2.30 with an İstanbulkart).

⇒ **Fom Eyüp** Buses 36CE, 44B, 48E, 99, 99Y and 399B/C travel to Eminönü from the Necip Fazıl Kısaküre stop in front of the ferry via Balat, Fener and Karaköy. Bus 39C travels to Aksaray via Edirnekapı, allowing you to stop and visit the Kariye Museum.
⇒ **From Hasköy** Buses 36T, 54K or 54HT travel to Taksim. Buses 47, 47E or 47N travel to Eminönü.

Need to Know

⇒ **Area Code** ☏0212

SIGHTS

Few visitors to İstanbul have heard about the ferry route up and down the length of the Golden Horn (Haliç). Until recently, this stretch of water to the north of the Galata Bridge was heavily polluted and its suburbs offered little to tempt travellers. All that's changing these days, with the Haliç suburbs being gentrified and beautification work, including the creation of many parks, being undertaken along both sides of the waterway. The ferry trip to Eyüp offers magnificent views of the imperial mosques atop the Old City's hills, glimpses of the historic city walls and panoramas of ancient suburbs including Fener, Balat and Ayvansaray. On the opposite shore, vistas include Ottoman *mezarlıgıs* (cemeteries) and the remnants of Ottoman arsenals and naval docks.

Üsküdar to Kasımpaşa

After departing from Üsküdar on the Asian side, the ferry stops at the Haliç *iskelesıs* (Golden Horn ferry docks) at **Karaköy** and **Eminönü**. The Karaköy *iskele* is on the northern side of the Galata Bridge, before the large Kadıköy *iskele*. The Eminönü *iskele* is on the western side of the Galata Bridge behind a car park next to the bus station. From Eminönü, the ferry passes underneath the Haliç Metro Bridge and the Atatürk (aka Unkapanı) Bridge before stopping at **Kasımpaşa** on the opposite side of the Golden Horn. This area is where the Ottoman imperial naval yards were located between the 16th and early 20th centuries, and some of the original building stock remains. The palace-like building to the left of the *iskele* is the 19th-century **Bahriye Nezareti** (Map p172; ☒Kasımpaşa), where the Ministry for the Navy was once based. It is currently undergoing a major restoration. On the hill above is an 18th-century building with a clock tower. This was originally

DAY TRIPS THE GOLDEN HORN

Golden Horn Cruise

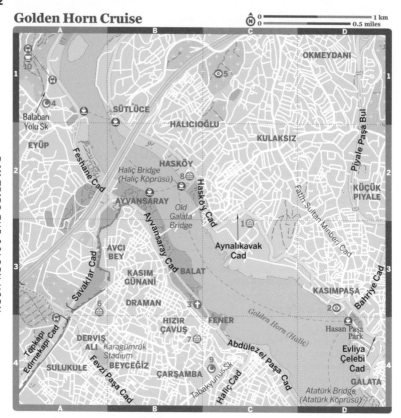

the Naval Academy but was converted to a hospital in the 1850s; French soldiers were treated here during the Crimean War. There are plans to redevelop the shipyards here into a huge complex including shops, hotels and restaurants, although locals seem sceptical that this will go ahead in the near future.

◉ Kasımpaşa to Hasköy

As the ferry makes its way to the next stop, Hasköy, you can see the fascinating Western District suburbs of **Fener** and **Balat** on the western (left) shore.

Fener is the traditional home of the city's Greek population and, although few Greeks are resident these days, a number of important Greek Orthodox sites remain. The prominent red-brick building with domed tower on the hill is the Phanar Greek Orthodox College (p118), the oldest

house of learning in İstanbul. The school has been housed in Fener since before the Conquest, but the present building dates from 1881–83. Sadly, it currently has a total enrollment of only 50 or so students. From this point, there are good views of the Yavuz Sultan Selim Mosque (p118) on the ridgeline and the Gothic Revival Church of St Stephen of the Bulgars (p121) on the waterfront, which has distinctive gilded copolas.

The next suburb, Balat, was once home to a large proportion of İstanbul's Jewish population, but is now crowded with migrants from the east of the country.

Passing the derelict remains of the original Galata Bridge on its way, the ferry then docks at **Hasköy**. For centuries a small, predominantly Jewish village, Hasköy became home to a naval shipyard and a sultan's hunting ground in the Ottoman period. Today it has two sights of interest to visitors, the Rahmi M Koç Museum, which is located directly to the left of the ferry stop

Golden Horn Cruise

(Hasköy İskelesi); and Aynalıkavak Kasrı, a short walk away.

The splendid **Rahmi M Koç Museum** (Rahmi M Koç Müzesi; Map p172; ☎0212-369 6600; www.rmk-museum.org.tr; Hasköy Caddesi 5; museum adult/student/child under 7yr ₺15/6/ free, steam-tug cruise ₺5/3/free, submarine adult/ student ₺7/5, planetarium ₺2; ⊙10am-5pm Tue-Fri, to 6pm Sat & Sun Oct-Mar, to 7pm Sat & Sun Apr-Sep; ⛴Hasköy) is dedicated to the history of transport, industry and communications in Turkey. Founded by the head of the Koç industrial group, one of Turkey's most prominent conglomerates, it exhibits artefacts from İstanbul's industrial past and is highly interactive, making it a particularly enjoyable destination for those travelling with children. The museum is in two parts: a new building constructed around a 19th-century dockyard on the Golden Horn side of the road, and a restored and converted Byzantine stone building known as the Lengerhane. The latter was used as a foundry by the Ottomans and now houses a planetarium and a large collection of model trains and boats. The exhibits concerned with forms of transport are particularly fascinating: you can admire a huge collection of mint-condition classic cars; climb aboard historic trams; take a cruise on a restored 1936 steam tug (summer weekends only); enter the cabin of a 1942 Douglas DC-3 Dakota; board a 1944 US naval submarine (advance bookings essential); or take a short trip on a working narrow-gauge railway (summer weekends only).

Excellent interpretive panels in Turkish and English are provided. There's also a Turkish restaurant right on the waterfront, a cafe in a restored 1953 ferry boat and a French restaurant in the Lengerhane.

The ornate 18th-century imperial hunting pavilion of **Aynalıkavak Kasrı** (Aynalıkavak Pavilion; Map p172; ☎0212-256 9750; www.millisaraylar.gov.tr; Aynalıkavak Caddesi; adult/student ₺5/1; ⊙9am-4.30pm Tue, Wed & Fri-Sun Apr-Oct, to 3.30pm Nov-Mar; ☐47, 47E, 47N from Eminönü; 36T, 54K, 54HT from Taksim), is set in a pretty garden and now houses a collection of historic musical instruments. To get there from the *iskele*, walk southeast (right) along Hasköy Caddesi, veer left into Okmeydanı Caddesi and then right into Sempt Konağı Sokak, which runs into Kasımpaşa-Hasköy Caddesi.

A number of historic cemeteries cling to the hills behind Hasköy. These include the **Hasköy Musevi Mezarlığı** (Map p172; ⛴Sütlüce), where many generations of Jewish İstanbullus have been buried.

⊙ Hasköy to Eyüp

The ferry's next stop is at **Ayvansaray** on the opposite shore. From here you can visit the Kariye Museum (Chora Church; p114) or walk up to Edirnekapı to see a well-preserved section of the historic city walls. It's possible to see part of the wall structure from the ferry.

From Ayvansaray, the ferry crosses to **Sütlüce** and returns to the western shore to terminate at **Eyüp**. This conservative suburb is built around the Eyüp Sultan Mosque (p118), one of the most important religious sites in Turkey.

✗ EATING & DRINKING

This isn't a part of town known for its eating and drinking options. Your best options for lunch are the cafes and restaurants in the Rahmi M Koç Museum complex (there are three of them). For a tea or coffee break, head to the Pierre Loti Café (p122) in Eyüp.

Princes' Islands

Explore

This is a great day trip, particularly as the ferry ride is so enjoyable. Lying 20km southeast of the city in the Sea of Marmara, there are nine islands in the group, five of which are populated (combined population 16,050). Most visitors head to the two largest, Büyükada and Heybeliada. If you manage to catch an early ferry, you will be able to spend the morning on Heybeliada and the afternoon on Büyükada (or vice versa). Note that many restaurants and most hotels are closed between November and April; and that ferry services are occasionally cancelled due to poor weather, resulting in visitors being stranded overnight. For further information, check the English-language website of the **Adalar Belediyesi** (www.adalar.bel.tr).

The Best...

➡ **Sight** Hagia Triada Monastery (p175), Heybeliada

➡ **Place to Eat** Teras Restaurant (p176), Büyükada

➡ **View** Yücetepe Kır Gazinosu Restaurant (p176), Büyükada

Top Tip

The islands can be oppressively crowded between May and October, when visitors number up to 50,000 per day on weekends. To avoid these crowds, visit on a weekday.

Getting There & Away

On summer weekends, board the ferry and grab a seat at least half an hour before departure time unless you want to stand the whole way. From the right side of the ferry you can view the various islands en route. Heading towards the Sea of Marmara, passengers are treated to fine views of Topkapı Palace, Aya Sofya and the Blue Mosque on the right and Kız Kulesi, Haydarpaşa train station and the distinctive minaret-style clock towers of Marmara University on the left. After a quick stop at Kadıköy, the ferry makes its way to the first island in the group, Kınalıada (30 minutes); then to Burgazada (15 minutes); to Heybeliada (15 minutes), the second-largest island; and to Büyükada (10 minutes), the largest island in the group. Be sure to check the websites of all companies as schedules and routes change regularly.

➡ **İstanbul Şehir Hatları** (p171) Runs at least eight ferry services daily to the islands from 6.50am to 11pm (to 9pm June to mid-September) from Kabataş. These depart from the Adalar İskelesi (Adalar Ferry

Dock). The most useful departure times for day-trippers are 8.40am and 10.40am (8.30am, 9.30am and 10.30am from June to mid-September). The trip costs ₺5.50 (₺4.40 with an İstanbulkart) to the islands and the same for each leg between the islands and for the return trip. Ferries return to İstanbul every two hours or so. Last ferries leave Büyükada at 6.15pm and 8.20pm and Heybeliada at 6.30pm and 8.35pm (9.15pm and 10.15pm from Büyükada and 9.30pm and 10.30pm from Heybeliada from June to mid-September).

➡ **İDO** (☑0850-222 4436; www.ido.com.tr) Offers two daily fast catamaran ferry services from Kabataş (₺11 *jeton* or ₺8.60 on İstanbulkart).

➡ **Dentur Avrasya** (p171) Operates regular small ferries stopping at Büyükada and Heybeliada (₺6); these leave from the dock behind the gas station at Kabataş.

➡ **Turyol** (☑0212-251 4421; http://turyol.com) Operates small ferry services between three and five times per day from both Karaköy and Eminönü to Büyükada (₺6).

Getting Around

One of the wonderful things about the Princes' Islands is that they are car-free zones. The main forms of transport are motorised carts, bicycles and *faytons* (horse-drawn carriages). The name *fayton* comes from the mythical Phaeton, son of the sun god Helios.

Need to Know

➡ **Area Code** ☑0216

 SIGHTS

Most İstanbullus refer to the Princes' Islands as simply The Islands (Adalar). Populated since the 4th century BC, the islands acquired their present name in the 6th century AD after coming into the possession of the Byzantine prince, Justin. The first Greek Orthodox monastery was established in 846 and regular ferry services from İstanbul began in 1846. Wealthy İstanbullus then began to purchase holiday villas here. Büyükada and Burgaza were popular with families of Greek and Jewish heritage; Heybeliada was predominantly Greek.

Popular island activities include cycling or walking along the attractive villa-lined streets, and exploring the protected pine-scented forests, which cover 50% of the landscape on both Büyükada and Heybeliada. Swimming is also popular, with the best beaches being on Büyükada; note that the water quality is regularly tested between May and October and the beaches only open when given an all-clear.

◉ Kabataş to the Islands

After boarding, try to find a seat on the right side of the ferry so that you can view the various islands as the ferry approaches them. Heading towards the Sea of Marmara, passengers are treated to fine views of Topkapı Palace (p61), Aya Sofya (p54) and the Blue Mosque (p72) on the right and **Kız Kulesi** (adult/student ₺20/10; ◷9am-6.45pm; 🚊Üsküdar, Ⓜ️Üsküdar), Haydarpaşa Railway Station (p158) and the distinctive minaret-style clock towers of Marmara University (p82) on the left.

◉ Heybeliada

Heybeliada (Heybeli for short and Halki in Greek) is the prettiest island in the Adalar group, replete with ornate 19th-century timber villas and offering gorgeous sea views from myriad viewpoints. It's extremely popular with day-trippers from İstanbul, who flock here on weekends to walk in the pine groves and swim from the tiny and usually crowded beaches.

As you arrive, you'll see the Deniz Lisesi (Turkish Navel Academy) to the left of the *iskele*. This was founded in 1824.

The island's major landmark is the **Hagia Triada Monastery** (Aya Triada; 📞0216-351 8563; Ümit Tepesi; ◷daily by appointment; 🚊Heybeliada), which is perched above a picturesque line of poplar trees in a spot that has been occupied by a Greek monastery since Byzantine times. This 1844 complex housed a Greek Orthodox theological school until 1971, when it was closed on the government's orders; the Ecumenical Orthodox Patriarchate is waging an ongoing campaign to have it reopened. There's a small church with an ornate altar and an internationally renowned library that houses many old and rare manuscripts. To visit the library, you'll need to gain special permission from the abbot, Metropolitan Elpidophoros. A *fayton* will charge around ₺30 to bring you here from the centre of town.

The delightful walk from the *iskele* up to the Merit Halki Palace hotel at the top of Refah Şehitleri Caddesi passes a host of large wooden villas set in lovingly tended gardens. Many laneways and streets lead to picnic spots and lookout points.

Bicycles are available for rent in several of the town's shops (₺10 /30 per hour/day). The *fayton* stand is on Araba Meydanı behind the Atatürk statue. Hire one for a one-hour tour of the island (*büyük turu*, ₺63) or a 25-minute tour (*küçük turu*, ₺50).

◉ Büyükada

The largest island in the Adalar group, Büyükada (Great Island) is impressive viewed from the ferry: gingerbread villas climb up the slopes of the hill and the bulbous twin cupolas of the Splendid Palas Hotel provide an unmistakable landmark. There's plenty to keep visitors occupied for a full day, with an excellent museum showcasing every aspect of island life, streets dotted with handsome 19th-century timber villas, heavily wooded pine forests with walking tracks, a spectacularly located Greek Orthodox monastery and a number of clean beaches.

You'll disembark the ferry at the island's attractive Ottoman Revival–style *iskele* (ferry dock) building, which dates from 1915 and features attractive Kütahya tiles.

The island's main drawcard is the Greek Orthodox Church and Monastery of St George, located on a 203m-high hill known as Yücetepe. To walk here, head from the ferry to the clock tower in İskele Meydanı (Dock Sq). The shopping district (with cheap eateries) is left along Recep Koç Sokak. Bear right onto 23 Nisan Caddesi, then head along Çankaya Caddesi up the hill to the monastery; when you come to a fork in the road, veer right. The walk, which takes at least one hour, takes you past a long progression of impressive wooden villas set in gardens. After 40 minutes or so you will reach a reserve called Luna Park by the locals. The monastery is a 25-minute walk up an extremely steep hill from here. As you ascend, you'll sometimes see pieces of cloth tied to the branches of trees along the path – each represents a prayer, most made by female supplicants visiting the monastery to pray for a child. Once a year, on 23 April, thousands of pilgrims – Greek Orthodox and Muslim – make their way up the hill to pay their respects to St George.

There's not a lot to see at the monastery, but the panoramic views from its terrace make the hour-long trek worthwhile. A small and gaudy church is the only building of note, so most visitors spend their time at the pleasant **Yücetepe Kır Gazinosu Restaurant** (✆0216-382 1333; Monastery of St George; mains ₺14-20; ✆daily Apr-Oct, Sat & Sun only Nov-Mar). Its outdoor tables have views to İstanbul and the nearby islands of Yassıada and Sivriada.

Relegated to an isolated site next to Aya Nikola Beach on the southeastern side of the island, the excellent **Museum of the Princes' Islands** (Adalar Müzesi; ✆0216-382 6430; www.adalarmuzesi.org; Yılmaz Türk Caddesi; adult/student ₺5/3, Wed free ; ✆9am-6pm Tue-Sun Apr-Oct, to 5pm Nov-Mar; ▣Büyükada) is often overlooked by visitors but we highly recommend making the effort to visit it. Multimedia exhibits focus on the history and culture of the Adalar and cover every aspect of island life, including geology, flora, religious heritage, food, architecture, music, festivals and literature. Interpretative panels and videos are in both Turkish and English, and there are objects galore to admire.

To get to the museum from the *iskele* (dock), head towards the clock tower and then walk straight ahead before turning left into Çınar Caddesi, right at the first fork into Alparslan Caddesi and then right at the second fork into Malül Gazi Caddesi and onto Yılmaz Türk Caddesi. The museum is located next to the Yıldırımspor Kulübü Deneği sports club. It's a pleasant 3km walk or a ₺35 *fayton* ride.

Büyükada has some good swimming beaches, but you'll need to pay for the privilege of using them. Try Nakibey, Yörükali and Viranbağ, where you'll pay between ₺20 and ₺40 per day per person, including use of a sun lounge and umbrella. Bicycles are available for rent in several of the town's shops (₺10/30 per hour/day). The *fayton* stand is to the left of the clock tower. Hire one for a 70-minute tour of the town, hills and shore (*büyük turu*, ₺95) or a shorter tour (*küçük turu*, ₺80).

 EATING & DRINKING

✖ Heybeliada

The best eateries are on the waterside promenade opposite the Mavi Marmara *iskele*. Many are closed for the winter season, and all should be booked ahead on summer weekends. Shops on İşgüzar Sokak in front of the *iskele* can provide picnic supplies.

HEYAMOLA ADA LOKANTASI TURKISH €€

(✆0216-351 1111; www.heyamolaadalokantasi.com; Mavi Marmara Yalı Caddesi 30b; mezes ₺10-22, salads ₺10-14, mains ₺22-40; ✆9am-11pm, closed Mon Nov-Apr; ▣Heybeliada) Opposite the İDO ferry dock, this busy place wows customers with a generous array of vegetable, yoghurt and seafood mezes. Those unsure of what to order can rely on the mixed meze plates (small/large ₺30/50) followed by a couple of hot seafood dishes. In summer, there's sometimes live music on weekend nights.

✖ Büyükada

Many restaurants are closed from November to Easter; during summer advance reservations are recommended, especially on weekends. Fast-food joints and ice-cream stands are clustered around the *iskele;* restaurants tend to be located next to the water. Picnic supplies can be purchased at the shops on Çınar Caddesi.

TERAS RESTAURANT TURKISH €€

(Eskibağ Teras; ✆0535 521 2724; Halık Koyu Beach; brunch ₺30, mains from ₺30; ✆10am-11pm; ▦; ▣Büyükada) Overlooking Büyükada's longest beach, Teras is a fabulous spot for leisurely year-round weekend brunches or summer dining (arrive before sunset). Brunch includes favourites such as *menemen* (scrambled eggs with peppers, tomatoes and sometimes cheese) and *börek* (filled pastry); dinner features spit-roast lamb and ultrafresh fish. It's a five-minute walk from Luna Park (take the road near the donkey park); a *fayton* costs ₺45.

PRINKIPO MEYHANE €€€

(✆0216-382 3591; Gülistan Caddesi 11; set menu incl alcohol ₺125; ✆11am-midnight; ▣Büyükada) Operated by local character Fıstık Ahmet, this long-standing favourite near the port is known for its excellent mezes and lavish pourings of alcohol (it's not the type of place that will appeal to teetotallers). Bookings are essential during summer, especially on Friday and Saturday nights when there is live music.

 Sleeping

Every accommodation style is available in İstanbul. You can live like a sultan in a world-class luxury hotel, bunk down in a dorm bed or settle into a stylish boutique establishment. The secret is to choose the neighbourhood that best suits your interests and then look for accommodation that will suit your style and budget – there are loads of options to choose from.

Accommodation Trends

Despite what certain members of the EU may think, İstanbul is a European city and accommodation styles and prices here are similar to those in most major European capitals. Recent trends have seen customers moving from small midrange and budget hotels that dominate Sultanahmet towards the apartments and boutique hotels that have been opening in Beyoğlu. Some of these hotels offer chic bars, spas, gyms and other trappings of the international designer lifestyle.

Accommodation Styles

The boutique hotels in Beyoğlu and along the Bosphorus are hip rather than historic, even though many of them occupy handsome 19th-century apartment blocks. Most have been fitted out by architects versed in international modernism, and have interiors that would suit Stockholm or Sydney as much as they do İstanbul. In most of Sultanahmet's hotels, the decor is different. These places are often owned and run by locals who are originally from the east of the country and have a resolutely Anatolian aesthetic – you'll see lots of carpets and kilims (pileless woven rugs), silk bedspreads and *nazar boncuks* (blue glass beads that Turks believe protect against the evil eye). That said, there are a number of Sultanahmet hotels that have melded the best of both worlds, delivering quietly elegant interiors with Anatolian or Ottoman flourishes.

Rates & Reservations

Hotels here are busy, so book your room as far in advance as possible, particularly if you are visiting during the high season (Easter/May, September/October and Christmas/New Year). Recent years have seen significant fluctuations in tourist numbers in İstanbul, so most hotels use yield management systems when setting their rates, meaning that in quiet times prices can drop sometimes by as much as 50% and in busy times they can skyrocket. As a result, treat our prices as a guide only – it is possible that the price you are quoted will be quite different. Note that most hotels in İstanbul set their prices in euros, and we have listed them as such here.

In-Hotel Dining

Breakfast is almost always included in the room rate. A standard Turkish breakfast buffet includes bread, jams, yogurt, sheep's milk cheese, boiled eggs, olives, tomatoes, cucumber and tea/coffee. Often cakes, cereals and *böreks* (filled pastries) are added. Most of the city's luxury hotels and many of its boutique choices have a bar and restaurant. The best of these are found at the Four Seasons Istanbul at Sultanahmet, Karaköy Rooms, Marmara Pera and the Four Seasons Istanbul at the Bosphorus.

Lonely Planet's Top Choices

Hotel Empress Zoe (p181) Atmospheric boutique choice near Aya Sofya perfectly balancing charm and comfort.

Hotel Ibrahim Pasha (p181) Chic contemporary style with Ottoman overtones; overlooks the Blue Mosque.

Karaköy Rooms (p183) Stylish and well-sized rooms are the main draw, with a lavish breakfast spread an added extra.

Louis Appartements (p182) Keenly priced and well-equipped suites and rooms near Galata Tower.

Marmara Guesthouse (p180) Friendly, family-run budget pension in the heart of Sultanahmet.

Sirkeci Mansion (p181) Wonderful family choice with impressive service, entertainment program and facilities.

NEED TO KNOW

Prices
We use the following coding to indicate the high-season price per night of a double room with breakfast.

€ under €90

€€ €90–200

€€€ more than €200

Airport Transfers
Many hotels will provide a free airport transfer from Atatürk International Airport if you stay three nights or more. This sometimes only applies to bookings made through hotel websites.

Discounts
Some hotels offer a discount of between 5% and 10% for cash payments if you book through the hotel website rather than a booking site. Room rates in the low season (November to Easter, excluding Christmas and New Year) are usually heavily discounted.

Tax
Value-added tax of 8% is added to all hotel bills. This is usually included in the price quoted when you book.

Casa di Bava (p183) Design hotel with well-equipped rooms and an arty vibe.

Best by Budget

€
Louis Appartements (p182) Classy and comfortable rooms with kitchenettes.

Marmara Guesthouse (p180) Three-star rooms for one-star prices.

€€
Hotel Ibrahim Pasha (p181) Exemplary boutique hotel with a great location off the Hippodrome.

Karaköy Rooms (p183) Hip location, decor and vibe.

€€€
Four Seasons Istanbul at the Bosphorus (p184) Restaurants, impressive spa, luxe rooms and spectacular pool.

Pera Palace Hotel (p184) Exceptional levels of service and comfort in historic surrounds.

Best for Families

Ahmet Efendi Evi (p180) Homey atmosphere and DVD player in family rooms.

Four Seasons Istanbul at the Bosphorus (p184) Babysitting service, a pool and a garden.

Hamamhane (p183) Family suite with kitchenette, washing machine and garden access.

Sarı Konak Hotel (p182) Kitchenettes and bathtubs in some rooms and suites.

Sirkeci Mansion (p181) Indoor pool, family rooms with bathtub and in-house dining.

Best Rooftop VIews

Arcadia Blue Hotel (p182) Bar-restaurant overlooking Aya Sofya, the Blue Mosque, the Bosphorus and the Sea of Marmara.

Four Seasons Istanbul at Sultanahmet (p182) Spectacular views of Aya Sofya and the Blue Mosque from the A'YA Rooftop Lounge.

Hotel Ibrahim Pasha (p181) Intimate rooftop bar overlooking the Blue Mosque and Palace of İbrahim Paşa.

TomTom Suites (p183) Bar-restaurant with spectacular view of the Bosphorus and Old City.

Marmara Pera (p184) Panoramic 360-degree views from the rooftop swimming pool and bar.

Vault Karaköy (p183) Golden Horn and Old City panorama from the rooftop bar-restaurant.

Where to Stay

NEIGHBOURHOOD	FOR	AGAINST
Sultanahmet & Around	Most of the major monuments and museums are located here, so it's convenient for sightseeing; a handy tram service travels to Beyoğlu.	Carpet touts can be annoying, but the biggest drawback is the lack of decent places to eat and drink.
Bazaar District	You'll be close to the shopping action in the Grand Bazaar and within walking distance of the major sights in Sultanahmet.	Many streets are deserted at night and on Sundays, so security can be an issue. Most restaurants and cafes only operate during the day.
Western Districts	This part of town is mainly residential, so you'll get a real feel for local life. Prices in eateries and shops are considerably lower than in the tourist areas.	Public transport is limited, so you'll have to rely on buses and taxis to get to other neighbourhoods. Eating and drinking options are also limited.
Beyoğlu	The best bars, restaurants and clubs are here, as is the greatest concentration of boutique hotels and apartment rentals. Tram and metro services connect it with the Historic Peninsula, and the ritzy shopping and residential suburbs to its northeast.	Lots of bars and nightclubs mean the streets around İstiklal Caddesi and in Cihangir and Karaköy can be noisy.
Kadıköy	The city's best produce market is located here, making it great for self-caterers; loads of bars and restaurants; lovely ferry ride, or a quick metro trip, to the Old City.	Streets around the market can be noisy in the morning and at night; you're dependent on public transport and taxis to explore the city.
Beşiktaş, Nişantaşi & Ortaköy	Rooms and restaurants overlooking the water are romantic, and there's something magical about hopping aboard hotel launches to criss cross the Bosphorus.	The distance from the Historic Peninsula is considerable, so the trip back to your hotel can be tiring after a full day of sightseeing. Eating and drinking choices can be limited.

🛏 Sultanahmet & Around

⭐**HOTEL ŞEBNEM** HOTEL €

Map p240 (☎0212-517 6623; www.sebnemhotel.net; Adliye Sokak 1, Cankurtaran; s €50, d €70-80, tr €90, f €110; ☀✴@☎; ☐Sultanahmet) An appealing sense of simplicity and intimacy pervades the Şebnem. Antiques dot the 15 smart rooms, which have wooden floors, modern bathrooms and comfortable beds; two have a private courtyard garden. The large terrace upstairs has a cafe-bar and views over the Sea of Marmara.

⭐**HOTEL ALP GUESTHOUSE** HOTEL €

Map p240 (☎0212-517 7067; www.alpguesthouse.com; Adliye Sokak 4, Cankurtaran; s/d €55/80; ☀✴☎; ☐Sultanahmet) This wooden building lives up to its location in Sultanahmet's premier small-hotel enclave, offering attractive, well-priced single, double, triple and family rooms. Bathrooms are small but very clean, and there are plenty of amenities. The roof terrace is one of the best in this area, with great sea views, comfortable indoor and outdoor seating, and free tea and coffee.

⭐**METROPOLIS HOSTEL** HOSTEL €

Map p240 (☎0212-518 1822; www.metropolishostel.com; Terbıyık Sokak 24, Cankurtaran; dm €15-16, d €60-65, s/d/tw/tr without bathroom €44/46/49/68; ℗☀✴☎; ☐Sultanahmet) Located in a quiet street where a good night's sleep is assured, the friendly Metropolis offers four- to six-bed dorms, including a female-only en-suite option with six beds and sweeping Sea of Marmara views. The rooftop terrace has a bar and sea views to equal many pricier hotels, and the busy entertainment program includes summer barbecues and belly dancing. Showers and toilets are clean but in limited supply, and the steep stairs could be challenging for some travellers.

★ MARMARA GUESTHOUSE PENSION €

Map p240 (☏0212-638 3638; www.marmaraguest
house.com; Terbıyık Sokak 15, Cankurtaran; d €65-
85, tr €80-100, f €95-115; ✸✱🕸; 🚇Sultanahmet)
Few of Sultanahmet's family-run pensions
can compete with the cleanliness, comfort
and thoughtful details here. The team goes
out of is way to welcome guests, offering advice and serving a delicious breakfast on the
vine-covered, sea-facing roof terrace. Rooms
have four-poster beds with Turkish hangings, good bathrooms (small in some cases)
and double-glazed windows. Members of the
same family operate the similarly impressive
Saruhan Hotel (p182) in the predominantly
residential pocket of Kadırga.

AHMET EFENDI EVI PENSION €

Map p240 (☏0212-518 8465; www.ahmetefendievi.
com; Keresteci Hakkı Sokak 23, Cankurtaran; s
€45-65, d €50-80, f €70-95; P✸✱🕸; 🚇Sultan-
ahmet) Mr Ahmet's House has an appealing
home-away-from-home feel and is a great
choice for families. In a predominantly residential area (a rarity in Sultanahmet), its
nine rooms of various sizes have modern decor and fittings; one has a terrace with views
of the Blue Mosque and Sea of Marmara.

HOTEL NOMADE BOUTIQUE HOTEL €

Map p240 (☏0212-513 8173; www.hotelnomade.
com; Ticarethane Sokak 15, Alemdar; s/d/tr €40/45/
70; P✸✱🕸; 🚇Sultanahmet) Designer style
and budget pricing don't often go together,
but Nomade bucks the trend. A few steps off
busy Divan Yolu, it offers simple rooms that
some guests find too small – request the largest possible. Everyone loves the roof-terrace
bar though (bang in front of Aya Sofya).

CHEERS LIGHTHOUSE HOSTEL €

Map p240 (☏0212-458 2324; www.cheerslight
house.com; Çayıroğlu Sokak 18, Küçük Ayasofya;
dm/s/d/tr €20/45/70/90; P✸✱🕸; 🚇Sultan-
ahmet) Part of a cheerfully named accommodation group, Cheers Lighthouse is in a quiet
neighbourhood. Reached via steep stairs,
rooms have sea views and options include a
loft-style suite with terrace and sauna. Bar-
restaurant **Cheers Soul Kitchen** (mezes ₺15,
mains ₺35; ⊙11am-10pm; 🕸) is an appealing
spot to watch the world go by, or to gaze at
the Bosphorus from the rear terrace.

ZEYNEP SULTAN HOTEL HOTEL €

Map p238 (☏0212-514 5001; www.zeynepsultan
hotel.com; Zeynep Sultan Camii Sokak 25, Alemdar;
s/d/tr €50/60/75; P✸✱🕸; 🚇Sultanahmet

or Gülhane) There aren't many hotels in the
world that can boast a Byzantine chapel in
the basement, but the Zeynep Sultan can. Its
22 renovated rooms have a modern, white
look and include fridges, tea and coffee facilities, and attractive marble finish in the
bathrooms. Breakfast is served on the rear
terrace with Aya Sofya views.

BIG APPLE HOSTEL HOSTEL €

Map p240 (☏0212-517 7931; www.hostelbigapple.
com; Bayram Fırını Sokak 12, Cankurtaran; dm
€15-45, r €30-75; ✸✱@🕸; 🚇Sultanahmet) It
may lack a traveller vibe, but the compen-
sations at this comfortable hostel include
six-bed air-conditioned dorms (including a
female-only option) with comfortable beds
and private bathroom, as well as hotel-style
private rooms with satellite TV, fridge and
bathroom. Added to this is a rooftop bar-
breakfast room with sea views.

AGORA GUESTHOUSE HOSTEL €

Map p240 (☏0212-458 5547; www.agoraguest
house.com; Amiral Tafdil Sokak 6, Cankurtaran;
dm €17-25, r €80-90; P✸✱🕸; 🚇Sultanahmet)
The friendly Agora is worth considering for
its comfortable bunk beds (with lockers big
enough for backpacks underneath); clean,
modern bathrooms, and roof terrace. The
main drawbacks are an inadequate number
of showers and toilets and a lack of natural
light in the basement dorms.

HOTEL PENINSULA HOTEL €

Map p70 (☏0212-458 6850; www.hotelpeninsula.
com; Adliye Sokak 6, Cankurtaran; d €35-50, tr €60,
f €65-100; ✸✱@🕸; 🚇Sultanahmet) Hallmarks
here are friendly staff, comfortable rooms
and bargain prices. Start your day on the sea-
facing roof terrace with its sociable breakfast
room and outdoor tables. Basement rooms
are dark, but have reduced prices (double
€35, family €65). The same crowd operates
the **Hanedan** (Map p240; ☏0212-516 4869;
www.hanedanhotel.com; Adliye Sokak 3; s €45, d
€50-55, tr €70, f €85-95; ✸✱@🕸) opposite
and the **Hotel Grand Peninsula** (Map p240;
☏0212-458 7710; www.grandpeninsulahotel.com;
Cetinkaya Sokak 3; d €50-65, s/tr/f €40/80/90;
P✸✱🕸) nearby, both also recommended.

BAHAUS HOSTEL HOSTEL €

Map p240 (☏0212-638 6534; www.bahaus
istanbul.com; Bayram Fırını Sokak 7, Cankurtaran;
dm €15-21, r €50; P✸✱@🕸; 🚇Sultanahmet)
Small, clean and secure, Bahaus stands in
stark and welcome contrast to the institu-

tional style hostels on nearby Akbıyık Caddesi. The four- to 14-bed dorms (including a female-only en-suite option) have curtained bunks with good mattresses, reading lights and lockers; they can be hot in summer. Top marks go to the plentiful bathrooms, entertainment program and rooftop terrace bar.

★HOTEL IBRAHIM PASHA   BOUTIQUE HOTEL €€

Map p240 (📞0212-518 0394; www.ibrahimpasha. com; Terzihane Sokak 7, Sultanahmet; r standard/ deluxe €125/175; ➌❄@🛜; 🚇Sultanahmet) Cultural tomes are piled in reception and throughout the 24 rooms of this exemplary design hotel, which also has a comfortable lounge with open fire, and a terrace bar with knockout views of the nearby Blue Mosque and Hippodrome. Rooms are gorgeous but some are small, with more space in the deluxe options and those in the new section.

★HOTEL EMPRESS ZOE   BOUTIQUE HOTEL €€

Map p240 (📞0212-518 2504; www.emzoe.com; Akbıyık Caddesi 10, Cankurtaran; s €140-160, tr €150, ste €180-300; ➌❄🛜; 🚇Sultanahmet) Named after the feisty Byzantine empress, this is one of İstanbul's most impressive boutique hotels. The four buildings house 26 diverse rooms. The garden suites overlook a 15th-century hamam and the gorgeous flower-filled courtyard where breakfast is served in warm weather. You can enjoy an evening drink there, or while admiring the sea view from the terrace.

★SIRKECI MANSION   HOTEL €€

Map p238 (📞0212-528 4344; www.sirkecimansion. com; Taya Hatun Sokak 5, Sirkeci; s €110-247, d €149-247, tr €199, f €209-224; ➌❄@🛜❄; 🚇Gülhane) Travellers love this terrific-value hotel overlooking Gülhane Park, with its impeccably clean, well-sized and amenity-laden rooms, some with balconies. It has a restaurant where a lavish breakfast is served, an indoor pool and hamam. Top marks go to the attention to detail, helpful staff and the complimentary entertainment program, which includes walking tours and afternoon teas.

★HOTEL AMIRA   BOUTIQUE HOTEL €€

Map p240 (📞0212-516 1640; www.hotelamira. com; Mustafapaşa Sokak 43, Küçük Ayasofya; r €129-159; ➌❄@🛜) A consistent performer, Amira has 32 attractive rooms with Ottoman flourishes. It's a relaxing haven after a long day of sightseeing, complete with tea and coffee, slippers, a safe and bottled water aplenty. Adding further appeal are the atten-

tive service, a spa, a roof terrace overlooking the Little Aya Sofya and the Sea of Marmara, and complimentary afternoon tea is served in the sunken lounge. The only difference between standard and deluxe rooms is size, with poky bathrooms in the former.

HOTEL ALILASS   DESIGN HOTEL €€

Map p240 (📞0212-516 8860; www.hotelalilass. com; Bayram Fırını Sokak 9, Cankurtaran; s €60-90, d €70-100; ➌❄🛜; 🚇Sultanahmet) This well-priced hotel has 22 small but stylish rooms, with low-hanging lights, black-and-white photos of old İstanbul, and bathrooms featuring Ottoman tiles and glass walls. Facilities include a cafe, roof terrace and conservatory-like breakfast room in the back garden.

OSMAN HAN HOTEL   HOTEL €€

Map p240 (📞0212-4587702; www.osmanhanhotel. com; Çetinkaya Sokak 1, Cankurtaran; s/d standard €160/170, deluxe €180/190; ➌❄🛜; 🚇Sultanahmet) Amenity levels at this friendly little hotel are high: rooms have comfortable beds, minibars, tea and coffee facilities, and satellite TV, while the breakfast room and terrace have sea views. The difference between standard and deluxe rooms is space, with cramped bathrooms in the former. The ground-floor rooms (single/double €130/140) are right next to reception. Weekend rates are €10 higher per room.

OTTOMAN HOTEL IMPERIAL   HOTEL €€

Map p238 (📞0212-513 6151; www.ottomanhotel imperial.com; Caferiye Sokak 6; r from €100; ➌❄@🛜; 🚇Sultanahmet) This four-star hotel is in a wonderfully quiet location outside Topkapı Palace walls. Its large and comfortable rooms have plenty of amenities, including minibars and coffee machines, and are decorated with Ottoman-style *objets d'art*; opt for one facing the neighbouring Aya Sofya or in the rear annexe. No roof terrace, but on-site Matbah (p84) restaurant is excellent.

DERSAADET HOTEL   HOTEL €€

Map p240 (📞0212-458 0760; www.hotelder saadet.com; Kapıağası Sokak 5, Küçük Ayasofya; s from €70, d €84-152, ste €180-200; ➌❄@🛜; 🚇Sultanahmet) 'Dersaadet' means 'Place of Happiness' in Turkish – and guests are inevitably happy at this well-run place with Ottoman-style decor and Sea of Marmara views throughout. A restored mansion, its 17 comfortable rooms include a sumptuous penthouse suite. Amenities include a lift and a terrace with panoramic views.

SARI KONAK HOTEL

BOUTIQUE HOTEL €€

Map p240 (☎0212-638 6258; www.istanbulhotel sarikonak.com; Mimar Mehmet Ağa Caddesi 26, Cankurtaran; r €104-134, tr/f/ste €154/234/234; P❄✱@🛜; 🚇Sultanahmet) Guests here enjoy relaxing on the roof terrace with its Sea of Marmara and Blue Mosque views, but also take advantage of the comfortable lounge and courtyard downstairs. With Ottoman touches and prints of old İstanbul, bedrooms are similarly impressive.

ARCADIA BLUE HOTEL

HOTEL €€

Map p240 (☎0212-516 9696; www.hotelarcadia blue.com; İmran Öktem Caddesi 1, Bindirbirek; r economy/standard/sea view/deluxe from €63/108/129/171; P❄✱🛜; 🚇Sultanahmet) This modern hotel has memorable views of Aya Sofya, the Blue Mosque, the Bosphorus and the Sea of Marmara from its roof-terrace bar-restaurant, and a ground-floor cafe where complimentary afternoon tea is served. There's also a hamam and a gym. Rooms are extremely comfortable; all are a good size but the sea-view options are worth their higher price tag.

FOUR SEASONS ISTANBUL AT SULTANAHMET

HOTEL €€€

Map p240 (☎0212-402 3000; www.fourseasons. com/istanbul; Tevkifhane Sokak 1, Cankurtaran; r from €400; P❄✱@🛜; 🚇Sultanahmet) This luxurious hotel has an excellent position near Aya Sofya and the Blue Mosque, with views of both and of the Bosphorus from its rooftop bar-restaurant. Facilities include a spa and an excellent restaurant in the leafy inner courtyard, while even the entry-level superior rooms are serene havens with original Turkish artworks and handwoven kilims (pileless woven rugs).

🛏 Bazaar District

BURCKIN SUITES HOTEL

HOTEL €

Map p242 (☎0212-638 5521; www.burckinhotel. com; Klodfarer Caddesi 18, Binbirdirek; s €59-64, d €64-69, f €109-119; P❄✱🛜; 🚇Sultanahmet) Readers have criticised the small size of Burckin's rooms and their bathrooms, but the decor is attractive and there are plenty of amenities. The main draw is the rooftop-terrace restaurant-bar, which has a wonderful view of Aya Sofya and the Sea of Marmara.

SARUHAN HOTEL

HOTEL €

Map p242 (☎0212-458 7608; www.saruhanhotel. com; Cinci Meydanı Sokak 34, Kadırga; s/d/f €70/75/105; ❄✱@🛜; 🚇Çemberlitaş) Hitherto bereft of hotels, the quiet residential pocket of Kadırga is inching its way into the limelight, courtesy of impressive family-run operations like this one. The Saruhan offers 17 comfortable and well-equipped rooms and a lovely terrace with a sea view. It's 20 minutes' walk to the sights in Sultanahmet and a shorter (but steep) walk to the Grand Bazaar.

🛏 Western Districts

AKIN HOUSE

APARTMENT €

Map p252 (☎0212-533 3023; www.akin-house. com; Vodina Caddesi 40, Balat; s/d €25/35, with kitchenette €35/45; P❄🛜; 🚌99, 99A, 99Y from Eminönü, 55T from Taksim) To properly appreciate the area's neighbourhood feel, stay at one of these self-catering apartments, spread across neighbouring houses near the Fener bus stop. Exposed brick, antique and modern furnishings, the odd painted wooden ceiling and views of Phanar Greek Orthodox College or the Golden Horn add bags of character. The Turkish-Australian managers are very helpful. Suites generally have a fridge and kettle; some have a kitchenette.

🛏 Beyoğlu

★LOUIS APPARTEMENTS

HOTEL €

Map p248 (☎0212-293 4052; www.louis.com. tr/galata; İlk Beladiye Caddesi 10, Şişhane; d/ste €90/200; ❄✱@🛜🚹; Ⓜ Şişhane, ✪Tünel) The top-floor suite at this meticulously maintained and keenly priced hotel near the Galata Tower is the knockout option among the 12 suites and rooms on offer. All have a large bed, TV/DVD player, ironing set-up and kitchenette equipped with appliances, including an espresso machine. Decor is understated but pleasing; staff are helpful. An optional breakfast costs €9 per person.

RAPUNZEL HOSTEL

HOSTEL €

Map p248 (☎0212-292 5034; www.rapunzel istanbul.com; Bereketzade Camii Sokak 3, Galata; dm €14-24, s €35, tw €40-70; ✱@🛜; Ⓜ Şişhane, ✪Tünel) This intimate hostel near Galata Tower is blessed with informed, friendly and enthusiastic staff, making it a great choice for budget travellers. Dorms and rooms are small but have air-con, clean private bathrooms, reading lights and power points; mixed and female dorms also have lockers. There's a cosy TV room and a roof terrace with view of the Historical Peninsula.

WORLD HOUSE HOSTEL HOSTEL €

Map p248 (📞0212-293 5520; www.worldhouse istanbul.com; Galipdede Caddesi 85, Galata; dm €9-22, d €36-68, tr €48-78; @🛜; Ⓜ️Şişhane, 🚇Tünel) Tucked behind the Latife Cafe, this long-standing and justly popular hostel is close to Beyoğlu's entertainment strips but not too far from the sights in Sultanahmet. Nonstandard hostel features include double-glazed windows and an in-house *lokanta* (serving ready-made food; lunch ₺10). All dorms are mixed (the best are in the front building) and bathrooms are clean (one shower/toilet for every nine beds).

★**KARAKÖY ROOMS** BOUTIQUE HOTEL €€

Map p248 (📞0212-252 5422; http://karakoy rooms.com; Galata Şarap İskelesi Sokak 10, Karaköy; standard r €80-130, studio €130-200; 😊🌸🛜; 🚇Karaköy) Occupying five floors above one of the city's best-loved restaurants, this splendid hotel has only 12 rooms – book well in advance. The double and deluxe rooms are spacious, comfortable, well-equipped and offer exceptional value for money. The pricier studios are enormous, with well-equipped kitchenettes. Decor is super-stylish throughout and the breakfast (served in the restaurant) is lavish and delicious.

★**CASA DI BAVA** BOUTIQUE HOTEL €€

Map p247 (📞0538-377 3877; www.casadibava istanbul.com; Bostanbaşı Caddesi 28, Çukurcuma; economy €140, 1-bedroom apt €180, 2-bedroom penthouse €320; 😊🌸🛜🐾; Ⓜ️Taksim) The two-bedroom penthouse apartment at this recently opened suite hotel is an absolute knockout, and the 11 one-bedroom apartments in the 1880s building are impressive, too. All are stylishly decorated and well-appointed, with original artworks, fully equipped kitchenettes and washing machines. The basement suites are smaller and less expensive; all have daily maid service. In-room breakfast costs €6 per person.

★**TOMTOM SUITES** BOUTIQUE HOTEL €€

Map p248 (📞0212-292 4949; www.tomtomsuites. com; Tomtom Kaptan Sokak 18, Tophane; standard ste €150-170, deluxe ste €170-325; 😊🌸@🛜🐾; 🚇Tophane) We're more than happy to beat the drum about this hotel, occupying a former Franciscan nunnery off İstiklal Caddesi. Its contemporary decor is understated but elegant, levels of service are high and the suites are spacious and beautifully appointed. A delicious and generous breakfast is served in the rooftop restaurant with its panoramic view. Sadly, dinner is considerably less impressive.

★**WITT ISTANBUL HOTEL** BOUTIQUE HOTEL €€

Map p248 (📞0212-293 1500; www.wittistanbul. com; Defterdar Yokuşu 26, Cihangir; d ste €125-285, terrace ste €195-450; 🌸@🛜; Ⓜ️Taksim, 🚇Tophane) Showcasing nearly as many designer features as an issue of *Monocle*, this stylish apartment hotel in Cihangir offers spacious suites with seating area, CD/DVD player, espresso machine, king-size bed and swish bathroom. Most have kitchenettes and a few have panoramic terraces (there's also a communal rooftop terrace). It's a short but steep climb from the Tophane tram stop.

BANKERHAN HOTEL BOUTIQUE HOTEL €€

Map p248 (📞0212-243 5617; www.bankerhan.com; Banker Sokağı 2, Galata; standard s/d €79/99, tw €120, king & loft r €120-129; 😊🌸@🛜; 🚇Karaköy) Budget and boutique aren't concepts that sit comfortably together, but this recently opened hotel on the edge of Galata and Karaköy can legitimately claim to be both. The owners have a notable contemporary-art collection that is scattered throughout the building, and the 36 rooms are both stylish and comfortable. The cheapest options are cramped – upgrade if possible.

HAMAMHANE BOUTIQUE HOTEL €€

Map p248 (📞0212-293 4963; www.hammamhane. com; Çukurcuma Caddesi 45, Çukurcuma; studio €110, f & ste €140; 😊🌸@🛜🐾; 🚇Tophane) Çukurcuma is one of the few enclaves in Beyoğlu to retain an authentic neighbourhood feel, so it's a great spot for a city sojourn. Each of the spacious studios and suites at this keenly priced hotel come with a fully equipped kitchenette and clothes washer/dryer. Decor is Ikea-stylish and there's an extremely pleasant ground-floor dining room and terrace. It's worth noting that the owners have plans to renovate and open the adjoining hamam. While this occurs, construction noise and dust may be a problem.

VAULT KARAKÖY BOUTIQUE HOTEL €€

Map p248 (📞212-244 6434; www.thehousehotel. com; Bankalar Caddesi 5, Karaköy; s €109-209, d €134-234, ste €159-959; 🌸@🛜🛜; Ⓜ️Şişhane, 🚇Karaköy) This flagship property of İstanbul's fashionable House Hotel group is a stylish and evocative meld of old and new. Occupying a grand bank building complete with vaults (hence the name), facilities include a gym, hamam, lobby bar/restaurant

SLEEPING BEYOĞLU

and rooftop lounge. Rooms are comfortable and well-equipped (opt for a deluxe if possible, as classic and superior rooms are slightly cramped).

ISTANBUL PLACE APARTMENTS
APARTMENT €€

(✆0506 449 3393; http://istanbulplace.com; apt 1-bed €80-121, 2-bed €109-230, 3-bed €115-270; ✳🏠) Operated by a British-Turkish couple, this apartment rental company has nine well-appointed and beautifully presented properties in historic buildings across Galata and Taksim.

MARMARA PERA
HOTEL €€

Map p248 (✆0212-251 4646; www.themarmara hotels.com; Meşrutiyet Caddesi 1, Tepebaşı; r/f/ste €120/240/300; P🏊✳@🏠🏊🚼; MŞişhane, 🚇Tünel) A great location in the midst of Beyoğlu's major entertainment enclave makes this high-rise modern hotel an excellent choice. Added extras include a health club, a tiny outdoor pool, a truly fabulous buffet breakfast spread (€15 per person) and the fashionable Mikla (p136) rooftop bar and restaurant. Rooms with a sea view are approximately 30% more expensive.

★ PERA PALACE HOTEL
HISTORIC HOTEL €€€

Map p248 (✆0212-377 4000; www.perapalace. com; Meşrutiyet Caddesi 52, Tepebaşı; r €150-325, ste €330-550; P🏊✳@🏠🚼✳; MŞişhane) This famous hotel underwent a €23-million restoration in 2010 and the result is simply splendiferous. Rooms are luxurious and extremely comfortable, and facilities include an atmospheric bar and lounge (the latter often closed for private functions), spa, gym and restaurant. The most impressive feature of all is the service, which is both friendly and efficient. Breakfast costs €25.

🛏 Beşiktaş, Nişantaşi & Ortaköy

FOUR SEASONS ISTANBUL AT THE BOSPHORUS
LUXURY HOTEL €€€

Map p250 (✆0212-381 4000; www.fourseasons. com/bosphorus; Çırağan Caddesi 28, Beşiktaş; r from €600; P🏊✳@🏠🚼; 🚌Bahçeşehir Ünv. or Çırağan) One of two Four Seasons choices in İstanbul, this hotel incorporates an Ottoman building known as the Atik Paşa Konak. Service here is exemplary; rooms are luxurious; and the setting on the Bosphorus is truly magical. Add to this an excellent spa,

a restaurant, a terrace bar-cafe and a huge outdoor pool overlooking the Bosphorus and you are left with an unbeatable package.

SOFA HOTEL
BOUTIQUE HOTEL €€€

Map p250 (✆0212-368 1818; www.thesofahotel. com; Teşvikiye Caddesi 41, Nişantaşı; s/d from €180/200; 🏊✳🏠; MOsmanbey) The Sofa offers comfortable rooms packed with amenities, a spa (with relaxation pool), a cafe-cum-bookshop, a rooftop bar-restaurant, and excellent service down to the 'anytime, anything' button in the rooms. The terrace suites are beautiful open-plan spaces leading to balconies overlooking the neighbourhood. Be warned that street-facing rooms can be a bit noisy. Rates include an aromatherapy massage.

🛏 Kadıköy

HUSH HOSTEL LOUNGE
HOSTEL €

Map p253 (✆0216-450 4363; www.hushhostels. com; Rıhtım Caddesi 46, Yeldeğirmeni; dm €18, s without bathroom €24, d €52, without bathroom €36, tr €48; 🏊✳🏠; 🚢Kadıköy) Spread over two buildings in the up-and-coming Yeldeğirmeni district near the *iskele*, this well-run hostel is the more staid of the Hush Group's two Kadıköy properties and has a multi-age clientele. Dorms have reading lights and power points; lockers are in hallways. Facilities include clean bathrooms, communal kitchen, rear garden and lounge/TV room with book exchange. Wi-fi can be spotty. The hostel is always full on weekends, when locals keen to spend a weekend partying in the neighbourhood sleep over rather than relying on dolmuşes to get home. If staying on a Friday, be sure to take advantage of the free two-hour walking tour of the district.

HUSH HOSTEL MODA
HOSTEL €

Map p253 (✆0216-330 1122; www.hushhostels. com; Güneşlibahçe Sokak 50b, Moda; dm €18, s without bathroom €24, d €52, d without bathroom €36, tr €48; 🏊✳@🏠; 🚢Kadıköy) Located in the thick of Kadıköy's entertainment district, this is the party animal of the Hush group's two local hostels – expect plenty of noise. Private rooms with bathroom have air-con (dorms and rooms without bathroom don't) and there's a convivial terrace bar. The produce market is conveniently close, so the hostel's communal kitchen sees lots of cooking action.

Understand İstanbul

İstanbul Today

As the 21st century hits its stride, İstanbul is in an economic and political holding pattern. Two decades of growth and prosperity brought with it a number of challenges, chief among which was strain on the city's transport infrastructure by the growing population. While government has improved the city's roads and public transport, it still has a long way to go before the notorious traffic gridlock, which contributes to significant air pollution, is resolved. Even more challenging is the unsettled political environment, with a spate of bombings and an unsuccessful military coup d'état occurring here in 2016. Ramifications for the city's vital tourism industry has been disastrous.

Best in Music

BaBa ZuLa These darlings of the local alternative music scene play traditional Turkish instruments to create their unique sound, which melds electronica, reggae and dub. Their best known album is 2005's *Duble Oryantal* and their most recent release is 2014's *34 Oto Sanayi*.

Fazıl Say The internationally renowned pianist and composer has innumerable compositions and recordings to his credit, including the 2007 violin concerto *1001 Nights in The Harem*, the 2010 *İstanbul Symphony (Symphony No 1)* and the 2015 *Grand Bazaar Rhapsody for Orchestra (Opus 65)*.

İlhan Erşahin The Turkish-Swedish jazz saxophonist and composer performs and records with his Istanbul Sessions ensemble. Their five albums are *Istanbul Sessions featuring Erik Truffaz* (2010), *Istanbul Sessions: Bosphorus* (2010), *Istanbul Sessions* (2011), *Night Ride Remixes* (2012) and *Istanbul Underground* (2015).

Mercan Dede Known for his distinctive Sufi-electronic techno-fusion, Dede's albums include *Sufi Traveller* (2003), *Su* (Water; 2004), *Nefes* (Breath; 2006) and *Dünya* (Earth; 2013).

Civil Unrest and the Security Situation

The ramifications of the unsuccessful military coup d'état staged in July 2016 have been severe, with any opposition to the ruling AKP party and its leader, President Recep Tayyip Erdoğan, being emphatically suppressed. AKP supporters see the defeat of the coup as a triumph of democracy, but many secularist, left-leaning and Kurdish members of the community hold grave fears that free speech, independent media and basic human rights including the right to peaceful protest will fall victim to post-coup politics.

At the same time, political tensions within the country and the region have led to terrorist incidents including bomb attacks in areas frequented by tourists, resulting in a dramatic drop in tourist arrivals. This has had a devastating effect on the local economy. Visitors should monitor their country's travel advisories and stay alert at all times.

Infrastructure Upgrades

Over the past two decades the growing population has placed a huge strain on the city's public transport system. Fortunately, the local authorities and Ankara anticipated this problem and in 2005 commenced works on a hugely ambitious transportation infrastructure program that is ongoing. Works have included building an underwater railway link between the European and Asian suburbs, erecting a railway bridge over the Golden Horn, and integrating the new rail and metro lines with other city transport options. Construction has been slowed by constant archaeological discoveries, but the first phase of the project opened at the end of 2013; a third bridge was completed over the Bosphorus in 2016; and a huge new international airport is scheduled to open in 2018. Newly announced projects include a metro link between Kabataş and Mahmutbey (due for completion 2017), a traffic tunnel under the

Golden Horn (2018) and a pedestrian tunnel linking Kabataş in Beyoğlu with Üsküdar on the Asian shore.

Heritage Initiatives

A massive program of heritage restoration has been undertaken in recent years, focusing on the imperial mosques. These are being magnificently restored, but we're sorry to report that the city's Byzantine building stock hasn't received the same level of attention. Some important Byzantine buildings have been all but destroyed (the historic land walls), some left to fall into disrepair (Anemas Zindanları in Ayvansaray) and others are being subjected to restorations that can only be described as reprehensible (Church of the Monastery of Christ Pantokrator). Some Byzantine buildings that have been converted into mosques have been restored, but have lost much of their original character in the process. Most worrying is a push by a small but vocal sector of the community to overturn Atatürk's decision to designate Unesco-listed Aya Sofya as a museum and have it once again function as a mosque. This could place its acclaimed mosaics and frescoes in peril and would greatly upset members of the local and international Christian communities.

An Exciting Cultural Landscape

During the past decade the city's big banks, businesses and universities have built and endowed an array of cutting-edge museums and cultural centres, many of which have been designed by local architectural practices with growing international reputations. Joining mightily impressive cultural centres such as İstanbul Modern, SALT Galata, ARTER and Borusan Contemporary on the Bosphorus will be the Antrepo 5 Museum of Contemporary Art, a visually arresting building in Tophane designed by high-profile local architectural firm Emre Arolat.

These and a number of other institutions (large and small, public and private) aim to nurture a new and exciting generation of Turkish artists. Complementing exhibition, lecture and performance programs, the city's festival circuit, spearheaded by the impressive İstanbul Foundation for Culture and Arts, is now one of the busiest in Europe.

And Some Dodgy Developments

The city's skyline is in many ways its signature, but in the past decade some modern – and mind-blowingly ugly – developments have been added to it. In order to accommodate this 'urban regeneration', some residents – a good percentage of whom, critics have noted, are members of minority social groups – have been forcibly removed from their homes in inner-city suburbs and relocated to purpose-built high-rise housing in outer suburbs. Local environmental and heritage activists are quick to point out that many of the developments are being built by consortia with strong ties to the ruling AKP.

population per sq km

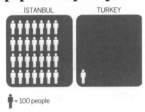

İSTANBUL   TURKEY

👤 ≈ 100 people

if İstanbul were 100 people

65 would live on the European side
35 would live on the Asian side

Ages
(% of population)

31   Under 20
38   20-39
23   40-60
8   Over 60

History

In its guises of Byzantium and Constantinople, İstanbul was ruled by Greeks, Romans and their descendants, many of whom left their stamp on the city's built heritage. After the fall of Byzantium, the city functioned as the capital of the world's most powerful empire and benefited from the riches associated with this. Its politics have given us the descriptor 'Byzantine' and its patrons have endowed it with a legacy of buildings and artefacts that certainly brings history to life.

Byzantium

The name İstanbul probably derives from 'eis ten polin' (Greek for 'to the city'). Though the Turks kept the name Constantinople after the Conquest, they also used other names, including İstanbul and Dersaadet (City of Peace and/or Happiness). The city's name was officially changed to İstanbul by Atatürk in the early republican years.

Legend tells us that the city of Byzantium was founded around 667 BC by a group of colonists from Megara, northwest of Athens. It was named after their leader, Byzas.

The new colony quickly prospered, largely due to its ability to levy tolls and harbour fees on ships passing through the Bosphorus, then as now an important waterway. A thriving marketplace was established and the inhabitants lived on traded goods and the abundant fish stocks in the surrounding waters.

In 512 BC Darius, Emperor of Persia, captured the city during his campaign against the Scythians. Following the retreat of the Persians in 478 BC, the town came under the influence and protection of Athens and joined the Athenian League. Though this was a turbulent relationship, Byzantium stayed under Athenian rule until 355 BC, when it gained independence.

By the end of the Hellenistic period, Byzantium had formed an alliance with the Roman Empire. It retained its status as a free state, and kept this even after being officially incorporated into the Roman Empire in AD 79 by Vespasian. Life was relatively uneventful until the city's leaders made a big mistake: they picked the wrong side in a Roman war of succession following the death of Emperor Pertinax in AD 193. When Septimius Severus emerged victorious over his rival Pescennius Niger, he mounted a three-year siege of the city, eventually massacring Byzantium's citizens, razing its walls and burning it to the ground. Ancient Byzantium was no more.

TIMELINE	1000 BC	667 BC	512 BC
	Thracian tribes found the settlements of Lygos and Semistra; Plinius mentions the founding of Semistra in his histories and traces of Lygos remain near Seraglio Point.	Legend tells us that Byzas, a citizen of the city of Megara, northwest of Athens, travels up the Bosphorus and founds Byzantium on the site of Lygos.	The army of the Persian emperor Darius captures the city; after the Persians' retreat in 478 BC, Byzantium chooses to join the Athenian League for protection.

The new emperor was aware of the city's important strategic position, and soon set about rebuilding it. He pardoned the remaining citizens and built a circuit of walls enclosing a city twice the size of its predecessor. The Hippodrome was built by Severus, as was a colonnaded way that followed the present path of Divan Yolu. Severus named his new city Augusta Antonina and it was subsequently ruled by a succession of emperors, including the great Diocletian (r 284–305).

Constantinople

Diocletian had decreed that after his retirement, the government of the Roman Empire should be overseen by co-emperors Galerius in the east (Augusta Antonina) and Constantine in the west (Rome). This resulted in a civil war, which was won by Constantine in AD 324 when he defeated Licinius, Galerius' successor, at Chrysopolis (the present-day suburb of Üsküdar).

With his victory, Constantine (r 324–37) became sole emperor of a reunited empire. He also became the first Christian emperor, though he didn't formally convert until he was on his deathbed. To solidify his power he summoned the First Ecumenical Council at Nicaea (İznik) in 325, which established the precedent of the emperor's supremacy in Church affairs.

Constantine also decided to move the capital of the empire to the shores of the Bosphorus, where he had forged his great victory and where the line between the Eastern and Western divisions of the Empire had previously been drawn. He built a new, wider circle of walls around the site of Byzantium and laid out a magnificent city within. The Hippodrome was extended and a forum was built on the crest of the second hill, near today's Nuruosmaniye Mosque. The city was dedicated on 11 May 330 as New Rome, but soon came to be called Constantinople.

Constantine died in 337, just seven years after the dedication of his new capital. His empire was divided up between his three sons: Constantius, Constantien and Constans. Constantinople was part of Constantius' share. His power base was greatly increased in 353 when he overthrew both of his brothers and brought the empire under his sole control.

Constantius died in 361 and was succeeded by his cousin Julian. Emperor Jovian was next, succeeded by Valens (of aqueduct fame).

The city continued to grow under the rule of the emperors. Theodosius I ('the Great'; r 379–95) had a forum built on the present site of Beyazıt Meydanı (Beyazıt Sq) and erected the Obelisk of Theodosius at the Hippodrome. His grandson Emperor Theodosius II (r 408–50),

HISTORY CONSTANTINOPLE

Ruling Dynasties

Since being declared the capital of the Roman Empire in AD 330, the city has been ruled by 85 Byzantine emperors, five Latin emperors and 32 Ottoman sultans.

Mehmet the Conqueror (Fatih) became Ottoman sultan for the first time in 1444, aged only 12, but was subsequently forced from power by a powerful grand vizier. He regained the throne in 1451, aged 19, and reigned until his death in 1481, aged 49.

335 BC	AD 79	330	380
Byzantium is granted independence but stays under the Athenian umbrella, withstanding with Athenian help a siege by Philip, father of Alexander the Great, in 340 BC.	Byzantium is officially incorporated into the Roman Empire ruled by the soldier-emperor Vespasian; it retains its status as a free state but pays high taxes to the empire.	Constantine the Great declares Byzantium the capital of the Roman Empire; the city soon becomes known as Constantinople.	Theodosius I declares Christianity the imperial religion; a year later, he summons an ecumenical council to Constantinople to define Church orthodoxy.

The Bosphorus Bridge

The first bridge built over the Bosphorus opened in 1973 and was initially named after the waterway. It was renamed Martyrs of July 15 Bridge after the attempted coup d'état in 2016.

threatened by the forces of Attila the Hun, ordered that an even wider, more formidable circle of walls be built around the city. Encircling all seven hills of the city, the walls were completed in 413, only to be brought down by a series of earthquakes in 447. They were hastily rebuilt in a mere two months – the rapid approach of Attila and the Huns acting as a powerful stimulus. The Theodosian walls successfully held out invaders for the next 757 years and still stand today, though they are in an increasingly dilapidated state of repair.

Theodosius died in 450 and was succeeded by a string of emperors, including the most famous of all Byzantine emperors, Justinian the Great. A former soldier, he and his great general Belisarius reconquered Anatolia, the Balkans, Egypt, Italy and North Africa. They also successfully put down the Nika riots of 532, killing 30,000 of the rioters in the Hippodrome in the process.

Three years before taking the throne, Justinian had married Theodora, a strong-willed former courtesan who is credited with having great influence over her husband. Together, they further embellished Constantinople with great buildings, including SS Sergius and Bacchus, now known as Küçük (Little) Aya Sofya, Hagia Eirene (Aya İrini) and Hagia Sophia (Aya Sofya), which was completed in 537.

From 565 to 1025, a succession of warrior emperors kept invaders such as the Persians and the Avars at bay. Though the foreign armies often managed to get as far as Chalcedon (the present-day suburb of Kadıköy), none were able to breach Theodosius' land walls. The Arab armies of the nascent Islamic empire tried in 669, 674, 678 and 717–18, each time in vain.

In 1071 Emperor Romanus IV Diogenes (r 1068–1071) led his army to eastern Anatolia to do battle with the Seljuk Turks, who had been forced out of Central Asia by the encroaching Mongols. However, at Manzikert (Malazgirt) the Byzantines were disastrously defeated, the emperor captured and imprisoned, and the former Byzantine heartland of Anatolia thus thrown open to Turkish invasion and settlement. Soon the Seljuks had built a thriving empire of their own in central Anatolia, with their capital first at Nicaea and later at Konya.

As Turkish power was consolidated to the east of Constantinople, the power of Venice – always a maritime and commercial rival to Constantinople – grew in the West. This coincided with the launch of the First Crusade and the arrival in Constantinople of the first of the Crusaders in 1096. Soldiers of the Second Crusade passed through the city in 1146 during the reign of Manuel I, son of John Comnenus II 'the Good' and his empress, Eirene, both of whose mosaic portraits can be seen in the gallery at Aya Sofya.

527	548	565	620
Justinian takes the throne; his introduction of heavy taxes leads to the Nika riots of 532 and half of the city is destroyed.	Theodora dies; during her reign she was known for granting women more rights in divorce cases, allowing women to own property, and enacting the death penalty for rape.	Justinian dies; his lasting memorial is the church of Hagia Sophia (Aya Sofya), which would be the centre of Eastern Orthodox Christianity for many centuries.	Heraclius I (r 610–41) changes the official language of the eastern empire from Latin to Greek, inaugurating what we now refer to as 'The Byzantine Empire'.

In 1204 soldiers of the Fourth Crusade led by Enrico Dandolo, Doge of Venice, attacked and ransacked the city. They then ruled it with an ally, Count Baldwin of Flanders, until 1261, when soldiers under Michael VIII Palaiologos, a Byzantine aristocrat in exile who had risen to become co-emperor of Nicaea, successfully recaptured it. The Byzantine Empire was restored.

İstanbul

Two decades after Michael reclaimed Constantinople, a Turkish warlord named Ertuğrul died in the village of Söğüt near Nicaea. He left his son Osman, who was known as Gazi (Warrior for the Faith), a small territory. Osman's followers became known in the Empire as Osmanlıs and in the West as the Ottomans.

Osman died in 1324 and was succeeded by his son Orhan. In 1326 Orhan captured Bursa, made it his capital and took the title of sultan. A victory at Nicaea followed, after which he sent his forces further afield, conquering Ankara to the east and Thrace to the west. His son Murat I (r 1362–89) took Adrianople (Edirne) in 1371.

Murat's son Beyazıt (r 1389–1402) unsuccessfully laid siege to Constantinople in 1394, then defeated a Crusader army 100,000 strong on the Danube in 1396. Though temporarily checked by the armies of Tamerlane and a nasty war of succession between Beyazıt's four sons that was eventually won by Mehmet I (r 1413–21), the Ottomans continued to grow in power and size. By 1440 the Ottoman armies under Murat II (1421–51) had taken Thessalonica, unsuccessfully laid siege to Constantinople and Belgrade, and battled Christian armies for Transylvania. It was at this point in history that Mehmet II 'The Conqueror' (r 1451–81) came to power and vowed to attain the ultimate prize – Constantinople.

In four short months, Mehmet oversaw the building of Rumeli Hisarı (the great fortress on the European side of the Bosphorus) and also repaired Anadolu Hisarı, built on the Asian shore half a century earlier by his great-grandfather Beyazıt I. Together these fortresses controlled the strait's narrowest point.

The Byzantines had closed the mouth of the Golden Horn with a heavy chain to prevent Ottoman boats from sailing in and attacking the city walls on the northern side. Not to be thwarted, Mehmet marshalled his boats at a cove (where Dolmabahçe Palace now stands) and had them transported overland by night on rollers, up the valley (present site of the Hilton Hotel) and down the other side into the Golden Horn at Kasımpaşa. Catching the Byzantine defenders by surprise, he soon had the Golden Horn under control.

The founder of modern nursing, Florence Nightingale, arrived at the Selimiye Army Barracks near Üsküdar in 1854 to nurse soldiers wounded in the Crimean War and stayed for three years. Her nickname 'The Lady with the Lamp' was inspired by her solitary late-night medical rounds through the barrack wards.

717	1204	1261	1432
Leo III, a Syrian, becomes emperor after deposing Theodosius III; he introduces edicts against the worship of images, ushering in the age of iconoclasm.	Enrico Dandolo, Doge of Venice, leads the Crusaders of the Fourth Crusade in a defeat of Constantinople; they sack the city and plunder many of its treasures.	Constantinople is recaptured by Michael VIII Palaiologos, a Byzantine aristocrat in exile who had risen to become co-emperor of Nicaea; the Byzantine Empire is restored.	Mehmet II, son of the Ottoman sultan Murad II, is born in Edirne; he succeeds his father as sultan, twice – once in 1444 and then permanently in 1451.

The last great obstacle was provided by the city's mighty walls. No matter how heavily Mehmet's cannons battered them, the Byzantines rebuilt the walls by night and, come daybreak, the impetuous young sultan would find himself back where he'd started. Finally, he received a proposal from a Hungarian cannon founder called Urban who had

POWERS BEHIND THE THRONE

Many powerful women have featured in İstanbul's imperial history. Here are our favourites:

Theodora

The wife of Justinian, Theodora (500–548) was the daughter of a bear-keeper at the Hippodrome and, if we are to believe Herodotus, had been a courtesan before she married. She subsequently became extremely devout and endowed a number of churches in the city. Justinian was devoted to her and she was widely acknowledged by contemporary historians to be the true power behind the throne. During her time as consort, she established homes for ex-prostitutes, granted women more rights in divorce cases, allowed women to own and inherit property, and enacted the death penalty for rape.

Zoe

Zoe (978–1050) was 50 years old and supposedly a virgin when her dying father, Constantine VIII, insisted she marry the aged Romanus III Argyrus. Romanus had been happily married for 40 years but Zoe and her father threatened him with blinding if he didn't consent. When Constantine died, Romanus was crowned emperor and Zoe empress. Zoe then took as her lover the much younger Michael the Paphlagonian. After Romanus mysteriously drowned in his bath in 1034, Zoe quickly married her companion, who joined her on the throne as Michael IV. Eight years later, after Michael died from an illness contracted while on campaign, Zoe and her sister Theodora ruled as empresses in their own right. At age 64 Zoe was married again, this time to an eminent senator, Constantine IX Monomachus, who outlived her.

Roxelana

The wife of Süleyman the Magnificent, Hürrem Sultan (1506–58) was more commonly known as Roxelana. She was beautiful, clever and ruthless. Though allowed four legal wives and as many concubines as he could support by Islamic law, Süleyman was devoted to Roxelana alone. Secure in her position, she mastered the art of palace intrigue and behind-the-scenes manipulation, even convincing the sultan to have İbrahim Paşa, Süleyman's lifelong companion and devoted grand vizier, strangled when he objected to her influence. She also ensured her drunken son, Selim the Sot, would succeed to the throne by having the able heir apparent, Prince Mustafa, strangled.

1453	1520	1556	1574
Mehmet's army takes İstanbul and he assumes power in the city, becoming known as Fatih ('The Conqueror'); he dies in 1481 and is succeeded by his son Beyazıt II.	Beyazıt's grandson Süleyman, who would come to be known as 'The Magnificent', ascends the throne and soon builds a reputation for his military conquests.	Süleyman dies while on a military campaign in Hungary; his son Selim II assumes the throne and becomes known as 'The Sot' for obvious reasons.	Selim II drowns after falling into his bath while drunk and is succeeded by his son Murat III, who orders the murder of his five younger brothers to ensure his succession.

come to help the Byzantine emperor defend Christendom against the infidels. Finding that the Byzantine emperor had no money, Urban was quick to discard his religious convictions and instead offered to make Mehmet the most enormous cannon ever seen. Mehmet gladly accepted and the mighty cannon breached the western walls, allowing the Ottomans into the city. On 28 May 1453 the final attack began and by the evening of the 29th the Turks were in complete control of the city. The last Byzantine emperor, Constantine XI Palaiologos, died fighting on the walls.

Seeing himself as the successor to great emperors such as Constantine and Justinian, the 21-year-old conqueror at once began to rebuild and repopulate the city. Aya Sofya was converted to a mosque; a new mosque, the Fatih (Conqueror) Camii, was built on the fourth hill; and the Eski Saray (Old Palace) was constructed on the third hill, followed by a new palace (Topkapı) on Sarayburnu a few years later. The city walls were repaired and a new fortress, Yedikule, was built. İstanbul, as it began to be known, became the new administrative, commercial and cultural centre of the ever-growing Ottoman Empire.

Under Mehmet's rule, Greeks who had fled the city were encouraged to return and an imperial decree calling for resettlement was issued; Muslims, Jews and Christians all took up his offer and were promised the right to worship as they pleased. The Genoese, who had fought with the Byzantines, were pardoned and allowed to stay in Galata, though the fortifications that surrounded their settlement were torn down. Only Galata Tower was allowed to stand.

Mehmet died in 1481 and was succeeded by Beyazıt II (r 1481–1512), who was ousted by his son, the ruthless Selim the Grim (r 1512–20), famed for executing seven grand viziers and numerous relatives during his relatively short reign.

The building boom that Mehmet kicked off was continued by his successors, with Süleyman the Magnificent (r 1520–66) and his architect Mimar Sinan being responsible for an enormous amount of construction. The city was endowed with buildings commissioned by the sultan and his family, court and grand viziers; these include the city's largest and grandest mosque, the Süleymaniye (1550). Later sultans built mosques and a series of palaces along the Bosphorus, among them Dolmabahçe.

However, what had been the most civilised city on earth in the time of Süleyman eventually declined along with the Ottoman Empire, and by the 19th century İstanbul had lost much of its former glory. Nevertheless, it continued to be seen by many Europeans as the 'Paris of the East' and, to affirm this, the first great international luxury express

Although he was instrumental in moving the capital of Turkey from İstanbul to Ankara, Atatürk loved the city and spent much of his time here. He kept a set of apartments in Dolmabahçe Palace and died there on 10 November 1938.

The Empress Theodora makes a great subject in Stella Duffy's rollicking biographical novel *Theodora: Actress. Empress. Whore.* (2010) and the palace intrigues orchestrated by Süleyman the Magnificent's consort Roxelana make for great TV drama in the enormously popular prime-time Turkish show *Muhteşem Yüzyıl* (The Magnificent Century).

1729	1826	1839	1853–56
A huge fire sweeps through the city, destroying 400 houses and 140 mosques, and causing 1000 deaths.	The Vakayı Hayriye, or 'Auspicious Event', is decreed, under which the corrupt and powerful imperial bodyguard known as the Janissary Corps is abolished.	Mahmut II implements the Tanzimat reforms, which integrate non-Muslims and non-Turks into Ottoman society through civil liberties and regulations.	The Ottoman empire fights in the Crimean War against Russia; Florence Nightingale arrives at the Selimiye Army Barracks near Üsküdar to nurse the wounded.

train, the famous *Orient Express,* connected İstanbul and the French capital in 1883.

The city's decline reflected that of the sultanate. The concept of democracy, imported from the West, took off in the 19th century and the sultans were forced to make concessions towards it. In 1876 Sultan Abdül Hamid II allowed the creation of an Ottoman constitution and the first-ever Ottoman parliament. However, these concessions didn't last long, with the sultan disabling the constitution in 1876 and suspending the parliament in 1878. A group of educated Turks took exception to this and established the Committee for Union and Progress (CUP), better known as the Young Turks, to fight for the reformation of the Ottoman sultanate and the introduction of democratic reform. In 1908 they forced the sultan to abdicate, reinstated the constitution and assumed governance of the empire.

One of the factors leading to the the Young Turks' decision to ally themselves with the Central Powers in WWI was their fear that the Allies (particularly Russia) coveted İstanbul. Unfortunately, the alliance led to their political demise when the Central Powers were defeated. The Young Turk leaders resigned, fled İstanbul and went into exile, leaving the city to be occupied by British, French and Italian troops placed there in accordance with the Armistice of Mudros, which ended Ottoman participation in the war. The city was returned to Ottoman rule under the 1923 Treaty of Lausanne, which defined the borders of the modern Turkish state.

The post-WWI campaign by Mustafa Kemal (Atatürk) for independence and the reinstatement of Turkish territory in the Balkans was directed from Ankara. After the Republic was founded in 1923, the new government was set up in that city. Robbed of its status as the capital of a vast empire, İstanbul lost much of its wealth and atmosphere. The city's streets and neighbourhoods decayed, its infrastructure was neither maintained nor improved and little economic development occurred there for the next half-century.

Great Reads

Byzantium (Judith Herrin; 2007)

Constantinople (Philip Mansel; 1995)

Inside the Seraglio (John Freely; 1999)

A Short History of Byzantium (John Julian Norwich; 1997)

The Recent Past

The weak economic position of İstanbul was reflected in the rest of the country, and this – along with some anger about Turkey's strengthening alliance with the USA – led to growing dissatisfaction with a succession of governments. There were military coups in 1960 and 1971, and the late 1960s and 1970s were characterised by left-wing activism and political violence. This reached a shocking crescendo on 1 May (May Day) 1977, when there was a flare-up between rival political factions at

1914	1915	1922	1923
The government allies itself with the Central Powers and joins WWI; the Bosphorus and Dardenelles are closed to shipping, leading to the Allies' decision to attack Gallipoli.	Many prominent members of the city's 164,000-strong Armenian population have their property confiscated and are deported from the city.	The Turkish Grand National Assembly abolishes the Ottoman sultanate; the last sultan, Mehmet VI, leaves the country on a British warship.	The Grand National Assembly relocates the nation's capital from İstanbul to Ankara; shortly afterwards, it proclaims the Turkish Republic.

a huge demonstration in Taksim Meydanı (Taksim Sq). Security forces intervened and approximately 40 protesters were killed.

Under the presidency of economist Turgut Özal, the 1980s saw a free-market-led economic and tourism boom in Turkey and its major city. Özal's government also presided over a great increase in urbanisation, with trainloads of people from eastern Anatolia making their way to İstanbul in search of jobs in the booming industrial sector. The city's infrastructure couldn't cope back then and is still catching up, despite nearly four decades of large-scale municipal works being undertaken.

The municipal elections of March 1994 were a shock to the political establishment, with the upstart religious-right Refah Partisi (Welfare Party) winning elections across the country. Its victory was seen in part as a protest vote against the corruption, ineffective policies and tedious political wrangles of the traditional parties. In İstanbul Refah was led by Recep Tayyip Erdoğan (b 1954), a proudly Islamist candidate. He vowed to modernise infrastructure and restore the city to its former glory.

In the national elections of December 1996, Refah polled more votes than any other party (23%), and eventually formed a government vowing moderation and honesty. Emboldened by political power, Prime Minister Necmettin Erbakan and other Refah politicians tested the boundaries of Turkey's traditional secularism, alarming the powerful National Security Council, the most visible symbol of the centrist military establishment's role as the caretaker of secularism and democracy.

In 1997 the council announced that Refah had flouted the constitutional ban on religion in politics and warned that the government should resign or face a military coup. Bowing to the inevitable, Erbakan did as the council wished. In İstanbul, Mayor Erdoğan was ousted by the secularist forces in the national government in late 1998.

National elections in April 1999 brought in a coalition government led by Bülent Ecevit's left-wing Democratic Left Party. After years under the conservative right of the Refah Partisi, the election result heralded a shift towards European-style social democracy.

Unfortunately for the new government, there was a spectacular collapse of the Turkish economy in 2001, leading to its electoral defeat in 2002. The victorious party was the moderate Adalet ve Kalkınma Partisi (Justice and Development Party; AKP), led by phoenix-like Recep Tayyip Erdoğan. In İstanbul, candidates from the AKP were elected into power in most municipalities, including the powerful Fatih Municipality, which includes Eminönü.

Elections in 2007 and 2011 had the same result, as did the municipal election in 2014. The result of the 2014 election was a disappointment

The author of many books about İstanbul, American-born academic John Freely arrived in the city in 1960 and spent decades exploring its historic neighbourhoods. His 1972 book *Strolling Through İstanbul*, which was written with Hilary Sumner-Boyd, is still in print and is essential reading for İstanbul-bound history and architecture buffs.

HISTORY THE RECENT PAST

1925	1934	1942	2006
The Republican government bans Dervish orders; many of the city's historic *tekkes* (Dervish lodges) are demolished.	Women are given the vote; by 1935 4.6% of the national parliament's representatives are female.	A wealth tax is introduced on affluent citizens. Ethnic minorities are taxed at a higher rate than Muslims; many are bankrupted and forced to leave the city.	İstanbul successfully bids to become a European Capital of Culture for 2010, and launches a program of heritage restoration and cultural development that continues for the next decade.

to many secular and left-leaning İstanbullus, as well as to former AKP supporters who had changed their political allegiance as a result of the government's handling of the 2013 Gezi Park protests. These protests, which were staged in and around Taksim Meydanı, were initially a public response to a plan to redevelop the park, on the northeastern edge of the square, but transformed into a much larger protest by İstanbullus against what they saw as an increasingly autocratic and undemocratic Turkish government. Called in to disperse the crowd, police used tear gas and water cannons, which led to violent clashes, 8000 injuries, at least four deaths and thousands of arrests.

After Gezi, local authorities cracked down on any political demonstrations that were seen as anti-government and made any large assemblies in or around Taksim Meydanı illegal. Local media outlets seen to be antigovernment were also targeted, with some being forceably closed or taken over by the government. Many İstanbul-based writers, journalists and editors were charged with serious crimes including membership of a terror organisation, espionage and revealing confidential documents. Charges under Article 301 of the Turkish penal code, which make it a punishable offence to insult Turkishness or various official Turkish institutions (including the president), were particularly prevalent.

A coup d'état staged by a small faction of the military in July 2016 was defeated when members of the public took to the streets to defend the democratically elected AKP government. Official reprisals against anyone suspected of being a coup perpetrator or supporter were draconian, with thousands of İstanbullus arrested, media outlets closed down and universities and schools purged. Unsurprisingly, tourist arrivals to the city plunged as a result of the turmoil and the local economy is still reeling as a result.

The current AKP-endorsed mayor of İstanbul, Kadir Topbaş (b 1945), is one of Erdoğan's former advisors and a former mayor of the Beyoğlu municipality. He has been mayor since 2004.

İstanbul's third bridge over the Bosphorus, the Yavuz Sultan Selim Bridge, opened in 2016. It is named after Sultan Selim I (r 1517–20), who acquired his nickname 'Selim the Grim' after dethroning his father Beyazıt II and ordering the deaths of his brothers and nephews to ensure his succession to the throne.

2011	2013	2014	2016
The ruling soft-Islamist Justice and Development Party (AKP), led by İstanbul-born prime minister Recep Tayyip Erdoğan, wins a third term in government.	Large demonstrations by İstanbullus protesting a plan to redevelop Gezi Park on the northeastern edge of Taksim Meydanı (Taksim Sq) are met with a violent response by the government.	After a long stint as the country's prime minister, Recep Tayyip Erdoğan wins Turkey's presidential election and consolidates his position at the helm of both the AKP and the country.	A small group of the military stage an unsuccessful coup d'état during which hundreds are killed; government reprisals against anyone thought to be a coup sympathiser are swift and severe.

Architecture

Architects and urban designers wanting to study the world's best practice need go no further than İstanbul. Here, delicate minarets reach towards the heavens, distinctive domes crown hills, elegant mansions adorn the water's edge and edgy art spaces claim contemporary landmark status. The skyline has wow factor in spades and the historical layers of the built environment are both handsome and fascinating – together, these offer travellers an exhilarating architectural experience.

Byzantine Architecture

After Mehmet the Conquerer stormed into İstanbul in 1453 many churches were converted into mosques; despite the minarets, you can usually tell a church-cum-mosque by the distinctive red bricks that are characteristic of all Byzantine churches.

Above: Ceiling, Blue Mosque (p72)

İstanbul's Old City is included in Unesco's World Heritage List for its mix and wealth of Byzantine and Ottoman architectural masterpieces and its incomparable skyline.

During Justinian's reign (527–65), architects were encouraged to surpass each other's achievements when it came to utilising the domed, Roman-influenced basilica form. Aya Sofya is the supreme example of this.

Early Byzantine basilica design used rectangular external walls; inside was a centralised polygonal plan with supporting walls and a dome. Little Aya Sofya (Küçük Aya Sofya Camii), built around 530, is a good example. Later, a mixed basilica and centralised polygonal plan developed. This was the foundation for church design from the 11th century until the Conquest and many Ottoman mosques were inspired by it. The Monastery of Christ Pantokrator is a good example.

The Byzantines also had a yen for building fortifications. The greatest of these is the still-standing land wall. Constructed in the 5th century by order of Emperor Theodosius II, it was 20km long and protected the city during multiple sieges until it was finally breached in 1453.

Constantine the Great, the first Byzantine emperor, named his city 'New Rome'. And like Rome it was characterised by great public works such as the stone aqueduct built by Emperor Valens between 368 and 378. The aqueduct fed a series of huge cisterns built across the city, one being the Basilica Cistern.

Like Rome, the city was built on seven hills and to a grid pattern that included ceremonial thoroughfares such as Divan Yolu and major public spaces such as the Hippodrome.

Ottoman Architecture

After the Conquest, the sultans wasted no time in putting their architectural stamp on the city. Mehmet didn't even wait until he had the city under his control, building the monumental Rumeli Hisarı on the Bosphorus in 1452, the year before his great victory.

Unfortunately, İstanbul notches up regular mentions in the World Monuments Fund's watchlist of heritage in danger. Recent entries include Haydarpaşa train station, the historic city walls and the Rum (Greek) Orphanage on Büyükada.

Once in the city, Mehmet kicked off a centuries-long Ottoman building spree, constructing a number of buildings, including a mosque on the fourth hill. After these he started work on the most famous Ottoman building of all: Topkapı Palace.

Mehmet had a penchant for palaces, but his great-grandson, Süleyman the Magnificent, was more of a mosque man. With his favourite architect, Mimar Sinan, he built the greatest of the city's Ottoman imperial mosques. Sinan's prototype mosque form has a forecourt with a şadırvan (ablutions fountain) and domed arcades on three sides. On the fourth side is the mosque, with a two-storey porch. The main prayer hall is covered by a central dome surrounded by smaller domes

THE GREAT SINAN

None of today's star architects come close to having the influence over a city that Mimar Koca Sinan had over Constantinople during his 50-year career.

Born in 1497, Sinan was a recruit to the devşirme, the annual intake of Christian youths into the janissaries. He became a Muslim (as all such recruits did) and eventually took up a post as a military engineer in the corps. Süleyman the Magnificent appointed him the chief of the imperial architects in 1538.

Sinan designed a total of 321 buildings, 85 of which are still standing in İstanbul. He died in 1588 and is buried in a self-designed türbe (tomb) located in one of the corners of the Süleymaniye Mosque, the building that many believe to be his greatest work.

Harem (p62), inside Topkapı Palace

and semidomes. There was usually one minaret, though imperial mosques had more.

Each imperial mosque had a *külliye* (mosque complex) clustered around it. This was a philanthropic complex including a *medrese* (seminary), hamam, *darüşşifa* (hospital), *imaret* (soup kitchen), *kütüphane* (library), *tabhane* (inn for travelling dervishes) or *kervansaray* (caravanserai) and cemetery with *türbes* (tombs). Over time many of these *külliyes* were demolished; fortunately, a number of the buildings in the magnificent Süleymaniye and Atik Valide complexes remain intact.

Later sultans continued Mehmet's palace-building craze. No palace would rival Topkapı, but Sultan Abdül Mecit I tried his best with the grandiose Dolmabahçe Palace and Abdül Aziz I built the extravagant Çırağan Palace and Beylerbeyi Palace. These and other buildings of the era have been collectively dubbed 'Turkish baroque'.

These mosques and palaces dominate the landscape and skyline of the city, but there are other quintessentially Ottoman buildings: the hamam and the Ottoman timber house. Hamams were usually built as part of a *külliye*, and provided an important point of social contact as well as facilities for ablutions. Architecturally significant hamams include the Ayasofya Hürrem Sultan Hamamı, the Çemberlitaş Hamamı, the Cağaloğlu Hamamı and the Kılıç Ali Paşa Hamamı. All are still functioning.

Wealthy Ottomans and foreign diplomats built many *yalıs* (waterside, usually timber, mansions) along the shores of the Bosphorus; city equivalents were sometimes set in a garden but were usually part of a crowded, urban streetscape. Unfortunately, not too many of

Two family dynasties have played major roles in İstanbul's architectural scene: the Balyans, who worked in the 18th and 19th centuries, and the Tabanlıoğlus, in the 20th and 21st centuries.

Şakirin Mosque (p160) in Üsküdar; designed by Hüsrev Tayla, with the interior design by Zeynep Fadıllıoğlu

these houses survive, a consequence of the fires that regularly raced through the Ottoman city.

Ottoman Revivalism & Modernism

In the late 19th and early 20th centuries, architects created a blend of European architecture alongside Turkish baroque, with some concessions to classic Ottoman style. This style has been dubbed 'Ottoman Revivalism' or First National Architecture.

The main proponents of this style were architects Vedat Tek (1873–1942) and Kemalettin Bey (1870–1927). Tek is best known for his Central Post Office in Sirkeci (1909) and Haydarpaşa İskelesi (Haydarpaşa Ferry Dock; 1915–17). Kemalettin Bey's Bebek Mosque (1913) and Fourth Vakıf Han (1912–26), a bank building in Eminönü that now houses the Legacy Ottoman Hotel, are his best-known works.

When Atatürk proclaimed Ankara the capital of the Republic, İstanbul lost much of its glamour and investment capital. Modernism was played out on the new canvas of Ankara, while İstanbul's dalliances went little further than the İstanbul City Hall in Fatih, designed by Nevzat Erol and built in 1953; the İstanbul Hilton Hotel, designed by SOM and Sedad Hakkı Eldem and built in 1952; the Atatürk Library in Gümüşsuyu, also by Eldem; and the much-maligned Atatürk Cultural Centre by Hayati Tabanlıoğlu, built from 1956 to 1957 and currently threatened with demolition as part of the redevelopment proposal for Gezi Park.

Recent architecture in the city can hardly be called inspiring. One building of note is Kanyon, a mixed residential, office and shopping development in Levent, designed by the LA-based Jerde Partnership with local architects Tabanlıoğlu Partnership. The nearby Loft Gardens residential complex and İstanbul Sapphire tower, both by Tabanlıoğlu Partnership, are also impressive, as is the terraced plaza and underground car park in Şişhane by Şanal Architecture. Notable contemporary religious buildings are few and far between, with the only exceptions being the extraordinary Sancaklar Mosque in Büyükçekmece outside the city, which was designed by Emre Arolat; and the sleek Şakirin Mosque in Üsküdar by Hüsrev Tayla and Zeynep Fadıllıoğlu.

Many art museums and cultural centres around town feature impressive new wings or inspired architectural conversions of industrial or commercial spaces. The best of these are İstanbul Modern, by Tabanlıoğlu Partnership; SALT Galata, by Mimarlar Tasarım; the Sakıp Sabancı Museum, by Savaş, Erkel and Çırakoğlu; the İstanbul Naval Museum in Beşiktaş, by Mehmet Kütükçüoğlu; and santralistanbul in Sütlüce on the Golden Horn, by Emre Arolat, Nevzat Sayın and Han Tümertekin. Tabanlıoğlu Partnership's Beyazıt State Library restoration and Emre Arolat's Eyüp Cultural Centre and Marriage Hall are also noteworthy.

At the time of writing, a number of projects by high-profile international firms were on the drawing board or in the first stages of construction. These included the city's new airport designed by Grimshaw Architects with Haptic Architects, which features a tulip-shaped traffic control tower.

Nevzat Erol's 1953 İstanbul Belediye Sarayı (İstanbul City Hall), located opposite the Şehzade Mehmet Mosque on Şehzadebaşı Caddesi in Fatih, was the first International Style building in the city.

ARCHITECTURE OTTOMAN REVIVALISM & MODERNISM

İstanbul on Page & Screen

Replete with colours, characters, sounds and stories, İstanbul has been inspiring writers and artists for as long as it has been seducing first-time visitors (and that's a very long time indeed). Those keen to indulge in some inspirational predeparture research should consider reading a book set in the city, or watching a film that has been shot here – there are many to choose from, both local and foreign.

Lord Byron spent two months in Constantinople in 1810 and wrote about the city in his satiric poem *Don Juan*.

İstanbul in Print

Turkey has a rich but relatively young literary tradition. Its brightest stars tend to be based in İstanbul and are greatly revered throughout the country. Fortunately, many of their works are now available in English translation.

It's not only Turks who are inspired to write about the city. There are a huge number of novels, travel memoirs and histories by foreign writers.

Literary Heritage

Under the sultans, literature was really a form of religious devotion. Ottoman poets, borrowing from the great Arabic and Persian traditions, wrote sensual love poems of attraction, longing, fulfilment and ecstasy in the search for union with God.

By the late 19th century the influence of Western literature began to be felt. This was the time of the Tanzimat political and social reforms initiated by Sultan Abdül Mecit, and in İstanbul a literary movement was established that became known as 'Tanzimat Literature'.

This movement was responsible for the first serious attacks on the ponderous cadences of Ottoman courtly prose and poetry, but it wasn't until the foundation of the Republic that the death knell for this form of literature finally rang. Atatürk decreed that the Turkish language should be purified of Arabic and Persian borrowings, and that in the future the nation's literature should be created using the new Latin-based Turkish alphabet. Major figures in the new literary movement (dubbed 'National Literature') included poet Yahya Kemal Beyatli (1884–1958) and novelist Halide Edib Adıvar (1884–1964).

Though not part of the National Literature movement, İrfan Orga (1908–70) is probably the most famous Turkish literary figure of the 20th century. His 1950 masterpiece *Portrait of a Turkish Family* is his memoir of growing up in İstanbul at the start of the century and is among the best writing about the city ever published.

Politician, essayist and novelist Ahmet Hamdi Tanipar (1901–62) wrote *A Mind at Peace* in 1949. Set in the city at the beginning of WWII, it is beloved by many Turks. Another of his novels, *The Time Regulation Institute,* was released in an English-language edition for the first time in 2014.

Contemporary Novelists

The second half of the 20th century saw a raft of İstanbul-based writers and poets published locally and internationally. Many were socialists, communists or outspoken critics of the government, and spent long and repeated periods in jail. The two most famous were Nâzım Hikmet (1902–63), whose masterwork is the five-volume collection of lyric and epic poetry entitled *Human Landscapes from My Country;* and Yaşar Kemal (b 1923), whose best-known work is *Mehmed, My Hawk.* Two of Kemal's novels – *The Birds Are Also Gone* and *The Sea-Crossed Fisherman* – are set in İstanbul.

High-profile writer Elif Şafak was born in Strasbourg in 1971 to Turkish parents and now divides her time between London and İstanbul. Her best-known novels are *The Flea Palace* (2002), *The Saint of Incipient Insanities* (2004), *The Bastard of Istanbul* (2006), *The Forty Rules of Love* (2010) and *Honour* (2012). Şafak's novels often address issues that are controversial in Turkey (eg honour killing, gay identity, the Armenian genocide, sex before marriage). Her most recent novel, *The Architect's Apprentice* (2014), revolves around the life of the Ottoman architect Mimar Sinan. It, *The Flea Palace* and *The Bastard of Istanbul* are all set in the city.

Arrested after the 1980 military coup, left-wing activist Izzet Celasin (b 1958) spent several years in a Turkish jail before being granted political asylum in Norway. His debut novel *Black Sky, Black Sea* (2012) is a semi-autobiographical story about young activists in İstanbul during the period of political unrest in the late 1970s. The timing of the novel's release (just before the Gezi protests of 2013) made it resonate both in Turkey and overseas.

> Turkish novelist, poet, songwriter and film director OZ Livaneli (b 1946) has written 15 bestsellers but only one, the acclaimed 2003 novel *Bliss* (*Mutluluk* in Turkish), is available in an English-language edition. Dealing with weighty issues such as honour killing and partially set in İstanbul, it was made into a film in 2007.

İSTANBUL ON PAGE & SCREEN İSTANBUL IN PRINT

ORHAN PAMUK

When the much-fêted Orhan Pamuk (b 1952) was awarded the 2006 Nobel Prize in Literature, the international cultural sector was largely unsurprised. The writing of the İstanbul-born, US-based novelist had already attracted critical accolades, including the IMPAC Dublin Literary Award, *The Independent* newspaper's Foreign Fiction Award of the Month and every local literary prize on offer.

In their citation, the Nobel judges said that in his 'quest for the melancholic soul of his native city' (ie İstanbul), Pamuk had 'discovered new symbols for the clash and interlacing of culture'. The only voices heard to criticise their judgement hailed from Turkey. Pamuk had been charged with 'insulting Turkishness' under Article 301 of the Turkish Criminal Code (the charges were dropped in early 2006), and some local commentators alleged that in his case the Nobel Prize was awarded for political (ie freedom of speech) reasons rather than purely on the merit of his literary oeuvre.

Pamuk has written 10 novels to date. His first, *Cevdet Bey & His Sons* (1982), is a dynastic saga of the İstanbul bourgeoisie. It was followed by *The House of Silence* (1983), *The White Castle* (1985) and *The Black Book* (1990). The latter was made into a film (*Gizli Yuz*) by director Omer Kavur in 1992. After this came *The New Life* (1995), *My Name is Red* (1998), *Snow* (2002), *The Museum of Innocence* (2009), *A Strangeness in His Mind* (2015) and *The Red-Haired Woman* (2016). In 2005 he published a memoir, *Istanbul: Memories of a City*, about the city he loves.

In 2012 Pamuk opened the Museum of Innocence (p131), his conceptual art project occupying an entire house in Cihangir. This was inspired by his novel of the same name, and has proved to be popular with locals and tourists alike. Grant Gee's 2015 documentary film *Innocence of Memories: Orhan Pamuk's Museum and Istanbul,* which is narrated by Pamuk, is set in the museum and at locations featured in the novel.

Selçuk Altun (b 1950) uses İstanbul as a setting in many of his novels. Sometimes mysteries, sometimes historical yarns, they include *Songs My Mother Never Taught Me* (2007), *Many and Many a Year Ago* (2008) and *The Sultan of Byzantium* (2011).

Other contemporary Turkish novelists of note include İstanbul-born Nobel Prize–winning novelist Orhan Pamuk (p203), Ahmet Ümit (b 1960) and Perihan Mağden (b 1960).

Through Foreign Eyes

Foreign novelists have long tried to capture the magic and mystery of İstanbul in their work. One of the earliest to do so was French novelist Pierre Loti (1850–1923), whose romantic novel *Aziyadé*, written in 1879, introduced Europe to Loti's almond-eyed Turkish lover and to the mysterious and all-pervasive attractions of the city itself.

After Loti, writers such as Harold Nicolson set popular stories in the city. Nicolson's 1921 novel *Sweet Waters* is a moving love story cum political thriller set in İstanbul during the Balkan Wars. Nicolson, who lived here as a diplomat, based the novel's main character on his wife, Vita Sackville-West.

Graham Greene's 1932 thriller *Stamboul Train* focuses on a group of passengers travelling between Ostend and İstanbul on the *Orient Express*. It was filmed in 1934 as *Orient Express*.

Thriller writer Eric Ambler used İstanbul as a setting in three highly regarded novels: *The Mask of Dimitrios* (1939), *Journey into Fear* (1940) and *The Light of Day* (1962).

THE DARK SIDE OF THE CITY

İstanbul features as the setting for some great crime novels:

The Inspector İkmen novels Barbara Nadel investigates the city's underbelly in a suitably gripping style. Whether they're set in Balat or Beyoğlu, her books are always evocative and well researched. Start with *Belshazzar's Daughter* (1999).

The Yashim the Ottoman Investigator novels Jason Goodwin writes historical crime novels with a protagonist who is a eunuch attached to the Ottoman court. Titles in the series include *The Janissary Tree* (2006), *An Evil Eye* (2011) and *The Baklava Club* (2014).

Murder on the Orient Express Hercule Poirot puts ze leetle grey cells to good use on the famous train in this 1934 novel by Agatha Christie. It was made into a film by Sidney Lumet in 1974 and features a few opening shots of İstanbul.

The Kamil Paşa novels These historical crime novels by Jenny White feature a magistrate in one of the new Ottoman secular courts. Titles include *The Sultan's Seal* (2006), *The Abyssinian Proof* (2009) and *The Winter Thief* (2010).

Island Crimes Lawrence Goodman's series of comic mystery novels set on the Princes' Islands includes *Sweet Confusion on the Princes' Islands, Sour Grapes on the Princes' Islands, A Grain of Salt on the Princes' Islands* and *Something Bitter on the Princes' Islands*.

The Hop-Çıkı-Yaya novels Mehmet Murat Somer's series of gay crime novels feature a transvestite amateur sleuth. Titles include *The Prophet Murders* (2008), *The Kiss Murders* (2009) and *The Wig Murders* (2014).

The Kati Hirschel Murder mysteries Written in Turkish and translated into English, these novels by Esmahan Aykol feature a German amateur sleuth who owns a bookshop in Galata. Titles include *Hotel Bosphorus* (2011) and *Baksheesh* (2013).

A Memento for İstanbul Three local policemen look to the city's history to solve a string of bizarre killings in this 2010 novel by Ahmet Ümit.

Historical novels set here include *The Rage of the Vulture* (Barry Unsworth; 1982), *The Stone Woman* (Tariq Ali; 2001), *The Calligrapher's Night* (Yasmine Ghata; 2006) and *The Dark Angel* (Mika Waltari; 1952). Young readers will enjoy *The Oracle of Stamboul* (Michael David Lukas; 2011).

Although best known as award-winning author Orhan Pamuk's English translator and as the daughter of American author John Freely, Maureen Freely is also a writer of fiction. Two of her best-known novels, *The Life of the Party* (1986) and *Sailing Through Byzantium* (2013), are semi-autobiographical tales set in İstanbul.

Alan Drew's 2008 novel *Gardens of Water* follows the lives of two families in the aftermath of the devastating earthquake that struck western Turkey (including İstanbul's outskirts) in 1999.

Joseph Kanon's 2012 thriller *Istanbul Passage* is set just after the end of WWII, when espionage is rife and Mossad is attempting to illegally transport Jewish refugees through the city en route to Palestine.

Travel Writing

....

Constantinople (Edmondo De Amici; 1878)

....

Constantinople in 1890 (Pierre Loti; 1892)

....

The Innocents Abroad (Mark Twain; 1869)

....

The Turkish Embassy Letters (Lady Mary Wortley Montagu; 1837)

Cinema

Turks are committed cinema-goers and the local industry continues to go from strength to strength. Local directors, many of whom are based in İstanbul, are now fixtures on the international festival circuit.

Local Stories

Oddly enough, few masterpieces of Turkish cinema have been set in İstanbul. Acclaimed directors including Metin Erksan, Yılmaz Güney and Erdan Kıral tended to set the social-realist films they made in the 1960s, '70s and '80s in the villages of central or eastern Anatolia.

This started to change in the 1990s, when many critical and popular hits were set in the city. Notable among these were the films of Zeki Demirkubuz, Omer Kavur, Yeşim Ustaoğlu, Mustafa Altıoklar and Yavuz Turgul.

Contemporary directors of note include Ferzan Özpetek, who has a growing number of Turkish-Italian co-productions to his credit. His 1996 film *Hamam,* set in İstanbul, was a big hit on the international festival circuit and is particularly noteworthy for addressing the hitherto hidden issue of homosexuality in Turkish society.

The issue of discrimination against Kurdish members of the community is investigated in Yeşim Ustaoğlu's powerful 1999 film *Journey to the Sun,* which is set in the city.

Yavuz Turgul's 2005 film *Lovelorn* is the story of idealist Nazim, who returns home to İstanbul after teaching for 15 years in a remote village in eastern Turkey and starts a doomed relationship with a single mother who works in a sleazy bar. It's particularly notable for the soundtrack by Tamer Çıray, which features the voice of Aynur Doğan.

Kutluğ Ataman's 2005 film *2 Girls* and Reha Erdem's 2008 film *My Only Sunshine* are both dramas in which the city provides an evocative backdrop.

Turkish-German director Fatih Akın received a screenwriting prize at Cannes for his 2007 film *The Edge of Heaven,* parts of which are set in İstanbul. His 2005 documentary about the İstanbul music scene – *Crossing the Bridge: The Sound of Istanbul* – was instrumental in raising the Turkish music industry's profile internationally.

Erdem Tepegöz' bleakly realistic 2013 film *Zerre* (*Particle*) follows single working woman Zeynep as she searches for a job to support her mother and disabled daughter. The film was shot in Tarlabaşı, near Beyoğlu.

İSTANBUL ON PAGE & SCREEN CINEMA

Clamour over Galata Tower, Aya Sofya's dome, the minarets of the Blue Mosque and the roof of Topkapı Palace while playing the popular PS3/Xbox 360 video game *Assassin's Creed: Revelations,* which is set in Constantinople in 1511.

Filiz Alpgezmen's *Yabancı (Stranger;* 2013) tells the story of Özgür, who was raised in Paris but returns to her parents' home town of İstanbul to bury her father, in the process discovering much about her family and herself.

Turkey's most acclaimed director, Nuri Bilge Ceylan, was awarded the 2014 Palme d'Or at Cannes for his film *Winter Sleep,* which is set in Cappadocia. At the awards ceremony, he dedicated his prize to 'all the young people of Turkey, including those who lost their lives over the past year', a clear statement of support for the anti-government protests at Gezi Park (p194) in 2013. Ceylan has directed three films set in İstanbul: *Distant* (2002), *Climates* (2006) and *Three Monkeys* (2008).

The final scenes in Deniz Gamze Ergüven's award-winning 2015 film *Mustang* are set in İstanbul.

Through Foreign Eyes

Many of the foreign-made films with scenes featuring İstanbul have been thrillers. These include James Negulesco's *The Mask of Dimitrios* (1944); Norman Foster's 1943 film *Journey into Fear;* Tomas Alfredson's 2011 film *Tinker Tailor Soldier Spy,* based on John Le Carré's 1974 novel; Olivier Megaton's *Taken 2* (2012); and three James Bond films: *From Russia with Love* (1974), *The World Is Not Enough* (1999) and *Skyfall* (2012).

Other films to look out for are Jacques Vierne's 1961 film *Tintin and the Golden Fleece;* Alain Robbe-Grillet's 1963 film *L'Immortelle;* Alan Parker's 1978 hit *Midnight Express;* and Jules Dassin's 1964 crime spoof *Topkapi,* which was based on Eric Ambler's novel *In the Light of Day.*

Greek director Tassos Boulmetis set part of his popular 2003 arthouse film *A Touch of Spice* here.

In 2014 Australian–New Zealand actor Russell Crowe released his directorial debut *The Water Diviner,* which tells the story of an Australian father who makes his way to İstanbul to ascertain the fate of his three sons, all missing in action after the Battle of Gallipoli in 1915.

Parts of Mira Nair's 2012 *The Reluctant Fundamentalist* and Hossein Amini's 2014 *The Two Faces of January* were also shot here.

Survival Guide

Transport

ARRIVING IN İSTANBUL

It's the national capital in all but name, so getting to İstanbul is easy. There are currently two international airports and a new and improved third airport is due to open in 2018. When it does, Atatürk International Airport will be retired from use. There is one *otogar* (bus station) from which national and international services arrive and depart. At the time of research there were no international rail connections, but this situation may change when upgrades to rail lines throughout the country are completed and when the security situation in Turkey's east and in Syria improves.

Flights, cars and tours can be booked online at www.lonelyplanet.com/bookings.

Air

Atatürk International Airport

The city's main airport, **Atatürk International Airport** (IST, Atatürk Havalimanı; ☎0090 444 9828; www.ataturkairport.com), is located in Yeşilköy, 23km west of Sultanahmet. The international terminal (Dış Hatlar) and domestic terminal (İç Hatlar) operate at or close to capacity, which has prompted the Turkish Government to announce construction of a new, much larger, airport 50km north of the city centre. The first stage of the new airport's construction is due to be completed by 2018 but the facility won't be fully operational until 2025.

The airport has car-rental desks, exchange offices, stands of mobile-phone companies, a 24-hour pharmacy, ATMs and a PTT (post office) at the international arrivals area. A 24-hour supermarket is located on the walkway to the metro.

Left-luggage A booth to your right as you exit customs offers luggage storage and charges ₺20 per suitcase or backpack per 24 hours; it's open around the clock.

Tourist information There's a small office in the international arrivals hall that is open from 9am to 9pm. It provides maps and advice.

METRO & TRAM

There's an efficient metro service between the airport and Yenikapı, from where you can connect to the M2 metro to Hacıosman. This stops at Vezneciler in the Bazaar District, and in Şişhane and Taksim in Beyoğlu en route. Another service, the Marmaray to Ayrılık Çeşmesi, stops at Sirkeci near the Eminönü ferry docks and in Üsküdar on the Asian shore en route.

To get to Sultanahmet, alight from the metro at Zeytinburnu, from where it's easy to connect with the tram to Sultanahmet, Eminönü and Kabataş. From Kabataş, there's a funicular to Taksim Meydanı (Taksim Sq). Note that if you are going to the airport from the city centre you should take the Bağcılar

---

CLIMATE CHANGE & TRAVEL

Every form of transport that relies on carbon-based fuel generates CO_2, the main cause of human-induced climate change. Modern travel is dependent on aeroplanes, which might use less fuel per kilometre per person than most cars but travel much greater distances. The altitude at which aircraft emit gases (including CO_2) and particles also contributes to their climate change impact. Many websites offer 'carbon calculators' that allow people to estimate the carbon emissions generated by their journey and, for those who wish to do so, to offset the impact of the greenhouse gases emitted with contributions to portfolios of climate-friendly initiatives throughout the world. Lonely Planet offsets the carbon footprint of all staff and author travel.

service rather than the Cevizlibağ one, which terminates before Zeytinburnu.

The metro station is on the lower ground floor beneath the international departures hall – follow the 'Metro/Subway' signs down the escalators and through the underground walkway. You'll need to purchase a *jeton* (ticket token; ₺4) for each individual metro trip or purchase and recharge an İstanbulkart (travel card; ₺10, including ₺4 credit) from the machines at the metro entrance. Services depart every six to 10 minutes from 6am until midnight. If you get off the metro at Zeytinburnu, the tram platform is right in front of you. You'll need to buy another token (₺4) to pass through the turnstiles.

AIRPORT BUS

If you are staying in Beyoğlu, the **Havataş** (Map p244; ✆444 2656; http://havatas.com) airport bus from Atatürk International Airport is probably the most convenient option. This departs from outside the arrivals hall. Buses leave every 30 minutes between 4am and 1am; the trip takes between 40 minutes and one hour, depending on traffic. Tickets cost ₺11 and the bus stops in front of the Point Hotel on Cumhuriyet Caddesi, close to Taksim Meydanı. Note that signage on the buses and at stops sometimes reads 'Havaş' rather than 'Havataş'.

A public bus service (No 96T) travels from a stop next to the Havataş buses outside the arrivals hall and travels to Taksim Meydanı (₺4, two hours, six daily); check the İETT website for departure times. To travel on this bus, you must have an İstanbulkart. These are available at the machines at the metro station entrance on the lower ground floor.

TAXI

A taxi from the airport costs around ₺45 to Sultanahmet,

PUBLIC TRANSPORT OPERATORS

İstanbul Elektrik Tramvay ve Tünel (İETT, İstanbul Electricity, Tramway and Tunnel General Management; www.iett.gov.tr) is responsible for running public buses, funiculars and historic trams in the city. Its website has useful timetable and route information in Turkish and English. Metro and tram services are run by **İstanbul Ulaşım** (www.istanbul-ulasim.com.tr), ferry services are run by **İstanbul Şehir Hatları** (İstanbul City Routes; www.sehirhatlari.com.tr), **Dentur Avrasya** (✆444 6336; www.denturavrasya.com) and **Turyol** (✆0212-251 4421; www.turyol.com), and seabus and fast-ferry services are operated by **İstanbul Deniz Otobüsleri** (İDO; ✆0850 222 4436; www.ido.com.tr).

₺55 to Beyoğlu and ₺80 to Kadıköy.

HOTEL SHUTTLE

Many hotels will provide a free pick-up service from Atatürk International Airport if you stay with them for three nights or more. There are also a number of very slow shuttle-bus services from hotels to the airport for your return trip; these cost around ₺25. Check details with your hotel.

Sabiha Gökçen International Airport

The city's second international airport, **Sabiha Gökçen International Airport** (SAW, Sabiha Gökçen Havalimanı; ✆0216-588 8888; www.sgairport.com), is at Pendik/Kurtköy on the Asian side of the city.

It has ATMs, car-rental desks, stands of mobile-phone companies, exchange offices, a mini-market and a PTT in the international arrivals hall.

Left-luggage A booth in the international arrivals hall offers luggage storage.

Tourist information There's a small office in the international arrivals hall that is open from 9am to 7pm. It provides maps and advice.

AIRPORT BUS

Havataş (Map p244; ✆444 2656; http://havatas.com) airport buses travel from the

airport to Taksim Meydanı (Taksim Sq) between 3.30am and 1am. There are also services to Kadıköy between 4am and 1am. Tickets cost ₺14 to Taksim (1½ hours) and ₺9 to Kadıköy (one hour). If you're heading towards the Old City from Taksim, you can take the funicular from Taksim to Kabataş (₺4) followed by the tram from Kabataş to Sultanahmet (₺4). From Kadıköy, ferries travel to Eminönü (₺4).

TAXI

Taxis from this airport to the city are expensive. To Beyoğlu you'll be looking at around ₺140; to Sultanahmet around ₺155.

HOTEL SHUTTLE

Hotels rarely provide free pick-up services from Sabiha Gökçen. Shuttle-bus services from hotels to the airport cost up to ₺75 but are infrequent – check details with your hotel. The trip can take up to two hours, so allow plenty of time.

Boat

Cruise ships currently arrive at a temporary dock near the Fındıklı tram stop.

Bus

The **Büyük İstanbul Otogarı** (Big İstanbul Bus Station; ✆0212-658 0505;

www.otogaristanbul.com) is the city's main bus station for both intercity and international routes. Often called simply 'the Otogar' (Bus Station), it's located at Esenler in the municipality of Bayrampaşa, about 10km west of Sultanahmet. The metro service between Aksaray and Atatürk International Airport stops here (Otogar stop). From the Otogar you can take the metro to Zeytinburnu and then easily connect with a tram (₺4) to Sultanahmet or Kabataş/Taksim. If you're going to Beyoğlu, bus 830 leaves from the centre of the Otogar every 15 minutes between 6am and 10.50pm and takes approximately one hour to reach Taksim Meydanı. The trip costs ₺4 and is slower than the metro/tram alternative. A taxi will cost approximately ₺35 to both Sultanahmet and Taksim.

There's a second, much smaller, otogar at Alibeyköy, where buses from central Anatolia (including Ankara and Cappadocia) stop en route to Esenler. From here passengers can take a *servis* (service bus) to Taksim; the transfer is included in the ticket cost. The only problem with this option is that service drivers rarely speak English and passengers sometimes have to wait for a *servis* – it's probably easier to go to Esenler. Note that no *servises* go to Sultanahmet.

The city's third otogar is in Ataşehir, on the Asian side at the junction of the O-2 and O-4 motorways. From Ataşehir, *servises* transfer passengers to Asian suburbs, including Kadıköy and Üsküdar.

Train

At the time of research, no international train services were leaving İstanbul – the daily Bosfor Ekspresi service to Bucharest via Sofia was by bus between İstanbul and Sofia and then by train between Sofia and Bucharest. It departs at 10pm daily (₺65 to Sofia, ₺125 to Bucharest).

A fast-train service operates between Ankara and Pendik, 20km southeast of Kadıköy on the Asian side of the city. This takes approximately 3½ hours and ticket prices start at ₺70. Unfortunately, Pendik is difficult to access. You'll need to take the metro from Sirkeci to Ayrılık Çeşmesi and then change to the M4 metro and travel to the end of the line at Kartal. From Kartal bus 17B and taxis travel the last 6km to Pendik Garı. There are future plans to extend the M4 to Pendik and Kaynarca, but a timetable for this has yet to be announced.

Car & Motorcycle

Sensible locals never drive into or within the city due to the horrendous traffic conditions, and we recommend you follow their lead.

GETTING AROUND İSTANBUL

Public transport is cheap and efficient. Purchasing an İstanbulkart (transport card) is highly recommended.

Tram Run from Bağcılar, in the city's west, to Kabataş, in Beyoğlu, stopping at the Grand Bazaar, Sultanahmet, Eminönü and Karaköy en route. Connect with the metro at Zeytinburnu and Sirkeci, with ferries at Eminönü and with funiculars at Karaköy and Kabataş.

Metro The M1A connects Yenikapı with the airport; the M2 connects Yenikapı

İSTANBULKARTS

İstanbul's public transport system is excellent, and one of its major strengths is the İstanbulkart, a rechargeable travel card similar to London's Oyster Card, Hong Kong's Octopus Card and Paris' Navigo.

İstanbulkarts are simple to operate. As you enter a bus or pass through the turnstile at a ferry dock or metro station, swipe your card for entry and the fare will automatically be deducted from your balance. The cards offer a considerable discount on fares (₺2.20 to ₺2.45 according to the destination, as opposed to the usual ₺4, with additional transfers within a two-hour journey window – ₺1.75 for the first transfer, ₺1.60 for the second and ₺1.40 for all subsequent transfers). They can also be used to pay for fares for more than one traveller (one swipe per person per ride).

The cards can be purchased from machines at metro and funicular stations for a non-refundable charge of ₺10, which includes ₺4 in credit. If you buy yours from a street kiosk near a tram or bus stop (look for an 'Akbil', 'Dolum Noktası' or 'İstanbulkart' sign), you will pay ₺8 for one with a plastic cover, or ₺7 without. These won't include any credit.

Cards can be recharged with amounts between ₺5 and ₺150 at kiosks or at machines at ferry docks, metro and bus stations.

KABATAŞ İSKELE CLOSURE

In August 2016 the various *iskelesi* (ferry docks) at Kabataş were closed for an indefinite period so that construction works for an underwater pedestrian tunnel linking Kabataş and Üsküdar could commence. During the closure, ferry services will be relocated as listed below:

Princes' Islands (Adalar) ferries Ferries operated by İstanbul Şehir Hatları will depart from/arrive at Eminönü (Katip Çelebi *iskele*) and Beşiktaş. Ferries operated by İDO now depart from/arrive at Beşiktaş and Yenikapı.

Kadıköy İstanbul Şehir Hatları ferries will depart from/arrive at Eminönü (Katip Çelebi *iskele*) and Beşiktaş.

Üsküdar Dentur ferries will use the *iskele* near the Karaköy fish market, on the western side of the Galata Bridge.

Bursa İDO seabuses will depart from the former Karaköy İDO pier.

Bosphorus & Golden Horn Dentur Avrasya had not announced the plans for the relocation of its hop-on, hop-off services to the Bosphorus and Golden Horn and its regular services to the Princes' Islands. These will probably depart from/arrive at Beşiktaş, but you should check the company's website for details.

with Hacıosman via Taksim; and the Marmaray connects Kazlıçeşme, west of the Old City, with Sirkeci before crossing under the Bosphorus to Üsküdar and Ayrılık Çeşmesi.

Ferry Travel between the European and Asian shores, along the Bosphorus and Golden Horn, and to the Adalar (Princes' Islands).

Bus Along the Bosphorus and the Golden Horn and between Üsküdar and Kadıköy.

Tickets & Passes

➡ *Jetons* can be purchased from ticket machines or offices at tram stops, *iskelesi* and funicular and metro stations, but it's much cheaper and easier to use an İstanbulkart.

➡ You must have an İstanbulkart to use a bus.

➡ Pay the driver when you take a dolmuş (shared minibus); fares vary according to destination and length of trip.

➡ Ticket prices are usually the same on public and private ferry services; İstanbulkarts can be used on some private ferries, but not all.

➡ İstanbulkarts cannot be used to pay for Bosphorus ferry tours.

Tram

An excellent *tramvay* (tramway) service runs from Bağcılar, in the city's west, to Zeytinburnu (where it connects with the metro from the airport) and on to Sultanahmet and Eminönü. It then crosses the Galata Bridge to Karaköy (to connect with the Tünel) and Kabataş (to connect with the funicular to Taksim Meydanı). A second service runs from Cevizlibağ, closer to Sultanahmet on the same line, through to Kabataş. Both services run every five minutes from 6am to midnight. The fare is ₺4; *jetons* are available from machines on every tram stop and İstanbulkarts can be used.

A small antique tram travels the length of İstiklal Caddesi in Beyoğlu from a stop near Tünel Meydanı to Taksim Meydanı (7am to 10.20pm). Electronic tickets (₺4) can be purchased from the ticket office at the Tünel funicular, and İstanbulkarts can be used.

Another small tram line follows a loop through

Kadıköy and the neighbouring suburb of Moda every 10 minutes between 6.55am and 9.20pm. *Jetons* cost ₺4 and İstanbulkarts can be used.

Ferry

The most enjoyable way to get around town is by ferry. Crossing between the Asian and European shores, up and down the Golden Horn and Bosphorus, and over to the Princes' Islands, these vessels are as efficient as they are popular with locals. Some are operated by the government-owned İstanbul Şehir Hatları; others by private companies, including **Dentur Avrasya** (☑444 6336; www.denturavrasya.com) and **Turyol** (☑0212-251 4421; www.turyol.com). Timetables are posted at *iskelesi* (ferry docks).

On the European side, the major ferry docks are at the mouth of the Golden Horn (Eminönü and Karaköy), at Beşiktaş and next to the tram stop at Kabataş, 2km past the Galata Bridge.

The ferries run to two annual timetables: winter (mid-September to May) and summer (June to mid-September). Tickets are

FERRY TRAVEL

Ferries ply the following useful two-way routes:

➜ Beşiktaş–Kadıköy
➜ Beşiktaş–Üsküdar
➜ Eminönü–Anadolu Kavağı (Bosphorus Cruise)
➜ Eminönü–Kadıköy
➜ Eminönü–Üsküdar
➜ Kabataş–Kadıköy
➜ Kabataş–Kadıköy–Kınalıada–Burgazada–
Heybeliada–Büyükada (Princes' Islands ferry)
➜ Kabataş–Üsküdar
➜ Karaköy–Kadıköy (some stop at Haydarpaşa)
➜ Karaköy–Üsküdar
➜ Sarıyer–Rumeli Kavağı–Anadolu Kavağı
➜ Üsküdar–Karaköy–Eminönü–Kasımpaşa–Hasköy–
Ayvansaray–Sütlüce–Eyüp (Golden Horn Ferry)

There are also limited services to, from and between
the Bosphorus suburbs.

cheap (usually ₺4) and it's possible to use an İstanbulkart on most routes.

There are also *deniz otobüsü* and *hızlı feribot* (seabus and fast ferry) services, but these ply routes that are of less interest to the traveller and are also more expensive than the conventional ferries. For more information, check **İstanbul Deniz Otobüsleri** (İDO; ☑0850 222 4436; www.ido.com.tr).

Taxi

İstanbul is full of yellow taxis. Some drivers are lunatics, others are con artists; most are neither. If you're caught with the first category and you're about to go into meltdown, say *'yavaş!'* (slow down!). Drivers in the con-artist category tend to prey on tourists. All taxis have digital meters and must run them, but some of these drivers ask for a flat fare, or pretend the meter doesn't work so they can gouge you at the end of the trip. The best way to counter this is to tell them no meter, no ride. Avoid the taxis waiting

for fares near Aya Sofya Meydanı – we have received reports of rip-offs.

Taxi fares are very reasonable and rates are the same during both day and night. It costs around ₺15 to travel between Beyoğlu and Sultanahmet.

Few taxis have seat belts. If you take a taxi from the European side to the Asian side over one of the Bosphorus bridges, it is your responsibility to cover the toll (₺4.75). The driver will add this to your fare. There is no toll when crossing from Asia to Europe.

Metro

Metro services depart every five minutes between 6am and midnight. *Jetons* cost ₺4 and İstanbulkarts can be used.

One line (the M1A) connects Yenikapı, southwest of Sultanahmet, with the airport. This stops at 16 stations, including Aksaray and the Otogar, along the way.

Another line (the M2) connects Yenikapı with Taksim, stopping at three stations

along the way: Vezneciler, near the Grand Bazaar; on the new bridge across the Golden Horn (Haliç); and at Şişhane, near Tünel Meydanı in Beyoğlu. From Taksim it travels northeast to Hacıosman via nine stations. A branch line, the M6, connects one of these stops, Levent, with Boğaziçi Üniversitesi near the Bosphorus.

A fourth line, known as the Marmaray, connects Kazlıçeşme, west of the Old City, with Ayrılık Çeşmesi, on the Asian side. This travels via a tunnel under the Sea of Marmara, stopping at Yenikapı, Sirkeci and Üsküdar en route and connecting with the M4 metro running between Kadıköy and Kartal. A small number of İstanbullus refuse to use this tunnel link, believing that safety standards were compromised during its construction so as to expedite its opening.

Funicular & Cable Car

There are two funiculars (*funıküleri*) and two cable cars (*teleferic*) in the city. All are short trips and İstanbulkarts can be used.

A funicular called the Tünel carries passengers between Karaköy, at the base of the Galata Bridge (Galata Köprüsü), to Tünel Meydanı, at one end of İstiklal Caddesi. The service operates every five minutes between 7am and 10.45pm and a *jeton* costs ₺4.

The second funicular carries passengers from Kabataş, at the end of the tramline, to Taksim Meydanı, where it connects to the metro. The service operates every five minutes from 6am to midnight and a *jeton* costs ₺4.

A cable car runs between the waterside at Eyüp to the Pierre Loti Café (8am to 10pm). Another travels between Maçka (near Taksim) downhill to the İstanbul Technical University in Taşkışla (8am to 7pm). *Jetons* for each cost ₺4.

Bus

The bus system in İstanbul is extremely efficient, though traffic congestion in the city means that bus trips can be very long. The introduction of Metrobüs lines (where buses are given dedicated traffic lanes) aims to relieve this problem, but these tend to service residential suburbs out of the city centre and are thus of limited benefit to travellers. The major bus stands are underneath Taksim Meydanı and at Beşiktaş, Kabataş, Eminönü, Kadıköy and Üsküdar, with most services running between 6am and 11pm. Destinations and main stops on city bus routes are shown on a sign on the right (kerb) side of the bus *(otobüs)*, or on the electronic display at its front. You must have an İstanbulkart before boarding.

The most useful bus lines for travellers are those running along both sides of the Bosphorus and the Golden Horn, those in the Western Districts and those between Üsküdar and Kadıköy.

Dolmuş

A dolmuş is a shared minibus. It waits at a specified departure point until it has a full complement of passengers (in Turkish, *dolmuş* means full) then follows a fixed route to its destination. Destinations are displayed in the window of the dolmuş. Passengers flag down the driver to get on and indicate to the driver when they want to get off, usually by saying *'inecek var!'* (someone wants to get out!). Fares vary (pay on board) but are usually the same as municipal buses. Dolmuşes are almost as comfortable as taxis, run later into the night in many instances, and often ply routes that buses and other forms of transport don't service. Most travellers are unlikely to take a dolmuş during their visit to the city. The only routes they are likely to find useful are Kadıköy–Taksim, Kadıköy–Üsküdar, Beşiktaş–Harbiye and along the Bosphorus shores.

Bicycle

You would be putting your life at serious risk – don't even think about it.

Directory A–Z

Customs Regulations

İstanbul's Atatürk International Airport uses the red and green channel system, randomly spot-checking passengers' luggage. You're allowed to import the following without paying duty:

Alcohol 1L of alcohol exceeding 22% volume, 2L of alcoholic beverages max 22% volume

Tobacco 600 cigarettes

Food 1kg of chocolate or candy; 1kg of coffee and tea

Currency No limit

Perfume & Cosmetics 5 bottles max 120mL

Note that it's illegal to take antiquities out of the country. Check www.gumruk.gov.tr for more information.

Discount Cards

Most visitors spend at least three days in İstanbul and cram as many museum visits as possible into their stay, so purchasing a **discount pass** (http://www.muze.gov.tr/en/museum-card) is worth considering. Valid for 120 hours (five days) from the first museum you visit, it costs ₺85 and allows one entrance to each of Topkapı Palace and Harem, Aya Sofya, Aya İrini, the İstanbul Archaeology Museums, the Museum of Turkish and Islamic Arts, the Great Palace Mosaics Museum, the Kariye Museum (Chora Church), Galata Mevlevi Museum, Fethiye Museum, Rumeli

Hisarı, Yıldız Sarayı and the İstanbul Museum of the History of Science & Technology in Islam. Purchased individually, admission fees to these sights will cost ₺260, so the pass represents a possible saving of ₺175. It sometimes allows you to bypass ticket queues, too.

As well as giving entry to these government-operated museums, the pass also provides discounts on entry to privately run museums such as the Museum of Innocence, the Pera Museum and the Rahmi M Koç Museum.

The pass can be purchased through some hotels and from the ticket offices of all of the museums it covers.

Emergency

Ambulance	☏112
Fire	☏110
Police	☏155

Insurance

It's sensible to organise travel insurance, including health cover, before arriving. Worldwide travel insurance is available at www.lonely planet.com/travel-insurance. You can buy, extend and claim online anytime – even if you're already on the road.

Electricity

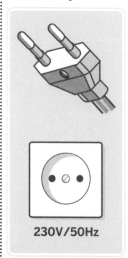

230V/50Hz

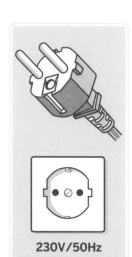

230V/50Hz

Internet Access

As is the case elsewhere in Europe, the proliferation of personal communications devices has led to internet cafes becoming a dying breed. Wi-fi connections are ubiquitous in hotels and hostels, and common in cafes, bars and restaurants.

The Turkish government has a well-documented track record in blocking access to social media platforms such as Twitter and Facebook during and immediately after security situations such as terrorist attacks. Many locals get around this by using VPNs.

If using a local computer, you may have to use a Turkish keyboard. When doing so, be aware that Turkish has two 'i's: the familiar dotted 'i' and the less familiar dotless 'ı'. Unfortunately the one in the usual place is the dotless 'ı' on a Turkish keyboard; you will need to make sure you use the correct dotted 'i' when typing in a web or email address. To create the @ symbol, hold down the 'q' and the right-hand ALT keys at the same time.

Legal Matters

➡ The age of consent in Turkey is 18, as is the legal age for voting, driving and drinking.

➡ Technically, you should carry your passport at all times. Many travellers choose to carry a photocopy and leave the actual document in their hotel safe.

➡ It is illegal to take antiquities out of the country.

➡ In recent years, local politics has become increasingly socially conservative. This has manifested itself in a number of ways, including police crackdowns on gay venues across the city, especially gay hamams and spas, which are regularly accused of breaching public-decency laws. If you visit one of these hamams,

there is a chance that you could be caught up in a police raid.

LGBT Travellers

Homosexuality isn't illegal in Turkey, but neither is it officially legal. There's a generally ambivalent attitude towards it among the general population, although there are sporadic reports of violence towards gay people, and conservative İstanbullus frown upon open displays of affection between persons of the same sex. Useful websites include the following:

IstanbulGay.com Handy guide to the gay, lesbian and transgender scenes in the city. It includes plenty of information about gay-friendly clubs, bars and hotels.

Lambda (www.lambdaistanbul. org/s) Turkish branch of the international Gay, Lesbian, Bisexual and Transgender Liberation Group. Its office is in Kadıköy.

Pride Travel (✆0212-527 0671; www.travelagencyturkey. com; 4th fl, Ates Pasaji, İncili Çavuş Sokak 15) Well-regarded, gay-owned and gay-run travel agency specialising in booking accommodation and tours for gay travellers.

Trans X Turkey (www.transx turkey.com/en) Advocacy group for Turkey's transgender community.

Media

The free media in Turkey has been undergoing something of a trial by ordeal over recent years, and the situation seems to be getting worse rather than better. This government interference has made sourcing impartial news a real challenge. There are now only two mainstream English-language newspapers: the *Hürriyet Daily News* (www.hurriyetdaily news.com) and *Daily Sabah*

(www.dailysabah.com). The *Hürriyet Daily News* is secularist and the *Daily Sabah* is unashamedly – many would say scandalously – pro-AKP.

The Guide İstanbul (www. theguideistanbul.com) is a listings-heavy bimonthly guide to the city that is available both online and in magazine format. Many of the city's hotels offer copies of it in guest rooms.

Money

ATMs

ATMs are everywhere in İstanbul. Virtually all of them offer instructions in English, French and German and will pay out Turkish liras when you insert your bank debit (cash) card. They will also pay cash advances on Visa and MasterCard. The limit on cash withdrawals is generally ₺600 to ₺800 per day, though this varies from bank to bank.

Changing Money

➡ The 24-hour *döviz bürosus* (exchange bureaux) in the arrivals halls of the international airports usually offer competitive rates.

➡ US dollars and euros are easily changed at exchange bureaux. They are sometimes accepted in carpet shops and hotels.

➡ Turkish liras are fully convertible, so there is no black market.

Credit Cards

Most hotels, car-hire agencies, shops, pharmacies, entertainment venues and restaurants will accept Visa and MasterCard; Amex isn't as widely accepted and Diner's is often not accepted. Inexpensive eateries usually accept cash only.

Currency

Türk Lirası (Turkish lira; ₺). Coins come in amounts of

one, five, 10, 25 and 50 kuruş and one lira; notes come in five, 10, 20, 50, 100 and 200 lira.

Opening Hours

Opening hours vary wildly across businesses and services in İstanbul. The following is a very general guide.

Bars Afternoon to early morning

Nightclubs 11pm till late

Post Offices & Banks 8.30am–5pm Monday to Friday

Restaurants & Cafes Breakfast 7.30am–10.30am, lunch noon–2.30pm, dinner 6.30pm–10pm

Shops 10am–7pm Monday to Saturday

Post

➡ Post offices are known as PTTs (peh-teh-teh; Posta, Telefon, Teleğraf) and have black-and-yellow signs.

➡ İstanbul's **Central Post Office** (Merkez Postane; Map p238; ☑444 1788; www.ptt. gov.tr; Büyük Postane Caddesi; ☺8.30am-5pm; ☒Sirkeci) is several blocks southwest of Sirkeci train station.

➡ The *yurtdışı* slot is for mail to foreign countries, *yurtiçi* is for mail to other Turkish cities, and *şehiriçi* is for mail within İstanbul.

➡ Mail delivery is fairly reliable. For more information on PTT services, go to www.ptt.gov.tr.

Public Holidays

Banks, offices and government services close for the day on the following secular public holidays.

New Year's Day 1 January

National Sovereignty & Children's Day 23 April

Labor & Solidarity Day 1 May

Commemoration of Atatürk, Youth & Sports Day 19 May

Democracy and Freedoms Day 15 July

Victory Day 30 August

Republic Day 29 October

Religious festivals are celebrated according to the Muslim lunar Hejira calendar. Two of these festivals (Şeker Bayramı and Kurban Bayramı) are also public holidays. Şeker Bayramı is a three-day festival at the end of Ramazan, and Kurban Bayramı, the most important religious holiday of the year, is a four-day festival whose date changes each year. During these festivals, banks and offices are closed and hotels, buses, trains and planes are heavily booked.

Though most restaurants and cafes open to serve non-Muslims during the holy month of Ramazan (called Ramadan in other countries), it's polite to avoid smoking, eating and drinking in the street during this period.

Smoking

Officially forbidden in all hotels and enclosed restaurant and bar spaces.

Telephone

If you are in European İstanbul and wish to call a number in Asian İstanbul, you must dial ☑0216 before the number. If you are in Asian İstanbul and wish to call a number in European İstanbul, use ☑0212. Do not use a prefix (that is, don't use the ☑0212/6) if you are calling a number on the same shore.

Country code	☑90
European İstanbul	☑0212
Asian İstanbul	☑0216
Code to make an intercity call	☑0 + local code

International access code	☑00
Directory inquiries	☑118
International operator	☑115

Mobile Phones

➡ Mobile phone reception is excellent in İstanbul.

➡ All mobile phone numbers start with a four-figure code beginning with ☑05.

➡ There are three major networks: **Turkcell** (www.turkcell.com.tr), **Vodafone** (www.vodafone.com.tr) and **Avea** (www.avea.com.tr). Each has shops throughout the city selling prepaid SIM cards *(kontürlü SIM karts)* that can be used in foreign phones. The cards operate for up to 120 days and cost around ₺85 (including ₺30 in local call credit). An internet data pack with the SIM will cost around ₺25/30/40/60 for 1/2/4/8 GB and a pack for international calls will cost an extra ₺30/60 or so for one/two hours credit. Ask the staff in the shop to suggest the most cost-effective solution for your needs. Once you have the SIM, it can be recharged with *kontürs* in amounts of ₺20 upwards.

➡ When you purchase the SIM, ask the staff to organise the activation for you (you'll need to show your passport). The account should activate almost immediately.

➡ Note that Turkey uses the standard GSM network operating on 900MHz or 1800MHz, so not all US and Canadian phones work here.

Time

İstanbul time is Eastern European Time (EET), three hours ahead of Coordinated Universal Time (UTC, alias GMT). The Turkish government decided in September 2016 to retain daylight-saving (summer) time year-round. Turks use the 24-hour clock.

Toilets

Most public toilets are of the Western sit-down variety; those in mosques are exceptions and are mainly squat style. Toilets near transport hubs and stations and in and around major sights usually charge a fee of ₺1.

There are handy public toilets in the Grand Bazaar, on the Hippodrome in Sultanahmet, and in the underpasses next to the ferry docks at Eminönü and Karaköy.

Tourist Information

The **Ministry of Culture & Tourism** (www.turizm.gov. tr) currently operates three tourist information offices or booths in the city and has booths at both international airports. In our experience, the Sirkeci office is the most helpful and the Sultanahmet office is the least helpful.

Tourist Office – Atatürk International Airport (📞0212-465 3547; International Arrivals Hall, Atatürk International Airport; ⏰9am-9pm)

Tourist Office – Sabiha Gökçen International Airport (📞0216-588 8794; ⏰8am-7pm)

Tourist Office – Sirkeci Train Station (Map p238; 📞0555 675 2674, 0212-511 5888; Sirkeci Gar, Ankara Caddesi, Sirkeci; ⏰9.30am-6pm mid-Apr–Sep, 9am-5.30pm Oct–mid-Apr; 🚆Sirkeci)

Tourist Office – Sultanahmet (Map p240; 📞0212-518 8754; Hippodrome, Sultanahmet; ⏰8.30am-6.30pm mid-Apr–Sep, 9am-5.30pm Oct–mid-Apr; 🚆Sultanahmet)

Tourist Office – Taksim (Map p244; 📞0212-233 0592; www.

kulturturizm.gov.tr; ground fl, Seyran Apartmanı, Mete Caddesi, Taksim; ⏰9.30am-6pm mid-Apr–Sep, 9am-5.30pm Oct–mid-Apr; Ⓜ Taksim)

Travellers with Disabilities

İstanbul can be challenging for mobility-impaired travellers. Roads are potholed and footpaths are often crooked and cracked. Fortunately the city is attempting to rectify this.

Government-run museums are free of charge for people with a disability. Public and private museums and sights that have wheelchair access and accessible toilets include Topkapı Palace, the İstanbul Archaeology Museums, İstanbul Modern, the Pera Museum and the Rahmi M Koç Museum. The last three of these also have limited facilities to assist accessibility for vision-impaired visitors.

Airlines and most four- and five-star hotels have wheelchair access and at least one room set up for guests with a disability. All public transport is free, and the metro and trams can be accessed by people in wheelchairs.

FHS Tourism and Event (www.accessibleturkey.org) is an İstanbul-based travel agency that has a dedicated department organising accessible travel packages and tours.

Visas

At the time of research, nationals of the following countries (among others) could enter Turkey for up to three months with only a valid passport (no visa required): Denmark, Finland, France, Germany, Greece, Israel, Italy, Japan, New Zealand, Sweden and Switzerland. Russians could enter for up to 60 days.

Nationals of the following countries (among others) needed to obtain an **electronic visa** (www. evisa.gov.tr) before their visit: Australia, Canada, China, Ireland, Mexico, Netherlands, Norway, Portugal, Spain, Taiwan, UK and USA. These visas were valid for between 30 and 90 days and for either a single entry or multiple entry, depending on the nationality. Visa fees cost US$25 to US$70, depending on nationality.

Indian nationals needed to 'meet certain conditions' before being granted an electronic visa.

Your passport must have at least six months' validity remaining, or you may not be admitted into Turkey. See the website of the **Ministry of Foreign Affairs** (www. mfa.gov.tr) for the latest information.

Women Travellers

Travelling in İstanbul as a female can be easy and enjoyable, provided you follow some simple guidelines. Tailor your behaviour and your clothing to your surrounds – outfits that are appropriate for neighbourhoods such as Beyoğlu and along the Bosphorus (skimpy tops, tight jeans etc) are not appropriate in conservative suburbs such as Üsküdar, for instance.

It's a good idea to sit in the back seat of a taxi rather than next to the driver. If approached by a Turkish man in circumstances that upset you, try saying *Ayıp!* (ah-*yuhp*), which means 'Shame on you!'

You'll have no trouble finding sanitary napkins and condoms in pharmacies and supermarkets in İstanbul; tampons can be a bit difficult to access. Bring a shawl to cover your head when visiting mosques.

Language

Turkish belongs to the Ural-Altaic language family. It's the official language of Turkey and northern Cyprus, and has approximately 70 million speakers worldwide.

Pronouncing Turkish is pretty simple for English speakers as most Turkish sounds are also found in English. If you read our coloured pronunciation guides as if they were English, you should be understood just fine. Note that the symbol ew represents the sound 'ee' pronounced with rounded lips (as in 'few'), and that the symbol uh is pronounced like the 'a' in 'ago'. The Turkish r is always rolled and v is pronounced a little softer than in English.

Word stress is quite light in Turkish – in our pronunciation guides the stressed syllables are in italics.

BASICS

Hello.
Merhaba. mer·ha·ba

Goodbye.
Hoşçakal. hosh·cha·kal
(said by person leaving)
Güle güle. gew·le gew·le
(said by person staying)

Yes.
Evet. e·vet

No.
Hayır. ha·yuhr

Excuse me.
Bakar mısınız. ba·kar muh·suh·nuhz

Sorry.
Özür dilerim. er·zewr dee·le·reem

Please.
Lütfen. lewt·fen

Thank you.
Teşekkür ederim. te·shek·kewr e·de·reem

You're welcome.
Birşey değil. beer·shay de·eel

How are you?
Nasılsınız? na·suhl·suh·nuhz

Fine, and you?
İyiyim, ya siz? ee·yee·yeem ya seez

What's your name?
Adınız nedir? a·duh·nuhz ne·deer

My name is ...
Benim adım ... be·neem a·duhm ...

Do you speak English?
İngilizce konuşuyor musunuz? een·gee·leez·je ko·noo·shoo·yor moo·soo·nooz

I understand.
Anlıyorum. an·luh·yo·room

I don't understand.
Anlamıyorum. an·la·muh·yo·room

ACCOMMODATION

Where can I find a ...?	Nerede ... bulabilirim?	ne·re·de ... boo·la·bee·lee·reem
campsite	kamp yeri	kamp ye·ree
guesthouse	misafirhane	mee·sa·feer·ha·ne
hotel	otel	o·tel
pension	pansiyon	pan·see·yon
youth hostel	gençlik hosteli	gench·leek hos·te·lee

How much is it per night/person?
Geceliği/Kişi başına ne kadar? ge·je·lee·ee/kee·shee ba·shuh·na ne ka·dar

Is breakfast included?
Kahvaltı dahil mi?   kah·val·*tuh* da·*heel* mee

Do you have a ...?	**... odanız**	**... o·da·nuz**
	var mı?	var muh
single room	*Tek kişilik*	tek kee·shee·*leek*
double room	*İki*	ee·*kee*
	kişilik	kee·shee·*leek*

air conditioning	*klima*	*klee·*ma
bathroom	*banyo*	*ban·*yo
window	*pencere*	*pen·*je·re

DIRECTIONS

Where is ...?
... nerede?   ... ne·re·de

What's the address?
Adresi nedir?   ad·re·*see* ne·deer

Could you write it down, please?
Lütfen yazar   lewt·fen ya·*zar*
mısınız?   muh·suh·*nuhz*

Can you show me (on the map)?
Bana (haritada)   ba·*na* (ha·ree·ta·*da*)
gösterebilir   gers·te·re·bee·leer
misiniz?   mee·seen·*neez*

It's straight ahead.
Tam karşıda.   tam kar·shuh·*da*

at the traffic lights
trafik   tra·*feek*
ışıklarından   uh·shuhk·la·ruhn·*dan*

at the corner	*köşeden*	ker·she·*den*
behind	*arkasında*	ar·ka·suhn·*da*
far (from)	*uzak*	oo·*zak*
in front of	*önünde*	er·newn·*de*
near (to)	*yakınında*	ya·kuh·nuhn·*da*
opposite	*karşısında*	kar·shuh·suhn·*da*
Turn left.	*Sola dön.*	so·*la* dern
Turn right.	*Sağa dön.*	sa·*a* dern

EATING & DRINKING

What would you recommend?
Ne tavsiye   ne tav·see·*ye*
edersiniz?   e·der·see·neez

What's in that dish?
Bu yemekte neler var?   boo ye·mek·*te* ne·ler var

I don't eat ...
... yemiyorum.   ... ye·mee·yo·room

Cheers!
Şerefe!   she·re·*fe*

That was delicious!
Nefisti!   ne·*fees*·tee

The bill/check, please.
Hesap lütfen.   he·*sap* lewt·fen

KEY PATTERNS

To get by in Turkish, mix and match these simple patterns with words of your choice:

When's (the next bus)?
(Sonraki otobüs)   (son·ra·*kee* o·to·*bews*)
ne zaman?   ne za·*man*

Where's (the market)?
(Pazar yeri) nerede?   (pa·zar ye·ree) ne·re·de

Where can I (buy a ticket)?
Nereden (bilet   ne·re·den (bee·*let*
alabilirim)?   a·*la*·bee·lee·reem)

I have (a reservation).
(Rezervasyonum)   (re·zer·vas·yo·*noom*)
var.   var

Do you have (a map)?
(Haritanız)   (ha·ree·ta·*nuhz*)
var mı?   var muh

Is there (a toilet)?
(Tuvalet) var mı?   (too·va·*let*) var muh

I'd like (the menu).
(Menüyü)   (me·new·*yew*)
istiyorum.   ees·tee·yo·room

I want to (make a call).
(Bir görüşme   (beer ger·rewsh·*me*
yapmak)   yap·*mak*)
istiyorum.   ees·tee·yo·room

Do I have to (declare this)?
(Bunu beyan   (boo·noo be·*yan*
etmem) gerekli mi?   et·*mem*) ge·rek·*lee* mee

I need (assistance).
(Yardıma)   (yar·duh·*ma*)
ihtiyacım var.   eeh·tee·ya·*juhm* var

I'd like a table for ...	**... bir masa**	**... beer ma·*sa**
	ayırtmak	a·yuhrt·*mak*
	istiyorum.	ees·tee·yo·room
(eight) o'clock	*Saat (sekiz)*	sa·*at* (se·*keez*)
	için	ee·*cheen*
(two) people	*(İki)*	(ee·*kee*)
	kişilik	kee·shee·*leek*

Key Words

appetisers	*mezeler*	me·ze·*ler*
bottle	*şişe*	shee·*she*
bowl	*kase*	*ka·*se
breakfast	*kahvaltı*	kah·val·*tuh*
(too) cold	*(çok) soğuk*	(chok) so·*ook*
cup	*fincan*	feen·*jan*
delicatessen	*şarküteri*	shar·kew·te·*ree*
dinner	*akşam yemeği*	ak·*sham* ye·me·ee
dish	*yemek*	ye·*mek*

food	*yiyecek*	yee·ye·jek
fork	*çatal*	cha·tal
glass	*bardak*	bar·dak
grocery	*bakkal*	bak·kal
halal	*helal*	he·lal
highchair	*mama sandalyesi*	ma·ma san·dal·ye·see
hot (warm)	*sıcak*	suh·jak
knife	*bıçak*	buh·chak
kosher	*koşer*	ko·sher
lunch	*öğle yemeği*	er·le ye·me·ee
main courses	*ana yemekler*	a·na ye·mek·ler
market	*pazar*	pa·zar
menu	*yemek listesi*	ye·mek lees·te·see
plate	*tabak*	ta·bak
restaurant	*restoran*	res·to·ran
spicy	*acı*	a·juh
spoon	*kaşık*	ka·shuhk
vegetarian	*vejeteryan*	ve·zhe·ter·yan

Meat & Fish

anchovy	*hamsi*	ham·see
beef	*sığır eti*	suh·uhr e·tee
calamari	*kalamares*	ka·la·ma·res
chicken	*piliç/ tavuk*	pee·leech/ ta·vook
fish	*balık*	ba·luhk
lamb	*kuzu*	koo·zoo
liver	*ciğer*	jee·er
mussels	*midye*	meed·ye
pork	*domuz eti*	do·mooz e·tee
veal	*dana eti*	da·na e·tee

Fruit & Vegetables

apple	*elma*	el·ma
apricot	*kayısı*	ka·yuh·suh
banana	*muz*	mooz
capsicum	*biber*	bee·ber
carrot	*havuç*	ha·vooch
cucumber	*salatalık*	sa·la·ta·luhk
fruit	*meyve*	may·ve
grape	*üzüm*	ew·zewm
melon	*kavun*	ka·voon
olive	*zeytin*	zay·teen
onion	*soğan*	so·an
orange	*portakal*	por·ta·kal

peach	*şeftali*	shef·ta·lee
potato	*patates*	pa·ta·tes
spinach	*ıspanak*	uhs·pa·nak
tomato	*domates*	do·ma·tes
watermelon	*karpuz*	kar·pooz

Other

bread	*ekmek*	ek·mek
cheese	*peynir*	pay·neer
egg	*yumurta*	yoo·moor·ta
honey	*bal*	bal
ice	*buz*	booz
pepper	*kara biber*	ka·ra bee·ber
rice	*pirinç/ pilav*	pee·reench/ pee·lav
salt	*tuz*	tooz
soup	*çorba*	chor·ba
sugar	*şeker*	she·ker
Turkish Delight	*lokum*	lo·koom

Drinks

beer	*bira*	bee·ra
coffee	*kahve*	kah·ve
(orange) juice	*(portakal) suyu*	(por·ta·kal soo·yoo)
milk	*süt*	sewt
mineral water	*maden suyu*	ma·den soo·yoo
soft drink	*alkolsüz içecek*	al·kol·sewz ee·che·jek
tea	*çay*	chai
water	*su*	soo
wine	*şarap*	sha·rap
yoghurt	*yoğurt*	yo·oort

Signs	
Açık	Open
Bay	Male
Bayan	Female
Çıkışı	Exit
Giriş	Entrance
Kapalı	Closed
Sigara İçilmez	No Smoking
Tuvaletler	Toilets
Yasak	Prohibited

Question Words		
How?	Nasıl?	na-seel
What?	Ne?	ne
When?	Ne zaman?	ne za-man
Where?	Nerede?	ne-re-de
Which?	Hangi?	han-gee
Who?	Kim?	keem
Why?	Neden?	ne-den

ATM	bankamatik	ban-ka-ma-teek
credit card	kredi kartı	kre-dee kar-tuh
post office	postane	pos-ta-ne
signature	imza	eem-za
tourist office	turizm bürosu	too-reezm bew-ro-soo

EMERGENCIES

Help!
İmdat! — eem-dat

I'm lost.
Kayboldum. — kai-bol-doom

Leave me alone!
Git başımdan! — geet ba-shuhm-dan

There's been an accident.
Bir kaza oldu. — beer ka-za ol-doo

Can I use your phone?
Telefonunuzu kullanabilir miyim? — te-le-fo-noo-noo-zoo kool-la-na-bee-leer mee-yeem

Call a doctor!
Doktor çağırın! — dok-tor cha-uh-ruhn

Call the police!
Polis çağırın! — po-lees cha-uh-ruhn

I'm ill.
Hastayım. — has-ta-yuhm

It hurts here.
Burası ağrıyor. — boo-ra-suh a-ruh-yor

I'm allergic to (nuts).
(Çerezlere) alerjim var. — (che-rez-le-re) a-ler-zheem var

SHOPPING & SERVICES

I'd like to buy ...
... almak istiyorum. — ... al-mak ees-tee-yo-room

I'm just looking.
Sadece bakıyorum. — sa-de-je ba-kuh-yo-room

May I look at it?
Bakabilir miyim? — ba-ka-bee-leer mee-yeem

The quality isn't good.
Kalitesi iyi değil. — ka-lee-te-see ee-yee de-eel

How much is it?
Ne kadar? — ne ka-dar

It's too expensive.
Bu çok pahalı. — boo chok pa-ha-luh

Do you have something cheaper?
Daha ucuz birşey var mı? — da-ha oo-jooz beer-shay var muh

There's a mistake in the bill.
Hesapta bir yanlışlık var. — he-sap-ta beer yan-luhsh-luhk var

TIME & DATES

What time is it?	Saat kaç?	sa-at kach
It's (10) o'clock.	Saat (on).	sa-at (on)
Half past (10).	(On) buçuk.	(on) boo-chook
in the morning	öğleden evvel	er-le-den ev-vel
in the afternoon	öğleden sonra	er-le-den son-ra
in the evening	akşam	ak-sham
yesterday	dün	dewn
today	bugün	boo-gewn
tomorrow	yarın	ya-ruhn
Monday	Pazartesi	pa-zar-te-see
Tuesday	Salı	sa-luh
Wednesday	Çarşamba	char-sham-ba
Thursday	Perşembe	per-shem-be
Friday	Cuma	joo-ma
Saturday	Cumartesi	joo-mar-te-see
Sunday	Pazar	pa-zar
January	Ocak	o-jak
February	Şubat	shoo-bat
March	Mart	mart
April	Nisan	nee-san
May	Mayıs	ma-yuhs
June	Haziran	ha-zee-ran
July	Temmuz	tem-mooz
August	Ağustos	a-oos-tos
September	Eylül	ay-lewl
October	Ekim	e-keem
November	Kasım	ka-suhm
December	Aralık	a-ra-luhk

TRANSPORT

Public Transport

At what time does the ... leave/arrive?	... ne zaman kalkacak/ varır?	... ne za-man kal-ka-jak/ va-ruhr
boat	Vapur	va-poor
bus	Otobüs	o-to-bews
plane	Uçak	oo-chak
train	Tren	tren

Numbers

1	bir	beer
2	iki	ee·kee
3	üç	ewch
4	dört	dert
5	beş	besh
6	altı	al·tuh
7	yedi	ye·dee
8	sekiz	se·keez
9	dokuz	do·kooz
10	on	on
20	yirmi	yeer·mee
30	otuz	o·tooz
40	kırk	kuhrk
50	elli	el·lee
60	altmış	alt·muhsh
70	yetmiş	et·meesh
80	seksen	sek·sen
90	doksan	dok·san
100	yüz	yewz
1000	bin	been

Does it stop at (Maltepe)?
(Maltepe'de)   (mal·te·pe·de)
durur mu?   doo·roor moo

What's the next stop?
Sonraki durak   son·ra·kee doo·rak
hangisi?   han·gee·see

Please tell me when we get to (Beşiktaş).
(Beşiktaş'a)   (be·sheek·ta·sha)
vardığımızda   var·duh·uh·muhz·da
lütfen bana   lewt·fen ba·na
söyleyin.   say·le·yeen

I'd like to get off at (Kadıköy).
(Kadıköy'de) inmek   (ka·duh·kay·de) een·mek
istiyorum.   ees·tee·yo·room

I'd like a ...	(Bostancı'ya)	(bos·tan·juh·ya)
ticket to	... bir bilet	... beer bee·let
(Bostancı).	lütfen.	lewt·fen
1st-class	Birinci mevki	bee·reen·jee mev·kee
2nd-class	İkinci mevki	ee·keen·jee mev·kee
one-way	Gidiş	gee·deesh
return	Gidiş-dönüş	gee·deesh·der·newsh

first	ilk	eelk
last	son	son
next	geleçek	ge·le·jek

I'd like a/an ... seat.	... bir yer istiyorum.	... beer yer ees·tee·yo·room
aisle	Koridor tarafında	ko·ree·dor ta·ra·fuhn·da
window	Cam kenarı	jam ke·na·ruh

cancelled	iptal edildi	eep·tal e·deel·dee
delayed	ertelendi	er·te·len·dee
platform	peron	pe·ron
ticket office	bilet gişesi	bee·let gee·she·see
timetable	tarife	ta·ree·fe
train station	istasyon	ees·tas·yon

Driving & Cycling

I'd like to hire a ...	Bir ... kiralamak istiyorum.	beer ... kee·ra·la·mak ees·tee·yo·room
4WD	dört çeker	dert che·ker
bicycle	bisiklet	bee·seek·let
car	araba	a·ra·ba
motorcycle	motosiklet	mo·to·seek·let

bike shop	bisikletçi	bee·seek·let·chee
child seat	çocuk koltuğu	cho·jook kol·too·oo
diesel	dizel	dee·zel
helmet	kask	kask
mechanic	araba tamircisi	a·ra·ba ta·meer·jee·see
petrol/gas	benzin	ben·zeen
service station	benzin istasyonu	ben·zeen ees·tas·yo·noo

Is this the road to (Taksim)?
(Taksim'e) giden   (tak·see·me) gee·den
yol bu mu?   yol boo moo

(How long) Can I park here?
Buraya (ne kadar   boo·ra·ya (ne ka·dar
süre) park   sew·re) park
edebilirim?   e·de·bee·lee·reem

**The car/motorbike has broken down
(at Osmanbey).**
Arabam/   a·ra·bam/
Motosikletim   mo·to·seek·le·teem
(Osmanbey'de)   (os·man·bay·de)
bozuldu.   bo·zool·doo

I have a flat tyre.
Lastiğim patladı.   las·tee·eem pat·la·duh

I've run out of petrol.
Benzinim bitti.   ben·zee·neem beet·tee

GLOSSARY

Below are some useful Turkish words and abbreviations:

ada(lar) – island

arasta – row of shops near a mosque

Asya – Asian İstanbul

Avrupa – European İstanbul

bahçe(si) – garden

bey – 'Mr'; follows the name

boğaz – strait

bulvar(ı) – often abbreviated to 'bul'; boulevard or avenue

caddesi – often abbreviated to 'cad'; road

cami(i) – mosque

çarşı(sı) – market, bazaar

çay bahçesi – tea garden

çeşme – spring, fountain

deniz – sea

deniz otobüsü – catamaran; sea bus

dervish – member of the Mevlevi Muslim brotherhood

dolmuş – shared taxi (or minibus)

döviz bürosu – currency-exchange office

eczane – chemist/pharmacy

eski – old (thing, not person)

ezan – Muslim call to prayer; also *azan*

fasıl – energetic folk music played in *meyhanes* (taverns)

fayton – horse-drawn carriage

feribot – ferry

hamam(ı) – Turkish steam bath

han – traditional name for a caravanserai

hastanesi – hospital

hısar(ı) – fortress or citadel

imam – prayer leader; Muslim cleric; teacher

iskele(si) – landing place, wharf, quay

kadın – wife

kale(si) – fortress, citadel

kapı(sı) – door, gate

karagöz – shadow-puppet theatre

KDV – *katma değer vergisi*; value-added tax (VAT)

kebapçı – place selling kebaps

keyif – relaxation

kilim – pileless woven rug

konak, konağı – mansion, government headquarters

köprü – bridge

köy(ü) – village

külliye – mosque complex

kuru temizleme – dry cleaning

mahfil – high, elaborate chair

Maşallah – Wonder of God! (said in admiration or to avert the evil eye)

medrese – Islamic school of higher studies

merkez postane – central post office

meydan(ı) – public square, open place

mihrab – niche in a mosque indicating the direction of Mecca

mimber – pulpit in a mosque

minaret – mosque tower from which Muslims are called to prayer

müezzin – the official who sings the *ezan*

müze(si) – museum

nargile – water pipe

oda(sı) – room

otel(ı) – hotel

otobüs – bus

otogar – bus station

Ottoman – of or pertaining to the Ottoman Empire, which lasted from the end of the 13th century to the end of WWI

padişah – Ottoman emperor, sultan

paşa – general, governor

pazar(ı) – weekly market, bazaar

PTT – Posta, Telefon, Teleğraf; post, telephone and telegraph office

Ramazan – Islamic holy month of fasting (Ramadan)

şadırvan – fountain where Muslims perform ritual ablutions

saray(ı) – palace

sebil – fountain

şehir – city; municipal area

selamlık – public/male quarters of a traditional household

Seljuk – of or pertaining to the Seljuk Turks, who in the 11th to 13th centuries created the first Turkish state to rule Anatolia

sema – dervish ceremony

semahane – hall where whirling-dervish ceremony is performed

sokak, sokağı – often abbreviated to 'sk' or 'sok'; street or lane

Sufi – Muslim mystic, member of a mystic (dervish) brotherhood

sultan – sovereign

tarikat – a Sufic order

tavla – backgammon

TC – Türkiye Cumhuriyeti (Turkish Republic); designates an official office or organisation

tekke – dervish lodge

tramvay – tram

tuğra – sultan's monogram, imperial signature

türbe – tomb

ücretsiz servis – free service

valide sultan – queen mother

vezir – vizier (minister) in the Ottoman government

yalı – waterside timber mansion

yeni – new

yıldız – star

yol(u) – road, way

FOOD GLOSSARY

General Terms

acı – spicy

afiyet olsun – bon appétit

aile salonu – family room; for couples, families and women in a Turkish restaurant

akşam yemeği – dinner

ana yemekler – main courses

bakkal – grocery store

balık restoran – fish restaurant

bardak – glass

bıçak – knife

börekçi – place selling pastries

büfe – snack bar

buz – ice

çatal – fork

dolma – vegetables stuffed with rice and/or meat

etyemez/vejeteryan – vegetarian

fasulyecı – restaurant serving cooked beans

fincan – cup

garson – waiter/waitress

hazır yemek lokanta – casual restaurant serving ready-made food

helal – halal

hesap – the bill

içmek – drink

İngilizce menu – menu in English

kaşık – spoon

kase/tas – bowl

kahvaltı – breakfast

kebapcı – kebap restaurant

köftecı – *köfte* (meatball) restaurant

koşer – kosher

lokanta – abbreviation of *hazır yemek lokanta*

mama sandalyesi – highchair

menü – menu

meyhane – tavern

meze – small dish eaten at the start of a meal; similar to tapas

ocakbaşı – fireside kebap restaurant

öğle yemeği – lunch

pastane – cake shop

pazar – market

peçete – napkin

pidecisi – pizza restaurant

porsiyon – portion, helping

restoran – restaurant

sade – plain

şarküteri – delicatessen

şerefe! – cheers!

servis ücreti – service charge

sıcak – hot; warm

şişe – bottle

tabak – plate

uç – tip

yarım porsiyon – half *porsiyon*

yemek – eat; dish

zeytinyağlı – food cooked in olive oil

Staples

ayva – quince

bal – honey

balık – fish

beyaz peynir – salty white cheese similar to fetta

biber – bell pepper

ceviz – walnut

ciğer – liver

çilek – strawberry

çorba – soup

dana eti – veal

domates – tomato

ekmek – bread

elma – apple

enginar – artichoke

erik – plum

et – meat

et suyu – meat stock

fistik – pistachio

hamsi – anchovy

havuç – carrot

incir – fig

ıspanak – spinach

kalamar – calamari

kalkan – turbot

kara/toz biber – black/white pepper

karpuz – watermelon

kaşar peyniri – cheddar-like sheep's milk cheese

kavun – melon

kayısı – apricot

kestane – chestnuts

kiraz – cherry

kuzu – lamb

levrek – sea bass

limon – lemon

lüfer – bluefish

mantar – mushroom

meyve – fruit

midye – mussels

muz – banana

pastırma – pressed beef preserved in garlic and spices

patates – potato

patlıcan – eggplant

peynir – cheese

pirinç/pilav – rice

portakal – orange

salata – salad

salatalık – cucumber

sebze – vegetables

şeftali – peach

şeker – sugar

sığır eti – beef

simit – sesame-encrusted bread ring

soğan – onion

tavuk/piliç – chicken

taze fasulye – green beans

tuz – salt

un – flour

uskumru – mackerel

üzüm – grape

vişne – sour cherry, morello

yumurta – egg

zeytin – olive Popular Dishes

FOOD GLOSSARY

Popular Dishes

MEZE

acılı ezme – spicy tomato and onion paste

ançüez – salted or pickled anchovy

barbunya piliki – red-bean salad

beyaz peynir – white cheese from sheep or goat

çacık – yoghurt dip with garlic and mint

çerkez tavuğu – Circassian chicken; made with chicken, bread, walnuts, salt and garlic

enginar – cooked artichoke

fasulye pilaki – white beans cooked with tomato paste and garlic

fava salatası – mashed broad-bean salad

haydari – yoghurt dip with roasted eggplant and garlic

humus – chickpea dip with sesame oil, lemon and spices

imam bayıldı – literally 'the imam fainted'; eggplant, onion, tomato and peppers slow-cooked in olive oil

kalamar tava – fried calamari

lakerda – strongly flavoured salted kingfish salad

midye dolma – stuffed mussels

muhammara – dip of walnuts, bread, tahini, olive oil and lemon juice; also known as *acuka* or *civizli biber*

patlıcan kızartması – fried eggplants with tomatoes

piyaz – white-bean salad

Rus salatası – Russian salad

semizotu salatası – green purslane with yoghurt and garlic

sigara böreği – deep-fried cigar-shaped pastries filled with white cheese

turşu – pickled vegetables

yaprak sarma/yaprak dolması – vine leaves stuffed with rice, herbs and pine nuts

yeşil fasulye – green beans

KEBAPS (KEBABS) & KÖFTE (MEATBALLS)

Adana kebap – a spicy version of *şiş köfte*

alinazik – eggplant purée with yoghurt and ground *köfte*

beyti sarma – spicy ground meat baked in a thin layer of bread and served with yoghurt

çiğ köfte – raw ground-lamb mixed with pounded bulgur, onion, spices and pepper

döner kebap – compressed meat (usually lamb) cooked on a revolving upright skewer and thinly sliced

fıstıklı kebap – minced lamb studded with pistachios

içli köfte – meatballs rolled in bulgur and fried

İskender (Bursa) kebap – döner lamb served on crumbled pide with yoghurt, topped with tomato and butter sauces

ızgara köfte – grilled meatballs

karışık ızgara – mixed grilled lamb

kebap – meat grilled on a skewer

köfte – meatballs

patlıcan kebap – cubed or minced lamb grilled with eggplant

pirzola – lamb cutlet

şiş kebap – small pieces of lamb grilled on a skewer

şiş köfte – meatballs wrapped around a flat skewer and barbecued

tavuk şiş – small chicken pieces grilled on a skewer

testi kebap – small pieces of lamb or chicken in sauce that is slow-cooked in a sealed terracotta pot

tokat kebap – lamb cubes grilled with potato, tomato, eggplant and garlic

Urfa kebap – a mild version of the Adana kebap served with lots of onion and black pepper

Other Dishes

Arnavut çiğeri – Albanian-style spicy fried liver

balık ekmek – sandwich of grilled fish and salad

börek – sweet or savoury filled pastry

çoban salatası – salad of tomatoes, cucumber, onion and pepper

gözleme – filled savoury pancake

hünkâr beğendi – literally 'sultan's delight'; lamb or beef stew served on a mound of rich eggplant purée

iç pilav – rice with onions, nuts and currants

işkembe çorbası – tripe soup

kısır – bulgur salad

kokoreç – seasoned, grilled lamb/mutton intestines

kuru fasulye – haricot beans cooked in a spicy tomato sauce

lahmacun – thin and crispy Arabic-style pizza

mantı – Turkish ravioli stuffed with beef mince and topped with yoghurt, garlic, tomato and butter

menemen – breakfast eggs cooked with tomatoes, peppers and white cheese

mercimek çorbası – lentil soup

pide – Turkish-style pizza

su böreği – lasagne-like layered pastry laced with white cheese and parsley

FOOD GLOSSARY

sucuk – spicy beef sausage
tavuk kavurma – roast chicken

Drinks & Desserts

Amerikan kahvesi – instant coffee
aşure – dried fruit, nut and pulse pudding
ayran – drink made with yoghurt and salt
baklava – layered filo pastry with honey or sugar syrup; sometimes made with nuts
beyaz şarap – white wine
bira – beer
bitki çay – herbal tea
çay – tea
dondurma – ice-cream
elma çay – apple tea, predominantly a tourist drink
fırın sütlaç – rice pudding

helva – sweet prepared with sesame oil, cereals and honey or sugar syrup
kadayıf – dough soaked in syrup and topped with a layer of kaymak (clotted cream)
kahve – coffee
kırmızı şarap – red wine
kiraz suyu – cherry juice
kola – cola-flavoured soft drink
künefe – shredded-wheat pastry with pistachios, honey and sugar syrup
limonata – lemonade
lokum – Turkish Delight
maden suyu – mineral water
mahallebi – sweet rice-flour and milk pudding
meyve suyu – fruit juice

rakı – strong aniseed-flavoured liquor
sahlep – hot drink made with crushed tapioca-root extract
şalgam suyu – sour turnip juice
şarap – wine
su – water
süt – milk
(taze) nar suyu – (fresh) pomegranate juice
(taze) portakal suyu – (fresh) orange juice
Türk kahvesi – Turkish coffee
...az şekerli – with a little sugar
...çok şekerli – with a lot of sugar
...orta şekerli – with medium sugar
...sade/şekersiz – no sugar

Behind the Scenes

SEND US YOUR FEEDBACK

We love to hear from travellers – your comments keep us on our toes and help make our books better. Our well-travelled team reads every word on what you loved or loathed about this book. Although we cannot reply individually to your submissions, we always guarantee that your feedback goes straight to the appropriate authors, in time for the next edition. Each person who sends us information is thanked in the next edition – the most useful submissions are rewarded with a selection of digital PDF chapters.

Visit **lonelyplanet.com/contact** to submit your updates and suggestions or to ask for help. Our award-winning website also features inspirational travel stories, news and discussions.

Note: We may edit, reproduce and incorporate your comments in Lonely Planet products such as guidebooks, websites and digital products, so let us know if you don't want your comments reproduced or your name acknowledged. For a copy of our privacy policy visit lonelyplanet.com/privacy.

OUR READERS

Many thanks to the travellers who used the last edition and wrote to us with helpful hints, useful advice and interesting anecdotes:
Aleksandr Shapovalov, Brian Wallis, Heather Monell, Kristof Rubens, Martine W, Michael Sheridan, Natasha Meissner, Simon Marks-Isaacs

WRITER THANKS

Virginia Maxwell

Many thanks to Pat Yale, Mehmet Umur, Emel Güntaş, Faruk Boyacı, Atilla Tuna, Görgün Taner, Tahir Karabaş, Jen Hartin, Eveline Zoutendijk, George Grundy, Ann Nevans, Tina Nevans, Jennifer Gaudet, Özlem Tuna, Monica Fritz, Leon Yildirimer, Luca Fritz, Teoman Göral, Meltem İnce Okvuran, Nurullah Çınar, Deniz Ova, Zeynep Unanç, Antony Doucet, Sabiha Apaydın, Saliha Yavuz and the many others who shared their knowledge and love of the city with me.

James Bainbridge

Çok teşekkürler to my İstanbullu friends old and new who helped me discover the best of the city, including Tahir, Jen and Charlie for showing me around Fener and Balat; Leyla Tabrizi for Nişantaşı advice; Gamze Artaman for Byzantine history; and Barış, Maşallah, Sergei and all the gang at my hotel (guys, that postcard from Cape Town is coming, promise). Cheers also to Cliff Wilkinson, Virginia Maxwell, everyone at Lonely Planet, and on the home front Leigh-Robin, Oliver and Thomas.

ACKNOWLEDGEMENTS

Cover photograph: Blue Mosque (Sultanahmet Camii), Alan Copson/AWL ©.

Illustrations: pp58-9 and pp64-5 by Javier Zarracina.

THIS BOOK

This 9th edition of Lonely Planet's *İstanbul* guidebook was researched and written by Virginia Maxwell and James Bainbridge. The previous two editions were also written by Virginia. This guidebook was produced by the following:

Destination Editors Lorna Parkes, Tom Stainer, Clifton Wilkinson
Product Editors Grace Dobell, Amanda Williamson
Senior Cartographer Corey Hutchison
Book Designer Clara Monitto
Assisting Editors Andrew Bain, Robyn Loughnane, Anne Mulvaney, Claire Naylor, Susan Paterson
Cover Researcher Naomi Parker
Thanks to Imogen Bannister, Bridget Blair, Liz Heynes, Andi Jones, Catherine Naghten, Karyn Noble, Kathryn Rowan, Tony Wheeler

Index

see also separate subindexes for:

🍴 **EATING P232**

🍷 **DRINKING & NIGHTLIFE P233**

☆ **ENTERTAINMENT P234**

🛍 **SHOPPING P234**

🏃 **SPORTS & ACTIVITIES P234**

🛏 **SLEEPING P235**

EATING

INDEX DRINKING & NIGHTLIFE

☆ **ENTERTAINMENT**

🛍 **SHOPPING**

İstanbul Maps

Sights

- Beach
- Bird Sanctuary
- Buddhist
- Castle/Palace
- Christian
- Confucian
- Hindu
- Islamic
- Jain
- Jewish
- Monument
- Museum/Gallery/Historic Building
- Ruin
- Shinto
- Sikh
- Taoist
- Winery/Vineyard
- Zoo/Wildlife Sanctuary
- Other Sight

Activities, Courses & Tours

- Bodysurfing
- Diving
- Canoeing/Kayaking
- Course/Tour
- Sento Hot Baths/Onsen
- Skiing
- Snorkelling
- Surfing
- Swimming/Pool
- Walking
- Windsurfing
- Other Activity

Sleeping

- Sleeping
- Camping

Eating

- Eating

Drinking & Nightlife

- Drinking & Nightlife
- Cafe

Entertainment

- Entertainment

Shopping

- Shopping

Information

- Bank
- Embassy/Consulate
- Hospital/Medical
- Internet
- Police
- Post Office
- Telephone
- Toilet
- Tourist Information
- Other Information

Geographic

- Beach
- Gate
- Hut/Shelter
- Lighthouse
- Lookout
- Mountain/Volcano
- Oasis
- Park
- Pass
- Picnic Area
- Waterfall

Population

- Capital (National)
- Capital (State/Province)
- City/Large Town
- Town/Village

Transport

- Airport
- Border crossing
- Bus
- Cable car/Funicular
- Cycling
- Ferry
- Metro station
- Monorail
- Parking
- Petrol station
- S-Bahn/Subway station
- Taxi
- T-bane/Tunnelbana station
- Train station/Railway
- Tram
- Tube station
- U-Bahn/Underground station
- Other Transport

Note: Not all symbols displayed above appear on the maps in this book

Routes

- Tollway
- Freeway
- Primary
- Secondary
- Tertiary
- Lane
- Unsealed road
- Road under construction
- Plaza/Mall
- Steps
- Tunnel
- Pedestrian overpass
- Walking Tour
- Walking Tour detour
- Path/Walking Trail

Boundaries

- International
- State/Province
- Disputed
- Regional/Suburb
- Marine Park
- Cliff
- Wall

Hydrography

- River, Creek
- Intermittent River
- Canal
- Water
- Dry/Salt/Intermittent Lake
- Reef

Areas

- Airport/Runway
- Beach/Desert
- Cemetery (Christian)
- Cemetery (Other)
- Glacier
- Mudflat
- Park/Forest
- Sight (Building)
- Sportsground
- Swamp/Mangrove

MAP INDEX

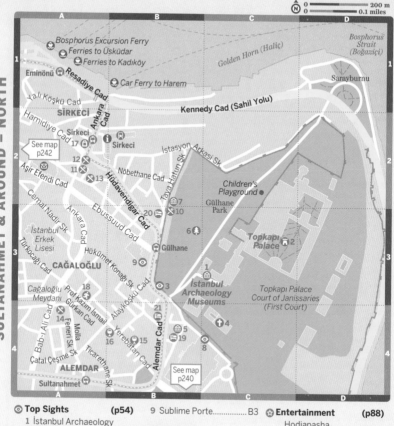

SULTANAHMET & AROUND – SOUTH *Map on p240*

SULTANAHMET & AROUND – SOUTH

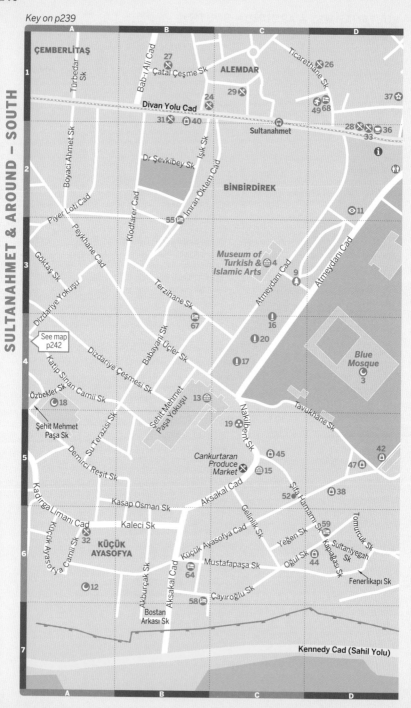

ÇEMBERLİTAŞ

Türbedar Sk

Bab-ı Ali Cad

27
Çatal Çeşme Sk

ALEMDAR

Ticarethane Sk

26

29

37

24
Divan Yolu Cad

49 68

31 40

28 33 36

Sultanahmet

Boyaci Ahmet Sk

Dr Şevkibey Sk

Işık Sk

İmran Öktem Cad

BİNBİRDİREK

11

Piyer Loti Cad

Klodfarer Cad

55

Museum of
Turkish &
Islamic Arts

4

9

Atmeydanı Cad

Atmeydanı Cad

Pelykhane Cad

Göktaş Sk

Dizdariye Yokuşu

Terzihane Sk

67

16

20

17

Blue
Mosque
3

See map
p242

Dizdariye Çeşmesi Sk

Babayani Üçler Sk

Şehit Mehmet
Paşa Yokuşu

13

Katip Sinan Camil Sk

Özbekler Sk
18

Şehit Mehmet
Paşa Sk

19

Makbent Sk

45

Tavukhane Sk

42

Su Terazisi Sk

Demirci Reşit Sk

Cankurtaran
Produce
Market

15

52

47

38

Kadırga Limanı Cad

Kasap Osman Sk

Aksakal Cad

Kaleci Sk

Sıfa Hamamı Sk

Tomurcuk Sk

Küçük Ayasofya Camil Sk

32

KÜÇÜK
AYASOFYA

Küçük Ayasofya Cad

Gelinlik Sk

Yeğen Sk

59

Sultaniyegah Sk

Kapağası Sk

Akburçak Sk

Aksakal Cad

Mustafapaşa Sk

Oğul Sk

44

Fenerlikapı Sk

64

12

58
Çayıroğlu Sk

Bostan
Arkası Sk

Kennedy Cad (Sahil Yolu)

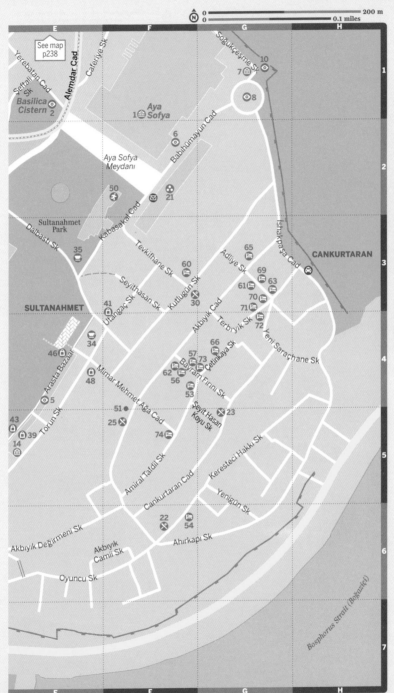

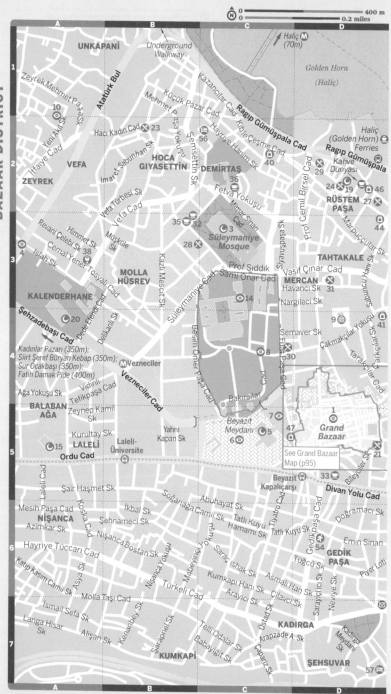

BAZAAR DISTRICT

Key on p246

BEYOĞLU – NORTHEAST

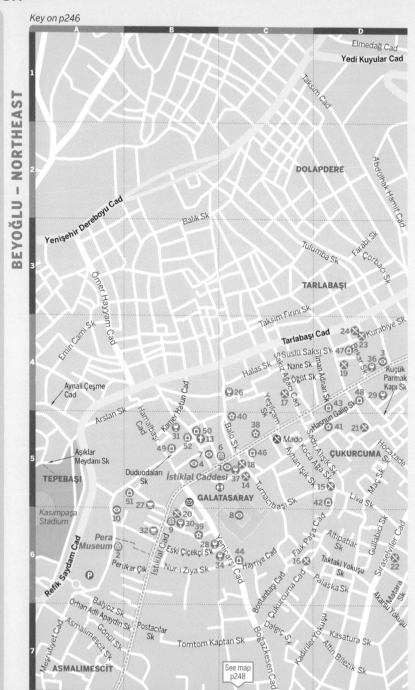

See map
p248

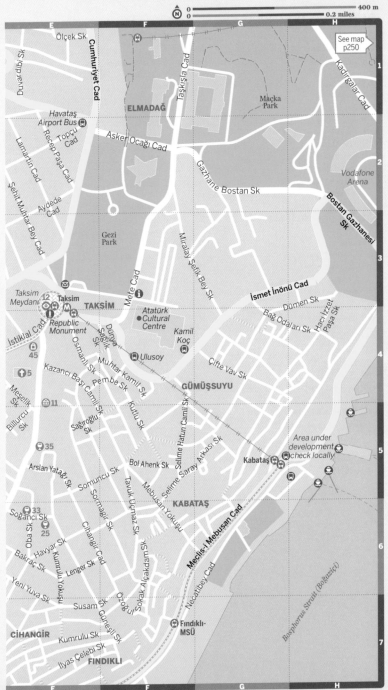

0   400 m
0   0.2 miles

See map
p250

Ölçek Sk

Cumhuriyet Cad

Taşkışla Cad

ELMADAĞ

Duvardıbı Sk

Havataş
Airport Bus

Asker Ocağı Cad

Topçu
Cad

Recep Paşa Cad

Lamartin Cad

Şehit Muhtar Bey Cad

Aydede
Cad

Gezi
Park

Gazhane Bostan Sk

Miralay Şefik Bey Sk

Mete Cad

Maçka
Park

Vodafone
Arena

Bostan Gazhanesi
Sk

İsmet İnönü Cad

Taksim
Meydanı

12 Taksim

TAKSİM

Republic
Monument

İstiklal Cad

45

5

Meşelik
Sk

Billurcu
Sk

11

35

Kazancı Başı Cami Sk

Osmanlı Sk

Dünya
Sağlık
Sk

Muhtar Kamil Sk

Pembe Sk

Sağıroğlu
Sk

Atatürk
Cultural
Centre

Kamil
Koç

Ulusoy

Kutlu Sk

GÜMÜŞSUYU

Dümen Sk

Bağ Odaları Sk

Hacı İzzet
Paşa Sk

Çifte Vav Sk

Selime Hatun Cami Sk

Saray Arkası Sk

Area under
development
check locally

Kabataş

Arslan Yatağı Sk

Somuncu Sk

Sofmağr Sk

Bol Ahenk Sk

Tavuk Uçmaz Sk

Mebusan Yokuşu

KABATAŞ

33

25

Soğancı Sk

Oba Sk

Havyar Sk

Kumrulu Yokuşu

Cihangir Cad

Lenger Sk

Bakraç Sk

Yeni Yuva Sk

Sokak Alçakdam Sk

Özoğul

Meclis-i Mebusan Cad

Necatibey Cad

Susam Sk

Güneşli Sk

CİHANGİR

Kumrulu Sk

İlyas Çelebi Sk

FINDIKLI

Fındıklı-
MSÜ

Bosphorus Strait (Boğaziçi)

BEYOĞLU – NORTHEAST *Map on p244*

BEYOĞLU – SOUTHWEST *Map on p248*

Key on p247

BEYOĞLU – SOUTHWEST

See map p244

TEPEBAŞI

Tepebaşı Cad
Asmalımescit Sk
Tepebaşı Akarca Sk

12
33
81
Balyoz
74
61
Orhan Adli Apaydin Sk
47
55
Postacılar Sk
2
83
25
ASMALIMESCİT
38
Gönül
50
17
18
Minare Sk

Hasan Paşa Park

Havuzbaşı Değirmen Sk
Tali Sk
Anbar Arkası Sk
Ayni Ali Baba Sk
Ali Baba Sk

Evliya Çelebi Cad

Refik Saydam Cad

Bedrettin Sk

TÜNEL

Jurnal Sk
Meşrutiyet Cad
Şimal Sk

15
26
49
23
Camcı Örmealtı Sk

36
16
37
Tünel Meydanı
Şişhane
46
Kumbaracı Yokuşu
Fevzi Sk

Şahkulu
71
Bostan Sk

ŞİŞHANE
57
Şişhane
Tünel (Upper Station)
67
6
4
Haci Mimi Külhanı Sk

Şişhane Pl
Şişhane

Şişhane
58
32
Dilek Sk

Paşa Çıplağı Sk
Yolcuzade İskender Cad
Şişhane Sk
80
11
Büyük Hendek Cad
İlk Belediye Cad
Galipdede Cad

Fürreyya Galata Balıkçısı
Serdar-ı Ekrem Cad
86
59
Ali Hoca Sk

Dik Sk
Tülcük Sk
Okçu Musa Cad
Laleli Çeşme Sk
19
24
48
64
Talat Beyi Sk

Mürver Sk
Yanıkkapı Sk
41
52
Galata Meydanı
Yüksek Kaldırım Cad
Lüleci Hendek Cad

Cevahir Çıkmazı
Yolcuzade Sk
3
7
51
65
Alageyik Sk
GALATA
Hoca Tahsin Sk

Seyahan 2
56
Cami Sk
82
Hacı Ali Sk

Yelkenciler Sk
Galata Mahkemesi Sk
Futuhat Sk
Hoca Hanim Sk
1
Bankalar Cad
Camondo Stairs
76

Hediye Sk
Nafe Sk
13
35
Perşembe Pazarı Cad
Zincirli Han Sk
Billur Sk
84
Söğüt Sk
40

Haliç (100m)

Bakir Sk
Tersane Cad
30
68
34
Kemankeş

Taflan Sk
Ziyali Sk
Kürekçiler Cad
31
Gümrük Sk
KARAKÖY
Necatibey Cad
Maliye Cad
Arapoğlan Sk

Tünel (Lower Station)
Karaköy
Karaköy Cad

Fermeneciler Sk
Fish Market (Balık Pazarı)
Turyol Ferries to Kadıköy & Üsküdar

Karaköy Meydanı
Rihtim Cad

Golden Horn (Haliç)
Haliç (Golden Horn) Ferries
Karaköy İskelesi (Ferry Dock)

Galata Bridge (Galata Köprüsü)

RÜSTEMPAŞA

Ragıp Gümüşpala Cad

See map p242

A B C D

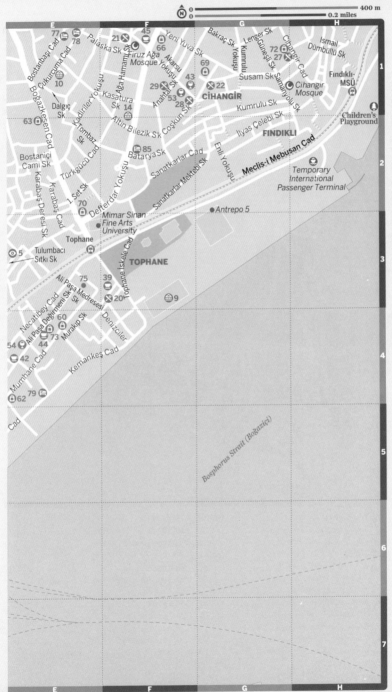

BEŞİKTAŞ, NIŞANTAŞI & ORTAKÖY

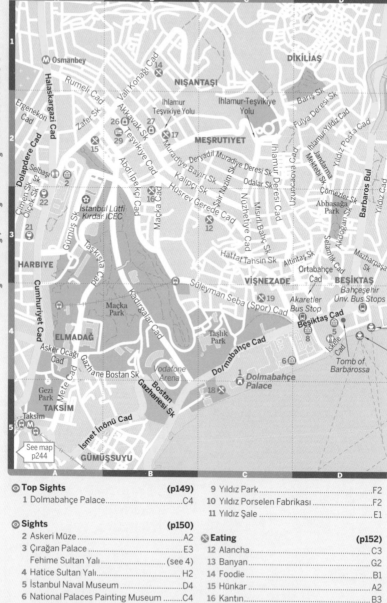

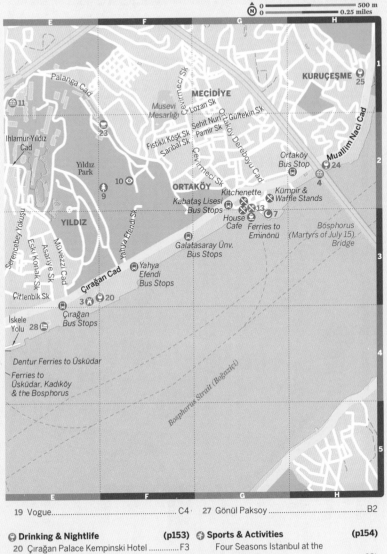

0 500 m
0 0.25 miles

WESTERN DISTRICTS

KADIKÖY

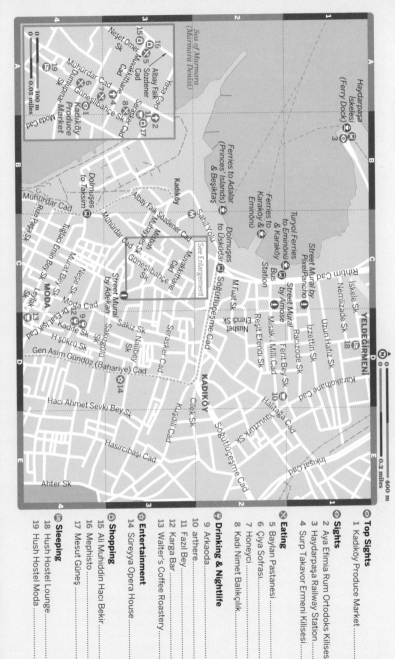

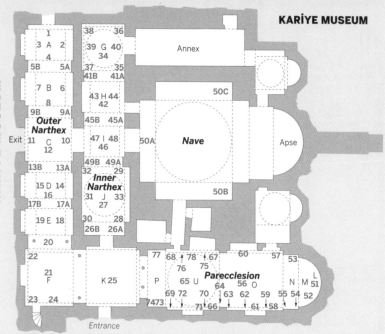

KARİYE MUSEUM

Annex

Nave

Apse

Outer Narthex

Exit

Inner Narthex

Pareclesion

Entrance

◉ Mosaics

1 The voyage of the Virgin to Bethlehem & the dream of Joseph

2 The census held for the enrolment for taxation & registration of Mary & Joseph in the presence of Cyrenius, Governor of Syria

3 Jesus going with Mary & Joseph to Jerusalem

4 Remains of mosaics – Jesus among the doctors in the temple

5A St Trachos

5B St Andronikus

6 The birth of Jesus

7 The return of the Virgin Mary with Jesus

8 The attempts of Satan to deceive Jesus

9A St Georgios

9B St Demetrius

10 Jesus & the inscription 'the dwelling-place of the living'

11 The prayer of the Virgin & the attendant angels

12 The wedding at Cana & the miracles

13A Depiction of the saints

13B Depiction of the saints

14 The Magi on their way to Jerusalem riding on horseback & the three Magi in audience with King Herod

15 Elizabeth & John the Baptist running away from a pursuing soldier

16 Remains of mosaics

17A Depiction of the saints

17B Depiction of the saints

18 The scene of King Herod's investigation & a guard standing

19 The mourning mothers

20 No mosaics left

21 A decorative medallion

22 The meeting of Jesus with the Samaritan woman at the well

23 The healing of a paralysed person by Jesus

24 King Herod giving the order for the massacre of the innocents & the execution thereof

25 Remains of mosaics

26A The healing by Jesus of a young man with an injured arm

26B The healing by Jesus of leprous man

27 Twenty-four of the early ancestors of Jesus (Genealogy of Christ)

28 The healing by Jesus of a woman asking for the restoration of her health

29 The healing by Jesus of the mother-in-law of St Peter

30 The healing by Jesus of a deaf person

31 Dispersion of good health by Jesus to the people
32 The healing by Jesus of two blind men
33 The Khalke Jesus & the praying Virgin
34 Mary and the Baby Jesus surrounded by her ancestors
35 Joachim in the mountains praying to have a child
36 No mosaics left
37 The breaking of the good news of the birth of Jesus to Mary – The Annunciation
38 The chief priest Zacchariah judging the Virgin
39 Mary & Joseph bidding each other farewell
40 The breaking of the good news of the birth of Mary to Anne
41A The meeting of Anne & Joachim
41B Joseph bringing the Virgin into his house
42 Mary in the arms of Anne & Joachim & the blessing by the priests
43 Giving of the stick with young shoots indicating Joseph as Mary's fiancé
44 The birth of the Virgin Mary
45A The first seven steps of the Virgin & below, St Peter
45B The prayer of the chief priest Zacchariah in front of the 12 sticks
46 The presentation of Mary (age three) to the temple by her parents
47 The Virgin taking the skeins of wool to weave the veil for the temple
48 Theodore Metochites presenting a small model of the church to Jesus
49A The feeding of the Virgin by an angel & below, St Peter
49B Remains of mosaics – Directives given to the Virgin at the temple
50A The Assumption of the Virgin
50B Mary and the Baby Jesus
50C Jesus in a standing posture, holding the Bible in his hand

◉ **Frescoes**

51 The Anastasis
52 The Church fathers
53 The raising (resurrection of the widow's son)
54 The healing of the daughter of Jairus
55 The Virgin Elousa
56 The Last Judgement
57 Abraham & the beggar Lazarus on his lap
58 St George
59 Rich man burning in Hell's fire
60 Those entering Heaven & the Angel Seraphim with the semi-nude good thief
61 Depiction of Andronikus II & his family & the inscription & depiction above of Makarios Tornikes & his wife Eugenia
62 The Bearing of the Ark of the Covenant
63 St Demetrius
64 St Theodore Tiro
65 Mary & child Jesus with the 12 attending angels
66 Four Gospel Writers (Hymnographers): St Cosmos
67 Four Gospel Writers (Hymnographers): St John of Damascene
68 Four Gospel Writers (Hymnographers): St Theophanes
69 Four Gospel Writers (Hymnographers): St Joseph
70 St Theodore Stratelates
71 King Solomon & the Israelites
72 Placement into the temple of the Ark of the Covenant
73 The combat of an angel with the Asurians in the outskirts of Jerusalem
74 St Procopios, St Sabas Stratelates
75 Moses in the bushes
76 Jacob's ladder & the angels
77 Aaron & his sons carrying votive offerings, in front of the altar
78 St Samonas & Guiras

Our Story

A beat-up old car, a few dollars in the pocket and a sense of adventure. In 1972 that's all Tony and Maureen Wheeler needed for the trip of a lifetime – across Europe and Asia overland to Australia. It took several months, and at the end – broke but inspired – they sat at their kitchen table writing and stapling together their first travel guide, *Across Asia on the Cheap*. Within a week they'd sold 1500 copies. Lonely Planet was born.

Today, Lonely Planet has offices in Franklin, London, Melbourne, Oakland, Dublin, Beijing and Delhi, with more than 600 staff and writers. We share Tony's belief that 'a great guidebook should do three things: inform, educate and amuse'.

Our Writers

Virginia Maxwell
Bazaar District, Beyoğlu, Kadıköy, Day Trips

Although based in Australia, Virginia spends part of each year in Turkey. As well as working on the previous five editions of this city guide, she also writes Lonely Planet's *Pocket İstanbul*, covers İstanbul, İzmir and the North Aegean for the *Turkey* guide, and writes about the city for a host of international magazines and websites. Virginia also wrote the Plan, Understand and Survive sections of this guide.

James Bainbridge
Sultanahmet & Around, Western Districts, Beşiktaş, Nişantaşı & Ortaköy

James is a British writer based in South Africa's Cape Winelands, where he writes for publications worldwide. He has been working on Lonely Planet projects for more than a decade, including coordinating five editions of *Turkey*, writing the first edition of *Discover Turkey* and contributing a major feature on Turkey to Lonely Planet *Traveller* magazine. He was extremely happy to return to his old stomping ground of İstanbul, where he once lived and took a Turkish-language course.

Published by Lonely Planet Global Limited
CRN 554153
9th edition – February 2017
ISBN 978 1 78657 228 8
© Lonely Planet 2017   Photographs © as indicated 2017
10 9 8 7 6 5 4 3 2 1
Printed in China

Although the authors and Lonely Planet have taken all reasonable care in preparing this book, we make no warranty about the accuracy or completeness of its content and, to the maximum extent permitted, disclaim all liability arising from its use.